UNIVERSITY LIBRARY
UW-STEVENS POINT

DIAGNOSTIC-PRESCRIPTIVE TEACHING

John Stellern
University of Wyoming

EXCEPTIONAL PRESS/SAN JUAN CAPISTRANO, California

Typography & Production
by
The Capistrano Composing Room
San Juan Capistrano, California

Copyright © 1982 by

Exceptional Press, Inc., San Juan Capistrano, CA 92693-0344

All rights reserved. No part of this publication may be reproduced, stored in a retrieval system, or transmitted, in any form or by any means, electronic, mechanical, photocopying, recording, or otherwise, without the prior written permission of the publisher.

Printed in the United States of America.

ISBN 0-914420-56-9

TABLE OF CONTENTS

PART I.	Introduction to Diagnostic-Prescriptive Teaching and Programming	1
Chapter 1.	Philosophy and Background	3
Chapter 2.	An Overview of the Education Intervention and Management Model	4
PART II.	The First Component of the Education Intervention and Management Model: The Learner	7
SECTION I.	Formal Psychoeducational Testing and Assessment	9
Chapter 3.	Introduction to Psychoeducational Testing and Assessment	9
Chapter 4.	The Ethics of Psychoeducational Testing and Assessment	16
Chapter 5.	The Wechsler Intelligence Scale for Children (WISC); The Wechsler Intelligence Scale for Children-Revised (WISC-R); The Wechsler Adult Intelligence Scale (WAIS); and the The Wechsler Adult Intelligence Scale—Revised (WAIS-R) Wechsler Preschool and Primary Scale of Intelligence (WPPSI)	18
Chapter 6.	The Stanford-Binet Intelligence Scale	30
Chapter 7.	The Peabody Picture Vocabulary Test; and the Columbia Mental Maturity Scale	32
Chapter 8.	Wide Range Achievement Test (WRAT); Peabody Individual Achievement Test (PIAT); Auditory Discrimination Test; Test of Auditory Discrimination (TAD); Key Math Diagnostic Arithmetic Test; and the Test Battery Concept and Exercise	34
Chapter 9.	The Illinois Test of Psycholinguistic Abilities (ITPA); and Test Battery Interpretation Exercise	37
Chapter 10.	The Bender-Gestalt Test	43
Chapter 11.	The Draw-A-Person Test	89
SECTION II.	Informal Psychoeducational Testing and Assessment	124
Chapter 12.	The Stellern-Shaw Informal Learning Inventory (SILI)	124
Chapter 13.	The Comprehensive History	173
Chapter 14.	The Reinforcement Inventory	191
Chapter 15.	The Five Kinds of Necessary Learner Information	193
SECTION III.	A Theoretical Orientation to the Understanding of Personality	197
Chapter 16.	A Theretical Orientation to the Understanding of Personality	197

PART III.	The Second Component of the Education Intervention and Management Model: Behavioral-Instructional Objectives	205
	Chapter 17. An Orientation to Behavioral-Instructional Objectives	207
	Chapter 18. Analysis of the Ingredients of a Good Objective	209
	Chapter 19. Behavioral-Instructional Objectives; P.L. 94-142; and IEPs	213
PART IV.	The Third Component of the Education Intervention and Management Model: Task Analysis	215
	Chapter 20. Task Analysis	217
	Chapter 21. Sample Task Analyses	220
PART V.	The Fourth Component of the Education Intervention and Management Model: Individualization and Success	225
	Chapter 22. Prescriptive Teaching and Classroom Mechanics	227
	Chapter 23. Direct Instruction	266
	Chapter 24. The Physical Arrangement of the Classroom	272
	Chapter 25. Classroom Grouping Arrangements	280
PART VI.	The Fifth Component of the Education Intervention and Management Model: Baseline Measurement	300
	Chapter 26. The Theoretical Aspects of Baseline Measurement	301
	Chapter 27. The Mechanical Aspects of Baseline Measurement	305
PART VII.	The Sixth Component of the Education Intervention and Management Model: Behavior Modification and Change Agents	312
SECTION I.	Behavior Modification and Change Agents: General Application	313
	Chapter 28. Positive Reinforcement	313
	Chapter 29. Extinction Techniques	323
SECTION II.	Behavior Modification and Change Agents: Specific Application	327
	Chapter 30. Change Agents	327
PART VIII.	Legislation Relating to Special Education	338
	Chapter 31. Public Law 94-142	339
	Chapter 32. Procedures for Evaluating Specific Learning Disabilities: Supplement to the Education of the Handicapped Act	343

	Chapter 33.	Section 504 of the Rehabilitation Act of 1973	345
PART IX.	Diagnostic-Prescriptive Teaching and Programming As a Cross-Categorical Special Education Model		348
	Chapter 34.	D-PT Similarities and Differences Regarding Educationally Handicapped Individuals	349
	Chapter 35.	IEP Forms	355
	Chapter 36.	Group Program Form	360
PART X.	Sample IEPs		364
	Chapter 37.	Sample IEPs	364
APPENDIX I.	Selected Curriculum Materials Which Represent a Good D-PT Match		383
INDEX			405

ACKNOWLEDGMENTS

Grateful appreciation is expressed to those who are close to me and who temporarily suffered while this book was being written. Grateful appreciation of another kind is expressed to those colleagues and authorities, some of whom are identified in this book, who in various ways helped to shape the theoretical and practical orientation of the author.

John Stellern
Laramie, Wyoming
1982

PROLOGUE

This book deals with the theoretical as well as the practical aspects of Diagnostic-Prescriptive Teaching and Programming. The content of the book reflects the professional and personal biases and experiences of the author.

This book is written for those individuals who wish to increase the likelihood of successful intervention with learning or behavior problems by means of the application of systematic diagnostic-prescriptive teaching concepts. This book is also written for, and partially dedicated to, our undergraduate and graduate Diagnostic-Prescriptive Teaching majors at the University of Wyoming, whose keen questions and observations have helped increase our knowledge of systematic and successful intervention strategies.

PART I

INTRODUCTION TO DIAGNOSTIC-PRESCRIPTIVE TEACHING AND PROGRAMMING

The process of change begins with someone who cares. Yet to do nothing but care, however humanistic, is unproductive. Even to care with understanding, although humanistic and wise, is still unproductive. However, to do something positive, based on care and understanding, is not only humanistic and wise, but also productive.

Chapter 1

Philosophy and Background

Human life is dear and also complex. Such dearness and complexity dictate that the life process be treated with wisdom and care. Unfortunately, for some individuals with problems and for others who seek to resolve those problems, the necessary wisdom and care are lacking.

With the advent of P.L. 94-142 and Section 504 of the Rehabilitation Act or 1973, public education has entered an age of accountability. We define accountability as the measurable justification of behavior. We anticipate in the not too distant future that boards of education, superintendents, principals, pupil personnel workers, and teachers will be held accountable for their public school behavior relative to the responsibility with which they are vested. We further anticipate that the privilege of public education employment will be a function of the identification of professional objectives and the subsequent assessment of the degree to which those objectives are met.

Although special education has entered an age of accountability, it is threatened by an identity crisis. Traditional ways of working are being questioned and new ways of working are being advocated. Such a crisis situation, in part, is due to the conflicting evidence regarding whether the traditional operation of special education is academically and/or socially effective.

Out of a concern for the way in which the human life process is treated, an interest in educational accountability, and a fascination with the trend away from conventional special education practices, we developed and assembled various assessment and intervention strategies into an operational framework that we call diagnostic-prescriptive teaching and programming.

Diagnostic-prescriptive teaching and programming expresses itself in our education intervention and management model. The model is designed to facilitate successful IEP and IIP (individualized instruction program) intervention with learning or behavior problems. The focus of the model relates to school problems with learning or behavior and the resolution of those problems by school-related practitioners. However, the potential application of the model is wider in nature, and actually extends to a systems approach to any kind of learning or behavior problem resolution relative to anyone who wishes to apply the particular strategies involved. In its operational state, the model is accountability based because of the use of concepts of behavioral-instructional objectives, task analysis, and baseline measurement; and the model is cross-categorical in nature, in that its systems approach to problem resolution is not dependent on the presenting problem being of a certain nosological type.

Chapter 2

An Overview of the Education Intervention and Management Model

Diagnostic-prescriptive teaching and programming is defined as the accurate assessment of, and systematic and successful intervention with, learning or behavior problems. In order to convert diagnostic-prescriptive teaching ideas into operational mechanics, the education intervention and management model was developed. The model is a systems approach to learning or behavior problem resolution. The model is equally applicable to special education and regular education, and is equally appropriate for teachers, counselors, principals, and/or parents who wish to systematically intervene with learning or behavior problems by means of diagnostic-prescriptive teaching strategies.

Irrespective of the particular kind of learning or behavior problem, and regardless of the kind of individual seeking problem resolution, the model operates on a two-part plan:

1. Each major IEP-IIP intervention with a learning or behavior problem employs the formula, "assessment + prescription = correction." In order to justify intervening in the complex life-process of a human being, trial and error needs to be reduced, and the likelihood of intervention success needs to be increased. The likelihood of successful intervention can be increased by the practitioner accurately assessing, through the use of formal and informal techniques, the nature of the presenting problem; by the practitioner rendering meaningful prescriptions relative to the remediation of the presenting problem; and, based on those prescriptions, by the practitioner either systematically intervening with the presenting problem for the purpose of effective positive change, or supervising that intervention.

2. Each major intervention is conducted by systematically following the six components of the model, beginning with the learner, and progressing concentrically outward. In order to increase the likelihood of intervention success, learning or behavior problem resolution should be executed with as much precision as possible. Therefore, it is recommended that each major intervention be conducted by means of the systematic use of the model.

The model is composed of six major intervention components, as well as various intervention subcomponents. The first concentric ring of the model corresponds to the learner. Five kinds of information about each learner should be obtained by means of formal and informal assessment techniques. The five kinds of information are: the learner's obtained and potential problem-solving ability; learning characteristics; achievement data; those personality characteristics necessary to affect systematic environmental manipulation; and that which the learner regards as reinforcing and aversive.

The second concentric ring of the model refers to behavioral-instructional objectives. An objective is a written prescriptive teaching plan of action. An objective has three parts: (1) the performance-based identification of the terminal behavior expected of the learner; (2) the important conditions associated with that terminal behavior; and (3) the criteria of acceptable performance, in terms of time, accuracy, and difficulty level. The practitioner should identify a behavioral-instructional objective for each learner relative to each major intervention.

The third concentric ring of the model refers to task analysis. This involves the identification of the sequential steps necessary for the learner to get from the observed behavior to the terminal behavior. The task analysis approach permits a systematic way of identifying a precision entry level, thus increasing the likelihood of efficient intervention with learning or behavior problems.

The fourth concentric ring refers to individualization and success. This involves information necessary for the mechanical operation of the D-PT classroom.

The fifth concentric ring refers to baseline behavior measurement. Each practitioner should measure the frequency of target behavior by means of baseline measurement. The typical two-axis time and frequency

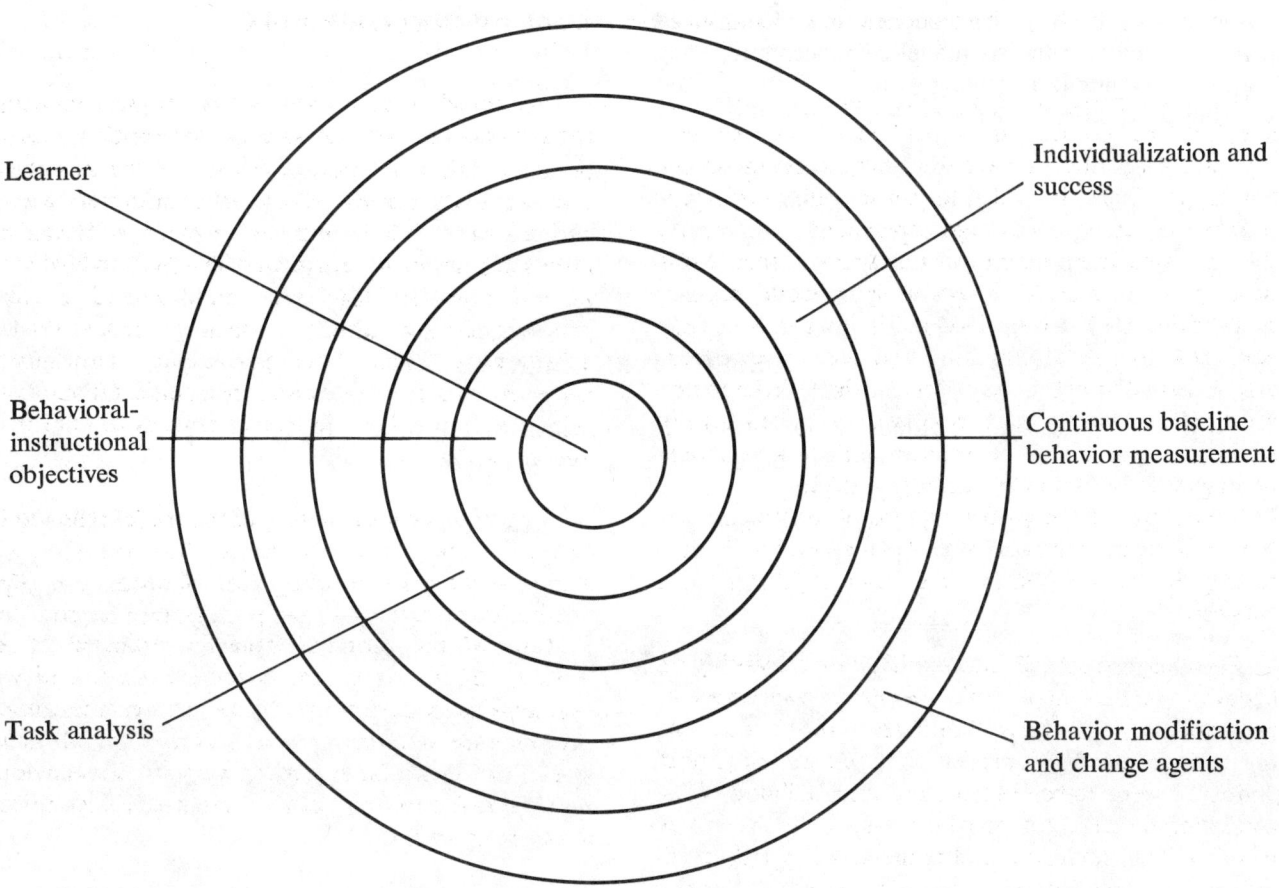

Figure I
Management Model

measurement grid, and learning contracts, are employed for the purpose of recording the pre-, continuing-, and postintervention frequency of that target behavior. Baseline measurement plays a central role in the operation of diagnostic prescriptive teaching, as it forms the accountability means by which the success of the learner and practitioner may be judged.

The sixth and last concentric ring of the model relates to behavior modification and change agents. Behavior modification and change agents refers to any agent of manipulation that is designed to effect systematic behavior change. So that each intervention may have an increased chance of success due to the use of change agents, the following intervention strategies are advocated: The use of the Thorndikian learning theory model, for the purpose of employing the practitioner as the stimulus that evokes the desired response; the various mechanics of positive reinforcement, negative reinforcement, and extinction techniques; contingency management; the reinforcing properties of high interest activities and materials; medication; time-out; the structured classroom; modeling; crisis intervention; the immediate feedback interview; student, parent, individual, and group counseling; body-image development; parent and student aides; token economy; the menu models; and chaining and reverse chaining.

In summary, diagnostic-prescriptive teaching is defined as the accurate assessment of, and the systematic intervention with, learning or behavior problems. The management model is a way of putting the diagnostic-prescriptive teaching concepts into action, and involves employing the six model components for each major intervention, beginning with the learner, and working concentrically outward. For each major intervention, the practitioner should obtain the five kinds of learner information, develop behavioral or instructional objectives, develop a task analysis for each objective, apply individualization and success principles, obtain baseline measurements, and then systematically apply behavior modification and change agents to increase the likelihood of intervention success.

SELECTED REFERENCES

Lindsley, O. "Direct Measurement and Prothesis of Retarded Behavior," *Journal of Education,* 1964, *147,* 62-81.

Peter, L. *Prescriptive Teaching*. New York: McGraw-Hill, 1965.

PART II

THE FIRST COMPONENT OF THE EDUCATION INTERVENTION AND MANAGEMENT MODEL:

The Learner

The managment model has six components. Of the six, the learner is the most important, since it is for the learner that diagnostic-prescriptive teaching concepts exist. In order to conduct effective IEP intervention, it is necessary to obtain five kinds of learner information. Psychoeducational testing and assessment can provide that information. Part II presents various formal and informal psychoeducational testing and assessment procedures as they relate to the learner and the nature of the presenting problem.

Section I

Formal Psychoeducational Testing and Assessment

Chapter 3

Introduction to Psychoeducational Testing and Assessment

Diagnostic-prescriptive teaching represents a collection of strategies that are designed to permit successful IEP and IIP intervention with learning or behavior problems. The management model represents an operational plan by which these intervention strategies may be put into action. The rationale of the management model is based on the assumption that human life intervention should be as thoughtfully planned and executed as possible so as to reduce the opportunity for trial-and-error behavior and to increase the likelihood of presenting problem resolution.

The model is composed of six components. We recommend that each major intervention with a learning or behavior problem be sequentially conducted by means of the six components, beginning with the learner, and progressing concentrically outward. the learner is the most important of the six model components since the diagnostic-prescriptive teaching concepts exist for the learner. Through five kinds of learner information the presenting problem is sufficiently understood to permit systematic problem resolution.

The learner component requires that five kinds of information be obtained about each learner for whom an IEP intervention is contemplated. These five kinds of information are: (1) the learner's obtained problem solving ability (obtained IQ), and potential problem ability (potential IQ); (2) learning characteristics (strengths and weaknesses relative to input, memory, meaning, output, attention span, physical factors, and self structuring ability); (3) achievement data; (4) sufficient information about the personality characteristics of the learner and family to permit systematic environmental manipulation; and (5) that which the learner regards as reinforcing and aversive, as such information is relevant to increasing the likelihood of intervention success by the use of behavior modification and change agents. All five kinds of information can be obtained through formal and/or informal psychoeducational testing and assessment procedures.

Psychoeducational refers to the contribution that the discipline of psychology can make to the discipline of education. Testing refers to an examination of an individual(s) for the purpose of achieving a greater understanding of that individual by means of the test results. And assessment refers to the translation of test result understanding into appropriate remedial and/or IEP prescriptions. Putting the three concepts together, psychoeducational testing and assessment refers to the contribution that psychological and educational theory and tests can make to the understanding of a learner and the consequent resolution of the presenting problem.

There are two basic kinds of psycho-educational tests: formal and informal. Formal psycho-educational tests have norms relative to which the test results are interpreted; the test results are expressed in the form of number scores, such as IQ, grade level, percentile, etc.; and the test questions or items are developed in relation to a carefully selected pool of individuals who form the standardization sample. Formal tests are known as norm referenced tests.

Informal psycho-educational tests have no standardization sample, no norms, and usually do not result in number scores. Rather, informal tests yield subjective information about the individual, such as: "is unable to discriminate between two similar consonant sounds." As such, the test subject is compared with himself, not a standardization sample. Informal tests are known as criterion referenced tests.

By way of introduction to psychoeducational testing and assessment, several important concepts should be considered.

The value and advantages of Psychological Testing

1. There are at least five kinds of information about the learner that are necessary for systematic IEP-IIP intervention. Psychoeducational testing can provide that information. While we concede that it is possible to conduct an intervention without the advantage of all five kinds of information, we contend that such an intervention would likely be characterized by undesirable trial-and-error procedures.
2. Psychoeducational testing permits the identification of subject learning characteristics, which permits the systematic individualization of instruction.
3. Psychoeducational testing facilitates the identification of the cause of the learner's presenting problem, and on that basis, the conduction of the appropriate presenting problem remediation.
4. Psychoeducational testing facilitates an understanding of subject personality dynamics in relation to the presenting problem, a situation which increases the likelihood of consequent remediation having a theoretically sound rationale, which in turn increases the likelihood of treatment success.
5. Psychoeducational testing permits an identification of learner problem-solving strengths and weaknesses, a situation which permits homogeneous learner grouping.
6. Psychoeducational testing facilitates the distinction between the learner's obtained and problem-solving ability. This distinction permits a consideration of the learner in terms of potential strength, and a subsequent programming upward of that individual toward greater problem-solving fulfillment. Such a learner-strength orientation would not be possible if only the obtained IQ was considered important.
7. Psychoeducational testing permits the identification of the learner's prognosis, especially regarding presenting problem resolution, course of study success, vocational success, etc.
8. Psychoeducational testing facilitates the identification of student educational readiness, a situation which facilitates appropriate grade placement as well as the conduction of orthogenic education for those students in a marginal state of educational readiness.

The Dangers of Psychoeducational Testing and Assessment

The dangers of psychoeducational testing can be immense, and unless care is taken, the dangers can outweigh the advantages. Therefore, it is urged that psychoeducational testing strategies be employed only by those individuals trained in those strategies, and only by those individuals who operate in an ethical and humanistic fashion.

One of the primary dangers of psychoeducational testing is that of invasion of privacy. We contend that every lawful human being has the right to privacy, which in this case means a right not to be invaded by testing practices. In the case of a minor subject, the right not to be invaded by testing practices should be executed by the parent of the minor.

The mere experience of being tested can cause subject and family anxiety. Such anxiety can create unwanted personal and family disruption, a situation which could be avoided by either not testing at all, or by a gradual and hence anxiety-reducing approach to the testing process.

Anxiety that is created by a testing experience can negatively influence subject test behavior, a situation which could result in inaccurate test result interpretation. Therefore, any subsequent remediation could be inappropriate, a situation that could cause increased anxiety for the subject and family.

Another danger is that misinterpretation of test data could result in the self-fulfilling prophecy (Rosenthal and Jacobson, 1968). We contend that people relate to each other on the basis of the way in which they perceive each other. As such, test data misinterpretation could result in an inappropriate label (for example, mentally retarded) being attached to a student, who subsequently is inaccurately perceived in terms of that label. Unfortunately, such a situation is common to special education, as too many students are misdiagnosed on the basis of minimal evidence as being mentally retarded (when in fact they are not mentally retarded), placed in an EMR class, perceived by the teacher as being mentally retarded because of the MR label, and therefore taught as if they really were mentally retarded. We contend that such self-fulfilling prophecy can result in personal, family, and educational anguish, as well as result in a limitation of the opportunity of that student to ascend from the perceived level of problem solving to a level of problem solving more compatible with the student's potential. For this reason, it is contended that major educational decisions should not be made on the basis of one test result alone, but rather on the basis of a battery of test results in combination with as much learner information as possible.

Another danger involves the inappropriate use of confidential test result information, a situation which could incur a variety of unfortunate emotional injuries to the subject and family.

A danger can occur in relation to the security-maturity level of the test examiner. An examiner who is emotionally disturbed, anxious, prejudiced, immature, etc., not only can thereby cause subject anxiety, which in turn can negatively influence subject test behavior, but also can cause examiner misinterpretation of the test result data, a situation which could have harmful effects on subsequent subject remediation. The kind of person the test examiner is can make a difference relative to the degree to which a test subject feels comfortable in the test situation, and therefore able to problem solve at the subject's normal level of ability. Also, the kind of person the test examiner is can make a difference relative to the accuracy with which the subject's test behavior is interpreted by that examiner. A "sick" examiner could inappropriately interpret normal test results as peculiar, bizarre, sick, etc., due to the personality projection of the sick examiner. Similarly, a rigid examiner could interpret normal test results in the context of the examiner's rigidity, a situation which could result in hollow, wooden, and thus misleading test-result interpretations.

Test Subject Attitude

A third important concept in relation to psychoeducational testing is the powerful influence that the attitude of a test subject can have on test results. Although a particular test result is almost always valid with respect to the test subject, at the particular time, relative to the particular test, and under the stress of the particular testing situation, it is important to realize that any unusual test subject attitude can spuriously deflate typical problem-solving ability. Unless the examiner is alert to the attitude of the subject and the impact that subject attitude can have on typical problem-solving ability, incorrect examiner interpretation of test performance can result. There are five different kinds of unusual test subject attitudes which occur with sufficient frequency to justify their discussion here, and which tend to spuriously deflate typical problem-solving ability.

Subject anxiety. Anxiety can interrupt thought processes, and cause hyperactivity or hypoactivity, attention and concentration difficulty, perceptual problems, visual-motor coordination problems, etc., and is likely to interfere with typical problem-solving ability. The test results of an anxious subject should be considered only in the context of the degree to which the anxiety has impaired the subject's ability to problem solve.

Subject submission. Some test subjects, because of authority figure difficulty, submit to the examiner in such a way that they relinquish their best problem-solving ability. In such situations, the test results could be spuriously low, and should be interpreted only in the context of the subject's authority-problem based submissiveness.

Subject resentment. Some test subjects, because of an authority problem and/or poorly controlled anger, relate to the test examiner with resentment and anger. Such a subject attitude can minimally manifest itself in reduced problem-solving ability, and maximally manifest itself in open defiance and refusal to continue the testing program. Such test results need to be interpreted only in the context of the subject's ability to cope with authority-figure relationships and/or the poorly controlled anger.

Subject perplexity. Some test subjects are so confused by the testing program that they react with bewilderment. Such a subject attitude can dramatically impair typical problem-solving ability.

Subject hyperactivity. Some subjects, either because of anxiety, poor controls, and/or a central nervous system dysfunction, react to stress and testing with hyperactivity. Such a subject attitude can manifest itself in visual-motor coordination difficulties, perceptual problems, motor problems, thought process difficulty, etc., and can seriously obscure typical problem-solving ability. Such a test performance should be interpreted only in relation to the subject's hyperactivity.

Motivation To Become a Test Examiner

Another important concept in relation to psychoeducational testing is the recognition that, in general, people engage in behavior in order to satisfy internal and external needs. The disciplines of psychology and psychometry are no exception, and thus we can assume that many psychologists and psychometrists occupy their professional positions in order to satisfy certain needs. It becomes important to understand that individuals who engage in psychoeducational testing for unhealthy needs can have a destructive impact on the test subject, either directly on the subject at the time of testing and thus negatively influence the test performance, or indirectly on the subject and thus influence the future of the subject by means of inappropriate test performance interpretation.

Some unhealthy reasons why people engage in psychoeducational testing, and the consequences of those unhealthy reasons, are presented below.

1. Some individuals become test examiners in order to compensate for feelings of insecurity and loss of power. Such compensation often expresses itself in the adverse manipulation of the captive test subject, not only during the test program itself, but also subsequent to that program in terms of inappropriate educational placement recommendations, inappropriate recommendations regarding exemption from school, inappropriate institutional-placement recommendations, inappropriate treatment recommendations, etc.

2. Some individuals become test examiners in order to compensate for feelings of personal inadequacy. Such compensation often expresses itself in terms of the examiner actively looking for, and finding, faults or evidence of test subject inadequacy. This kind of examiner often inappropriately finds something wrong with the test subject, and therefore feels better about himself.

3. Some individuals become test examiners in order to master their personal problems by the reassurance that other people (test subjects) also have problems. This kind of examiner is the psychometric voyeur, or peeping Tom, and feels better to the degree that his problems are matched in scope by problems of the test subject. This kind of unhealthy test examiner is less damaging than the type who must find faults, since the voyeur type needs only the reassurance given by the fact that people, because they are people, have problems.

IQ Controversies

A fifth important concept in relation to psychoeducational testing is the nature of the IQ, and an examination of some of the concepts and controversies that exist relative to the IQ.

The IQ concept refers to a measure of problem-solving ability. Since there are many different kinds of problem-solving ability (verbal, numerical, spatial, mechanical, etc.), it follows that an IQ is meaningless unless interpreted in relation to the particular test from which the IQ was obtained.

Many test examiners are interested in the IQ only for the number that it represents (IQ 126, IQ 63, etc.). However, our orientation is that the IQ number, in isolation, is almost meaningless, in that the number reveals only the degree to which the subject performed above or below normal, on that particular day, relative to the particular test, and with respect to the particular test-stress of the moment. We contend that a richer approach to IQ interpretation is in terms of how that IQ was derived. This is known as the clinical orientation to the IQ, as opposed to the number orientation to the IQ. We contend that in order to make the IQ number meaningful, it is necessary to determine the learning, problem-solving, and personality strengths and weaknesses that were employed by a subject in the process of acquiring that particular number. Thus, it is rather sterile to describe a nine-year-old subject simply as having a IQ of 85. It is a much richer description of that same subject to report that he has an obtained IQ of 85, abstract verbal problem-solving ability commensurate with a normal eleven year old, a potential verbal IQ of 125, visual discrimination, visual storage, and visual sequential memory abilities compatible with an average five year old, intact and well-functioning auditory channel processes, first grade tool-subject ability due to marked visual discrimination and memory problems, and a healthy personality that is coping as well as possible with the frustration of chronic failure.

A controversy exists about whether the IQ is stable from age to age. We contend that the IQ is a statistically stable concept, and is likely to change from age to age only in relation to a change in the subject's problem-solving ability. Thus, if a subject experiences increased anxiety, a sudden memory problem, brain damage, etc., the subject's problem-solving ability could commensurately change, in which case the IQ would reflect that change.

IQs that result from different tests are not always directly comparable. This exists because different IQ-test authors have different definitions of IQ, as well as different intentions regarding the purpose of the IQ tests. Therefore, IQs that result from different tests often differ in terms of what they measure, and as such are not directly comparable. As a rule, it is safe to compare IQs only when those IQs are derived from the same instrument (or instruments purporting to measure the same concept), when those IQs are derived within one year of each other and if no major trauma occurred in the interim, and when the subject entertained the same test attitude for both IQ test administrations. If these rather pure test conditions exist, it is then relatively safe to compare the IQ test results for growth or deterioration purposes.

Although some IQ tests appear to be similar in nature, the meaning of the test results can be different depending on the type of individuals on whom the test was standardized. An extreme example of this situation would be the application of the results of an IQ test that was standardized on gifted American Caucasian children to Australian Aborigine adults. A not-so-extreme example of this situation would be the application of an IQ test which was standardized on middle-class Caucasian individuals to ghetto non-Caucasian individuals. In order to justify the use of an IQ test, the socioeconomic level, age, ethnic or racial origin, geographic location, and educational background of a test subject should be represented in the standardization sample of the test.

IQ test results have different meanings to the degree that the tests from which the results accrue measure different factors. An IQ of 109 achieved from a test that measures a verbal factor does not have the same meaning as an IQ of 109 achieved from a test that measures a numerical factor. With respect to such a case, the correct interpretation would be that the test subject has high-average verbal problem-solving ability, as well as high-average numerical problem-solving ability. The two identical IQ numbers are conceptually different. Thus, IQs should not be compared unless the tests from which the IQs derive purport to measure the same factor. The reader should be aware of the large number of factors that are purportedly measured by various tests, thus making it necessary to identify what a particular test purports to measure before comparing the results of one test with the results of another.

There are many acceptable ways of interpreting the numerical meaning of the IQ. One of the most common is the following:

IQ	130+	Gifted
IQ	120–129	Superior
IQ	110–119	Bright-Normal
IQ	90–109	Normal
IQ	80– 89	Dull-Normal
IQ	70– 79	Borderline
IQ	69–	Mentally Retarded

Desirable Test Examiner Personality Traits

Another important concept in relation to psychoeducational testing is that of desirable test examiner personality traits. A test examiner occupies a position of immense power and responsibility relative to a test subject, not only during the actual time of testing but also subsequent to that time in terms of treatment recommendations. We contend that a test examiner, like other professional behavioral scientists, should be uniquely qualified to occupy that position of power and responsibility. We regard the following personality characteristics and professional traits as being essential to the appropriate discharge of the test examiner responsibility:

1. Emotional health and security.
2. Humor.
3. Flexibility.
4. The ability to relate well to people.
5. An orientation to problem resolution that involves understanding the meaning of test results, as opposed to an interest only in a test result number.
6. We consider it important for a test examiner to have developed a sound theoretical orientation to the explanation of behavior. Such an orientation makes it possible for an examiner to conceptualize a subject's presenting problem in a consistent way. This in turn makes it possible for the examiner to select a complementary battery of tests which are designed to provide a rich understanding of the presenting problem. Lastly, such an orientation allows the test examiner to understand the clinical meaning of the test results. By understanding the nature of the presenting problem, selecting the right tests based on that understanding, and then understanding the test results in relation to the presenting problem, the examiner is in a better position to make and execute appropriate remedial suggestions.
7. The mechanical skill necessary to execute whatever tests are selected for use.

Phenomenology of Testing

Another important concept in relation to psychoeducational testing is that which we identify as the phenomenology of testing. Phenomenology (Snygg and Combs, 1979) refers to the ability to understand the internal frame of reference of the other person. In essence, this means to understand things the way the other person understands them. The phenomenology of testing refers to the ability to understand the way the test subject feels and understands. We contend that by understanding the internal frame of reference of the test subject, the examiner has a richer opportunity to effect a meaningful presenting problem resolution.

The phenomenology of testing is not as easy to practice as it may initially seem. The phenomenology process involves being sensitive to the verbal and nonverbal language of the other individual, and then comprehending that language in terms of the symbolic meaning involved. This process appears to be relatively easy for some secure, empathic, and perceptive people who naturally seem to operate at a meaning level of interpersonal understanding. On the other hand, the phenomenology process seems to be difficult for many people, particularly those who are insecure, defensive, and threatened, and consequently find the meaning level of interpersonal involvement anxiety provoking. This threatened type of person often operates at a shallow level of interpersonal understanding, and never really perceives the beauty (and pain) which lies submerged behind words, body actions, facial gestures, etc. The threatened test examiner is often unable to engage in phenomenology, and can see only the shell of the test subject, and makes recommendations that are consequently shallow and sterile. On the other hand, the secure test examiner is often able to engage in phenomenology, and can see the richness and depth of the subject, and makes recommendations that are alive with creative presenting-problem resolution suggestions.

The Purpose of Testing

The last important introductory concept that should be considered is the purpose of testing. We consider human life intervention as a private and delicate process. Such an intervention should be contemplated only when as many variables as possible have been controlled, and only after a great deal of thought has been devoted to the intervention rationale. It becomes important to place psychoeducational testing in its appropriate context.

We contend that psychoeducational testing should be conducted only under the following conditions:

1. The only justification for testing is to acquire information that will assist with the resolution of a presenting problem. We contend that the efficiency with which an intervention is conducted will effect the likelihood of intervention success. Intervention efficiency can be increased by means of understanding the presenting problem, through the use of formal and informal psychoeducational instruments. The more a presenting problem can be understood, the easier it will be to effect successful problem resolution. We argue that

psychoeducational testing is essential to the resolution of a presenting problem, but it is only for the purpose of such resolution that any test should be given.

2. Testing should not be conducted unless a specific presenting problem exists which has been sufficiently defined so as to permit the examiner to decide whether testing is appropriate. The only appropriate use of tests is for the purpose of acquiring specific information which is expected to help with the resolution of a presenting problem.

3. Testing can be justified only if the examiner (or interpreter) is capable of translating the test result information into meaningful IEPs and/or recommendations for the recipient of that information. It is wasteful to accumulate volumes of test result information unless that information can be translated into specific and helpful management strategies for the teacher, in teacher-language; for the parent, in parent-language; for the counselor, in counselor-language; for the employer, in employer-language; and so on.

4. In terms of diagnostic-prescriptive teaching and the operation of the management model, psychoeducational testing should not be considered except in the context of an intervention with a learning or behavior problem. Under such circumstances, testing and assessment is appropriate, but only in terms of the acquisition of that part of the learner information that is relevant to the resolution of the presenting problem.

5. No testing is justified unless the ethical considerations presented in the next chapter are appropriately employed.

SELECTED REFERENCES

Rosenthal, R., and Jacobson, L. *Pygmalion in the Classroom*. New York: Holt, Rinehart, and Winston, 1968.

Snygg, D., and Combs, A. *Individual Behavior*. New York: Harper and Row, 1979.

Chapter 4

The Ethics of Psychoeducational Testing and Assessment

Psychoeducational testing should not be conducted without employing the appropriate ethical principles (Ethical Standards of Psychologists, 1977). Identified below are those ethical principles that we regard as important.

1. It is necessary to obtain written parental permission to test (or counsel, or place in a special education class) a minor school subject. This principle exists for four reasons: (a) A lawful human being has the right not to have his privacy invaded. In the case of a minor subject, the parent, and in the case of a subject of majority age, the subject himself, has the right to refuse special professional attention which is not an immediate part of the normal instructional program. Although it may be unwise for such permission to be refused, it still is the prerogative of the individual not to have his privacy invaded. Written parental permission for testing, counseling, special education class placement, etc., represents a protection against future parent or subject claim of invasion of privacy. (b) We contend that it is not the school authorities but the parents of a minor subject who have the ultimate responsiblility for decisions that are made about that subject. It makes good ethical sense to obtain parental permission for any special professional attention that is contemplated for a minor subject, especially when that attention might result in change decisions which could affect the life of the subject and family. Written parental permission represents protection against future claims of change decisions being made without parental approval. (c) We contend that those minor subjects with learning or behavior problems who have the best prognosis for remedial success are the subjects whose parents are cooperative and willing to continue the school remedial program at home. As such, it is urged that admission to special education classes be, among other factors, a function of written parental approval, not only for the school based remedial program, but also for any school or home remedial process for which parental cooperation is necessary. Such parental process might involve parent group counseling, serving as a teacher-aide, providing reinforcement objects for teacher use, etc. In order to obtain written parental approval for such involvement, the proposed remedial process must have been explained to the parents, which is the first step in beginning problem resolution for the minor subject. (d) P.L. 94-142 requires written permission.

2. Do not discuss anxiety provoking test results with a minor subject. We contend that it is wrong to cause an individual stress by presenting emotionally loaded concepts which the individual is incapable of mastering.

3. Do not shock parents or teachers by reporting test results in terms of emotionally loaded words (Crazy, Brain-damaged, etc.), or in terms of deep psychodynamics. It is not defensible to increase the anxiety of the individual who is the object of professional attention. Furthermore, due to increased anxiety resulting from test results being reported in terms of emotionally loaded words, involved teachers or parents may be unable to carry out the recommended remedial program. Thus, when reporting test results, do so in the understandable language of the recipient.

4. Prior to testing, know why you are testing. This can be accomplished by obtaining from the referring individual a specific presenting problem and an indication as to the way in which testing can contribute to the resolution of the problem. If unmet, this ethical principle can result in a vast amount of wasted professional time.

5. Test results are confidential information and may not be released to unauthorized individuals. As a rule, written parental permission should be obtained prior to releasing test result information that involves a minor subject. Similarly, subject permission should be obtained prior to releasing such information if the subject has reached the age of majority.

6. Never test blind. Prior to any testing, acquire as much information about the subject as possible, so that the decision whether to test can appropriately be made, so that the appropriate test battery can be selected, and so that meaningful remediation can be prescribed.

7. Always be qualified to give the test that is being administered.

8. One's own children should not be used for the purpose of gaining practice with test administration and interpretation, especially regarding those tests the results of which could be anxiety provoking to the examiner-parent.

9. The ultimate responsibility for a minor subject belongs to the parents, not educators. Especially regarding a minor subject, we advise against the examiner promising to keep information confidential. Under certain circumstances information should be passed on to appropriate authorities, such as when there is danger to the life of the subject by the subject and when there is danger to the life or property of others by the subject.

10. Test results are confidential information, although they may be subpoenaed by a jurist. Depending on the laws of the state, the test examiner may be exempt from testifying in court regarding confidential information if that examiner is a licensed psychologist, social worker, medical doctor, or attorney. If the examiner is not licensed, that examiner may be required by the jurist to personally present in court the confidential information. In such a case, the examiner has the option of breaking the confidence or risking contempt of court charges.

11. The school cumulative record is public information. As such, confidential information, including test interpretation, should not be kept in the cum folder. We recommend keeping a private professional file for the inclusion of confidential information.

12. It is unethical to test friends, associates, or members of one's family for professional purposes. This principle exists in order to avoid a conflict of interest.

13. In many states it is illegal to represent oneself as a psychologist or psychometrist and counsel or test privately for a fee unless licensed by that state as a psychologist or psychometrist. This means, for example, that the mere acquisition of coursework in psycho-educational testing does not lawfully enable that person to represent himself as a psychologist or psychometrist and test privately for a fee, unless the individual is appropriately licensed.

14. A basic ethical principle is: do not make a client worse by means of the professional relationship.

15. Do not accept a testing responsibility when the presenting problem is beyond your professional ability. Similarly, if you have accepted a testing responsibility but wish to refer the subject to another professional person, your responsibility persists until the subject has been accepted by the individual to whom the referral is made.

16. It is unacceptable to refer a minor subject directly to a physician. Such a referral should be made through channels to the family, and then if the family elects, to a professional person of their choice.

17. Terminate a professional relationship when your services are no longer necessary or productive.

18. It is unethical now, and also probably illegal, to make a major educational change decision about a subject (for example, regular class to MR class) on the basis of IQ test results if the socio-economic, age, ethnic, etc., status of the subject is not represented in the test standardization.

SELECTED REFERENCES

Ethical Standards of Psychologists. Washington, D.C.: American Psychological Association, 1977.

Chapter 5

**The Wechsler Intelligence Scale for Children (WISC);
The Wechsler Intelligence Scale for Children—Revised (WISC-R)
The Wechsler Adult Intelligence Scale (WAIS);
The Wechsler Adult Intelligence Scale—Revised (WAIS-R);
and the
Wechsler Preschool and Primary Scale of Intelligence (WPPSI)**

The remaining chapters of the section present a discussion of formal psychoeducational testing instruments. By interpreting the results of these instruments, it is possible to gain four of the five kinds of learner information essential to effective diagnostic prescriptive teaching and IEP development: (a) obtained and potential problem-solving ability; (b) learning characteristics; (c) achievement data; and (d) sufficient personality information about the subject and family to permit systematic environmental manipulation.

WECHSLER INTELLIGENCE SCALE FOR CHILDREN (WISC)

Introduction

The Wechsler Intelligence Scale for Children (Wechsler, 1949) is an individual intelligence test which is designed for subjects from 5-0 years to 15-11 years of age. With a few exceptions, the WISC is the best individual intelligence test relative to subjects on whom it is standardized. The WISC is mechanically and interpretively similar to the WAIS, so that much of what is discussed herein about the WISC is applicable to the WAIS.

The WISC, WAIS, and WPPSI employ a global definition of intelligence. They measure a comprehensive kind of intelligence that involves traditional intelligence-task problem solving, but also the measurement of thought process, personality, and learning strengths and weaknesses. The WISC does not have a strong standardization, as it is standardized only on Caucasians. The Wechsler tests result in an IQ number. This number is computed by a special procedure, the concept of which differs from the old ratio IQ, and which is identified as the deviation IQ. The deviation IQ concept means that the Wechsler IQ test results of a subject of any given age are, for the purpose of IQ computation, compared with subjects of a similar age. Thus, the deviation IQ does not normally change with age.

Organization and Administration

The WISC is organized in terms of six verbal subtests, which through proration yield a verbal IQ, and six performance subtests, which through proration yield a performance IQ. In addition, the verbal IQ may be combined with the performance IQ to yield a full scale IQ. The WISC has a total of 12 subtests, although usually only ten subtests are employed in the determination of the full scale IQ.

When administering the WISC, each of the 12 subtests results in a raw score, which is the number of correct answers obtained by the subject on the particular subtest. Each of the 12 subtest raw scores can be translated into a scaled score by simple reference to a chart in the WISC manual. The verbal subtest scaled scores may be summed and converted to the verbal IQ by reference to a chart in the manual. Similarly, the performance subtest scaled scores may be summed and converted to the performance IQ. Lastly, the verbal scaled score sum may be added to the performance scaled score sum, resulting in a full scale scaled score sum, which in turn may be converted to the full scale IQ, by reference to the manual chart.

The average WISC verbal, performance, and full scale IQ is 100, and the standard deviation of each is 15. The average WISC subtest scaled score is 10, and the standard deviation of each is 3.

The WISC test form (as well as all other test forms) is called a protocol. In addition to administering the test and filling out the protocol in the prescribed way, it is recommended that the examiner continually take personal notes regarding any unusual subject behavior. These personal notes are confidential and should not be deposited in the subject's cum folder.

The Wechsler tests are psychological instruments and should be treated with ethical care. They require an extended length of time, under professional supervision, for administration and interpretation mastery.

The Wechsler tests employ a valuable but administratively cumbersome scoring feature, which is often employed by other psychoeducational instruments: the concepts of basal score and ceiling score. The basal score is that point in a particular test at which the subject incurs no test item failure. The ceiling score is that point in a particular test at which the subject is no longer able to achieve test item success. The basal score and the ceiling score represent, respectively, the places at which the scoring of the test begins and ends. Tests that employ the basal and ceiling concepts have a subject raw score range between the point of the basal (and the preceding points for which the subject is given credit) and that of the ceiling.

Interpretation

The WISC and WAIS, more than the WPPSI, are subject to three different kinds of clinical interpretation: (a) The quantitative difference between the verbal IQ and performance IQ, (b) the quantitative difference between the subtest scaled scores, and (c) the subtest verbalizations of the subject.

The quantitative difference between the Verbal IQ and the Performance IQ

The average verbal IQ, performance IQ, and full scale IQ is 100. However, this is a theoretical average, and it is unusual for a test-subject to achieve a verbal IQ of 100, a performance IQ of 100, and a full scale IQ of 100. Yet, since the theoretical average individual would have average (100) IQ scores, then the degree to which there is a difference between a subject's verbal IQ and performance IQ suggests a deviation from that theoretical average. Clinically, we regard a difference in either direction of 20 IQ points or more between the verbal and performance IQs as being an interpretively significant deviation. Regarding such a difference, the fact that the verbal IQ is higher than the performance IQ suggests a certain set of interpretative hypotheses, and the fact that the performance IQ is higher than the verbal IQ suggests a different set of interpretive hypotheses. Once again, beginning with a minimum difference of 20 IQ points, the greater the difference in either direction between the verbal and performance IQs, the more that difference deviates from the theoretical average, and the more likely that difference represents an interpretively significant deviation.

The following WISC-WAIS interpretive information (Table I) relates to the clinical meaning that is attached to the way in which a 20 or more IQ point difference manifests itself between the verbal and performance IQs. The following information represents guidelines only, and is not designed to represent hard rules of interpretation.

The reader is encouraged to visualize a horizontal line, which we will let represent the theoretical average IQ of 100. The following interpretive information relates to the way in which the verbal IQ differs from the performance IQ, above or below that average IQ line by 20 or more IQ points, and the interpretive hypotheses which are attached to that IQ score difference.

Table I

Interpretive Hypotheses Attached to Verbal IQ — Performance IQ
Difference of More Than 20 IQ Points.

Verbal IQ Above Performance IQ by 20 or more IQ points.

a. Verbal IQ up and high (e.g., 130-140), and performance IQ down (e.g., around 100), suggests: an academic and intellectual orientation, and not much of a motor or performance orientation; thus, not much of a doer. The more the verbal answers are stilted, an intellectualizing and perhaps obsessive-compulsive subject is suggested.

b. Verbal IQ slightly above 100 (although this varies), and performance IQ down (e.g., 80s), suggests: depression, particularly if the performance subtests are down due to a general slowness of the subject, and the verbal subtest answers are filled with verbalizations of self-punishment, evil, sin, etc.

c. Verbal IQ average or above (although this varies greatly), and performance IQ significantly below average (e.g., 85 or less, although this also varies greatly), with particularly low (7 and under) scaled scores in block design, coding, object assembly, and picture arrangement, in that order, suggests: brain damage, physiological immaturity, and/or poor eye-hand coordination, involving the visual-motor area of the brain.

d. Verbal IQ average or above (although this varies greatly), and performance IQ below average (although this too varies greatly), with particularly low scaled scores in digit span, coding, arithmetic, block design, object assembly, and picture arrangement, in that order, suggests: anxiety. Particular attention should be given to the digit span scaled score, as this is usually the subtest which is most vulnerable to anxiety. As a rule, and other variables being equal, the more digit span is significantly down due to anxiety, the greater the subject's anxiety. Conversely, the higher the digit span score, the more likely the subject is not anxious; i.e., emotionally bland.

Performance IQ above Verbal IQ by 20 or more IQ points

e. Performance IQ often above 100, and verbal IQ slightly below average (although this varies greatly), suggests: acting-out and/or delinquency, if the verbalizations are characterized by impulsive, aggressive, and destructive concepts. In its most nonpathological sense, this performance IQ-verbal IQ difference, without the aggressive verbalizations, could represent a performance oriented doer with limited verbal ability. In a learning disability sense, this performance IQ-verbal IQ difference could represent a verbal apraxia, which would manifest itself in marked expressive language problems with motor-performance strength. A differential diagnosis relative to these three conditions can be made by analyzing the content of the subject's verbalizations (aggression), as well as the ease with which those verbalizations are made.

f. Performance IQ slightly above 100, and verbal IQ often below 90, (although each of these can vary greatly), particularly when an analysis of the verbalizations reveals bizarre and out-of-context ideas, suggests: schizophrenia, usually of the childhood or simple type. The paranoid individual and the paranoid schizophrenic usually have more intact, but odd, thought processes, and their verbal IQ is usually higher than the performance IQ.

g. Performance IQ slightly above 100 (although this can vary greatly), and Verbal IQ often below 85, particularly when the verbalizations are impoverished and culturally poor suggests: cultural difference.

The following interpretative hypotheses relate not to verbal IQ — performance IQ difference, but rather to the similarity between the verbal and performance IQs.

h. Verbal IQ, performance IQ, and full scale IQ all up and high (e.g., 130+), suggests: a powerful problem solver, with equal strength in most areas of problem solving. In and by itself this kind of IQ relationship suggests a tremendous amount of intellectual ability, although before clinically eliminating possible problems from consideration the subject's verbalizations would need to be analyzed as well as the results of other test scores.

i. Verbal IQ, performance IQ, and full scale IQ all down and under 75, with all the scaled scores at 8 or below, suggests: mental retardation. If the IQs are between 50 and 75, and the scaled scores are between 5 and 8, an educable mental retardate is suggested; if the IQs are under 50, and the Scaled Scores are under 5, a trainable mental retardate is suggested.

j. A spatial score can be derived from the sum of the picture arrangement, block design, and object assembly scaled scores.

A conceptual score can be derived from the sum of the information, similarities, and vocabulary scaled scores.

And a sequencing score can be derived from the sum of the digit span and coding scaled scores.

The quantitative difference between the sub test Scaled Scores

Just as the theoretical average individual would achieve Verbal, Performance, and Full Scale IQs of 100, so would that theoretical average individual achieve a Scaled Score of 10 on each of the WISC subtests. This theoretical average result almost never occurs, and the Scaled Scores of most individuals fluctuate 3 or 4 points between each other. Yet, since the theoretical average subest Scaled Score is 10, then the degree to which any subtest Scaled Score deviates significantly from that average of 10 is the degree to which that deviation is diagnostically significant and clinically interpretable. In this context, we regard a Scaled Score deviation of 5 or more points from the theoretical average of 10 as being interpretively significant. Thus, a Scaled Score of 5 or less, or 15 or more, can be interpreted respectively in terms of the test subject having diagnostically significant problems with, or diagnostically significant strength in, the problem-solving ability purportedly measured by the subtest the Scaled Score of which deviates by being either down (5 or less), or up (15 or more).

By this particular interpretive technique, the down or up Scaled Scores are compared to the theoretical average of 10, and not to the performance of the subject. For this reason, we prefer another subtest Scaled Score interpretive technique, which analyzes Scaled Scores in relation to the performance of the subject. This technique involves obtaining the subject's average Verbal subtest Scaled Score, and the subject's average Performance subtest Scaled Score (the average Scaled Score is obtained by summing all the Verbal or Performance Scaled Scores and dividing the sum by the number, not the amount, of Scaled Scores). The examiner now has an average Verbal subtest, and an average Performance subtest, Scaled Score. If any of the Verbal Scaled Scores deviate from the subject's average Verbal Scaled Score by 4 or more points, that deviation is interpretatively significant, and can be understood in terms of a problem with, or strength in, the problem-solving ability purportedly measured by the subtest the Scaled Score of which deviates by either being significantly down (4 or more points below the subject's average Verbal Scaled Score), or significantly up (4 or more points above the subject's average Verbal Scaled Score). The same mechanics and interpretation apply to deviations from the subject's average Performance Scaled Score.

In order to interpret a subtest Scaled Score deviation, it is necessary to know what the various WISC and WAIS subtests purport to measure. The following discussion (Table II) relates to the twelve WISC subtests (as well as to the identical WAIS subtests), and what each subtest supposedly measures.

Table II

What the WISC Subtests Measure

VERBAL SUBTESTS.

INFORMATION: Measures a learned fund of knowledge and general facts. Correct answers are usually dependent on formal education.

COMPREHENSION: Measures judgment, common sense, and practical reasoning ability. Correct answers are dependent on having had a wide variety of practical experience.

ARITHMETIC: Measures number and arithmetic ability. This subtest also measures short-term auditory memory. Correct answers are dependent on concentration ability.

SIMILARITIES: Measures abstract verbal problem-solving ability. This subtest is a good predictor of middle-class, verbally oriented, school success.

VOCABULARY: Measures word or vocabulary knowledge. Correct answers are often dependent on formal education. This subtest is a good predictor of middle-class, verbally oriented, school success.

DIGIT SPAN: Measures short-term auditory sequential memory, and is dependent on concentration ability. This subtest is vulnerable to subject-anxiety.

PERFORMANCE SUBTESTS.

PICTURE COMPLETION: Measures the ability to visually identify common everyday details. This subtest also involves the ability to separate essential from nonessential visual details.

PICTURE ARRANGEMENT: Measures the visual-motor ability to fit parts to the whole, the ability to visually think sequentially, the ability to understand human behavior cause-effect relationship, and to some extent, social intelligence.

BLOCK DESIGN: Measures nonverbal abstract problem-solving ability, visual-motor coordination, and spatial relations. This subtest is probably the most powerful of the performance subtests in terms of measuring basic nonverbal intelligence.

OBJECT ASSEMBLY: Measures visual-motor coordination, spatial relations, and the ability to fit parts to the whole.

CODING: Measures visual-motor coordination, manual dexterity, and flexibility (the ability to conceptually shift). This subtest is thought to be an indication of new learning potential, as correct answers are partially dependent on subject flexibility (ability to shift). This subtest also measures visual memory.

MAZES: Measures planning and anticipation ability, and visual-motor coordination.

By determining the existence of a significant subtest Scaled Score deviation (up or down), and with reference to what the various subtests measure (Table II), it is possible to identify learner problem solving, personality, and learning strengths and weaknesses. Such a procedure is the beginning of the process by which it is possible to obtain the learner information necessary for effective diagnostic-prescriptive teaching.

An additional way of obtaining the necessary learner information, in relation to significant Scaled Score deviations, is presented by Table III. The interpretive hypotheses contained in Table III relate significant subtest Scaled Score deviations to the possible emotional disturbance, mental retardation, learning disability, and/or cultural difference cause of those deviations. As usual, a significant Scaled Score deviation is considered to mean a deviation of 5 or more points from the theoretical average of 10, or 4 or more points from the subject's average Verbal or Performance Scaled Score. Again, the following interpretative hypotheses represent guidelines only, to be confirmed or rejected by subsequent analysis.

By now, the reader should be aware of the interpretive power of psychoeducational tests. However, we wish to emphasize that unless care is exercised, an examiner can become so involved with the identification of subject pathology that the problem-resolution focus becomes unclear, and subject strength and adaptive-coping skills become lost. Thus, despite the fact that psychoeducational test procedures are designed to provide helpful information about presenting problems, and problems often involve pathology, we urge that the examiner initially approach psychoeducational test interpretation in terms of subject personality, problem solving, learning, etc., strength, and then if necessary, proceed to an analysis of weakness and presenting problem etiology. In this way, the subject's adaptive and coping strength will not become lost.

Relative to an analysis of presenting problems, the most benign explanation for a significant Scaled Score drop is fatigue, malingering, or a simple absence (genetic or learned) of the problem-solving ability purportedly measured by the subtest with the down Scaled Score. The examiner should look for simple explanations for Scaled Score deviations first, and then if necessary, move to the more complex (and more clinically tentative) explanation. Table III presents some of those more complex explanations.

Table III

Significant WISC (and WAIS) Subtest Scaled Score
Deviations in Terms of Possible Cause

	Scaled Score Increase, Due to Emotional Problems	Scaled Score Drop, Due to Emotional Problems, Cultural Difference, or Mental Retardation	Scaled Score Drop, Due to Learning Disability
Information:	Obsessive-compulsive personality, especially when the verbalizations are stilted.	Emotional disturbance: repression; poor reality testing; delinquency and/or control problems (acting out). Cultural difference (improverished answers). Mental retardation.	Auditory: input, memory, and/or meaning problems; verbal output disorder.
Comprehension:	Paranoid personality.	Emotional disturbance: delinquency and/or control problems; poor common sense; poor reality testing. Cultural difference. Mental retardation.	Auditory: input, memory, and/or meaning problems; verbal output disorder.
Arithmetic:	Obsessive-compulsive personality; sometimes the paranoid personality.	Emotional disturbance: anxiety; poor concentration; poor reality testing. Cultural difference. Mental retardation.	Short-term auditory memory disorder; verbal output problem.
Similarities:	Obsessive-compulsive personality, especially when the verbalizations are stilted; paranoid personality.	Mental retardation. Cultural difference. Emotional disturbance: poor reality testing; anxiety, and hence concrete thought processes; delinquency and/or control problems.	Auditory: input, memory, and/or meaning problems; verbal output disorder.
Vocabulary:	Obsessive-compulsive personality, especially when the verbalizations are stilted; paranoid personality.	Mental retardation. Cultural difference. Emotional disturbance: poor reality testing; anxiety; delinquency and/or control problems.	Auditory: input, memory, and/or meaning problems; verbal output disorder.

Table III (Continued)

Digit Span:	The alert paranoid personality.	Emotional disturbance: anxiety, which affects attention span; digits backward much better than digits forward suggests thought process difficulty. Mental retardation.	Short-term auditory sequential memory disorder; verbal output disorder.
Picture Completion:	The alert paranoid personality.	Emotional disturbance: poor reality testing, depression. Mental retardation. Cultural difference.	Visual: input, memory, and/or meaning problems; visual figure-ground disorder.
Picture Arrangement:	The ingratiating delinquent and/or con-man.	Emotional disturbance: anxiety; depression; poor reality testing. Mental retardation.	Visual-motor coordination (output) problem; visual input and/or meaning problems.
Block Design:	The perfectionist.	Mental retardation. Emotional disturbance: anxiety; depression.	Visual-motor coordination problem; visual figure-ground disorder; visual input and/or memory problems.
Object Assembly:	The perfectionist; sometimes, the ingratiating con-man.	Emotional disturbance: anxiety; depression; poor reality testing. Mental retardation.	Visual-motor coordination problem; visual figure-ground disorder; visual: input, memory, and/or meaning problems.
Coding:	The perfectionist.	Emotional disturbance: anxiety; depression; control problems. Mental retardation.	Visual-motor coordination problem; visual input and/or memory problems.
Mazes:	The perfectionist.	Emotional disturbance: anxiety; depression; control problems.	Visual-motor coordination problem; visual figure-ground disorder; visual input problem.

The subtest verbalizations of the subject

The WISC (and WAIS) is susceptible to at least three different kinds of clinical interpretation. The first two have been examined above and we shall discuss the third kind of clinical interpretation here. The third interpretation is that of the subject's verbalizations, that is, what the subject says (the particular words), and how the words are said. Although it is impossible to identify the infinite variety of ways in which different kinds of test subjects might express themselves on the WISC (or WAIS), a few illustrations follow.

The depressed subject often has verbalizations characterized by grief, melancholy, evil, sin, wanting to be hurt or to die, etc., and in general, is perceptually as well as motorically slow due to the depression.

The acting-out and/or delinquent subject often has verbalizations characterized by anger, destruction, impulsivity, lack of feeling or concern for others, etc., is often unconcerned about incorrect answers, and is often perceptually and motorically quick, although not concerned about the results of the quickness. Some delinquents, despite their aggressiveness, are ingratiating, and strive to at least superficially establish smooth rapport with the test examiner. This kind of rare individual is often characterized as the con-man.

The learning disabled subject with a low verbal IQ but average or above performance IQ (or the converse) is often revealed not only by the IQ differential and the implied problem-solving difficulty, but also by the fact that this individual usually tries hard to succeed. Unlike the delinquent, this individual usually cares about his performance, but is unable to perform normally, as opposed to the delinquent who often can perform, but will not.

The subject with poor reality testing who is probably somewhere on the continuum of psychosis, usually has verbalizations characterized by odd, out-of-context, and bizarre ideas. These kinds of verbalizations do not make sense when judged against conventional logic, and stand out as being grossly different. For example, a poor reality testing answer to the WISC Information question about who discovered America is, "The forest ranger, because he is outside when it thunders." This is a bizarre answer, that makes no context-sense.

The obsessive-compulsive, as well as the paranoid individual, are usually verbally bright, and have verbalizations that are super-thorough in their attempt to explain the question. This super-thoroughness gives the verbalizations a perfectionistic quality, and the thoroughness often bogs down into the use of huge words as substitutes for simpler words.

The culturally different subject usually has verbalizations that are impoverished and qualitatively poor in nature. Often, the verbalizations of the nonretarded culturally different subject and the mentally retarded subject are similar, although other indices such as the performance IQ, a few average subtest performances, the general nonverbal alertness of the culturally different subject, etc., make the differentiation between the nonretarded culturally different subject and the mentally retarded subject relatively easy.

The anxious subject often reveals the anxiety not so much by the choice of words, but by the way in which the words (as well as nonverbal behavior) are expressed. Thus, the anxious subject may stutter and stammer, be nervous and twitchy, flush and pale, perspire frequently, and on the performance subtests, be quick but motor-perceptually awkward due to the anxiety.

The legitimate mental retardate (not pseudo-MR) has verbalizations that are commensurate with the retarded mental age. The verbalizations are conceptually underdeveloped; slow to be delivered; and often confused, simple, and incorrect without implication of being bizarre.

Selected observations about test interpretation

1. The validity of IQ scores obtained under less than standardized conditions is often questioned. The argument is made that a test should not be given except under optimal conditions, thus assuring that the test results will be the best effort of the subject and therefore valid. Although we are sympathetic to this position, we recognize that optimal conditions in the field are often hard to arrange. Thus, we accept most test results as being valid, but only in relation to the subject, the subject and the particular test, and the stress of the particular moment. We argue that test results are always meaningful, but only in a context that is relative to the subject and the test-moment.

2. We stress the identification of the difference between the obtained and potential IQ. Obtained IQ refers to a subject's typical problem-solving ability. Potential IQ refers to a subject's best predicted problem-solving ability as an indication of what the subject might be capable of doing were problem-solving impediments

removed. We contend that many special education students have a marked difference between obtained and potential problem-solving ability. The importance of that difference, and the humanistic issue at stake, is that if a subject's potential problem-solving ability can be identified, then attempts can be made to program that subject up to that potential ability, as opposed to operating at a lesser rate of problem-solving fulfillment.

Obtained IQ corresponds to the acquired IQ. A subject with a Performance IQ of 121 has an obtained Performance IQ of 121, and other variables being equal, would likely perform at that (superior) level of problem-solving ability with respect to performance kinds of tasks.

On the other hand, and especially with respect to the Wechsler tests, since each subtest may measure a different aspect of problem solving, the highest Verbal or Performance subtest Scaled Score can be regarded as an indication of that subject's Verbal or Performance potential problem-solving ability. Although the Verbal or Performance potential problem-solving ability cannot be considered a level of problem solving which a subject will immediately (or ever) attain, the recognition of the potential level of ability permits a different consideration of the subject, which, if the focus were only on the obtained IQ, would otherwise be obscured.

As a rough rule, it is possible to convert separate subtest Scaled Scores into approximate IQ values by equating each Scaled Score point above or below 10 with five IQ points. Thus, the subject with the Performance IQ of 121 whose highest Performance Scaled Score is 19 on the Block Design subtest would have a potential Performance problem-solving ability of 145.

Applying the concept of potential problem-solving ability to the accurate identification of the condition of mental retardation, we can now understand that many presumed mentally retarded subjects are not mentally retarded at all. Although their Verbal and Performance IQs may be below 75, some Scaled Scores are often in the average range, thus suggesting average ability in those problem-solving areas as well as average Verbal or Performance potential problem-solving ability. Such average ability is incompatible with the label of mental retardation. In order to justify the label mental retardation, we argue that all MR subject IQs should be below 75 and all Scaled Scores by 8 or under.

In summary, we suggest identifying the high Scaled Scores and then equating them with problem-solving strength, and identifying the low Scaled Scores and equating them with problem-solving weakness.

3. We stress the identification of learning characteristics. Learning characteristics refer to auditory, visual, verbal, graphic, and/or haptic (the combination of tactual and kinesthetic), input, memory, meaning, and/or output processes. Strengths and weaknesses are psychometrically represented by high and low subtest scores. Although the WISC (and WAIS) can reveal learning characteristic strengths and weaknesses, as symbolized by the information contained in the third column of Table III, the Wechsler tests are not as good for this purpose as is the ITPA.

We suggest identifying the high and low Scaled Scores and attributing problem-solving strength to the high scores and problem-solving weakness to the low scores. However, the fact that a given Scaled Score is high or low does not necessarily imply a learning characteristic strength or weakness because other variables, such as emotional disturbance, cultural difference, mental retardation, malingering, etc., can cause high or low Scaled Scores. If other causes of high and low Scaled Scores can be ruled out, the examiner can hypothesize that high and low Scaled Scores reflect a learning characteristic strength or weakness.

4. The theoretical average individual would have no high or low Scaled Scores, but rather a flat profile. However, that theoretical average individual does not exist. As a rule, the more variable the Scaled Scores are in relation to each other (for example, each Scaled Score differing 5 or more points from each other), the more something that is not average is causing that variability. Such "between subtests variability" is known as intertest scatter. It is not unusual for emotionally disturbed subjects to have a great amount of intertest scatter. Similarly, within a particular subtest, the average test subject usually starts out accurately, and gradually runs out of appropriate problem-solving ability. On the other hand, the emotionally disturbed subject often displays within subtest variability by failing easy questions, passing hard questions, etc., without much consistency. This "within subtest variability" is known as intratest scatter. As a rule, emotionally disturbed subjects often display substantial inter as well as intratest scatter.

5. We have stated that the WISC, with a few exceptions,

is the best individual intelligence test relative to subjects on whom it is standardized. The two major qualifications to the exclusive use of the WISC are: a. The Stanford-Binet is a better instrument to use for the purpose of identifying the condition of mental retardation relative to individuals whose chronological age is under eight years. This is so because of the good standardization and clinical use of the Binet relative to individuals from two years to seven or eight years of age. Furthermore, the WISC is standardized only down to the age of five years, and a mental retardate whose chronological age is under eight years could well have a mental age below the level at which the WISC begins to measure intelligence. If such were the case, the WISC would not be capable of measuring the subject's true mental age.

b. The strength of the Stanford-Binet is in its ability to measure intelligence relative to individuals whose chronological age is from two years to seven or eight years. Since the WISC is weakest at the five- and possibly six-year levels, the Binet is preferred for the purpose of measuring the intelligence of the average five-year-old individual. However, to the degree that the five-year-old is precocious, the WISC probably has as much strength as the Stanford-Binet.

WISC interpretation exercises

The following WISC information is in the form of IQs and Scaled Scores. The reader is invited to analyze the four profiles in terms of the conditions that might have caused the nonaverage kind of high or low Scaled Scores and IQs.

1. Verbal IQ 67, Performance IQ 62, Full Scale IQ 65
   I (Information), 6; C, 5; A, 6; S, 4; V, 5; DS, 6; PC, 7; PA, 7; BD, 4; OA, 6; C, 4
2. Verbal IQ 96, Performance IQ 89, Full Scale IQ 93
   I, 9; C, 10; A, 5; S, 9; V, 9; DS, 3; PC, 10; PA, 8; BD, 5; OA, 8; C, 4
3. Verbal IQ 61, Performance IQ 52, Full Scale IQ 56
   I, 5; C, 6; A, 6; S, 10; V, 9; DS, 1; PC, 2; PA, 5; BD, 11; OA, 3; C, 2
4. Verbal IQ 107, Performance IQ 101, Full Scale IQ 104
   I, 11; C, 10; A, 9; S, 11; V, 12; DS, 10; PC, 9; PA, 11; BD, 11; OA, 10; C, 9

Answers: (1) mental retardation, (2) anxiety, (3) pseudomental retardation (this is a profile of a prepsychotic subject — the deviant verbalizations and marked Digit Span drop of which psychometrically suggest the prepsychosis), (4) normal

WECHSLER INTELLIGENCE SCALE FOR CHILDREN — REVISED (WISC-R)

The Wechsler Intelligence Scale for Children - Revised (Wechsler, 1974) is similar in philosophy and mechanics to the 1949 WISC. The WISC-R standardization sample is based on the 1970 census, and is controlled for race; the Verbal and Performance subtests are alternated; and, although the subtest names are the same as for the WISC, some of the subtest questions are different. The WISC-R has not been commercially available long enough to have been subjected to the same clinical and research experiences as the WISC. As such, it is premature to judge whether the clinical interpretation of the two tests is the same.

WECHSLER ADULT INTELLIGENCE SCALE (WAIS)

The Wechsler Adult Intelligence Scale (Wechsler, 1955) is an individual intelligence test which is designed for subjects sixteen years of age and up. The WAIS has a better standardization than the WISC in that the WAIS includes non-Caucasians. The WAIS administration is similar to the WISC. Likewise, the WAIS subtests are conceptually identical to the WISC, except that the WAIS has only eleven subtests: the WISC mazes have been left out of the WAIS.

The clinical interpretation of the WAIS is similar to the clinical interpretation of the WISC, and therefore we shall not repeat it here. Although the WISC and WAIS are both good individual tests of intelligence, the WAIS results are probably more credible, as the WAIS population is older and thus less variable than especially the lower end of the WISC population. We regard the WAIS as the best individual intelligence test currently commercially available.

WECHSLER PRESCHOOL AND PRIMARY SCALE OF INTELLIGENCE (WPPSI)

The Wechsler Preschool and Primary Scale of Intelligence (Wechsler, 1963) is an individual intelligence test that is designed for subjects between the ages of four and six and one-half years. The WPPSI has an acceptable standardization, but has not received the clinical use of the WISC and WAIS, due in part to the young age and hence variability of the population for which it is designed.

The WPPSI is administratively and interpretively similar to the WISC. The WPPSI has eleven subtests, eight of which are conceptually the same as the WISC. The WPPSI adds one entirely new subtest, and changes the name (and mechanics somewhat) of two other subtests. A major administrative difference between the WPPSI and the WISC is that on the WPPSI, the various Verbal and Performance subtests are presented in an alternating way, whereas on the WISC all the Verbal subtests are presented, then all the Performance subtests are presented. The interpretation of the WPPSI subtests is similar to the corresponding WISC subtests, and therefore will not be repeated here. However, the clinical interpretation of the WPPSI should be more cautiously made than that of the WISC because of the young age and hence variability of the WPPSi subjects, and also because the WPPSI has not had the same clinical use as the WISC.

We regard the WPPSI unfavorably. This is because the WPPSI age range competes with the WISC and Stanford-Binet tests, both of which have had more clinical use and are, in our opinion, better instruments. In addition, the WPPSI has a low ceiling with respect to intellectually gifted subjects; this means that very intelligent subjects are capable of getting all the WPPSI questions correct, a situation which results in an inaccurate assessment of the intellectual power of these individuals.

WECHSLER ADULT INTELLIGENCE SCALE-REVISED (WAIS-R)

The Wechsler Adult Intelligence Scale-Revised (Wechsler, 1981) is similar in philosophy and mechanics to the 1955 WAIS. The two tests apparently measure the same "abilities"; the content, administration, and scoring of the WAIS-R have been slightly changed; and the WAIS-R standardization is based on the 1970 (and more recent) Census data. The similarity of the two tests suggests that the clinical interpretation of the WAIS-R is the same as the WAIS.

SELECTED REFERENCES

Wechsler, D. *The Measurement and Appraisal of Adult Intelligence.* Baltimore: The Williams and Wilkins Company, 1972.

Wechsler Adult Intelligence Scale. New York: The Psychological Corporation, 1955.

Wechsler Adult Intelligence Scale - Revised. New York: The Psychological Corporation, 1981.

Wechsler Intelligence Scale for Children. New York: The Psychological Corporation, 1949.

Wechsler Intelligence Scale for Children - Revised. New York: The Psychological Corporation, 1974.

Wechsler Preschool and Primary Scale of Intelligence. New York: The Psychological Corporation, 1963.

Chapter 6

The Stanford-Binet Intelligence Scale

The Stanford-Binet Intelligence Scale (Terman & Merrill, 1972) is one of the oldest individual intelligence tests. It was originally (1905) designed in the form of the Binet-Simon Scale to identify French students who were "subnormal." In 1916, under the direction of L. M. Terman at Stanford University, the Binet-Simon Scale was adapted, a situation which resulted in the Stanford-Binet Intelligence Scale. Since that time, the test has been revised several times, although some of the test items are nonetheless outdated.

The Stanford-Binet Intelligence Scale (Binet) is designed to measure the general intelligence of individuals from the age of two years to about eighteen years. Originally the Binet employed the mental age concept for the purpose of reporting intelligence. However, at the time of its 1960 revision, IQ conversion charts were developed and included in the manual, a situation which permits an easy translation from mental age to a deviation IQ.

The Binet has some weaknesses: the Binet is awkward to administer, primarily because it is an age-scale type of test, and it employs the basal and ceiling score concepts, a combination of two procedures which can result in a protracted administration. The revised Binet standardization is weakened by the use of only Caucasians in the sample. The Binet is not as clinically useful as the Wechsler tests, particularly for the purpose of identifying personality characteristics. The WISC is a better intelligence test relative to normal subjects who are six years of age or older. And, the Binet method of calculating the mental age and IQ is more cumbersome than the Wechsler test method.

The Binet has many strengths: in our opinion, the Binet is the best individual intelligence test relative to standardization subjects between the ages of two and six years. The Binet provides a higher ceiling than most other individual intelligence tests, and therefore it is possible to test the intellectual power of very gifted young children (above the IQ of 150).

Another strength of the Binet relates to its mental age basis. Some individuals can better understand the meaning of intellectual problem-solving ability when that ability is presented in the form of mental age rather than IQ. This is so because the mental age concept is similar to the chronological age concept, which most people understand. For some teachers and parents in particular, it is often easier to comprehend the problem-solving ability of a five-year-old child when that child is described as having a mental age of six years, as opposed to an IQ of 120.

The mental age basis of the Binet accounts for another strength. The Binet is organized by mental age levels (2-year level, 2½-year level, 3-year level, etc.). Theoretically, the average individual has a mental age equal to his chronological age. This average individual on the Binet should be able to correctly solve all tasks included in the mental age level which is equivalent to his chronological age. This is tantamount to the concept of developmental tasks. For example, since the task "copying a circle" appears in the Binet three-year mental-age level, the average three-year-old should be able to copy a circle. The Binet provides developmental problem-solving tasks for the age levels utilized by the Binet, and if one were interested in, for example, what the normal three-year-old should be able to do (in relation to what the Binet measures), it would be appropriate to refer to the Binet three-year test level for the developmental tasks of a three-year-old.

Another Binet strength involves a rather rare application of the test. Between the mental ages of two and six, the Binet provides its only clinical strength, viz., identifying learning characteristic strengths and weaknesses. Based on a knowledge of what learning characteristics are measured by the various Binet questions, it is possible to analyze the questions failed, and therefrom hypothesize learning strengths and weaknesses.

Table IV presents the major learning characteristics thought to be measured by the Binet questions from the two-year level to the seven-year level. Such data represent hypotheses only, and are not offered as hard rules of interpretation.

Table IV

Learning Channels as Measured by Stanford-Binet Questions

Year II

1: Visual memory, visual-motor coordination (output)
2: Visual memory
3: Auditory memory, auditory-visual association
4: Visual-motor coordination
5: Visual memory, verbal output
6: Verbal output

Year II - 6

1: Auditory memory, auditory-visual association
2: Auditory memory, auditory-visual association
3: Visual memory (revisualization), verbal output
4: Visual memory, verbal output
5: Auditory sequential memory
6: Auditory sequential memory, motor output

Year III

1: Visual-motor coordination
2: Visual memory, verbal output
3: Visual-motor coordination
4: Visual memory
5: Visual-motor coordination
6: Visual-motor coordination

Year III - 6

1: Visual input, spatial relations
2: Visual-motor coordination, spatial relations
3: Visual input and memory
4: Visual meaning, verbal output
5: Visual-motor coordination
6: Auditory input and meaning, verbal output

Year IV

1: Visual memory, verbal output
2: Visual memory
3: Abstract verbal ability
4: Auditory-visual memory and association
5: Visual input and memory
6: Auditory input and meaning

Year IV - 6

1: Visual input and meaning
2: Abstract verbal ability
3: Visual input, auditory-visual association
4: Auditory input and meaning
5: Auditory sequential memory, motor output
6: Auditory input and meaning

Year V

1: Auditory-visual association, visual-motor coordination
2: Visual memory, visual-motor coordination
3: Auditory memory and meaning, verbal output
4: Visual-motor coordination
5: Visual input, auditory-visual association
6: Visual-motor coordination

Year VI

1: Auditory memory and meaning, verbal output
2: Abstract verbal ability
3: Visual input, memory, and meaning
4: Auditory input, memory, and meaning, visual-motor coordination
5: Abstract verbal ability
6: Visual input, auditory-visual association, visual-motor coordination

The learning channel strength and weakness assessment use of the Binet is rare. However, we regard the Binet as one of the two best commercial instruments for such an assessment purpose.

SELECTED REFERENCES

Terman, L., & Merrill, M. *Stanford-Binet Intelligence Scale: Manual for the Third Revision, Form L-M.* Boston: Houghton Mifflin, 1972.

Thorndike, R. L. *Monograph: 1972 Form L-M norms.* Boston: Houghton Mifflin, 1973.

Chapter 7

The Peabody Picture Vocabulary Test and Peabody Picture Vocabulary Test-Revised; and the Columbia Mental Maturity Scale

The Peabody Picture Vocabulary Test

The Peabody Picture Vocabulary Test (Dunn, 1965) is a quick, auditory-visual association, individual intelligence test which is designed for subjects between the ages of 2½ and 18 years. The Peabody Picture Vocabulary Test (Peabody) is capable of rendering IQ results from the IQ 10 to IQ 175.

The Peabody employs the concepts of basal and ceiling scores; it usually has a high subject interest factor; and the administration involves showing the subject a page with four different black and white pictures, saying a stimulus word, and asking the subject to point to one of the four pictures which best describes the stimulus word.

The Peabody has many advantages: (1) the ability to read is not necessary for the purpose of taking the test, (2) subject responses need not be oral, and as such the Peabody may be used with speech-impaired subjects, (3) the Peabody may be used with seriously physically impaired subjects, although at least one means of communication should be established between the subject and the examiner (for example, eye blink, finger movement, etc.), (4) the Peabody has been translated into foreign languages, (5) it is simple, quick, and untimed, (6) there are two alternate but equivalent forms, which permit a test-retest in rapid succession, (7) a simple formula is provided in the manual for the purpose of determining the IQ if a subject's problem-solving level is above or below the figures in the charts, (8) much clinical research has been done with the Peabody, and particularly regarding its use with mental retardates, and (9) since the Peabody is an auditory-visual association intelligence test, the results can be used to predict success in verbally oriented middle-class education (other variables being equal).

The Peabody has some disadvantages: (1) the standardization is regionally limited, and involves only Caucasians, (2) it has only a limited clinical use, and (3) in our experience, and with respect to the same subject, the Peabody IQ results are often 5–10 IQ points higher than the equivalent WISC or Binet IQs, and especially so with mental retardates. The implication is that an examiner should not rule out true mental retardation because of a Peabody IQ of 79 or 80, in that the Peabody tends to record high.

The PPVT-R (Dunn, 1981), is a measure of receptive vocabulary which yields age-based standard scores. The test retains its quick screen nature, the four multiple choice picture items, and easy translation from raw score to standard scores, although the stimulus pictures are new. The norms are based on a representative sample of 5000 individuals, who were matched relative to census data for ethnic group, parent occupation, sex, and geographical region. The standardization norms range from two years to 40 years of age.

COLUMBIA MENTAL MATURITY SCALE

The Columbia Mental Maturity Scale (Burgemeister et al., 1972) is an easy to administer, high interest, essentially nonverbal, individual intelligence test. It is standardized on children from three years, six months through nine years, eleven months of age. The Columbia requires no verbal response from the subject, and requires only a minimal motor response (eye blink, finger movement, etc.). It can be used meaningfully with subjects who are deaf, aphasic, with nonreaders, or seriously physically handicapped.

The Columbia is easy to score; it is not clinical in

nature; and it is untimed, and therefore a power test.

The Columbia operates on the basis of nonverbal symbol discrimination and reasoning ability. The test consists of 92 cards that are arranged in a series of eight overlapping levels. Each level has from 51 to 65 cards and normally a subject takes only the level that is appropriate for his chronological age. Each card has from three to five objects, one of which is different from the others. The subject is directed to select the one object that is different.

The Columbia expresses itself in five possible scores: (1) A raw score, which is not interpretable; (2) an age deviation score (ADS), which is somewhat similar to the deviation IQ concept, which has a range of 50 to 150, and which has a mean score of 100 and a standard deviation of 16. The ADS reflects the degree to which a subject's score deviates from the average score of subjects of a given chronological age; (3) a percentile score, based on the ADS; (4) a Stanine score, which has a range of 1 to 9, with a middle value of 5, and which is based on the ADS; and (5) a maturity index (MI), which is a number-letter value that expresses which one of 13 Columbia standardization age-groups the subject's score most closely resembles. All five of the possible Columbia scores are easy to obtain by means of manual charts.

We have found the Columbia effective for obtaining a rough indication of nonverbal problem-solving ability from subjects who, because of paralysis, aphasia, etc., had been thought to be untestable.

SELECTED REFERENCES

Burgmeister, B., Blum, L. H., & Lorge, I. *Columbia Mental Maturity Scale*. New York: Harcourt Brace Jovanovich, 1972.

Dunn, L. *Peabody Picture Vocabulary Test*. Minnesota: American Guidance Service, 1965.

Dunn, L., & Dunn, L. *Peabody Picture Vocabulary Test-Revised*. Minnesota: American Guidance Service, 1981.

Chapter 8

**Wide Range Achievement Test (WRAT);
Peabody Individual Achievement Test (PIAT):
Auditory Discrimination Test;
Test of Auditory Discrimination (TAD);
Key Math Diagnostic Arithmetic Test;
and the Test Battery Concept and Exercise**

WIDE RANGE ACHIEVEMENT TEST (WRAT)

The Wide Range Achievement Test (Revised) (Jastak and Jastak, 1978) measures achievement in written spelling, written arithmetic, and oral reading from nursery school to grade 18. Each of the three achievement tests has two levels, with Level I being appropriate for individuals from the chronological age of five years to 11-11 years, and Level II being appropriate for individuals who are 12 years of age and older. In addition, each of the three achievement tests employs a pretest, which is appropriate for individuals below a certain chronological age as well as individuals above that age who score below a certain minimum point.

The WRAT administration is initially cumbersome, although with practice it becomes easy, and usually takes less than 25 minutes to administer and score.

One of the cumbersome WRAT features involves the use of the basal and ceiling score concepts, which are different for each of the three achievement tests, and also different for the determination of when to give the pretests. The following information (Table V) is designed to make the basal and ceiling score operation more understandable.

We regard the WRAT as a good instrument for the purpose of measuring achievement in the areas of written spelling, arithmetic computation, and word recall. However, as with the Peabody and Columbia tests, without adaptation, the WRAT is not useful as a clinical tool since it provides only achievement results in the form of grade level scores.

Table V

WRAT Basal-Ceiling Scores for Tests and Levels

	Spelling	*Arithmetic*	*Reading*
Ceiling	10 consecutive failures	10 minutes	12 consecutive failures
Level I 5 years to 11-11 years	Prespelling test: 5 years to 7-11 years or less than 7 correct points	Prearithmetic test: 5 years to 7-0 years or less than 5 correct points	Prereading test: Under 8 years or failure on the first line
Level II 12 years and up	Prespelling test: Less than 5 correct points	Prearithmetic test: Less than 6 correct points	Prereading test: Less than 11 correct points

PEABODY INDIVIDUAL ACHIEVEMENT TEST (PIAT)

The Peabody Individual Achievement Test (Dunn and Markwardt, 1970) is a wide-range screening measure of achievement in mathematics, reading recognition, reading comprehension, spelling, and general information. The PIAT is an individual, and easy to administer, test; it measures achievement from kindergarten through grade 12; and it results in four types of derived scores, viz., grade equivalents, age equivalents, percentile ranks, and standard scores.

The PIAT items are arranged in order of their difficulty; the basal and ceiling scores are easy to use; demonstration and training exercises are available for each of the five tests, thus increasing the stability of the instrument, especially for young or immature subjects; and only a pointing or oral response is required for three of the five tests, thus making the PIAT an appropriate test for subjects who are unable to perform on written achievement tests.

We regard the PIAT as a good and somewhat innovative screening (but not diagnostic) achievement test.

AUDITORY DISCRIMINATION TEST

The Auditory Discrimination Test (Wepman, 1958) is an administratively quick instrument that is designed to measure auditory discrimination. It operates on the basis of two equivalent forms, each of which has 40 short word-pairs, 10 of which are the same (lack-lack), and 30 of which are different (tub-tug). The subject is turned with his back to the examiner, and the examiner pronounces the word-pairs. The subject is asked to indicate whether the word-pairs are the same or different. The dissimilar words are organized into an X column, and the similar words are organized into a Y column. Subject X and Y errors are recorded, then summed, and the total X error score is compared to the error norms. Those norms are:

For 5 year olds, X errors greater than six.
For 6 year olds, X errors greater than five.
For 7 year olds, X errors greater than four.
For 8 year olds and older, X errors greater than three.

By determining the subject's age and number of X errors, and by reference to the above norms, it is possible to determine whether the subject is thought to be within normal auditory discrimination limits, or whether the subject has an auditory discrimination problem.

The revised Auditory Discrimination Test (Wepman, 1973) is almost identical in context and operation to the 1958 Auditory Discrimination Test. The primary practical difference between the two versions is that interpretation of the 1973 test results is made on the basis of the "correct score," whereas interpretation of the 1958 test results is made on the basis of the "error score." Nonetheless, the 1973 test form and scoring standards are compatible with the 1958 test.

TEST OF AUDITORY DISCRIMINATION (TAD)

The Test of Auditory Discrimination (Goldman, Fristoe, and Woodcock, 1970) provides a measure of auditory discrimination under ideal listening conditions, and a measure of auditory discrimination in the presence of controlled background noise. The test is individually administered, and normed for subjects from four years of age to above 70 years; it operates on the basis of word-picture associations; no spoken or written response is required of subjects; and the test employs a training procedure which serves to familiarize subjects with the concept of word-picture associations.

The TAD involves the use of prerecorded tapes and a tape player, and the use of high-fidelity earphones is recommended; an attempt is made to reduce the possible effects of language development on the test results; the test is of short duration, but the use of hardware complicates the administration; and, for all practical purposes, the test results are expressed in percentile scores and standard scores.

We regard the TAD as operationally sound, and as a more complete but more administratively complicated, measure of auditory discrimination than the Wepman Auditory Discrimination Test.

KEY MATH DIAGNOSTIC ARITHMETIC TEST

Key Math is an individually administered diagnostic test of mathematics skill. The test items are divided into

14 subtests, which are organized into three major areas: Content, Operations, and Applications. The 14 subtests are:

Content

A. Numeration
B. Fractions
C. Geometry & Symbols

Operations	*Applications*
D. Addition	J. Word Problems
E. Subtraction	K. Missing Elements
F. Multiplicatioon	L. Money
G. Division	M. Measurement
H. Mental Computation	N. Time
I. Numerical Reasoning	

Key Math is designed to provide four levels of diagnostic information: total test performance, which is expressed in the form of a grade equivalent score; area performance; subtest performance; and item performance.

Key Math was normed on subjects from kindergarten grade through grade 7; the test materials are attractive and easy to use; the test takes about 30 minutes to administer; and the results of the test are recorded on a Diagnostic Record, which yields a diagnostic profile of mathematics performance.

One of the interesting features of the Key Math test is a written description, in behavioral objective form, of the mathematics skill measured by each of the 209 test items. It would be possible to begin a remedial mathematics program by using those behavioral objectives that relate to the individual's strengths and weaknesses, as revealed by the diagnostic profile.

INTRODUCTION OF THE TEST BATTERY CONCEPT

Presenting problem resolution is partially made possible by the acquisition of certain kinds of information about the learner. Such acquisition is often a matter of using a battery of tests which have been carefully selected so as to yield information necessary to help resolve the presenting problem. After the various tests have been administered, the results should be interpreted with respect to the way in which they corroborate each other relative to explaining the presenting problem. Thus, it is important to use cross-validated results from a test battery for the purpose of effecting problem remediation.

The following information represents an exercise in cross-validating test battery results. The reader should analyze the test results and form hypotheses as to the nature of the presenting problem, obtained and potential IQ, learning characteristics, personality strengths and weaknesses, and so on.

Subject: Margaret, chronological age 9-2, third grade.
Presenting problem: poor phonic reading, poor phonic spelling, and poor oral arithmetic ability; much better with visual and visual-motor tasks.
WISC: Verbal IQ 70, Performance IQ 132, Full Scale IQ 99.

I (Information), 6	PC, 14
C, 5	PA, 13
A, 4	BD, 16
S, 7	OA, 14
V, 6	C, 16
DS, 3	

Binet IQ: 89
Peabody IQ: 78
Columbia ADS: 120
Test of Auditory Discrimination: 14th percentile
WRAT: S, 1.0; A, 3.1; R, 1.2

SELECTED REFERENCES

Connolly, A., Nachtman, W., and Pritchett, M., *Key Math Diagnostic Arithmetic Test*. Minnesota: American Guidance Service, 1976.

Dunn, L., & Markwardt, F. *Peabody Individual Achievement Test*. Minnesota: American Guidance Service, 1970.

Goldman, R., Fristoe, M., & Woodcock, R. *Test of Auditory Discrimination*. Minnesota: American Guidance Service, 1970.

Jastak, J., & Jastak, R. *Wide Range Achievement Test Manual* (Revised). Delaware: Guidance Associates, 1978.

Wepman, J. *The Auditory Discrimination Test*. Chicago: Language Research Associates, 1958.

Wepman, J. *The Auditory Discrimination Test* (Revised edition). Chicago: Language Research Associates, 1973.

Chapter 9

The Illinois Test of Psycholinguistic Abilities (ITPA)

The Illinois Test of Psycholinguistic Abilities (Kirk, et al., 1968) is a diagnostic tool with which to identify learning channel and problem-solving strengths and weaknesses. It is highly structured, administratively cumbersome, and designed for individuals from 2½ years to 10 years of age.

The original version of the ITPA was published in 1961 as the Experimental Edition. The current version, the Revised Edition, is an improvement over the Experimental Edition partly because of the addition of three subtests. The Revised Edition employs three dimensions of cognitive ability: (1) channels of communication (learning channels), which involve the auditory, visual, manual-motor, and verbal channels; (2) psycholinguistic processes, which involve the receptive process (input), expressive process (output), and the integrative process (memory and meaning); and (3) levels of organization, which involve the representational level (the ability to use symbols in a meaningful way), and the automatic level (the ability to use nonsymbolic tasks in an automatic way). Thus, the ITPA is organized around three dimensions of cognitive abilities: channels of communication, psycholinguistic processes, and levels of organization.

The ITPA is a psycholinguistic test. Psycholinguistic refers to the relationship between psychology and language functions. The ITPA has 12 subtests, each of which appears to measure different psycholinguistic abilities. Table VI identifies these 12 subtests and what each subtest is thought to measure.

Table VI

ITPA Subtests and What They Measure

1.	Auditory Reception:	auditory input and discrimination
2.	Visual Reception:	visual input and discrimination, visual meaning
3.	Visual Sequential Memory:	visual sequential memory
4.	Auditory Association:	abstract verbal ability (like the Wechsler Similarities subtest)
5.	Auditory Sequential Memory:	auditory sequential memory (like the Wechsler Digit Span subtest)
6.	Visual Association:	the ability to comprehend relationships between ideas presented visually (visual meaning)
7.	Visual Closure:	the ability to recognize whole objects from visually presented parts of those objects (visual figure-ground)
8.	Verbal Expression:	expressive conceptual-verbal ability (somewhat similar to the Wechsler Vocabulary subtest, although Verbal Expression emphasizes quantity of expression more than quality)
9.	Grammatic Closure:	learned grammar habits
10.	Manual Expression:	the ability to translate visual ideas into their motor equivalent
11.	Auditory Closure:	the ability to supply missing sounds in words
12.	Sound Blending:	the ability to blend sounds

The ITPA administration is complicated and requires time and effort for mastery. This is due in part to a complex protocol and a set of cumbersome administrative directions. The protocol and directions involve: (1) the application of complicated basal and ceiling score concepts, which are numerically identified in the upper left corner of the protocol for each subtest; (2) a sampling technique, which is applicable to some of the subtests, which is identified by an asterisk immediately to the left of germane questions (e.g., Visual Sequential Memory, numbers 2, 5, 8, etc.), and which permits the examiner to administer only those asterisked questions until a certain ceiling has been established; (3) demonstration items, which are identified in the protocol by Demonstration I, and Demonstration II, which apply to the point at which the examiner begins the administration of the particular subtest, and which relate to, usually, Demonstration I being applicable for subjects under six years of age, and Demonstration II being applicable for subjects who are six years of age and older; (4) a novel way of indicating the correct answers on the protocol, which involves using bold face type to indicate the "yes" (**Y**) or "no" (**N**) correct answer, or using bold face type to indicate the correct number-answer; and (5) the Visual Reception and Visual Association subtest tasks and answers are presented in a clockwise pattern, with number one being on the examiner's right-front when the picture books are open and facing the subject.

The ITPA employs some new scoring concepts:
1. The Raw Score refers to the number of right answers with respect to each subtest, and is not interpretable.
2. The Age Score represents a subject's psycholinguistic age for each subtest and, like chronological age, is expressed in a year-month notation (e.g., 8 years, 3 months). As with mental age, the average standardization individual should achieve an Age Score that is equal to his chronological age. The Age Score is directly interpretable, and forms an excellent way of identifying whether a subject's problem-solving ability for any or all subtests is above or below his chronological age (or mental age). In other words, the Age Score reveals the subject's ITPA-based learning strengths and weaknesses.
3. The Scaled Score (like the Wechsler Scaled Score) is another way of identifying the subject's ITPA-based learning strengths and weaknesses. Scaled Scores (as well as Age Scores) are determined by entering a Manual chart with the particular subtest Raw Score. Scaled Scores, for each subtest, have an average score of 36, and a standard deviation of 6. The theoretical average individual would have ITPA subtest Scaled Scores of 36. As with the Wechsler tests, the degree to which a subject's Scaled Scores deviate from the average of 36 indicates the degree to which that subject is not-average with respect to those particular subtests and what they measure.
4. The Composite PLA (Psycholinguistic Age) represents an integration of the first ten subtest Age Scores into one composite Age Score, which is the Composite PLA. The Composite PLA expresses an overall psycholinguistic age. Since the average standardization individual should have a Composite PLA equal to his chronological age (and mental age), the Composite PLA represents another IPTA-based method of identifying whether a subject is psycholinguistically above average (above his chronological age), or below average (below his chronological age). The Composite PLA is determined by entering an appropriate Manual chart with the Sum of Raw Scores.
5. The Mean SS (Mean Scaled Score) is the subject's average Scaled Score for the first ten subtests (this excludes subtests 11 and 12, Auditory Closure and Sound Blending). The Mean SS is a critical ITPA concept, which is determined by summing the first ten subtest Scaled Scores and then dividing that sum by ten. The Mean SS represents the subject's Mean (average) Scaled Score. The subject's Mean SS should be distinguished from the average Scaled Score figure of 36 in that the 36 figure represents the theoretical average Scaled Score and in no way represents the subject's average Scaled Score. With the Mean SS figure, the examiner may enter the Profile of Abilities chart on the ITPA protocol, find the Mean SS figure in bold type on the extreme right-hand margin, and draw a line from that right-hand margin straight across to the left margin, ending at the bold-face double line. This Mean SS line represents the subject's Mean Scaled Score against

which the subject's subtest Scaled Scores may be compared. Next, the examiner plots (by means of dots) on the Profile of Abilities, each of the subject's subtest Scaled Scores, and connects the dots by a straight line. This will result in a profile of the subject's Scaled Score ability with respect to each ITPA subtest. The important interpretation of the Profile relates to the difference between each of the subject's subtest Scaled Scores and the subject's Mean Scaled Score (which is represented by the right-to-left drawn line). Specifically, a difference between any subtest Scaled Score and the subject's Mean Scaled Score (represented by the drawn line) of plus or minus six is within the normal range and should not be considered an indication of special ability or disability. A difference between a subtest Scaled Score and the subject's Mean SS of plus or minus seven, eight, or nine points is considered to suggest a borderline ability (plus) or disability (minus). A difference between a subtest SS and the subject's Mean SS of plus or minus 10 or greater is considered a substantial strength or weakness, and in the case of a weakness, sufficiently substantial to suggest the need for remediation.

In partial summary, the ITPA is a psycholinguistic instrument which measures learning channel and problem-solving strengths and weaknesses relative to subjects who are from 2½ to 10 years of age. There are three basic ITPA ways to assess learning strength and weakness: (1) by comparing the subject's subtest Age Scores with the subject's chronological age (or mental age), (2) by comparing the subject's subtest Scaled Scores with the theoretical average Scaled Score of 36 for each subtest (in which case the subject is being compared with the average standardization individual), and (3) by comparing the subject's subtest Scaled Scores with the subject's Mean Scaled Score (which is the comparison made by the Profile of Abilities), in which case the subject is being compared with himself. It is this latter comparison for which the interpretation of differences, which was discussed above, has been developed (Kirk, et al., 1968).

Another method of interpreting the ITPA is by examining which subtest Scaled Scores are significantly down (more than 6 Scaled Score points difference between the subtest Scaled Score and the subject's Mean Scaled Score). There are eight ways of interpreting the the meaning of down scores, all of which relate to problem-solving difficulty with the abilities measured by the down subtests.

1. If all, and only, the reception (input) subtest Scaled Scores are down, a decoding (input) disorder is suggested.
2. If all, and only, the expression (output) subtest Scaled Scores are down, an encoding (output) disorder is suggested.
3. If all, and only, the memory subtest Scaled Scores are down, a general memory disorder is suggested.
4. If all, and only, the association subtest Scaled Scores are down, a disorder in the meaning system is suggested.
5. If all, and only, the representational level (first six subtests) subtest Scaled Scores are down, a representational disorder is suggested (the inability to use symbols in a meaningful way).
6. If all, and only, the automatic level (last six subtests) subtest Scaled Scores are down, an automatic disorder is suggested (the inability to automatically use learned language patterns correctly).
7. If all, and only, the auditory channel (input, memory, association) or visual channel, etc., subtest Scaled Scores are down, an auditory, or visual, learning channel deficiency is suggested.
8. If, as is often the case, there appears to be no pattern to the subtest strengths and weaknesses, and if apparently unrelated subtest Scaled Scores are down, then problem-solving difficulty with the particular abilities measured by the down subtests is suggested.

We regard the ITPA as a good diagnostic instrument relative to its intended psycholinguistic purpose. Although we advocate regarding high ITPA Age Scores and Scaled Scores as an indication of learning and problem-solving strength, and low Age and Scaled Scores as an indication of learning and problem-solving weakness, the reader should be cautioned not to conclude that a low ITPA score means a learning disability. A low ITPA score usually indicates that the subject has difficulty with the particular subtest task, but that low score in and by itself does not indicate why the difficulty exists. That difficulty could exist because of emotional problems, sensory impairment, cultural difference, malingering, fatigue, and/or mental retardation, as well as a pure learning disability. Therefore, we suggest that the ITPA be regarded as an instrument which identifies learning or problem-solving strengths and weaknesses, but not as an instrument which identifies the reason for those strengths and weaknesses.

As with the WISC and WAIS, the ITPA subtests are vulnerable to certain kinds of test subject presenting problems. Table VII identifies for each of the twelve ITPA subtests the various presenting problems to which we consider the subtests vulnerable. In other words, Table VII presents information about the kind of problems that can result in marked difficulty with the various subtest tasks.

Although the ITPA test standardization relates only to subjects from the ages 2½ to 10 years, clinically, but without standardization procedures, it is possible to use the ITPA test relative to subjects who are older than 10 years. In so doing, it is assumed that subjects who are older than 10 years but who are unable to achieve the 10 year old subtest norms have problem-solving weaknesses in those particular subtest areas. One of the assets of the ITPA is that its use as a clinical tool has resulted in the buildup of many good ITPA-related remedial programs. It is quite possible to use an exclusive ITPA-related remedial program relative to subjects who demonstrate ITPA learning weakness. Although we support the appropriate use of such remedial programs, we do not recommend their exclusive use.

Table VII

Subject Presenting Problems to Which the ITPA Subtests Are Vulnerable

Auditory Reception	Deaf and hard of hearing Auditory: input, memory, and/or meaning problems Repression Cultural difference Mental retardation
Visual Reception	Blind and partially sighted Visual: input, memory, and/or meaning problems Mental retardation Control problem (acting out)
Visual Sequential Memory	Blind and partially sighted Anxiety Visual sequential memory disorder Mental retardation Control problem Visual-motor coordination (output) problem
Auditory Association	Deaf and hard of hearing Auditory: input, memory, and/or meaning problems Mental retardation Cultural difference Anxiety Concrete thought processes

Auditory Sequential Memory	Deaf and hard of hearing Auditory sequential memory problem Auditory input disorder Anxiety Poor attention and concentration Control problem Mental retardation Delinquents often do well here, usually indicating blandness
Visual Association	Blind and partially sighted Visual input and/or memory disorder Abstract visual meaning problem Cultural difference Mental retardation
Visual Closure	Blind and partially sighted Visual figure-ground problem Visual input and/or memory problem Mental retardation Some delinquents do well here
Verbal Expression	Auditory memory and/or meaning problem Mental retardation Cultural difference Expressive aphasia (output) Repression
Grammatic Closure	Deaf and hard of hearing Auditory: input, memory, and/or meaning problems Cultural difference Mental retardation Delinquency Poor readers and spellers
Manual Expression	Visual: input, memory, and/or meaning problems Motor apraxia (output) Cultural difference Mental retardation Subjects who learn-by-doing often do well here Some delinquents do well here, indicating their motor orientation
Auditory Closure	Deaf and hard of hearing Auditory input and/or memory problem Expressive aphasia Mental retardation Anxiety Auditory based reading problem

Sound Blending   Deaf and hard of hearing
Auditory input and/or memory problem
Anxiety
Auditory based reading problem
Expressive aphasia
Mental retardation

Test Battery Interpretation Exercise

The following data represent an invitation to the reader to use the previously discussed psychoeducational testing concepts for the purpose of interpreting the scores of each of the tests; then comparing the various test scores with each other for the purpose of cross-validating the test interpretations; arriving at an analysis of the subject's obtained and potential IQ, learning strengths and weaknesses, personality characteristics, and an assumption of the presenting problem; and lastly, initiating some thought about how that presenting problem might be resolved.

Subject: Pam; chronological age, 7.7; second grade.
Presenting problem: poor handwriting, poor written spelling, poor spatial ability, and poor fine-motor coordination; but good oral and auditory abilities, including good oral reading.
WISC: Verbal IQ, 116; Performance IQ, 65; Full Scale IQ, 91

I (Information),	10	PC,	7
C,	10	PA,	7
A,	11	BD,	2
S,	16	OA,	6
V,	15	C,	3
DS,	14		

Peabody IQ: 121
Columbia ADS: 77
WRAT: S, 1.0; A, 1.1; R, 3.1

Test of Auditory Discrimination: 88th percentile

ITPA:	CPLA, 7.6; MSS, 34
AR,	37
VR,	34
VSM,	19
AA,	39
ASM,	41
VA,	29
VC,	21
VE,	43
GC,	41
ME,	30
AC,	39
SB,	44

SELECTED REFERENCES

Bush, W., & Giles, M.T. *Aids to Psycholinguistic Teaching* (2nd ed.) Ohio: Charles Merrill, 1977.

Kirk, S., & Kirk, W. *Psycholinguistic Learning Disabilities: Diagnosis and Remediation.* Illinois: University of Illinois Press, 1971.

Kirk, S., McCarthy, J., & Kirk, W. *Illinois Test of Psycholinguistic Abilities.* (Rev. ed.) Illinois: The University of Illinois Press, 1968.

Chapter 10

The Bender-Gestalt Test

The Bender-Gestalt Test (Bender, 1938) is a paper-pencil test which is composed of nine geometric designs and which involves the subject copying those designs (Table VIII presents the Bender-Gestalt Test designs). Each design is placed on a separate 3 x 5 card, with the cards being numbered from A, through number 1, to number 8. The designs are somewhat sequentially arranged from beginning to end in terms of the difficulty of reproduction; the test usually involves about ten minutes of administration, and for the facile practitioner, less than that for interpretation; the test has no basal or ceiling age, except for the ability to copy; the test has a high subject interest factor and therefore is a good choice for beginning a test battery; the test has received extensive clinical use, and as such has a vast amount of practical and research experience associated with it; and the test is applicable to almost all subjects, assuming the ability to copy by means of pencil and paper.

The Bender Test is diagnostically powerful and is appropriate for many different assessment purposes. The test is a psychological instrument; it should be used only by individuals having the necessary professional training; and the test should not be used on one's own children for the purpose of gaining administration or interpretation experience.

In its richest use, the Bender Test is a projective test. This means that subjects project aspects of their personality into the way in which they solve the test tasks. In order to encourage as much subject projection as possible, the test administration directions should be kept to a minimum. The examiner should present the subject with a pile of as many white and unlined 8½ x 11 sheets of paper as there are test cards, and a sharpened No. 2 pencil with an eraser, and express the following directions: "I am going to show you some pictures (or designs for older subjects). I want you to copy them the way you see them." In addition, and consistent with the philosophy of personality projection, the examiner should refer back to the subject any questions asked by the subject, by means of saying, "Do the best you can." Nonetheless, there are two administrative limitations which should be expressed to the subject if the situation arises: (1) the subject should not move the stimulus (design) card from the original examiner-placed position and (2) the reproductions must be made free hand, i.e., without the use of mechanical aids.

As with all psychoeducational tests, we recommend that the examiner take clinical notes on a separate sheet of paper with respect to any unusual subject behavior. In particular, it is important for the examiner to make a caret (ʌ) that identifies the top of the test paper adjacent to any deviantly reproduced test design. This will serve as a record of whether the deviantly reproduced design was perceptually rotated, or reproduced correctly after the test paper was turned.

Psychoeducational Use of the Bender Test

The Bender Test has a variety of psychoeducational uses. The following discussion identifies those uses.

Mental Age. The Bender Test is capable of revealing a subject's mental age, up to a mental age of around 12. The test designs are somewhat sequentially arranged from beginning to end in terms of their difficulty of reproduction. The ability to reproduce the designs is maturational in nature, with the easiest designs requiring a mental age of seven or so for accurate reproduction, and with the most difficult designs (numbers 7 and 8) requiring a mental age of around 11 or 12 for accurate reproduction. By knowing the way in which the various designs are normally reproduced at the various ages between the advent of copying ability and around 12 years, the examiner can estimate the mental age of a subject by comparing the subject's design reproductions with normal reproductions for the subject's age. Another way of expressing this concept is that the normal individual of a given age up to 12 years will reproduce the Bender Test designs in a normal way for that age. If the examiner knows what is normal, then the subject's mental age can be evaluated in terms of the subject's design reproductions being more mature, or less mature, than the normal reproductions for that age. Table IX presents a Bender Test maturation chart, which is designed to assist the reader with the identification of normal test design reproductions at various maturational ages. By reference to the maturation chart, it is a simple matter to determine if a subject's design reproductions are compatible with normal design reproductions for the subject's age, and if not, then the determination of the maturational level of that subject's designs.

Mental retardation. The Bender Test is a good instrument for differentiating between the legitimate mental retardate and pseudomental retardate. Up to a chronological age of approximately sixteen years, the legitimate mental retardate will usually reproduce the test designs in a way compatible with the subject's retarded mental age. Thus, a chronologically 11-year-old legitimate mental retardate with an accurate IQ of 50 will reproduce the designs in a way compatible with a five- or six-year-old child. A true mental retardate should have a Bender Test mental age compatible with the subject's retarded mental age (See Table XII, Nos. 1 and 8). If not, and especially if the Bender test mental age is normal, then the subject is not mentally retarded (although he may be other things), and is more appropriately indentified as pseudomentally retarded.

Cultural Difference. The Bender Test is good for the purpose of differentiating between the true mental retardate and the culturally different subject who is not mentally retarded. Sometimes the IQ test results of these two kinds of subjects appear somewhat alike. However, because the Bender Test is usually more culture-fair than the typical IQ tests, the Bender Test of the culturally different subject who is not mentally retarded usually reflects that subject's higher and non-mentally retarded, nonverbal (Bender Test) mental age, thus distinguishing between the two kinds of subjects.

Brain damage. The Bender Test is helpful relative to identifying subjects with brain damage in the visual discrimination (input) and/or graphic output areas of the brain. The major Bender Test indices of brain damage are: (1) designs reproduced with "dog ears" (See Table X, No. 9c and Table XII, No. 2); (2) designs reproduced with their basic form destroyed, a situation which is referred to as destruction of the gestalt (See Table X, No. 9d and Table XII, No. 12); and (3) designs reproduced in rotated fashion (rotated more than 45 degrees from their correct angle), although in order for rotation to be an indication of brain damage, the rotation should be combined with dog ears and/or destruction of the gestalt (See Table X, Nos. 9 *a. b, c,* and *d*).

Typically, rotated Bender Test designs without dog ears and/or destruction of the gestalt suggest a visual processing disorder, whereas designs reproduced with or without rotation but with dog ears and especially destruction of the gestalt suggest a graphic output disorder. As a rule, and with respect to Bender Test designs reproduced with rotation, dog ears, and/or destruction of the gestalt, if the subject cannot recognize the difference between the design model and the subject's inaccurate reproduction, the difficulty is likely to be of an input nature; if the subject can recognize the difference between the design model and the subject's inaccurate reproduction but is unable to correct the inaccurate reproduction, the difficulty is likely to be of an output nature.

Three cautions should be expressed relative to the use of the Bender Test for the purpose of identifying brain damage: (1) There are many areas of the brain that can be damaged and consequently result in behavior or learning problems. However, the Bender Test is capable of revealing such damage only in the visual discrimination and graphic output areas of the brain. (2) Brain damage implies actual damage to the brain. The Bender Test brain damage indices are often expressed by subjects with frank brain damage, but also by young children who do not have brain damage but who are neurologically immature. These two kinds of subjects often have the same educational presenting problem (visual reading, written spelling, written arithmetic, motor coordination, and/or handwriting difficulty), but the immature subject often neurologically matures with time, which results in a dissipation of the presenting problem. Such neurological maturation and problem dissipation usually do not occur with the frank brain damage subject. (3) It is often contended that the mere presence of design rotation or design distortion is indicative of brain damage. In our experience, this is not always the case. Design rotation or distortion suggest a visual discrimination and/graphic output difficulty, which could be expressed in tool-subject problems (visual reading, handwriting, written spelling, written arithmetic, motor coordination problems). However,

Table VIII

Bender-Gestalt Test Designs

Design A

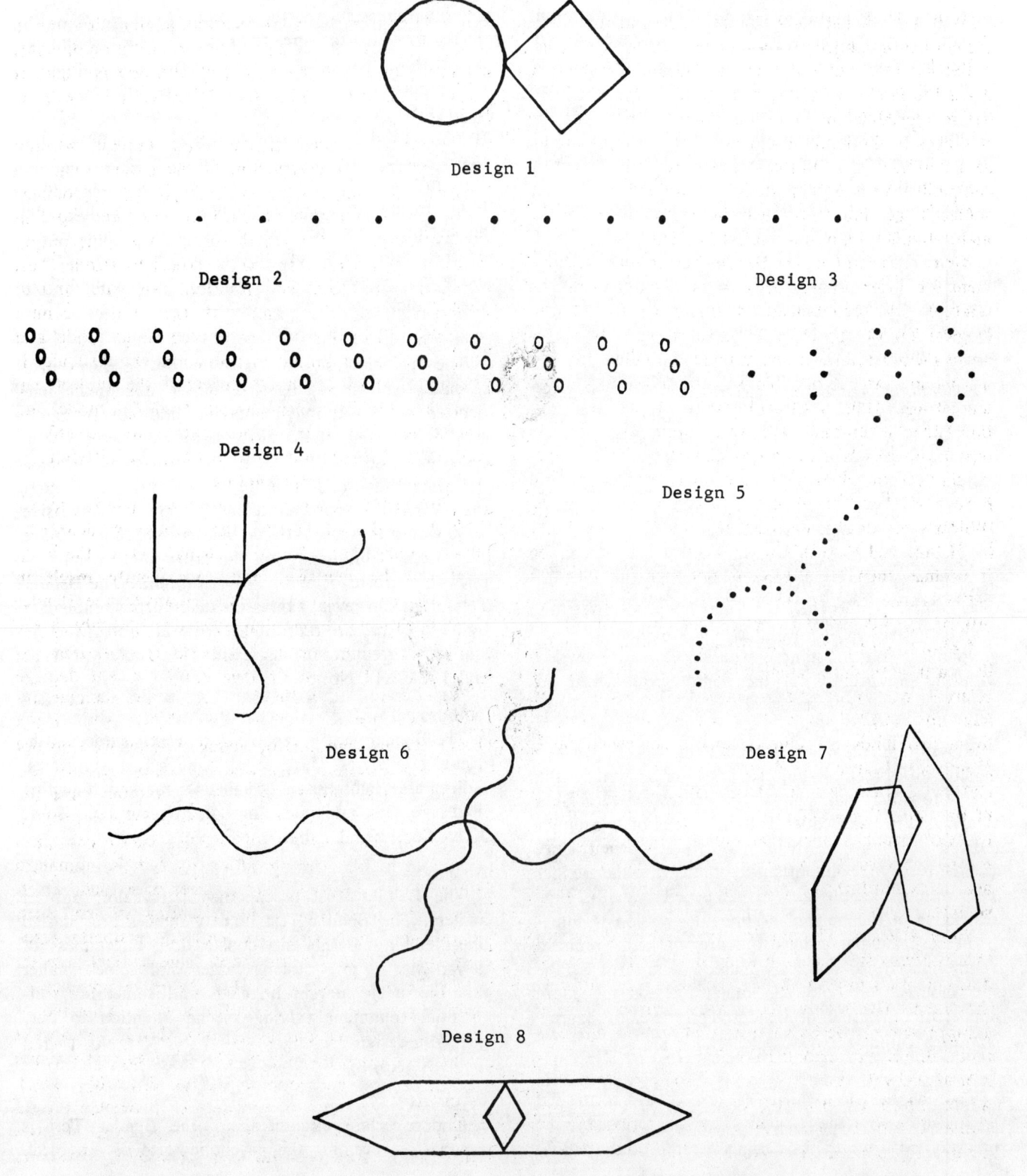

Design 1

Design 2

Design 3

Design 4

Design 5

Design 6

Design 7

Design 8

Reprinted from: Bender, Lauretta. "A Visual Motor Gestalt Test and its Clinical Use." Research Monograph No. 3, *American Orthopsychiatric Association*, 1938. Copyright, the American Orthopsychiatric Association, Inc. Reproduced by permission.

the mere Bender Test presence of visual discrimination and/or graphic output difficulty is insufficient reason to implicate brain damage. The cleaner the design reproductions, despite the rotations and/or distortions, the more likely the visual discrimination and/or graphic output difficulty is due to emotional stress rather than brain damage (See Table X, Nos. 9*a* and *b*). The importance of determining the cause of the difficulty relates to the remediation of the resulting tool-subject problems. Tool-subject problems caused by brain damage induced visual discrimination and/or graphic output difficulty should receive a different kind of educational remediation than the same tool-subject problems caused by emotional stress induced visual discrimination and/or graphic output difficulty.

Educational readiness. The Bender Test is good for the purpose of identifying those kindergarten students who are not maturationally ready to progress to the formal tool-subject programs of first-grade. The test design reproductions of this kind of individual are grossly immature, in terms of scribbling, lack of correct design-form for their age, and/or simply an inability to coordinate the eye-hand system despite near average, average, or even above-average overall intelligence (See Table XII, No. 14). It is our contention that this kind of individual should be retained in kindergarten, given appropriate readiness experiences, and provided with the opportunity for the neurological system to catch up with the chronological age.

Aggression, and control. The Bender Test is often capable of revealing subject aggression as well as the degree to which that aggression is controlled. Agression is revealed in the Bender Test by means of two major indices: (1) heavy, black, and bold pencil lines (which is why it is important to standardize the Bender Test with a medium-lead No. 2 pencil); and (2) irrespective of the bold black lines, aggression is sometimes revealed by designs that are markedly reduced (compressed), or markedly increased, in size. Of the two indices, the bold and black lines is the more important indication of Bender Test revealed aggression (See Table X, Nos. 3*c,* 3*d,* and 11).

The degree to which aggression is controlled is suggested by the Bender Test in terms of the precision with which the designs are reproduced. Bold and black lines suggest the amount of aggression to the degree to which the lines are bold and black. Nonetheless, if those lines are well-drawn, ordered, and precise, the implication is that the subject is controlling the aggression. Although the Bender Test does not directly reveal the following dynamics, it is also the implication that a subject who experiences such controlled aggression probably has or will develop psychosomatic symptoms or has an excellent means of sublimating that aggression. The more the reproduced designs suggest control, despite the amount of aggression, the more likely that aggression is controlled and/or dammed up (See Table X, No. 11).

Acting-out

The Bender Test often is good for the purpose of revealing subject acting-out and/or delinquent tendencies. Acting-out may or may not imply overt aggression. Irrespective of the aggression component, acting-out is expressed in the Bender Test by designs that lack the control factors of accuracy, order, and precision. If the designs are reproduced in a sloppy and impulsive way, with a not-care attitude, acting-out tendencies are suggested. Delinquency, on the other hand, often implies some form of aggressive acting-out. The Bender Test often can reveal aggressive delinquency tendencies by designs that are reproduced without control factors and with a great deal of aggression (See Table X, No. 11 and Table XII, No. 5).

Withdrawal

The Bender Test is capable of revealing subject withdrawal tendencies. The primary Bender Test withdrawal indices are: lightness of design line; marked reduction in design size; and often, margin hugging (See Table XII, No. 11 and Table X, No. 3*b*).

Anxiety

The Bender Test is capable of revealing subject anxiety. The Bender Test anxiety indices are: design line-sketching; design size-constriction; unevenness of design size (some designs larger and some smaller than normal); margin hugging; and sometimes, differential treatment (giving special attention to only part of a design or designs) (See Table XII, No. 11 and Table X, No. 6).

Psychosis

Under certain circumstances, the Bender Test is capable of revealing the psychotic state of a subject.

Table I X

The Maturational Characteristics of the
Bender-Gestalt Test Designs

	A	1	2	3	4	5	6	7	8
AVERAGE 12 YEAR OLD									
AVERAGE 11 YEAR OLD									
AVERAGE 10 YEAR OLD									
AVERAGE 9 YEAR OLD									
AVERAGE 8 YEAR OLD									
AVERAGE 7 YEAR OLD									
AVERAGE 6 YEAR OLD									
AVERAGE 5 YEAR OLD									
AVERAGE 4 YEAR OLD									
AVERAGE 3 YEAR OLD			SCRIBBLING						
AVERAGE 2 YEAR OLD			UNCOORDINATED & RANDOM SCRIBBLING						

The test cannot reveal psychosis unless the subject manifests the psychosis by means of the reality testing with which the designs are reproduced. Thus, the major Bender Test psychotic index is bizarre design reproductions. This means that the reproduced designs, like the subject himself, have little conventional logic attached to them, and are representative of the subject's state of poor reality testing. However, if a subject were sufficiently psychotic to manifest Bender Test psychotic indices, one would probably not need the test to render a diagnosis of psychosis.

The Bender Test as a projective test of personality

Based on the concept of personality projection, the Bender Test can be used as a projective test of personality. This use of the Bender Test is the most clinical of the previously discussed test uses, and the reader is cautioned not to employ the test for this purpose unless possessing the necessary professional training. Before presenting the Bender Test interpretive hypotheses, an important observation should be made. It is our conviction that the use of the Bender Test as a personality test should be preceded by the examiner-acquisition of a theoretical orientation to the understanding of human behavior and psychopathology. Only with the ability to relate the Bender Test personality interpretive hypotheses to a theoretical way of understanding those hypotheses is it possible to make sense out of a projective approach to the test.

The discussion of the use of the Bender Test as a projective test of personality is presented in two sections: personality interpretative hypotheses, and design symbolism. The reader should understand that the various test hypotheses are clinical in nature, and should be integrated with the examiner's theoretical orientation to the explanation of human behavior. As usual, these hypotheses should be regarded as guidelines only and not as hard rules of interpretation.

Bender Test personality interpretive hypotheses.
1. The sequence with which a subject reproduces the designs often relates to the subject's control, planning capacity, and ability to anticipate. The more logical and methodical the sequence, the more likely the subject is logical, controlled, and capable of anticipated planning. On the other hand, the more confused, irregular, or chaotic the sequence, the more likely the subject is confused, lacking in control, and in the extreme sense, poorly integrated (See Table X, No. 1).
2. The place on the paper where the subject draws the first design often relates to subject ego strength or weakness. The normal position is about 15 percent down from the top and 20 percent to the left of middle. The subject who draws the first design in the extreme upper left-hand corner is often anxious, insecure, and timid. The subject who draws the first design at the extreme bottom of the page is often depressed. The subject who draws the first design in the middle of the page and takes most of the page for so doing is often egocentric, often with compensatory acting-out tendencies (See Table X, No. 2).
3. The way in which a subject spaces the designs is often indicative of subject ego strength and control, particularly in relation to the continuum of withdrawal/acting-out. Specifically, the more compressed all the designs are into a very small space (for example, 10 percent of the page), the more likely the subject is rigid, anxious, constricted, and often with a great deal of dammed-up anger. On the other hand, the subject who uses a great deal of space, such as drawing each design on a separate page and using the entire page for that drawing, is usually egocentric, expansive, and, depending upon the amount of aggression and lack of control features involved with the drawings, delinquent. The normal spacing involves an orderly design placement on the page, with generally the use of about once or twice as much white space between the sequenced designs as the designs themselves are tall (See Table X, No. 3).
4. Collision means drawing the designs so that they collide with each other. Collision is rare and in a moderate form suggests strong dependency needs, poor planning capacity, and often, early authority-figure rejection. In the extreme form (each design drawn on top of each other), collision could suggest a psychotic state (See Table X, No. 4).
5. The subject who draws the designs hugging any of the margins (usually the left margin) often is anxious and insecure, and sees the margin

as an external aid in compensating for the insecurity, as well as, perhaps, feared loss of control (See Table X, No. 3b and Table XII, No. 11).

6. The subject who continually shifts the paper 90, 180, and/or 360 degrees, is often aggressive, in an oppositional, petulant, and/or stubborn way.

7. The marked reduction in size of any or all of the designs is suggestive of a subject with reduced external energy due to strong control. This hypothesis needs to be adjusted in relation to whether all the designs are reduced in size or whether just some of them are; in the latter case, the interpretation of reduced external energy due to control would be applied only to the symbolism of those particular designs which are reduced in size. Conversely, a marked increase in reproduced design size is suggestive of acting-out tendencies, compensatory tendencies, and/or expansiveness of mood. Depending on the control and aggression indicators, marked increase in size can be an indication of impulsivity and/or delinquency (See Table X, No. 5).

8. Differential treatment is a term used to express any special attention that a subject gives to any part of a given test (not just the Bender Test, but any test). Differential treatment often suggests a symbolic conflict with respect to whatever meaning the specially treated part of the design or test has for the subject. Differential treatment can manifest itself, on the Bender Test, in a variety of ways. Some of them are: profuse erasing, drawing a particular part over and over again, drawing a particular part of a design with very black lines and other parts of the design with very light lines, omission of part of a design (which probably is not accidental), omission of an entire design (which probably is not accidental), doodling, marked reduction and marked increase in design-part size within the same design, and so on. As a clinical rule, the direction of an exaggeration is interpretable, in terms of the vertical plane being symbolic of difficulty with authority figures and the horizontal plane being symbolic of difficulty with interpersonal and social relationships (See Table X, No. 6).

9. Closure difficulty means the tendency to draw unclosed designs when those designs are supposed to be reproduced closed. Such difficulty suggests problems with interpersonal relationships, particularly in terms of closeness: either a fear of that closeness, and/or a need for it. Closure difficulty manifests itself in, for example, the inability to complete the circle of Design A; the inability to join the circle and square of Design A; the inability to join the vertical and/or horizontal lines of Design 6; the inability to intersect the two figures of Design 7; and so on (See Table X, No. 7).

10. Changes in curvature means reducing or increasing the curves of the designs, and/or reducing or increasing the angle degree of the designs. A tendency to reduce the curves (which in its extreme form can manifest itself in making straight lines out of curved lines and which often appears with Design 6) is indicative of a reduction of emotional responsiveness (in its extreme form, withdrawal). The same is true with a tendency to decrease the angle degree of the designs, which often appears in Designs A, 6, and 7. A tendency to increase the curves of designs (which in its extreme form can manifest itself in snakelike curves that take the entire width and length of the page, particularly in relation to Design 6) is suggestive of an increased emotional responsiveness. The same is true with a tendency to increase the angles of designs (which often appears with Designs 6 and 7). The degree to which an increase in curvature or angulation is accompanied by a lack of control factors suggests that the increase in emotional responsiveness is likely not to be controlled, which suggests acting-out tendencies (See Table X, No. 8).

11. Rotation means reproducing a design in a way that is more than 45 degrees rotated with the stimulus card in the original examiner-placed position. Rotation implies perceptual rotation, not turning the stimulus card and then drawing the design correctly.

It is often contended that rotation is always indicative of brain damage. This, in our opinion, is not always the case. Brain damage rotation usually involves distortion of the gestalt and/or dog ears. A clean rotation is more likely to be a function of a perceptual or oppositional problem due to emotional stress. Often, emotionally-based rotation appears only with respect to one or two of the designs; in such a case, the rotation-suggested emotional stress should be interpreted in terms of the symbolism of the designs that are rotated.

With regard to brain damage rotation, sometimes the subject can recognize the difference between the model and the subject's own reproduction but is unable to correct it (output difficulty). By contrast, the subject who rotates for emotional reasons often can recognize the difference and can correct it.

Rotation is not turning the stimulus card (this should be prohibited), or turning the test paper, and then reproducing the design correctly. Rotation always involves drawing a rotated design despite the nonrotated stimulus card. In this context, rotation is usually indicative of a visual discrimination and/or graphic output problem, usually either organically or emotionally induced. In order to avoid any interpretation confusion, we recommend that the examiner use a caret (∧) to indicate the top of the page relative to each deviantly reproduced design. Such a caret indicates whether the deviant design is a legitimate rotation or a design reproduced correctly after the test-paper was turned (See Table X, Nos. 9 *a, b, c,* and *d*).

12. Retrogression means the conversion of the original design into a simpler form (for example, converting a series of dots to a straight line, a straight line to a sketchy line, a circle to a scribble, dots to unclosed loops). Retrogression suggests immaturity, in that the subject is unable or unwilling to deal with the reality of the task and chooses to simplify that task in immature ways (See Table X, No. 10).

13. Fragmentation is probably the most pathognomonic of all Bender Test hypotheses. Pathognomonic means an indication of pathology; and fragmentation means breaking the design into parts and reproducing the parts separately, sometimes with a great deal of illogical distance between those parts. True fragmentation is almost always an indication of brain damage or psychosis; it almost never occurs with a normal individual. Emotionally based fragmentation is usually indicative of a loss of integrative ability (See Table XII, No. 1).

14. Doodling is rare. If the doodling is bizarre it suggests a psychotic process. If the doodling is not bizarre, but indicative of lack of attention, it suggests malingering or lack of interest and/or rapport. Doodling is usually a pure projection of the subject, and as such may be interpreted in terms of the symbolism of the doodling.

15. Regarding the interpretation of hand-pencil movement, centrifugal (outward) movement suggests active tendencies, whereas centripetal (inward) movement suggests passive tendencies. On the Bender Test, these movement directions are manifested in the drawing of curves, circles, and lines.

16. Sketching is often indicative of anxiety and insecurity. Subjects with formal art training sometimes sketch and the anxiety hypothesis must be adjusted for these individuals, unless of course, they are also anxious.

17. Perseveration means the inappropriate repetition of a response. Perseveration, in general, and not with respect to the Bender Test, often manifests itself in three ways: (a) Ideational perseveration (which involves endless repetitive thinking of the same thought), (b) Motor or visual-motor perseveration (which involves endless repetition of the same motor or visual-motor behavior), and (c) Verbal perseveration (which involves endless repetition of the same word or sound). Bender Test perseveration is usually visual-motor perseveration and generally manifests itself on Designs 1, 2, and 5, relative to the inappropriate continuation of the dots. That is, the subject repetitively makes dots until he comes to the margin and can proceed no further. Perseveration may be emotionally or organically based. In either case, it suggests a rigidity and an inability to relinquish the stimulus (a situation often called stickiness). The rigidity associated with perseveration is to be interpreted differently depending upon whether the rigidity is emotionally or organically based. Nonetheless, to interrupt the perseverative response, it is often necessary for the practitioner to have prearranged with the

subject for the use of a neutral word (e.g., peanuts), and express that neutral word whenever the subject engages in the perseverative behavior. The prearranged neutral word sometimes helps the subject interrupt the perseveration (See Table XII, No. 13).

18. Overattention to small details suggests a pedantic and perfectionist individual.
19. Impulsively reproduced designs suggest an impulsive individual, and the more impulsively the designs are reproduced, the more, usually, the subject is impulsive (See Table XII, Nos. 5 and 12).
20. Subjects who draw boxes around each design (draw a design and then encase that design in a drawn box) are often insecure, guarded, rigid, and fearful. This Bender Test condition is rare, and although a few normal individuals do draw boxes, many box-drawing subjects are somewhat schizoid, paranoid, and/or rigid and compulsive. The symbolism of the boxes appears to be self-protection (See Table XII, No. 7).

Bender Test design symbolism. Due to the concept of personality projection, and by means of the previously discussed personality interpretive hypotheses, it is possible to interpret the meaning of any Bender Test design reproduction. It is possible to further increase the understanding of the meaning of design reproductions by interpreting the manner in which the designs are reproduced in relation to the symbolic meaning of those designs.

The following clinical but speculative hypotheses relate to the symbolism of the nine test designs. Although we regard each of the designs as having a unique symbolic pull or meaning, interpretation of the designs should not be a function of only the symbolism of those designs but rather an interpretation, by means of the personality interpretive hypotheses, of the manner in which the designs are reproduced (dark or light lines, large or small reproductions, perfect or sloppy reproductions, one part of the design larger than the other, etc.), in relation to the presumed symbolic meaning of the designs.

Two cautions should be noted: (1) the hypotheses regarding the design symbolism are subjective and should not be regarded as firm rules of interpretation and (2) the symbolism hypotheses, as well as the personality interpretive hypotheses, should be adjusted relative to a subject whose design reproductions are affected by graphic output difficulty due to brain damage. It makes no sense to try to interpret design reproduction distortion due to brain damage, a condition over which the subject has no personality projection control. However, it does make sense to try to interpret even bizarre design reproduction distortion when that distortion is due to psychopathology, as the subject, in such a context, still retains personality projection control.

The Basic Bender Test design symbolism are as follows.

a. Angles represent male symbolism, and curves-circles represent female symbolism. Thus, a distortion of the angle-part of Design A in relation to the correctly reproduced circle-part of Design A ( ) suggests some difficulty with the male part of the subject's male-female relationship.

b. The way in which a subject reproduces Design A is thought to symbolically relate to the nature of the subject's male-female relationships. In this context, it is interpretively meaningful if one part of Design A is larger, darker, away from, or penetrating the other part.

c. The way in which a subject reproduces Designs 1 and 2 is thought to symbolically relate to the nature of the subject's control system. In this context, it is interpretively meaningful if the dots and/or circles are reproduced with perfect alignment, size, and line color, or if they are reproduced in a sloppy, impulsive way (or any combination thereof). Generally, the more impulsive the way in which Designs 1 and 2 are reproduced, the more the subject has impulse problems (and the converse).

d. The way in which a subject reproduces Design 3 is thought to symbolically relate to the nature of the subject's sex-role identification. We have found that males with confused identity often reproduce Design 3 in a horizontally compressed but vertically elongated fashion ( ) ; conversely for females with confused identity ( ).

In this context, it is interpretively meaningful to pay attention to control factors (dots that are dark and heavy, or light, or impulsively reproduced) to determine the way in which the role-identity is integrated.

e. Like Design A, the way in which a subject reproduces Design 4 is thought to symbolically relate to the nature of the subject's male-female relationships. The Design 4 interpretation is the same as that for Design A, and will not be repeated here.

f. The way in which a subject reproduces Design 5 is thought to symbolically relate to the nature of the subject's dependency-affectional gratification. We have found that affectionally frustrated subjects often reproduce Design 5 with a flat arch, often with one leg considerably below the other, and often draw the arm not from the (normal) arch-top out, but from the outside into the arch (   ). In this context, it is interpretively meaningful to pay attention to control factors in order to determine the way in which the affectional frustration is integrated.

g. Like Designs 1 and 2, the way in which a subject reproduces Design 6 is thought to symbolically relate to the nature of the subject's control system. In this context, it is interpretively meaningful if the curves are markedly increased in frequency, if the curves are flattened into straight lines, if the design is impulsively reproduced, if the angle of the intersecting line is increased or flattened, and so on. Generally, markedly reducing the curve frequency and/or the degree of angulation suggests, minimally, a reduction of energy due to great control, and maximally, withdrawal (   ).

The converse is also true (   ). In this context, it is important to pay interpretive attention to the direction of line movement, as vertical line movement symbolically relates to authority-figure relationships (   ), and horizontal line movement symbolically relates to interpersonal or peer relationships (   ). Any reproduction deviation regarding vertical and/or horizontal line movement (increase or decrease in curvature, dark or light lines, control or impulsivity) can often be symbolically interpreted in terms of not only control of emotions, but also whether those emotions apply to authority figures and/or peers.

h. The way in which a subject reproduces Design 7 is thought to symbolically relate to the nature of the subject's male-authority relationships. We have found that the right figure of Design 7 often symbolically relates to the subject's perception of the primary authority-figure (usually the father), and the left figure often symbolically relates to the subject in relation to that authority-figure. In this context, it is interpretively meaningful if the two figures are close together, separated by a large amount of space, if the left figure is inside the right figure, if the points of either figure are blackened or reinforced, if one figure is large and the other small, or black and light, etc. It is also important to pay attention to the subject's use of control features to determine the way in which the authority-figure relationship is integrated.

The way in which a subject reproduces Design 8 is thought to symbolically relate to the nature of the subject's female-authority relationships. We have found that the diamond figure often symbolically relates to the subject's dependency and security-need satisfaction, in relation to the larger figure which often symbolically relates to the gratifying or not gratifying mother-figure. In this context, it is interpretively meaningful if the diamond is enveloped by the larger figure, if the diamond is much larger than the other figure, if the diamond-points have been omitted and/or if the points on the other figure are long and sharp, if one figure is dark and shaded and the other light and clear, etc. Again, it is important to pay attention to control factors to determine the way in which the subject's female-authority relationships are integrated.

Comments on the Use of the Bender Test as a Projective Test of Personality

With the speculative knowledge of the symbolic meaning of design angles and curves, the symbolic meaning of the nine designs, and with the knowledge of the personality interpretive hypotheses, it is possible to interpret the personality of any Bender Test subject. In this context, it should be remembered that all humans have needs or drives, all have ways of defending themselves against the recognition and/or expression of those needs or drives, and all have different ways of expressing the behavioral network which results from the drives and defenses: such is the uniqueness of human behavior. Since some of those drives, defenses, and ways of expressing the resulting behavioral network are projected by the subject into the Bender Test design reproduction, it is thus possible to interpret the personality of that subject irrespective of

Table X

Illustrations of the Bender-Gestalt Test Interpretative Hypotheses

1. Sequence of Designs

   Logical

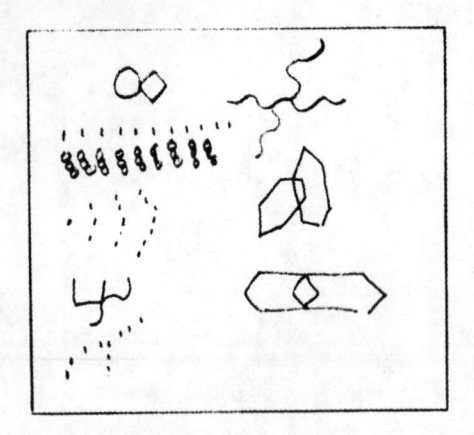

   Logical

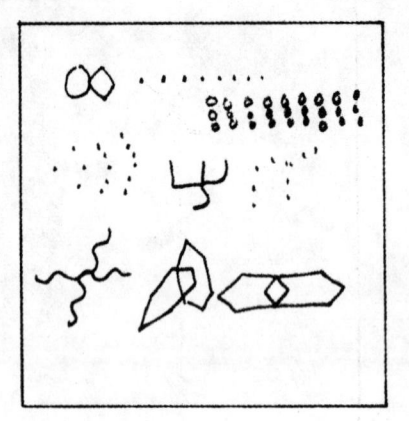

   Chaotic and Confused

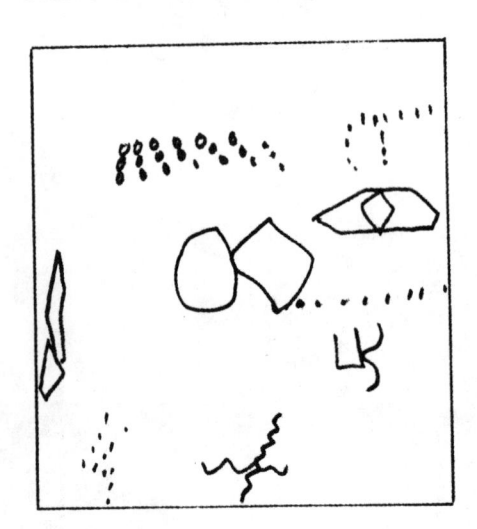

2. Placement of First Design

Normal

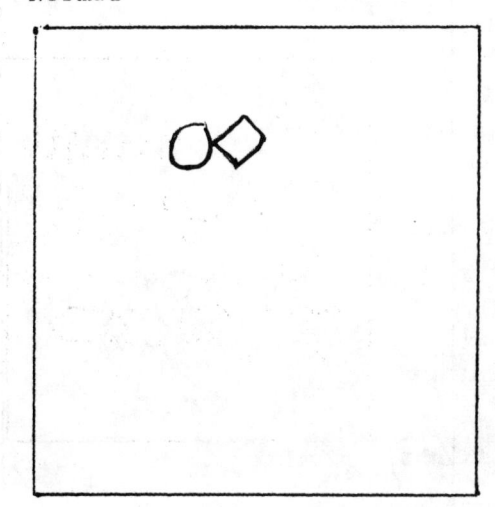

Anxious; Withdrawing; Insecure

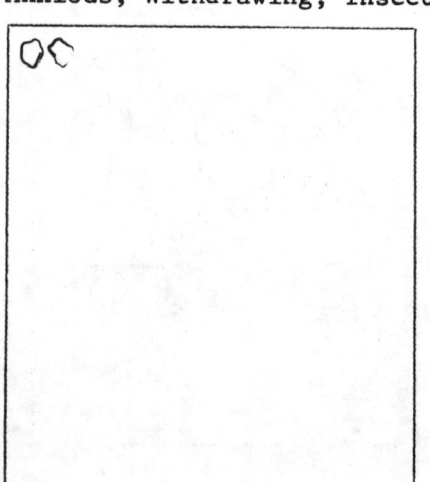

Depressed

Egocentric
Selfish; Grandiose

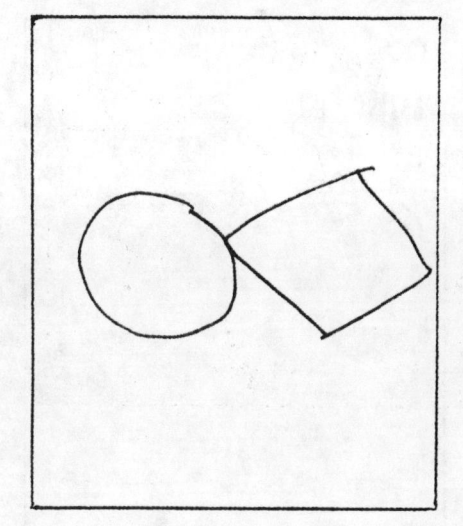

3. Spacing of Designs:

(a) Normal

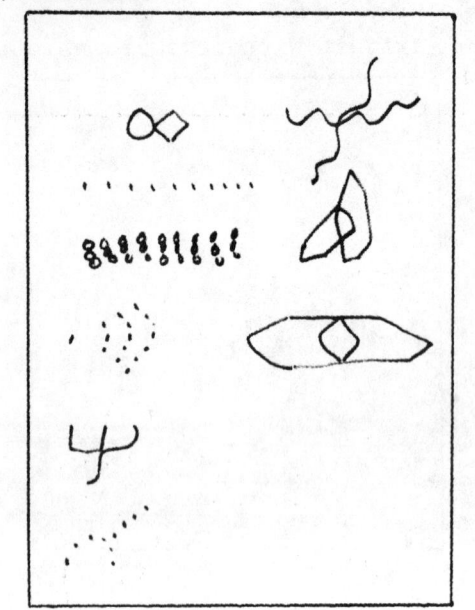

(b) Anxious; Withdrawing; Insecure

(c) Compressed Hostility

(d) Acting Out; Egocentric

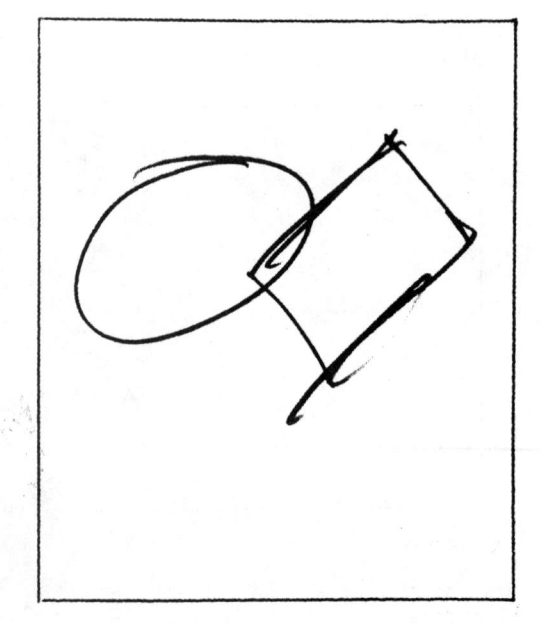

4. Collision

Moderate   Mild

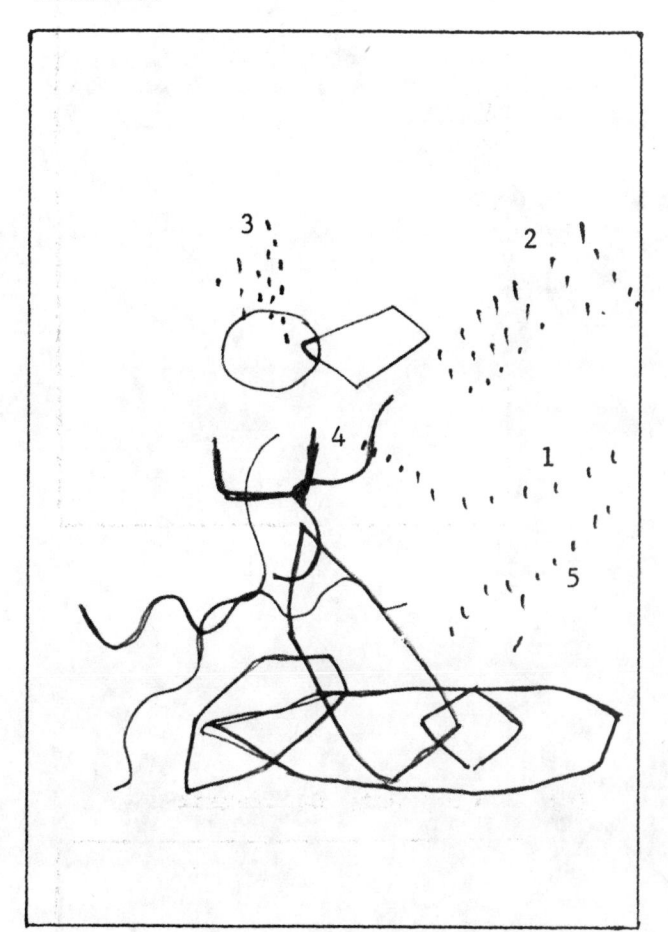

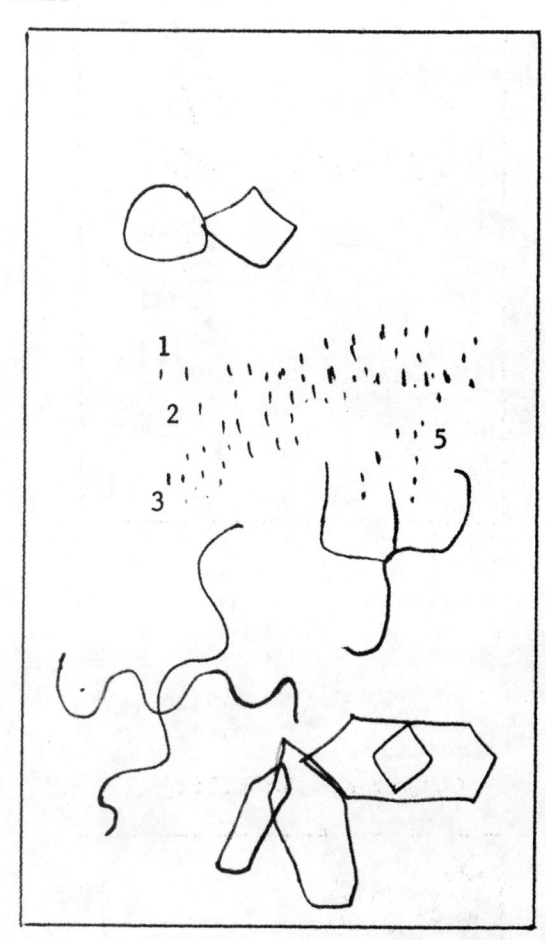

5. Change in Size of Designs:

   Reduction:

   from   to

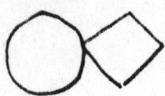

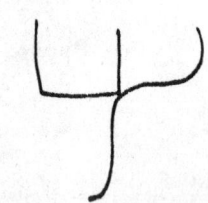

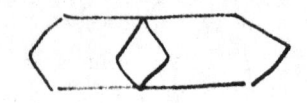

   Increase:

   from   to

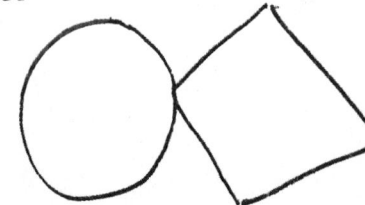

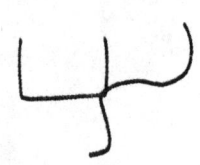

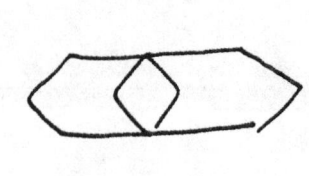

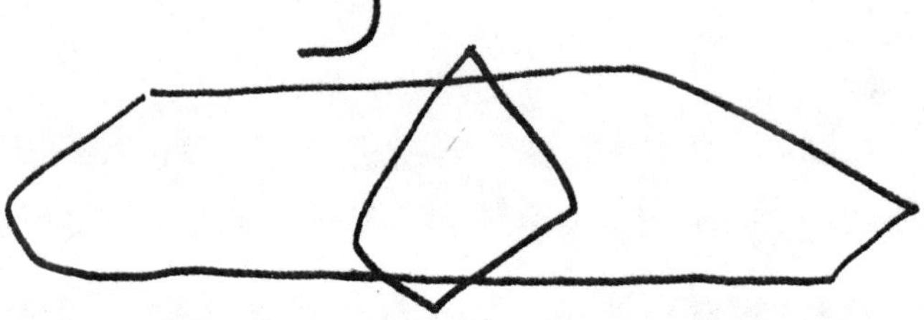

6. Differential Treatment

Design A:

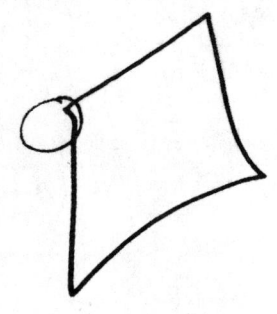

Design 4:

Design 1:

Design 5:

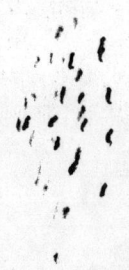

Design 3:

Design 6:

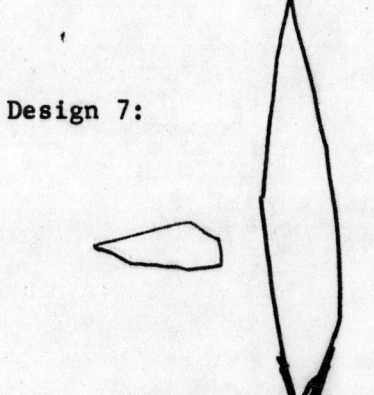

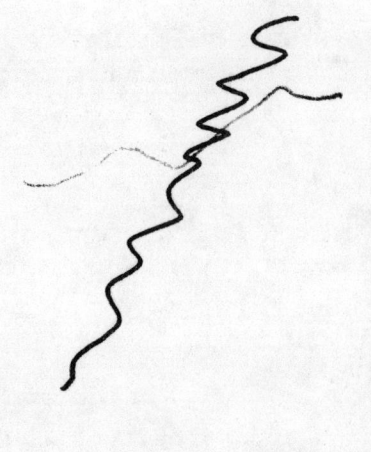

Design 7:

7. Closure Difficulty

Design A:

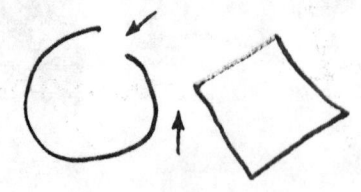

Design 6:

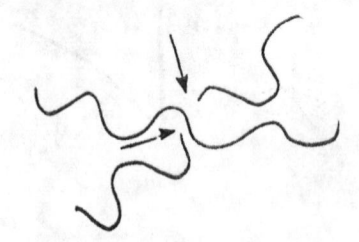

Design 2:

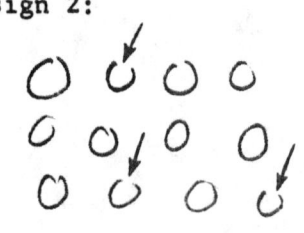

Design 8:

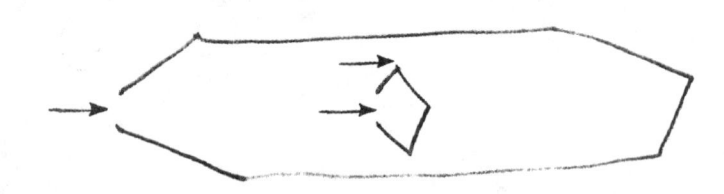

Design 4:

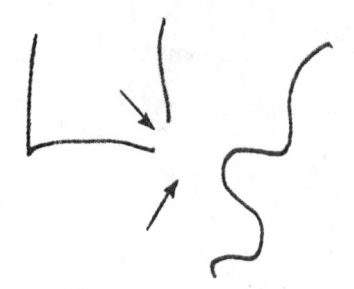

8. Increase and Decrease in Curvature

Design 6:

decrease   increase   both increase and decrease   both increase and decrease

Design 4:

decrease   increase

Design 5:

decrease   increase

61

9a. Design Rotation

General

Design A:

90° clockwise   90° counter clockwise

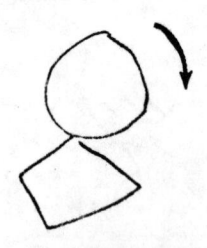

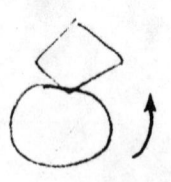

Design 1:   Design 8:

90°   90°

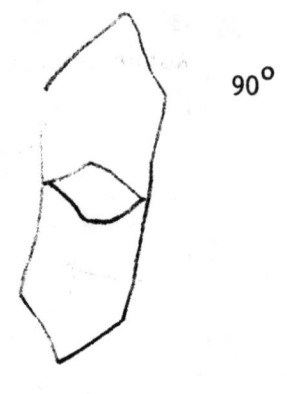

Design 4:

180°

Design 5:

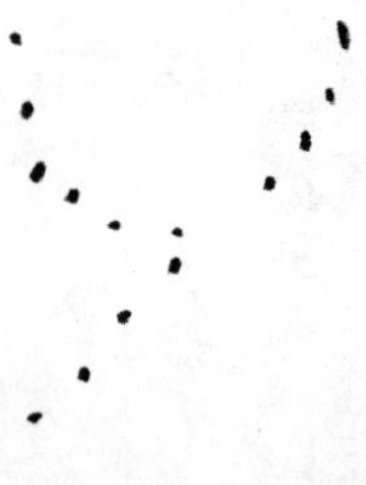

180°

62

9b. Design Rotation

Clean Rotation

9c. Design Rotation

Rotation Plus Dog Ears

Design A:

Design 4:

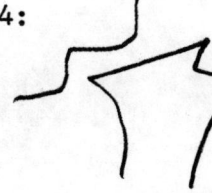

Design 8:

9d. Design Rotation

Rotation Plus Destruction of the Gestalt

Design A:

Design 4:

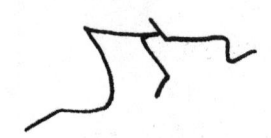

Design 8:

Design 7:

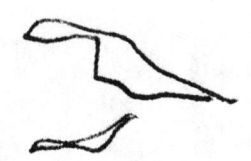

10. Retrogression

Design 1:

Design 1:

Design 2:

Design 3:

Design 4:

Design 5:

Design 6:

Design 7:

Design 8:

11. Controlled Aggression   Poorly Controlled Aggression

Design A

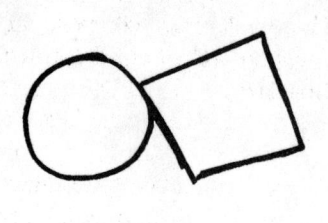

Design 1

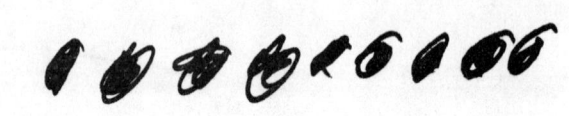

Design 4

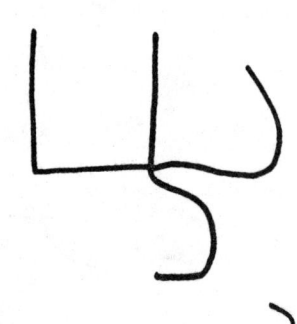

Design 6

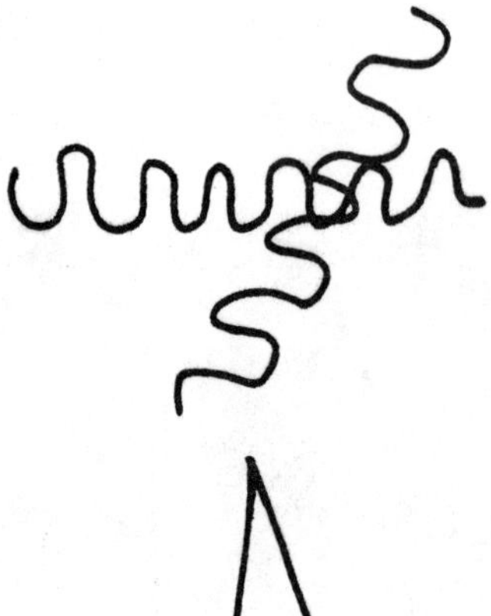

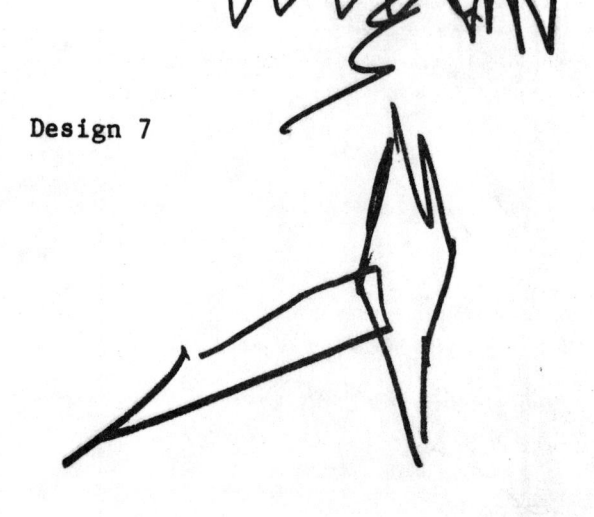

Design 7

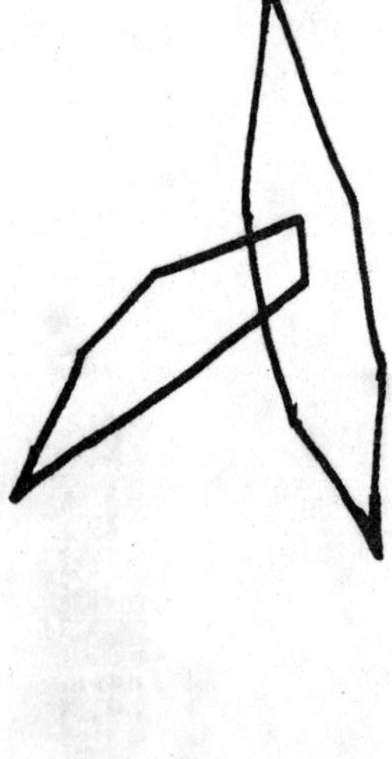

whether that subject is normal or not-normal. By means of such personality interpretation, the examiner is better able to program the subject, parents, teacher, principal, counselor, etc., with respect to presenting problem resolution.

Table XI presents the Koppitz Scoring System for the Bender-Gestalt Test. Although a facile Bender Test examiner analyzes the design reproductions without typically resorting to the time consuming scoring process, it is helpful sometimes to have a quantified way of interpreting the perceptual age and grade level of a Bender Test subject. The Koppitz Scoring System provides such a way, in terms of recording on the scoring sheet, for each of the nine designs, and by means of one point for each score-concept, whether specified design reproduction distortions exist. The examiner simply sums the scores, and applies the total error score to the perceptual age or grade level norms.

The Koppitz Scoring System provides interpretive security for the beginning Bender Test examiner and corroborative support for the veteran examiner. As such, we recommend its use whenever applicable.

Table XI

Koppitz Scoring System for the Bender-Gestalt Test*

Name_____ School_____ Grade_____

Teacher_____ Birthdate_____ Date_____ Age_____ Sex_____

Figure A. Score 1 point if following is observable	Score	Interpretation
1. Parts of Figure excessively distorted or misshapen; extra or missing angles.		
2. Disproportion between two parts of Figure; one must be at least twice the size of the other.		
3. Rotation of Figure or any part thereof by 45 degrees or more; rotation of stimulus card if then copied in rotated position; rotation of card and paper and then copied in correct position not scored.		
4. Failure to join two parts of Figure; curve and adjacent corner more than 1/8" apart; this applies to overlap.		

Figure 1

5. Five or more dots converted into circles; enlarged dots or partially filled in circles not scored.		
6. Rotation of Figure or any part thereof by 45 degrees or more; rotation of stimulus card if then copied in rotated position; rotation of card and paper and then copied in correct position not scored.		
7. Perserveration, more than fifteen dots in a row.		

Figure 2	Score	Interpretation

8. Rotation of Figure or any part thereof by 45 degrees or more; rotation of stimulus card if then copied in rotated position; rotation of card and paper and then copied in correct position not scored.

9. One or two rows of circles omitted, rows of dots of Figure 1 used as third row for Figure 2, five or more circles in majority of column.

10. More than 14 columns in a row.

Figure 3

11. Five or more dots converted into circles; enlarged dots or partially filled in circles not scored.

12. Rotation of Figure or any part thereof by 45 degrees or more; rotation of stimulus card if then copied in rotated position; rotation of card and paper and then copied in correct position not scored.

13. Shape of design lost; conglomeration of dots.

14. Continuous lines instead of series of dots.

Figure 4

15. Rotation of Figure or any part thereof by 45 degrees or more; rotation of stimulus card if then copied in rotated position; rotation of card and paper and then copied in correct position not scored.

16. Failure to join two parts of Figure; curve and adjacent corner more than 1/8" apart; this applies also to overlap.

Figure 5

17. Five or more dots converted into circles; enlarged dots or partially filled in circles not scored.

18. Rotation of figure or any part thereof by 45 degrees or more; rotation of stimulus card if then copied in rotated position; rotation of card and paper and then copied in correct position not scored.

19. Shape of design lost, conglomeration of dots.

20. Continuous lines instead of series of dots.

	Score	Interpretation

Figure 6

21. Three or more distinct angles substituted for curves.

22. No curves at all; one or two straight lines.

23. Two lines not crossing or crossing at the extreme end of one or both lines, that is less than 1/4" from end of line, two lines interwoven horizontally.

24. Perseveration; six or more sinusoidal curves in either direction.

Figure 7

25. Parts of figure excessively distorted or misshapen; extra or missing angles.

26. Disproportion between two parts of figure, one must be at least twice the size of the other.

27. Rotation of figure or any part thereof by 45 degrees or more; rotation of stimulus card if then copied in rotated position; rotation of card and paper and then copied in correct position not scored.

Figure 8

28. Hexagon or diamond excessively misshappen; extra or missing angles, diamond omitted.

29. Rotation of figure or any part thereof by 45 degrees or more; rotation of stimulus card if then copied in rotated position; rotation of card and paper and then copied in correct position not scored.

TOTAL SCORE

*Reprinted from: Koppitz, Elizabeth. "The Bender-Gestalt Test for Children, A Normative Study." *Journal of Clinical Psychology*, 1960, 16, 432–435. Reproduced by permission.

AGE NORMS

Perceptual Age	Mean Score	S.D.
5.0 — 5.5	13.6	3.61
5.6 — 5.11	9.8	3.72
6.0 — 6.5	8.4	4.12
6.6 — 6.11	6.4	3.76
7.0 — 7.5	4.8	3.61
7.6 — 7.11	4.7	3.34
8.0 — 8.5	3.7	3.60
8.6 — 8.11	2.5	3.03
9.0 — 9.5	1.7	1.82
9.6 — 9.11	1.4	1.43
10.0 — 10.5	1.5	1.31

GRADE NORMS

Grade	Mean Age	Mean B-G Score
Beginning kindergarten	5.4	13.5
Beginning first grade	6.5	8.1
Beginning second grade	7.5	4.7
Beginning third grade	8.7	2.2
Beginning fourth grade	9.8	1.5

Table XII presents a variety of actual Bender Test protocols, which illustrate many of the previously discussed interpretive hypotheses and concepts. The reader is invited to study the protocols for the purpose of applying those interpretive hypotheses and thereby gaining greater Bender Test interpretation facility.

Table XII

Sample Bender-Gestalt Test Protocols

1.

CA 8, IQ 46, Male.
Brain Damage
TMR

All

2.

CA 10, IQ 71, Male.
Organic Psychosis

A11 ∧

3.

CA 8, IQ 130
Normal Female

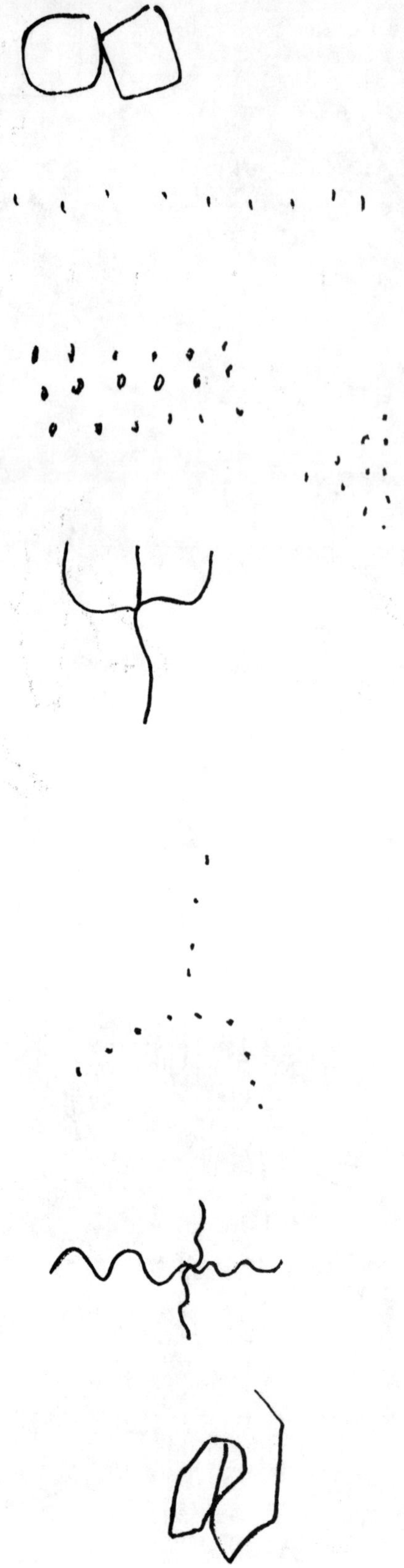

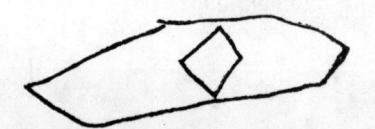

4.

CA 10, Male.
VIQ 95, PIQ 72
Brain Damage

5.

CA 18, IQ 89
Delinquent Male

6.

CA 8, IQ 68, Female.
Pseudo - MR
(average potential)

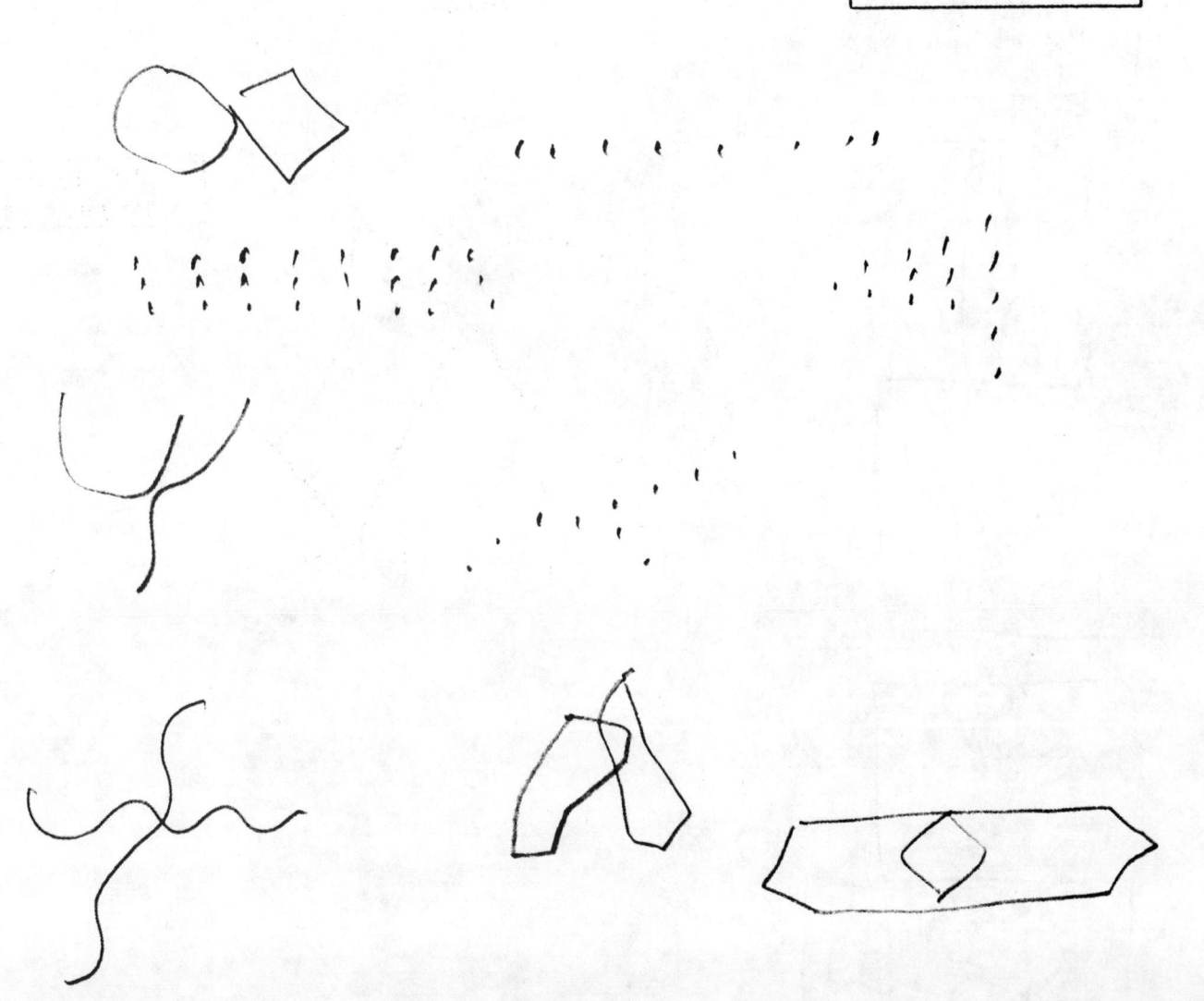

7.

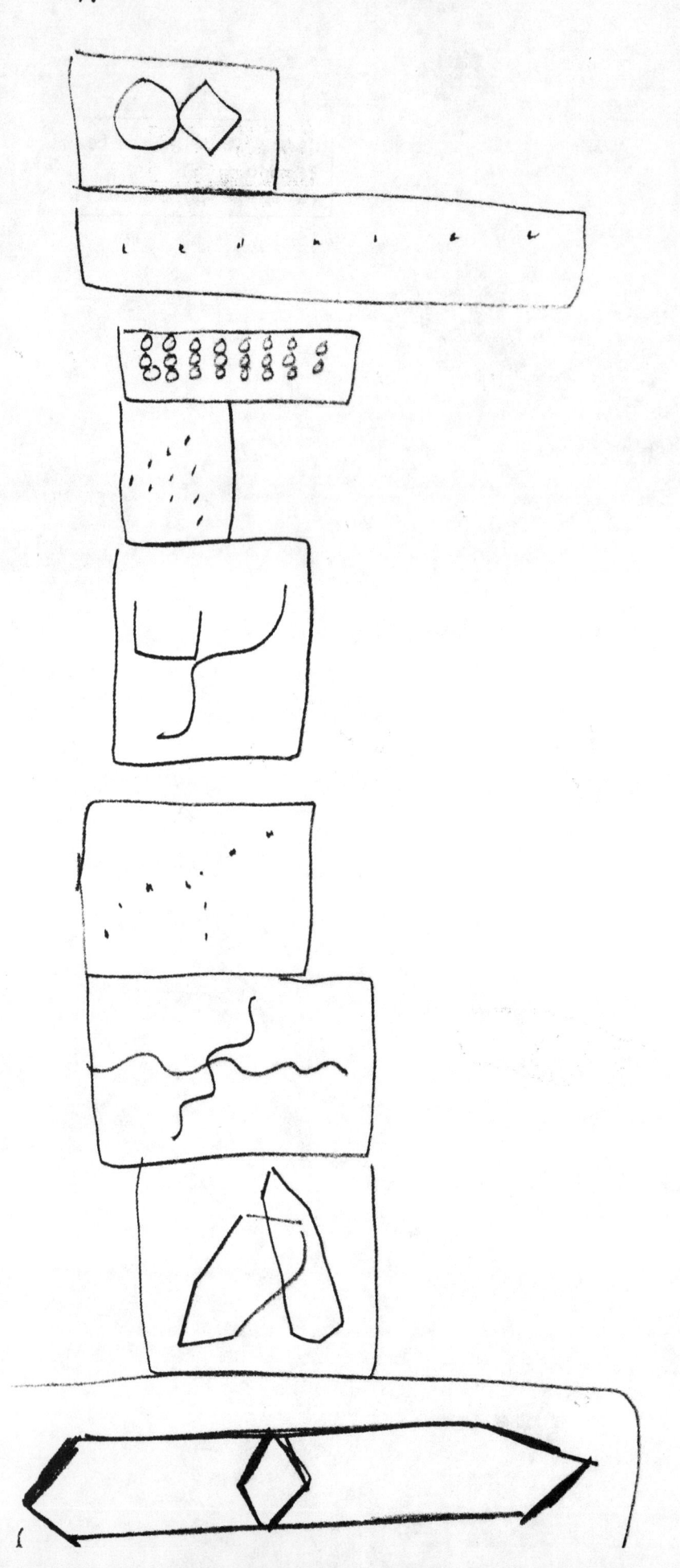

CA 27, IQ 119, Male.
Paranoid Schizophrenia

8.

CA 10, IQ 61
EMR: Male

9.

CA 6, IQ 125
Normal Male

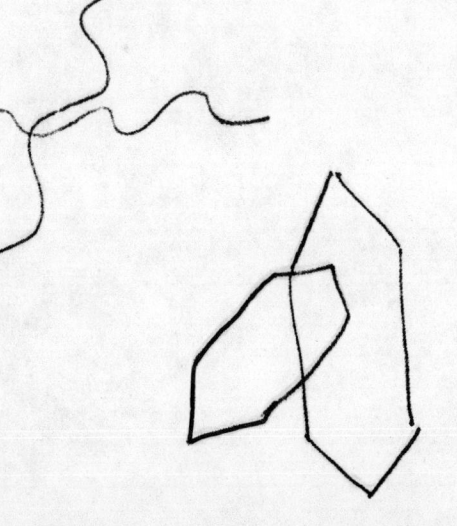

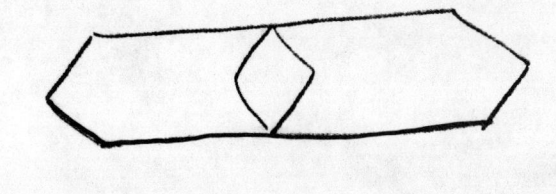

10.

CA 28, IQ 120
Normal Female

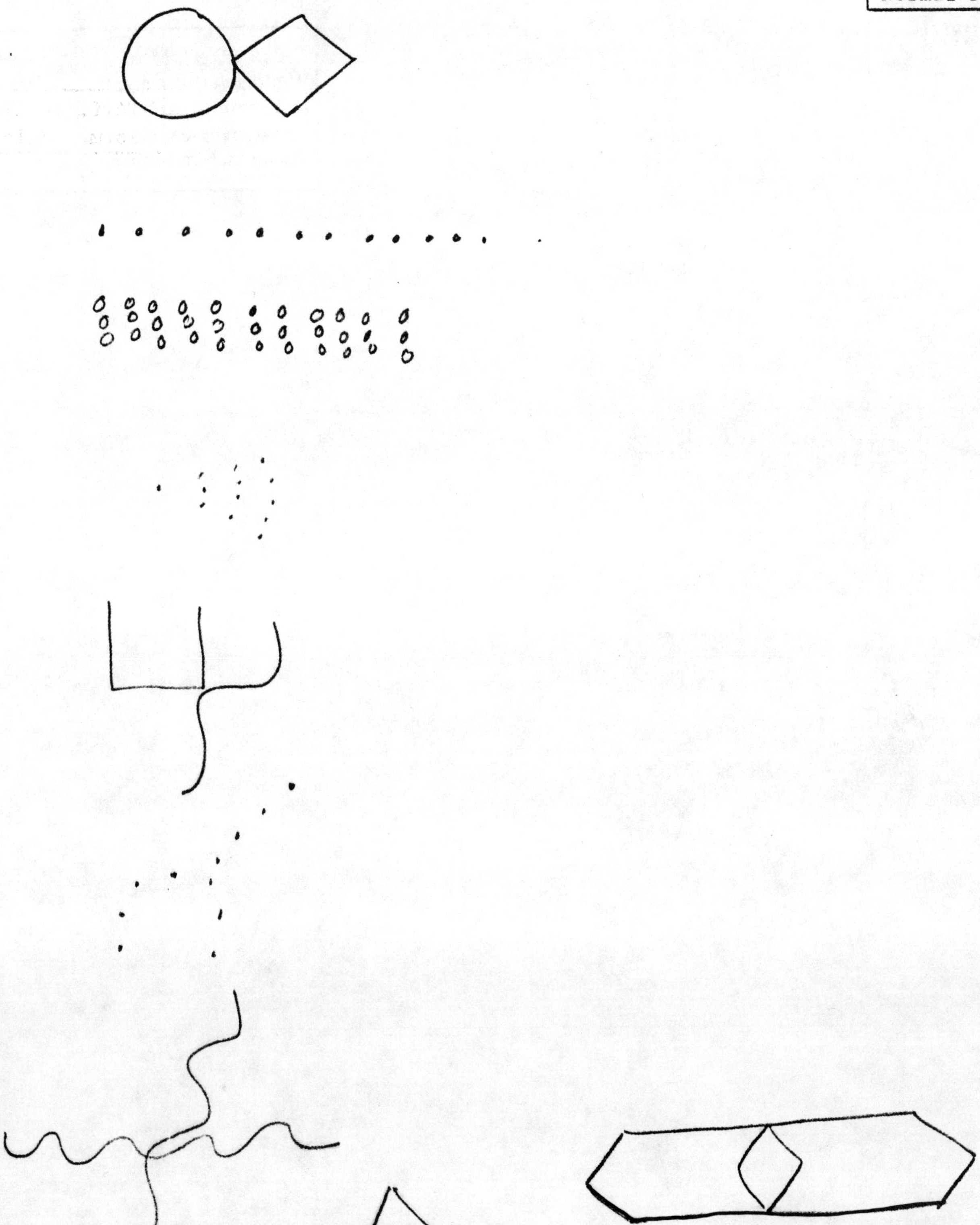

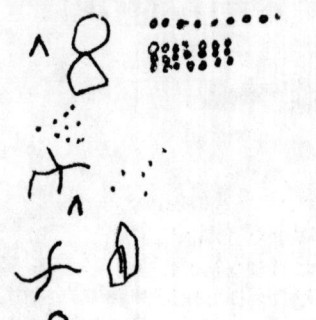

11.

CA 18, IQ 97, Male.
Withdrawal, anxiety,
and dammed-up hostility;
Emotionally-based visual
discrimination problem

12.

CA 12, Male.
VIQ 89, PIQ 47
Brain Damage
Marked impulse problems;
Moderate-severe visual
discrimination and graphic
output learning disability

85

13.

CA 11, Male.
VIQ 93, PIQ 57
Learning disability (visual discrimination and graphic output; presumed (but not) MR. Brain damage, and perservation.

14.

CA 6; Female. VIQ 89; PIQ 50. Maturationally Immature.

A.

SELECTED REFERENCES

Bender, Lauretta. "A Visual Motor Gestalt Test and Its Clinical Use." Research Monograph No. 3, *American Orthopsychiatric Association,* 1938.

Bender-Gestalt Test-Cards, The. New York: *The American Orthopsychiatric Association,* 1946.

Clawson, A. *Bender-Visual Motor Gestalt Test for Children.* California: Western Psychological Corporation, 1975.

Koppitz, E.M. *The Bender Gestalt Test for Young Children. Vol. II.* New York: Grune & Stratton, 1975.

Koppitz, E.M. "The Bender Gestalt Test for Children, a Normative Study." *Journal of Clinical Psychology,* 1960, *26.*

Chapter 11

The Draw-A-Person Test

The Draw-A-Person Test (Machover, 1978) is a versatile psychoeducational assessment tool and a projective test of personality. The power of this test to reveal personality variables is greater than almost all psychoeducational tests, including the Bender Test, but less than that of the Rorschach Test. The DAP is a psychological test and should be used only by individuals having the necessary training.

The DAP is easy to administer, and for the trained practitioner, easy to interpret. The test has no basal or ceiling age, except for the visual-motor ability to draw. The administrative procedures are: the subject should be provided with several sheets of white and unlined 8½ x 11 paper, and with a sharpened No. 2 pencil with an eraser. The only examiner directions are, "I want you to draw a person. Do the best you can." Note: the directions involve a request to draw a person, not a man or a woman; the subject should determine the sex of the person. As with the Bender Test, the examiner wishes to encourage as much subject personality projection as possible, and as such all subject questions should be referred back to the subject, in terms of, "Do the best you can." Also, as with the Bender Test, the subject may erase and may turn the test paper, but may not use mechanical drawing aids.

Within reason, the only DAP result that should be discouraged is the ultimate drawing of a stick figure. If a subject begins to draw a stick figure, it is usually desirable to permit the completion, but then ask the subject to draw a full figure.

After the subject has drawn the initial person, then if the examiner wishes to use the DAP to its fullest advantage, the examiner may give the subject another piece of unlined paper and ask the subject to draw a person of the opposite sex. We have found that almost as much personality information can be obtained from the first drawing as from both drawings, and under the usual circumstance of professional time-crunch, we have resorted to the use of only the first drawing.

The DAP is diagnostically sensitive; has a high subject-interest factor; and is easy and quick to administer. Since the clinical essence of both the Bender Test and DAP is the projective-based interpretation of paper-pencil drawings, there are many interpretive similarities between the Bender Test and DAP. Thus, a great deal of interpretive interchange between these two instruments is not only possible but should be encouraged.

The phenomenology of testing concept is particularly applicable to the DAP. Phenomenology means to gain the internal frame of reference of the other person; that is, to see and feel things the way the other person does. We contend that in order to engage in the phenomenology of testing or, for that matter, of life itself, a person should be perceptive and empathic. We have found that the defensive and insecure individual has difficulty engaging in phenomenology. This is so because to be sensitive to others and to use one's own barely conscious feelings to understand the delicate feelings of others can be threatening. We have found that it is usually the secure individual who is able to engage in the intuitiveness of phenomenology.

With the exception of the Rorschach Test, the phenomenology of testing concept is most applicable to the DAP. Although phenomenology complements the other tests discussed, we have found that the most successful DAP examiner is the individual who can not only feel how the subject himself feels as that subject is drawing the person, but who also can even feel how the person that is drawn might feel were that person to come alive. By means of this intuitive getting-inside the subject and drawn figure, the examiner has a richer understanding of subject-personality dynamics, which is necessary for effective presenting problem resolution.

DAP Personality Interpretive Hypotheses

The following discussion represents an analysis of the DAP personality interpretive hypotheses. These hypotheses are guidelines only and not hard rules of interpretation. We have found it helpful to systematize the DAP analysis and to recommend initially that the reader approach the DAP analysis by means of the following order.

Placement of the figure on the page

The normal placement is to the left of center, with the use of the space between 15 percent down from the top and 15 percent up from the bottom. Interpretively, placement to the extreme left suggests self-orientation, and to the extreme right suggests environment or other orientation. Low placement on the page suggests depression; and high placement on the page suggests enthusiasm. *Size of figure.* Very large figures suggest compensatory enthusiasm, and if the figures lack control features, they suggest acting-out tendencies. Small figures suggest low self-esteem, ego weakness, depression, and/or feelings of inadequacy. *The Sequence of drawing.* Most subjects begin with the head. Beginning with the feet suggests security or perhaps status problems. Drawing the head last often is indicative of a disturbance in interpersonal relationships. *Perspective.* Stick figures suggest evasiveness, probably based on insecurity, while profiles suggest a more subtle evasiveness. Profile head and full-view body often suggests a conflict regarding exhibitionism. Overdressed figures suggest compensation for body-image problems, and nude figures (very rare) suggest preoccupation with the body and/or sexuality. The control or lack of control features which accompany a nude drawing suggest whether the subject is likely to act-out his body concern or sexuality.

The Head and Neck

The head symbolizes the ego or self. Very large heads suggest a concern about identity, and very small heads suggest possible depression, anxiety, inadequacy, etc. Exaggerated heads have been drawn by individuals suffering from brain damage, or subsequent to brain surgery. Large heads drawn with precision and control often indicate intellectualization. The face expresses the feelings of the subject; specifically, a large gaping mouth may express dependency needs; a grim and straight-line mouth may express resentment, oppositionalism, and/or anger; the expression of teeth is rare, and often suggests oral aggression; a happy mouth suggests pleasantness. Unusually large ears suggest attention to the environment, and in particular, what people are saying, a situation which is often characteristic of paranoid states; very small ears may suggest an attempt to shut-out the auditory environment. An unusually large nose is often suggestive of phallic-aggression, and a very small nose is often suggestive of authority-figure induced feelings of inadequacy. Hair is often symbolic of virility, and as such, figures with an unusual amount of hair suggest sex-role confusion and possible bogus male or female compensatory activity; baldness often suggests resignation to feelings of sex-role inadequacy. The eyes are one of the most important DAP clinical cues, in that they reflect affect and mood as well as coping ability; the omission of eyes, or the omission of pupils but the drawing of eyes, suggests an attempt to shut out the world; the drawing of closed eyes suggests withdrawal and egocentricity; piercing eyes suggest aggression; wide open eyes suggest helplessness; etc. The neck symbolizes control, in that it physically exists between the head (ego) and the body (impulses); a long and thin neck suggests conscience control, and the opposite, no-neck, suggests the possibility of control problems and impulsive behavior (an interpretation which needs to be validated by other DAP indices of control difficulty). Things drawn around the neck (such as collar, necklace, choker, necktie, jewelry, etc.) suggest impulse control. Lastly, v-neck clothing suggests body curiosity.

Arms and hands

Arms and hands are personal-social contact features and are interpretively rich. Hands hidden in pockets, behind back, etc., suggest social and/or personal inadequacy and perhaps guilt; mittened or blunted fingers suggest social-personal inadequacy and perhaps guilt regarding aggression; arms drawn rigidly at the sides suggest social fear and rigidity; arms drawn out with palms up suggest dependency; arms folded suggest control; claw or stick fingers, and sharp finger nails, suggestion aggression; doubled fist suggests aggression; objects held by the hands can be interpreted in terms of the symbolism of those objects (gun: aggression; knife: aggression; furry cat: dependency; etc.).

Legs and feet

Legs and feet symbolically relate to security. Tiny feet suggest insecurity; feet spaced so that the figure would fall down were it real suggests feelings of inadequacy and insecurity; unusually large feet suggest arrogant behavior in compensation for feelings of inadequacy; legs pressed closely together suggest tenseness; legs and feet slightly apart and relaxed suggest self-comfort; legs and feet in any bizarre and unreal position suggest feelings of inadequacy and a fragile relationship with reality and the environment.

The torso

The torso is often symbolic of the strength of a subject's actual or wished-for impulses. A big, muscular torso suggests strong impulses; a weak torso suggests weak impulses. The control factors associated with a strong torso often indicate whether the subject is likely to act out the strong impulses. In this context, a belt is indicative of control.

Line qualities

The interpretive hypotheses associated with line qualities represent the DAP interpretive hypotheses which are most applicable to the Bender Test. Black and heavy lines suggest aggression; conversely, light and dim lines suggest withdrawal, uncertainty, and weakness; sketchy lines, except for the artist, suggest anxiety, uncertainty, and timidity; irrespective of the line quality, lines that are drawn impulsively and without care suggest acting-out tendencies; on the contrary, lines that are drawn with order, precision, and care suggest control regardless of whether they are bold, black, and angry looking. A subject who has a great deal of aggression that is rigidly controlled will probably develop psychosomatic symptoms unless appropriate means of sublimation are available. A midline emphasis (figure with emphasis on nose, tie, buttons, fly, and shoelaces) suggests body-image problems and even fears of falling apart. Line symmetry suggests control, but the more such symmetry is emphasized, the more the implication is of rigidity and compulsiveness; conversely, impulsivity, or the lack of symmetry, suggests acting-out tendencies.

Differential treatment

Differential treatment means giving special attention to parts of the drawing. The omission of any major body part is probably not accidental, and can be interpreted in terms of the subject coping with the threatening symbolism of the omitted body part by avoiding (omitting) that part; thus, omitted arms are often drawn by anxious individuals who fear rejection; facial features are often omitted by withdrawing individuals who have interpersonal problems; the crotch is often omitted by individuals who have sex-role problems; eyes are often omitted by withdrawing individuals who wish to shut out the world. Distortions, such as exaggerated size, heavy line emphasis, sharp points, reworking of part of the figure, etc., suggest a conflict regarding the symbolism of the distorted part of the body. Profuse erasing suggests a conflict with the symbolism of the body part erased. Shading suggests anxiety relative to the symbolism of the body part shaded (crotch, hands, and chest are the most commonly shaded body parts). Heavy dark shading suggests not only anxiety but also aggression relative to the symbolism of the shaded body part. And, stick figures suggest evasiveness and a reluctance to face problems.

Sex symbols

Some male sex symbols are: ties, pipes, cigarettes, shoes, guns, knives, and hats; some female sex symbols are: bows, jewelry, pockets, ribbons, laces, and purses. The interpretive implication is that males who draw an abundance of female sex symbols, and the converse, often have sex-role identification problems.

Figure sex

Subjects who draw figures of the opposite sex first may have, and are thereby expressing, sex-role identification confusion.

Overall impression of figure

To gain an overall impression of the drawn figure the examiner might ask, "What would that figure do were it to come alive?" Would it crumble because of weakness? Be angry? Cry? Run away? In general, the weaker and more shriveled the figure, as well as the opposite (for example, super muscles for males, and super beauty and curves for females), the more likely the subject has a rather shaky body-image.

Psychoeducational use of the DAP

The DAP is valuable for the purpose of assessing various kinds of learning and behavior problems. The following discussion presents the psychoeducational use and interpretive hypotheses of the DAP in relation to the assessment of those learning and behavior problems. As usual, the hypotheses represent interpretive guidelines only.

Mental age

Up to a mental age of about 14-15 years old, the ability to draw a person is maturational in nature;

therefore, DAP normalcy is a function of age. The DAP is roughly able to reveal a subject's mental age by the degree to which a subject's drawn figure matches the norm-figures for a given age (Goodenough, 1926; Harris, 1963). As a rule, the more appropriate specifications a drawn figure has, the brighter the subject (See Table XIII, Nos. 4 and 6). Table XIV is a DAP maturation chart, which is designed to assist the reader with the identification of normal DAP figures at various maturational ages. Although there is a greater variability within normal DAP figures than within normal Bender Test design reproductions, it is possible to determine, by reference to the DAP maturation chart, if a subject's DAP production is compatible with normal production for the subject's age, and if not, then the determination of the maturational level of that subject's DAP production.

Mental retardation

As with the Bender Test, the true mental retardate will usually have a DAP mental age that is compatible with the subject's retarded mental age (see Table XIII, No. 5). Many mental retardates are not true retardates, and this pseudomental retardation condition is manifested by greater Bender and DAP mental age than the obtained IQ would suggest.

Brain Damage

The Bender Test is a better instrument than the DAP for the purpose of detecting brain damage in the visual discrimination and/or graphic output areas of the brain. Nonetheless, the DAP can reveal such brain damage by the Bender Test signs of figure rotation, dog ears, and/or destruction of the gestalt (See Table XIII, Nos. 1 and 13). The Bender Test discussion of the relationship between rotation with dog ears and/or destruction of the gestalt and an input disorder, and the relationship between dog ears and/or destruction of the gestalt without rotation and an output disorder, applies here also.

Graphic output difficulty

Non-brain damage graphic output difficulty is often expressed on the DAP by paper-pencil sloppiness and immaturity without dog ears, rotation, and/or severe destruction of the gestalt. The etiology of the difficulty could be emotional stress or psychological immaturity. The subject with the emotionally based graphic output problem often can make the necessary corrections (although the subject may not want to), whereas the subject with the psysiologically based output problem may not be able to make the necessary corrections.

The DAP is a better instrument than the Bender Test for the purpose of determining whether a graphic output problem is due to emotional stress or to physiological immaturity. This differential diagnosis can be made on the basis of the number of DAP conflict indicators included in the drawn person. The more such conflict indicators are present, the more likely the problem is due to an emotional difficulty. This exists because the DAP is more of a personality test than the Bender Test, and thus, if there is a high stress loading on the DAP, and particularly if there is an absence of positive physiological cues in the subject's comprehensive history, the examiner can begin to hypothesize that the graphic output difficulty is due to emotional problems. The importance of determining etiology relates to appropriate remediation, in that tool-subject problems caused by emotionally based graphic output difficulty should receive a different kind of educational remediation than the same tool-subject problems caused by organically based graphic output difficulty.

School readiness

Like the Bender Test, the DAP can reveal pre-school or kindergarten subject immaturity and lack of readiness for formal education. This is shown by grossly immature visual-motor and pencil-paper coordination, as well as very immature drawings that often border on scribbling (See Table XIII, No. 13).

Aggression, and control

The DAP can reveal subject aggression by means of heavy, bold, and black lines; angry facial expressions; objects (for example, guns and knives) held by the drawn figure; figure size (often giant figures) and/or what the figure is doing (such as aggressive behavior) (See Table XIII, No. 3). However, irrespective of aggression indicators, control is suggested by the degree to which the DAP figure is drawn with order and precision. As with the Bender Test, the darker and heavier the lines, the greater (usually) the amount of aggression; yet the more the dark and heavy lines are drawn with precision and order, the greater (usually) the control over that aggression.

Acting out

The DAP can reveal subject acting-out tendencies in terms of figures that are drawn without the control factors discussed above. Impulsivity, a lack of order and structure, a lack of concern by the subject relative to what is drawn, and/or a general DAP sloppiness suggest lack of control. In combination with aggression indicators, lack of control suggests acting-out tendencies as well as possible delinquency (See Table XIII, No. 3).

Withdrawal

The DAP can reveal subject withdrawal and depression tendencies by means of the lightness of line, sketchiness, general weakness or shriveled quality of the drawn figure, a sad or empty facial expression, inactivity of the figure, or a markedly reduced size of the figure. A left and downward placement of the figure on the page reveals depression (See Table XIII, No. 10).

Anxiety

The DAP can reveal subject anxiety by means of the features discussed under "Withdrawal" above, plus such other features as marked differential treatment (especially erasures, shading, omissions, and distortions), unusual placement of the figure on the page, and especially a nonnatural position of the figure (See Table XIII, No. 10).

Psychosis

The DAP can reveal subject psychosis by means of bizarre qualities of the drawn figure. Any seriously drawn figure with bizarre and nonlogical qualities should alert the examiner to the possibility of a reality testing problem (See Table XIII, Nos. 2, 12a, and b).

Caution should be expressed: If a DAP subject has an organically based graphic output problem that results in a distorted DAP production, the examiner should not attempt to interpret the personality of that subject by means of the distorted figure as serious subject-personality misinterpretation could result.

The Draw-A-Family (DAF), and the House-Tree-Person (H-T-P) Tests

The DAF and HTP are variations on the theme of the DAP. All of the DAP and appropriate Bender Test interpretive hypotheses can be applied to the interpretation of the DAF and HTP. The DAF administration differs from the DAP only in that the subject is asked to draw his family. DAF interpretation can be made with respect to each of the figures drawn, as well as the placement of the drawn subject in relation to the placement of the drawn parents and siblings. Although we regard the DAP highly, we regard the DAF used in conjunction with the DAP as a waste of precious time in that not much more interpretive information can be gathered by means of the DAF used with the DAP (See Table XIII, No. 14).

Regarding the HTP (Buck, 1977), the subject is asked to draw a house, tree, and person. All questions are referred back to the subject. The subject may draw the three on one piece of paper (normal), on two pieces of paper, or on three pieces of paper. The usual DAP and Bender Test interpretive hypotheses apply to the HTP, and the only new interpretation procedure is that the house symbolizes the subject's dependency gratification, the tree symbolizes the subject's interpersonal and social relationships, and the person symbolizes the subject (in relation to the preceding DAP concepts). Regarding the house drawing, it is of interest to note whether the house is "alive" (windows, doors, curtains, window shades, chimney, smoke from the chimney, flowers, animals, pretty, etc.), or "dead" (sterile, drab, no life, no warmth, etc.), all of which relates to the way in which the subject regards his dependency or affectional gratification. Similarly, it is of interest to note whether the tree is "alive" (full of branches, bearing fruit, strong, big, blossoming, etc.), or "dead" (no blooms, no branches, no life, no bark, etc.), all of which relates to the nature of the subject's interpersonal and social relationships. The person of the HTP is interpreted as if it were the person of the DAP (See Table XIII, No. 15).

Table XIII presents a variety of actual DAP protocols which illustrate many of the previously discussed interpretive hypotheses and concepts. The reader is invited to study the protocols for the purpose of applying those interpretive hypotheses and thereby gaining greater DAP test interpretation facility.

Table XIV presents the DAP maturation chart.

Table XIII
Sample Draw-A-Person Protocols

1.

CA 8, Male.
VIQ 109, PIQ 71
Brain Damage

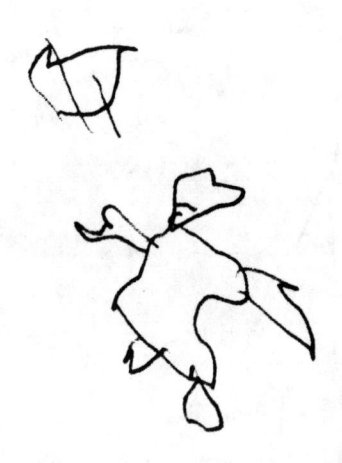

2.

CA 13, Male IQ 85
Schizophrenia

3.

CA 14, IQ 99
Male Delinquent

4.

CA 8, IQ 120
Normal Female

5.

CA 10, Male.
VIQ 66, PIQ 50
EMR

6.

CA 6, IQ 130
Normal Male

7.

CA 19, IQ 144 Male. Rigid: pre-paranoid; loner; excellent dresser; good student; suddenly went berserk.

8.

CA 18, IQ 93
Male; girl murderer

2nd attempt

1st attempt

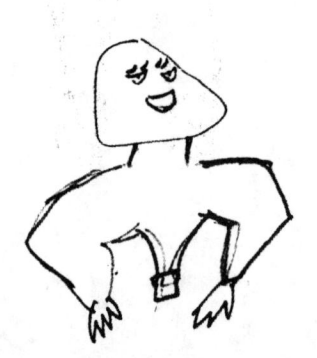

3rd attempt

102

9.

CA 16, IQ 104
Male. Presenting
problem was
fighting, drag
racing, truancy

10.

CA 18, Female, IQ 89
Depressed. with-
drawn, and anxious

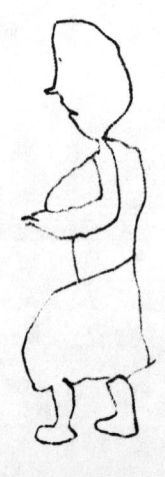

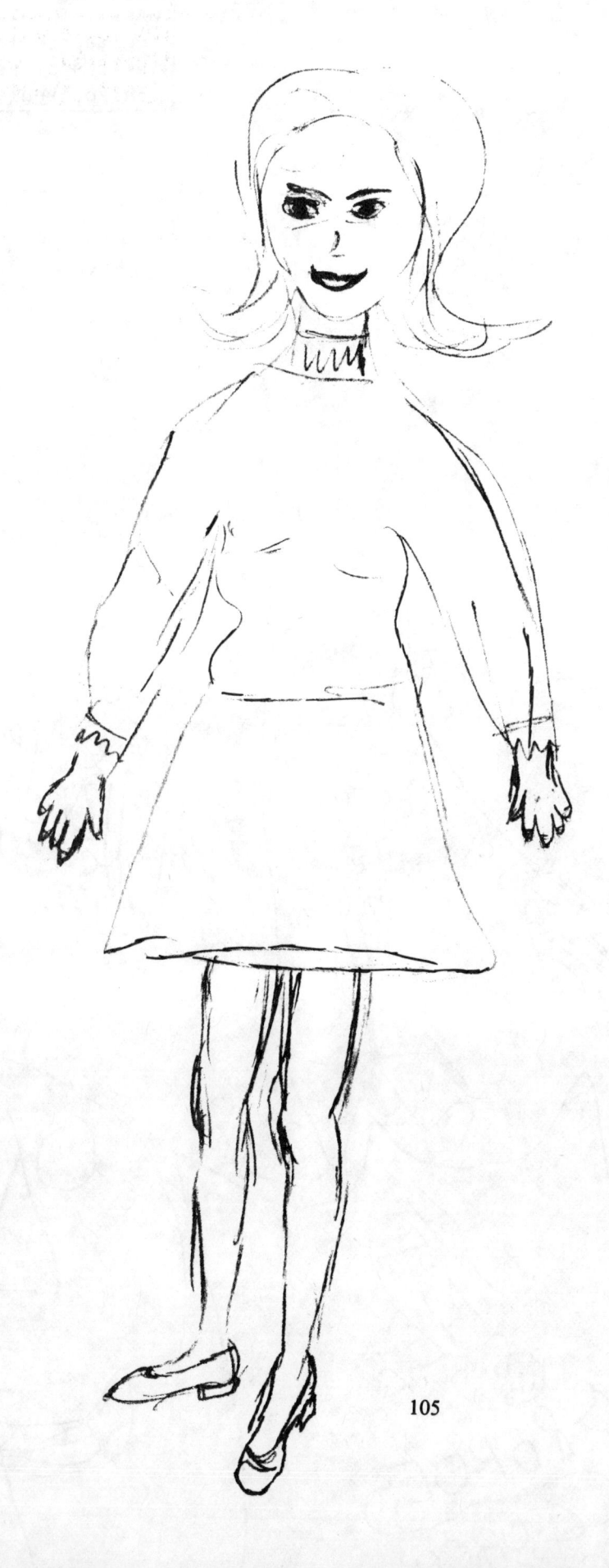

11.

CA 24 ; IQ 119
Normal Female

The same subject is responsible for drawing #12a and 12b. Two years separate the drawings.
12a.

> CA 10, IQ 92, Male.
> Schizophrenia (many
> indices of paranoid
> schizophrenia).

12b.

CA 12, IQ 86, Male.
Schizophrenia (more
indices of paranoid
schizophrenia).

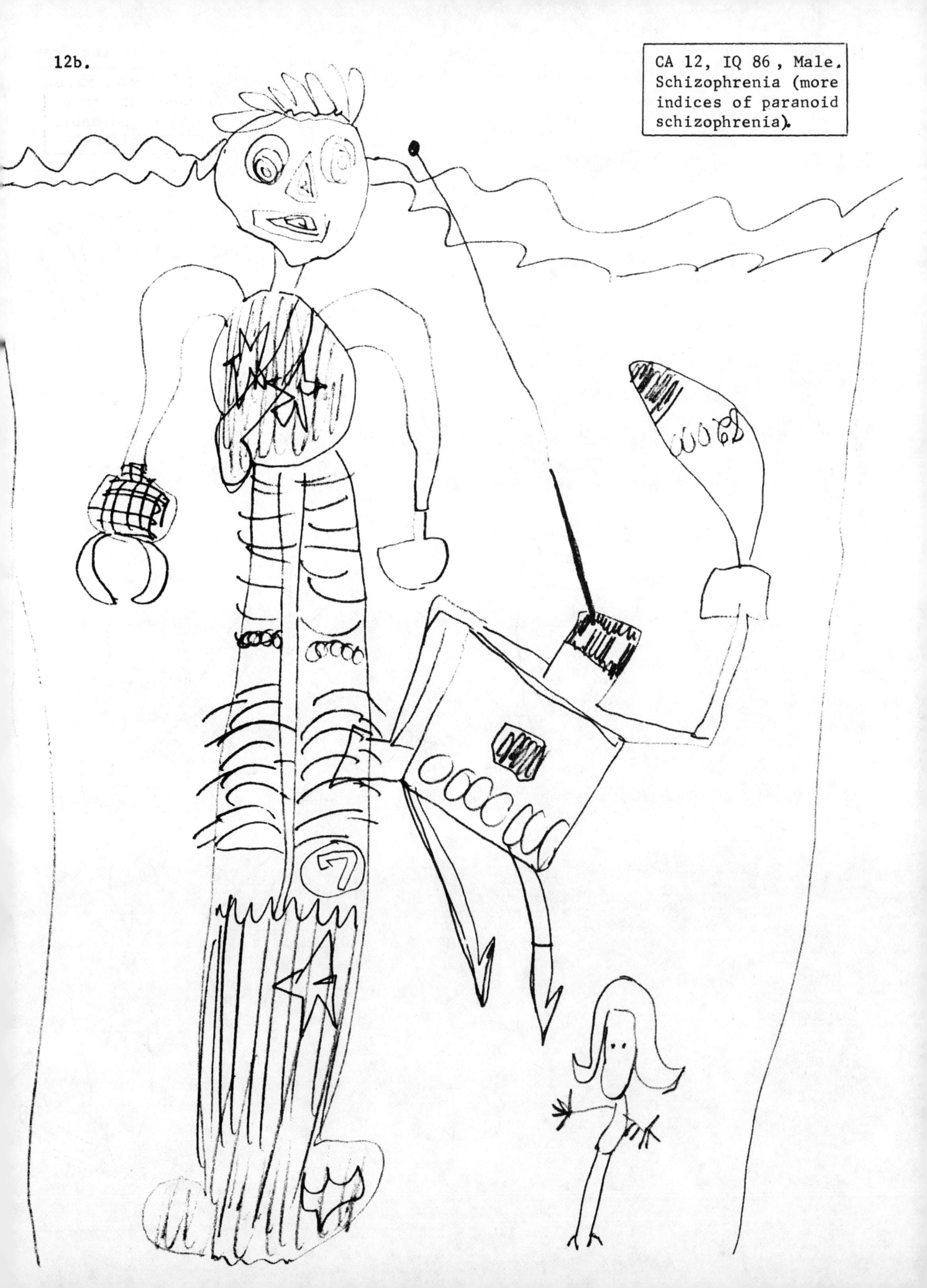

13.

CA 6; Male. VIQ 83, PIQ 52
Bizarre motor
and thought process
problems due to
brain damage

14.

Draw-a-Family
CA 29, IQ 123
Normal Female

15.

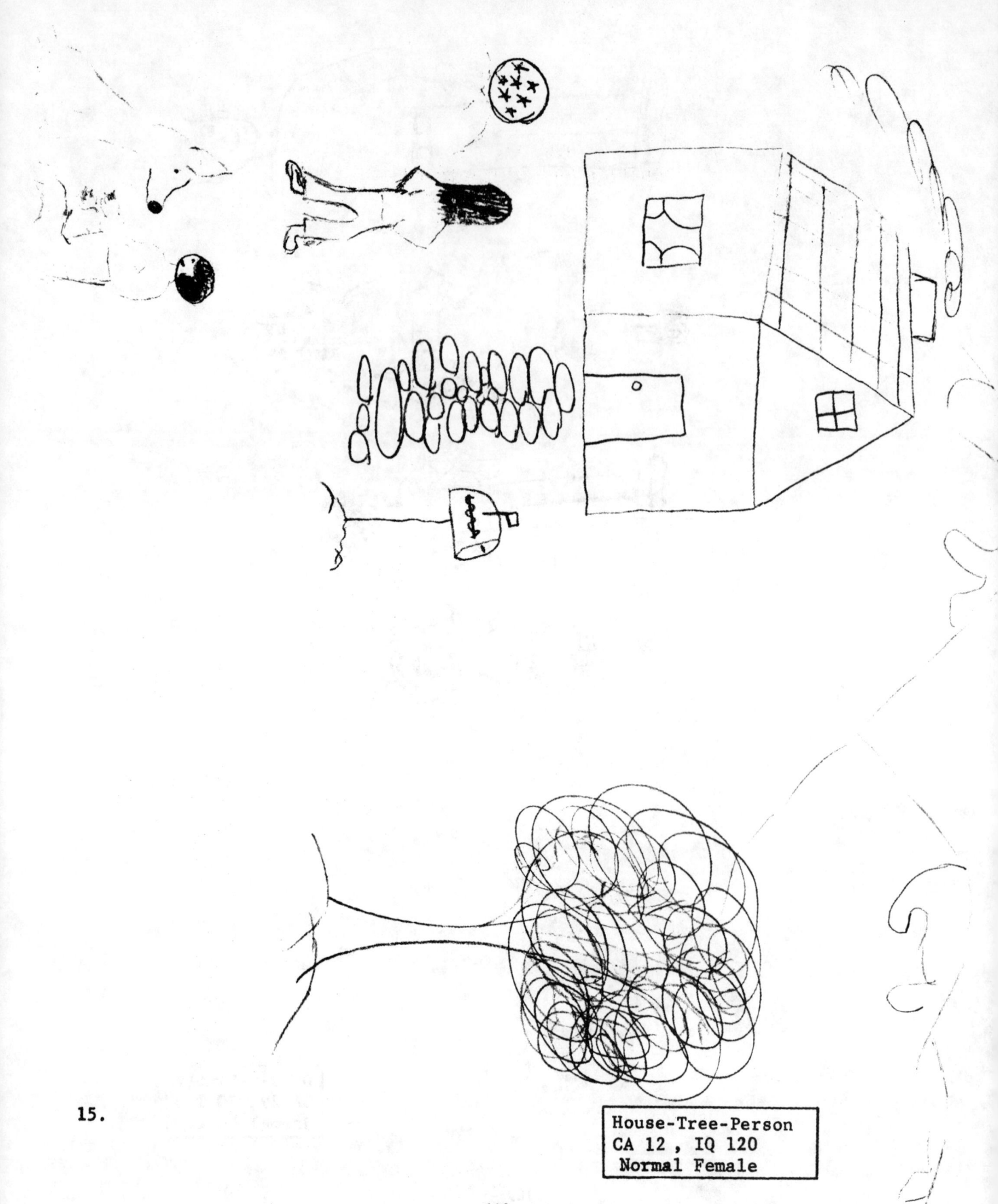

House-Tree-Person
CA 12 , IQ 120
Normal Female

Table XIV
Draw-A-Person Maturation Chart

CA 3.8, IQ 110
Normal Female

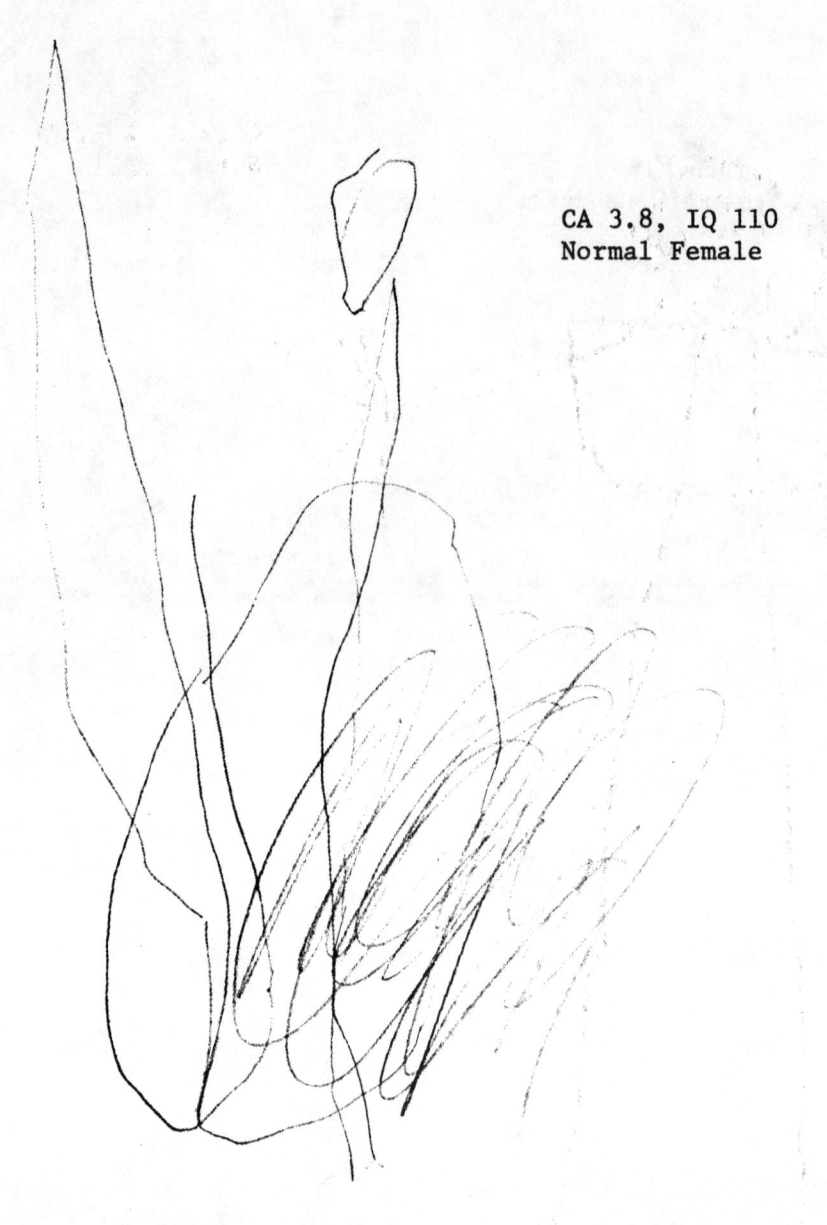

CA 4.0, IQ 97
Normal Male

CA 5.2, IQ 111
Normal Male

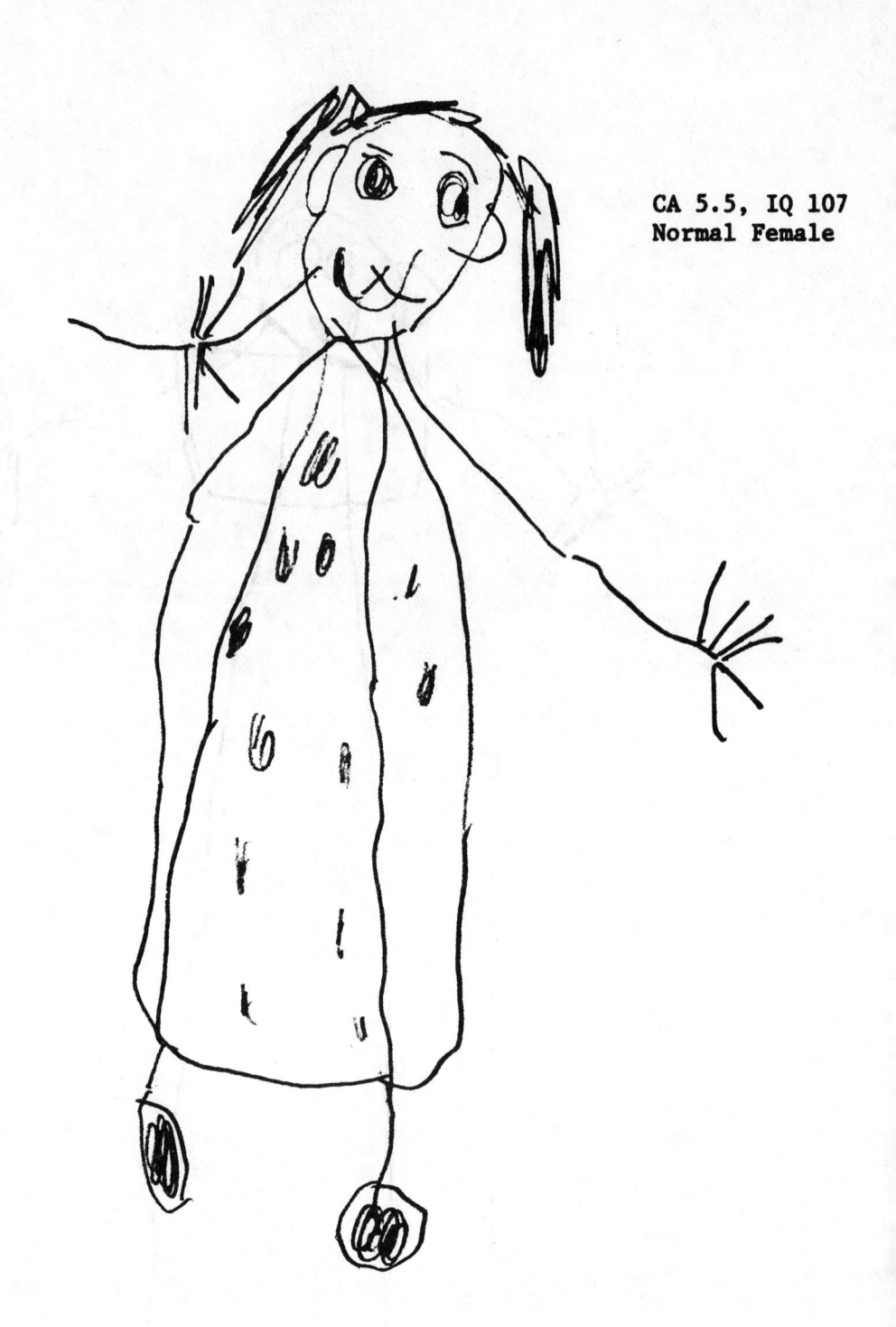

CA 5.5, IQ 107
Normal Female

CA 5.7, IQ 104
Normal Female

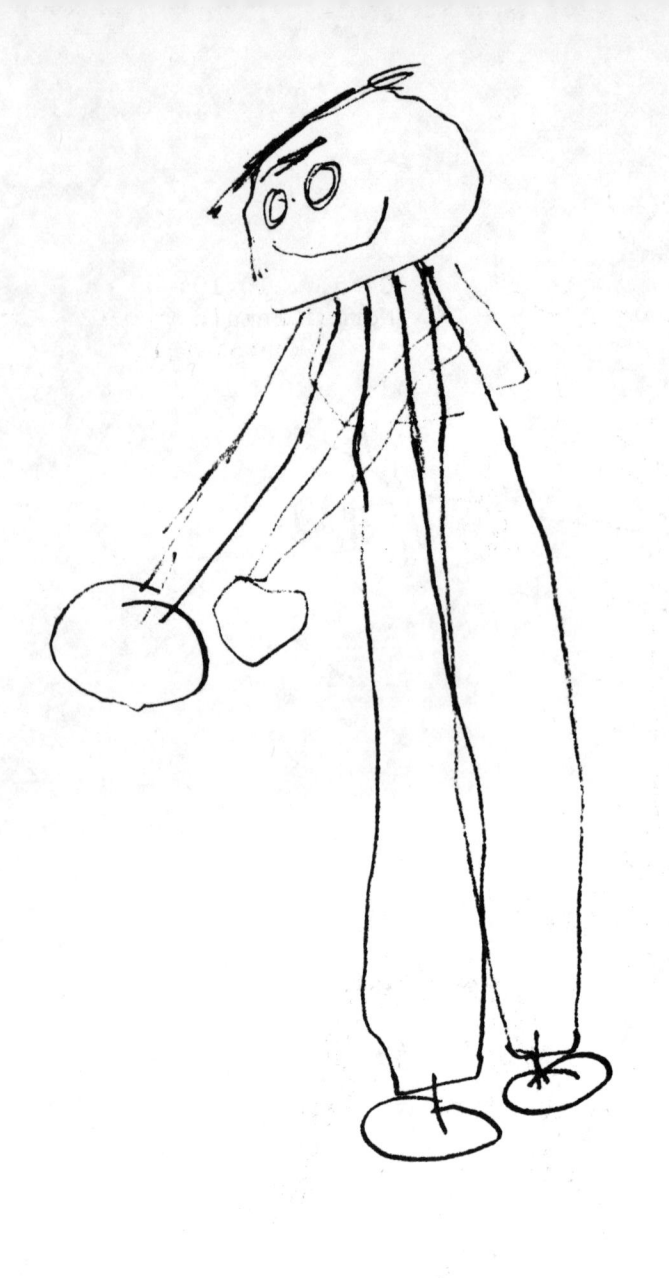

CA 5.9, IQ 115
Normal Male

CA 6.2, IQ 101
Normal Male

CA 6.11, IQ 95
Normal Male

CA 7.5, IQ 103
Normal Male

CA 8.4, IQ 99
Normal Female

CA 8.10, IQ 97.
Normal Male

CA 9.7, IQ 1
Normal Male

CA 10.3, IQ 102
Normal Female

CA 11.6, IQ 106
Normal Female

CA 12.2, IQ 108
Normal Female

CA 13.4, IQ 93
Normal Female

CA 14.1, IQ 111
Normal Female

CA 15.4, IQ 107
Normal Male

Section Summary

Diagnostic-prescriptive teaching represents a systematic way of intervening with learning or behavior problems. Successful programming is dependent on the acquisition of relevant information about the learner and presenting problem. There is no substitute for a professionally conducted psychoeducational testing program.

Part of the success of a testing program is due to the appropriate selection of tests that are designed to reveal what the examiner wishes to know about the presenting problem; part of the success of a testing program is due to the ability of the examiner to interpret the battery of tests and from them to seek cross-validated hypotheses that serve to explain the presenting problems; and part of the success of a testing program is due to the humanness, perceptiveness, and phenomenological capacity of the examiner.

SELECTED REFERENCES

Buck, J. *House-Tree-Person: Administration and Interpretation of H-T-P Test*. California: Western Psychological Services, 1977.

Goodenough, F. *Measurement of Intelligence by Drawings*. New York: World Book Company, 1926.

Harris, D. *Children's Drawings as Measures of Intellectual Maturity*. New York: Harcourt, Brace & World, 1963.

Machover, K. *Personality Projection in the Drawing of the Human Figure*. Illinois: Charles Thomas, 1978.

Section II
Informal Psychoeducational Testing and Assessment

Chapter 12

The Stellern-Shaw Informal Learning Inventory (SILI)

Certain information about the learner is necessary in order to conduct effective IEP-IIP intervention. Such information can be acquired by formal and/or informal psycho-educational testing techniques. Formal psychoeducational techniques involve the use of standardized instruments, which is the topic discussed in the previous section. Informal psychoeducational techniques involve the use of nonstandardized instruments.

In some instances, formal psychoeducational testing is not available or not possible. In such a case, obtaining the necessary learner information becomes a matter of informal assessment. In this and succeeding chapters of this section, various informal strategies for collecting the necessary learner information are discussed.

The Stellern-Shaw Informal Learning Inventory (SILI)

The Stellern-Shaw Informal Learning Inventory (SILI) is a subjective, unstandardized, but systematically arranged psychoeducational instrument which is designed to assist with the identification of learning characteristic strengths and weaknesses. There are no norms, except those which the practitioner develops by using the SILI. Although the SILI presents specific problem-solving tasks for each learning characteristic concept, the tasks are to be considered as conceptual guidelines only, and may be adjusted relative to the age, ability, particular presenting problem, etc., of the subject. The SILI is designed to be used either as a supplement to formal assessment instruments, or as a substitute for such instruments when the latter are not available or are not possible (e.g., parent refuses to permit formal testing).

We recommend that the SILI be used in its entirety, and in sequential order, relative to those subjects whose presenting problem is sufficiently global to resist the identification of specific areas of learning weakness. If the nature of a subject's learning weakness can be narrowed to a single channel (for example, the auditory channel), then only the appropriate part of the SILI may be used to further refine the particular nature of the learning defect.

As with other assessment instruments, we recommend that the examiner establish good rapport with the subject prior to commencing the SILI, and that the SILI be conducted in a quiet, distraction-free, and nonthreatening atmosphere. The examiner should have all necessary materials for the conduction of the SILI immediately available, because the entire instrument takes less than 30 minutes to administer, and the pace of the administration can be rapid.

Since the SILI has no norms on which to base test results, the examiner should pay close attention to the quality of subject answers. We recommend clinical note taking for the purpose of recording subject behavior and answers. If the answers reveal the possibility of a learning characteristic defect, but the SILI problem-solving tasks are not sufficiently refined to permit further evaluation, the examiner should feel free to innovate questions and procedures. It should be remembered that the SILI is an informal and unstandardized instrument designed for subjective-clinical use and can be adapted to meet the assessment needs of the examiner.

The Stellern-Shaw Informal Learning Inventory identifies an informal assessment procedure for classroom teachers, special educators, educational diagnosticians, etc. The SILI provides specific techniques for the assessment of auditory, visual, haptic, and multi-sensory input, memory, and meaning processes, as well as verbal, graphic, and haptic output processes.

OPERATIONAL DEFINITIONS

Auditory: A learning channel that involves the sense of hearing.

Visual: A learning channel that involves the sense of sight.

Tactual: A learning channel that involves the sense of touch.

Kinesthetic: A learning channel that involves the sense of body-muscle movement (e.g., tracing imaginary letters in the air with arm and hand).

Haptic: A learning channel that involves both the senses of touch and body-muscle movement (e.g., finger tracing).

Verbal: A learning channel that involves expressive language.

Graphic: A learning channel that involves paper-pencil activity.

Input: Decoding, reception, or input of stimuli by means of auditory, visual, and/or haptic channels.

Output: Encoding, responding, or output of stimuli by means of verbal, graphic, and/or haptic channels.

Auditory Processing: The ability to accurately take in, understand, and use stimuli acquired auditorially.

Visual Processing: The ability to accurately take in, understand, and use stimuli acquired visually.

Haptic Processing: The ability to accurately take in, understand, and use stimuli acquired haptically.

Tactual Processing: The ability to accurately take in, understand, and use stimuli acquired through the sense of touch.

Kinesthetic Processing: The ability to accurately take in, understand, and use stimuli acquired by means of body-muscle movement.

Multi-sensory Processing: The ability to accurately take in, understand, and use stimuli acquired by means of more than one input channel (e.g., auditory and visual).

Auditory Discrimination: The ability to discriminate similarities and differences between stimuli presented auditorially.

Visual Discrimination: The ability to discriminate similarities and differences between stimuli presented visually.

Haptic Discrimination: The ability to discriminate similarities and differences between stimuli presented haptically.

Auditory Storage Memory: The ability to remember single concepts, facts, and/or data when presented verbally over a short period of time.

Visual Storage Memory: The ability to remember single concepts, facts, and/or data when presented visually over a short period of time.

Haptic Storage Memory: The ability to remember single concepts, facts, and/or data when presented haptically over a short period of time.

Auditory Sequential Memory: The ability to remember, in the order given, a series of stimuli acquired auditorially.

Visual Sequential Memory: The ability to remember, in the order given, a series of stimuli acquired visually.

Haptic Sequential Memory: The ability to remember, in the order given, a series of stimuli acquired haptically.

Auditory Recall Memory (Reauditorization): The ability to spontaneously recall the names of objects that are presented non-verbally, as evidenced by the subject correctly naming the objects.

Visual Recall Memory (Revisualization): The ability to spontaneously recall how the names of words and/or objects presented verbally look in print, as evidenced by the subject graphically reproducing the target words or objects.

Auditory Meaning: The ability to gain meaning from stimuli acquired auditorially.

Visual Meaning: The ability to gain meaning from stimuli acquired visually.

Haptic Meaning: The ability to gain meaning from stimuli acquired haptically.

Verbal Output: The encoding, responding, or output of stimuli by means of expressive language.

Graphic Output: The encoding, responding, or output of stimuli by means of paper-pencil activity.

Haptic Output: The encoding, responding, or output of stimuli by means of a combination of tactual and kinesthetic activity (including visual-motor, gross-motor, and fine-motor activities).

Auditory Closure: The ability to verbally identify a whole or complete word from a verbal presentation of that word with one or more phonemes omitted.

Visual Closure: The ability to verbally identify (name) or graphically complete a visual stimulus (e.g., a word or picture), from a visual presentation of that stimulus, with one or more parts of the stimulus omitted.

Sound Blending: The ability to blend isolated sounds to make a word.

Auditory Figure-Ground: The ability to select an essential auditory stimulus among unessential and backgrund auditory stimuli.

Visual Figure-Ground: The ability to select an essential visual stimulus from unessential background visual stimuli

Visual Spatial Relationship: The ability to visualize positions of objects in space, as evidenced by correctly matching and/or reproducing three dimensional designs.

Convergence: The point at which two separate images received from the eyes become one; generally about sixteen inches from the eyes.

Visual Tracking: The ability to use both eyes in a coordinated and smooth manner when following a moving object.

Sound Location: The ability to identify the direction from which sounds originate.

General Health: A vitality that is apparent in muscular build, good color, abundance of energy, general well being, and freedom from disease, disorder, or illness.

Physical Characteristics: Physical information about a subject, the nature of which could influence the presenting problem (e.g., subject height, weight, visual and auditory acuity, general health and appearance, etc.).

Auditory Acuity: The accuracy with which one hears sounds.

Visual Acuity: The accuracy with which one sees visual symbols.

Color Vision: The ability to distinguish between color variations.

STELLERN-SHAW INFORMAL LEARNING INVENTORY TOPICS

Specific techniques are provided for the observation and assessment of the following topics:

A. PHYSICAL CHARACTERISTICS:
   1. Growth
   2. General Health
   3. Auditory Acuity
   4. Visual Acuity
   5. Color Vision

B. AUDITORY PROCESSING
   1. Auditory Discrimination
   2. Sound Location
   3. Auditory Storage Memory
   4. Auditory Sequential Memory
   5. Auditory Recall Memory
   6. Auditory Meaning
   7. Sound Blending
   8. Auditory Closure
   9. Auditory Figure-Ground
  10. Verbal Output

C. VISUAL PROCESSING
   1. Visual Tracking
   2. Convergence
   3. Visual Discrimination
   4. Visual Storage Memory
   5. Visual Sequential Memory
   6. Visual Recall Memory
   7. Visual Meaning
   8. Visual Closure
   9. Visual Figure-Ground
  10. Visual Spatial Relationship
  11. Graphic Output

D. HAPTIC PROCESSING
   1. Haptic Discrimination
   2. Haptic Storage Memory
   3. Haptic Sequential Memory
   4. Haptic Meaning
   5. Haptic Output

THE STELLERN-SHAW INFORMAL LEARNING INVENTORY

A. PHYSICAL CHARACTERISTICS

1. GROWTH

Definition: The general growth characteristics include height, weight, and frame.

Information such as height, weight, and frame may be obtained by comparing the subject to other subjects of the same age. The following table might serve as a basis for such a comparison.

		GROWTH CHARTS
TABLE I		WITH REFERENCE PERCENTILES FOR BOYS 2 TO 18 YEARS OF AGE

Stature for Age
Weight for Age
Weight for Stature

NAME _____   RECORD # _____

DATE OF BIRTH _____

Date of Measurement	Age Years	Months	Stature	Weight		

These charts to record the growth of the individual child were constructed by the National Center for Health Statistics in collaboration with the Center for Disease Control. The charts are based on data from national probability samples representative of boys in the general U.S. population. Their use will direct attention to unusual body size which may be due to disease or poor nutrition.

Measuring: Take all measurements with the child in minimal indoor clothing and without shoes. Measure stature with the child standing. Use a beam balance to measure weight.

Recording: First take all measurements and record them on this front page. Then graph each measurement on the appropriate chart. Find the child's age on the horizontal sale; then follow a vertical line from that point to the horizontal level of the child's measurement (stature or weight). Where the two lines intersect, make a cross mark with a pencil. In graphing weight for stature, place the cross mark directly above the child's stature at the horizontal level of his weight. When the child is measured again, join the new set of cross marks to the previous set by straight lines.

Do not use the weight for stature chart for boys who have begun to develop secondary sex characteristics.

Interpreting: Many factors influence growth. Therefore, growth data cannot be used alone to diagnose disease, but they do allow you to identify some unusual children.

Each chart contains a series of curved lines numbered to show selected percentiles. These refer to the rank of a measure in a group of 100. Thus, when a cross mark is on the 95th percentile line of weight for age it means that only five children among 100 of the corresponding age and sex have weights greater than that recorded.

Inspect the set of cross marks you have just made. If any are particularly high or low (for example, above the 95th percentile or below the 5th percentile), you may want to refer the child to a physician. *Compare* the most recent set of cross marks with earlier sets for the same child. If he has changed rapidly in percentile levels, you may want to refer him to a physician. Rapid changes are less likely to be significant when they occur within the range from the 25th to the 75th percentile.

In normal teenagers, the age of onset of puberty varies. Rises occur in percentile levels if puberty is early, and these levels fall if puberty is late.

BOYS FROM 2 TO 18 YEARS
STATURE FOR AGE

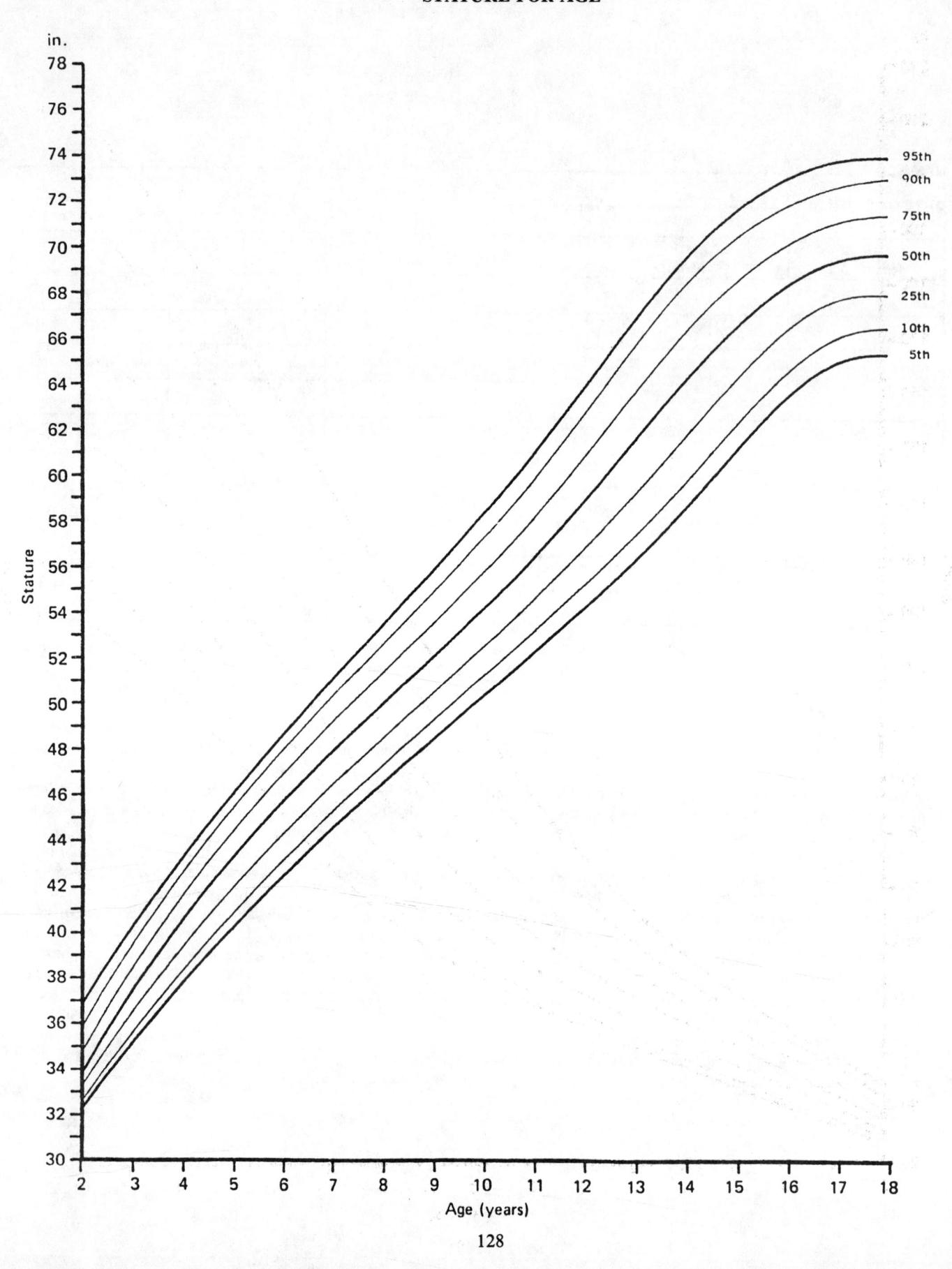

BOYS FROM 2 TO 18 YEARS
WEIGHT FOR AGE

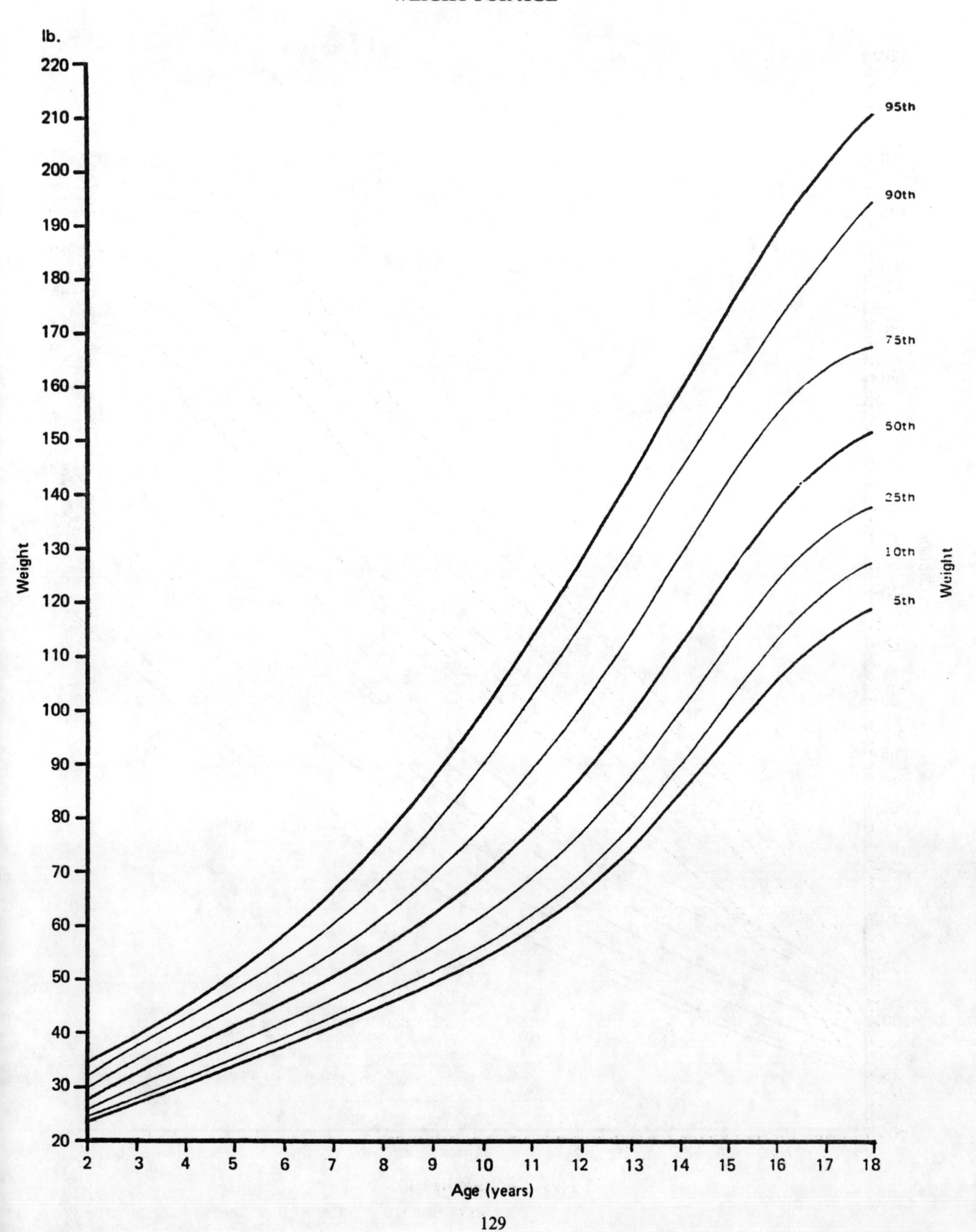

PRE-PUBERTAL BOYS FROM 2 TO 11½ YEARS
WEIGHT FOR STATURE

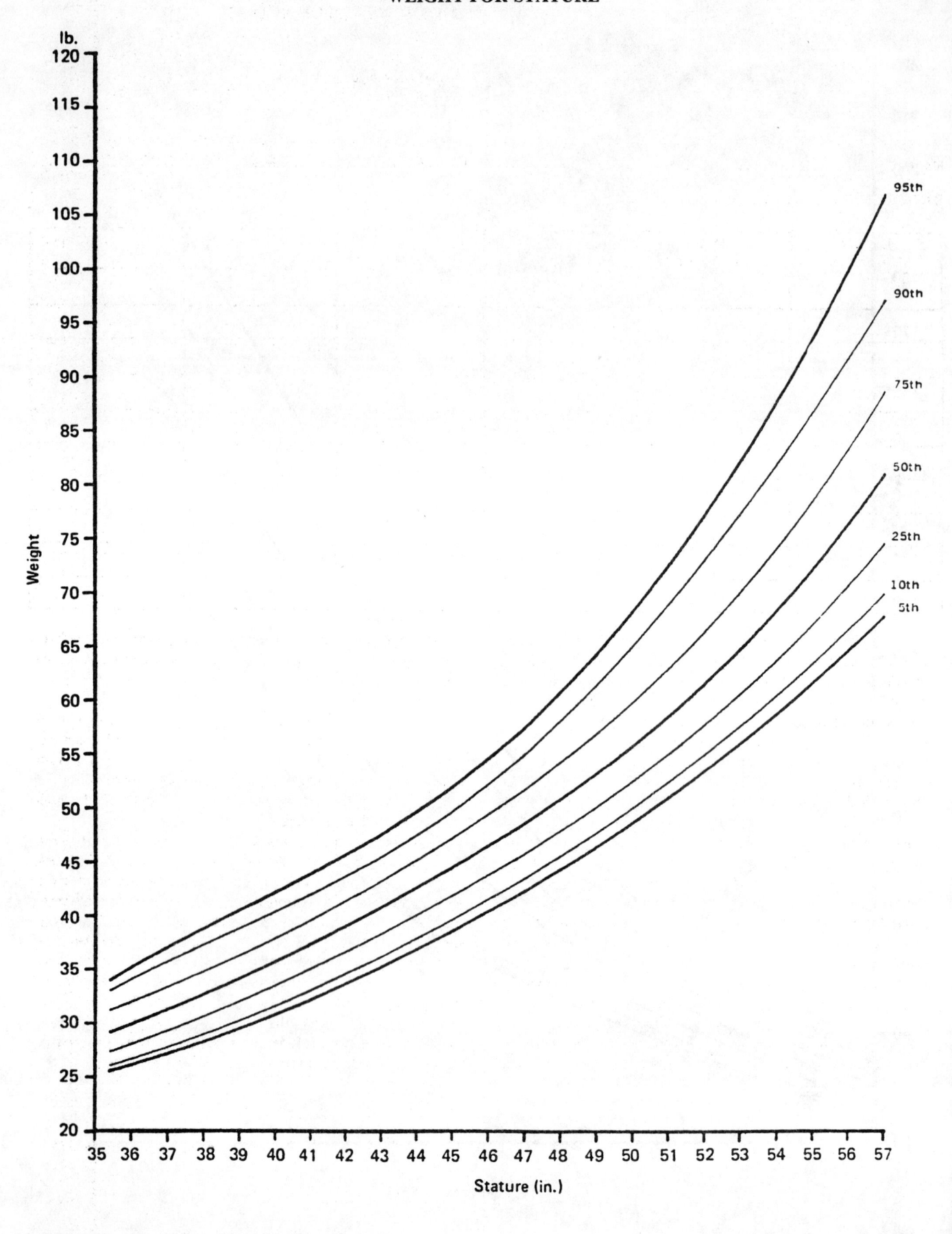

GROWTH CHARTS
WITH REFERENCE PERCENTILES
FOR GIRLS
2 TO 18 YEARS OF AGE

Stature for Age
Weight for Age
Weight for Stature

NAME _____   RECORD # _____

DATE OF BIRTH _____

Date of Measurement	Age Years	Age Months	Stature	Weight		

These charts to record the growth of the individual child were constructed by the National Center for Health Statistics in collaboration with the Center for Disease Control. The charts are based on data from national probability samples representative of girls in the general U.S. population. Their use will direct attention to unusual body size which may be due to disease or poor nutrition.

Measuring: Take all measurements with the child in minimal indoor clothing and without shoes. Measure stature with the child standing. Use a beam balance to measure weight.

Recording: First take all measurements and record them on this front page. Then graph each measurement on the appropriate chart. Find the child's age on the horizontal sale; then follow a vertical line from that point to the horizontal level of the child's measurement (stature or weight). Where the two lines intersect, make a cross mark with a pencil. In graphing weight for stature, place the cross mark directly above the child's stature at the horizontal level of his weight. When the child is measured again, join the new set of cross marks to the previous set by straight lines.

Do not use the weight for stature chart for girls who have begun to develop secondary sex characteristics.

Interpreting: Many factors influence growth. Therefore, growth data cannot be used alone to diagnose disease, but they do allow you to identify some unusual children.

Each chart contains a series of curved lines numbered to show selected percentiles. These refer to the rank of a measure in a group of 100. Thus, when a cross mark is on the 95th percentile line of weight for age it means that only five children among 100 of the corresponding age and sex have weights greater than that recorded.

Inspect the set of cross marks you have just made. If any are particularly high or low (for example, above the 95th percentile or below the 5th percentile), you may want to refer the child to a physician. *Compare* the most recent set of cross marks with earlier sets for the same child. If she has changed rapidly in percentile levels, you may want to refer her to a physician. Rapid changes are less likely to be significant when they occur within the range from the 25th to the 75th percentile.

In normal teenagers, the age of onset of puberty varies. Rises occur in percentile levels if puberty is early, and these levels fall if puberty is late.

GIRLS FROM 2 TO 18 YEARS

STATURE FOR AGE

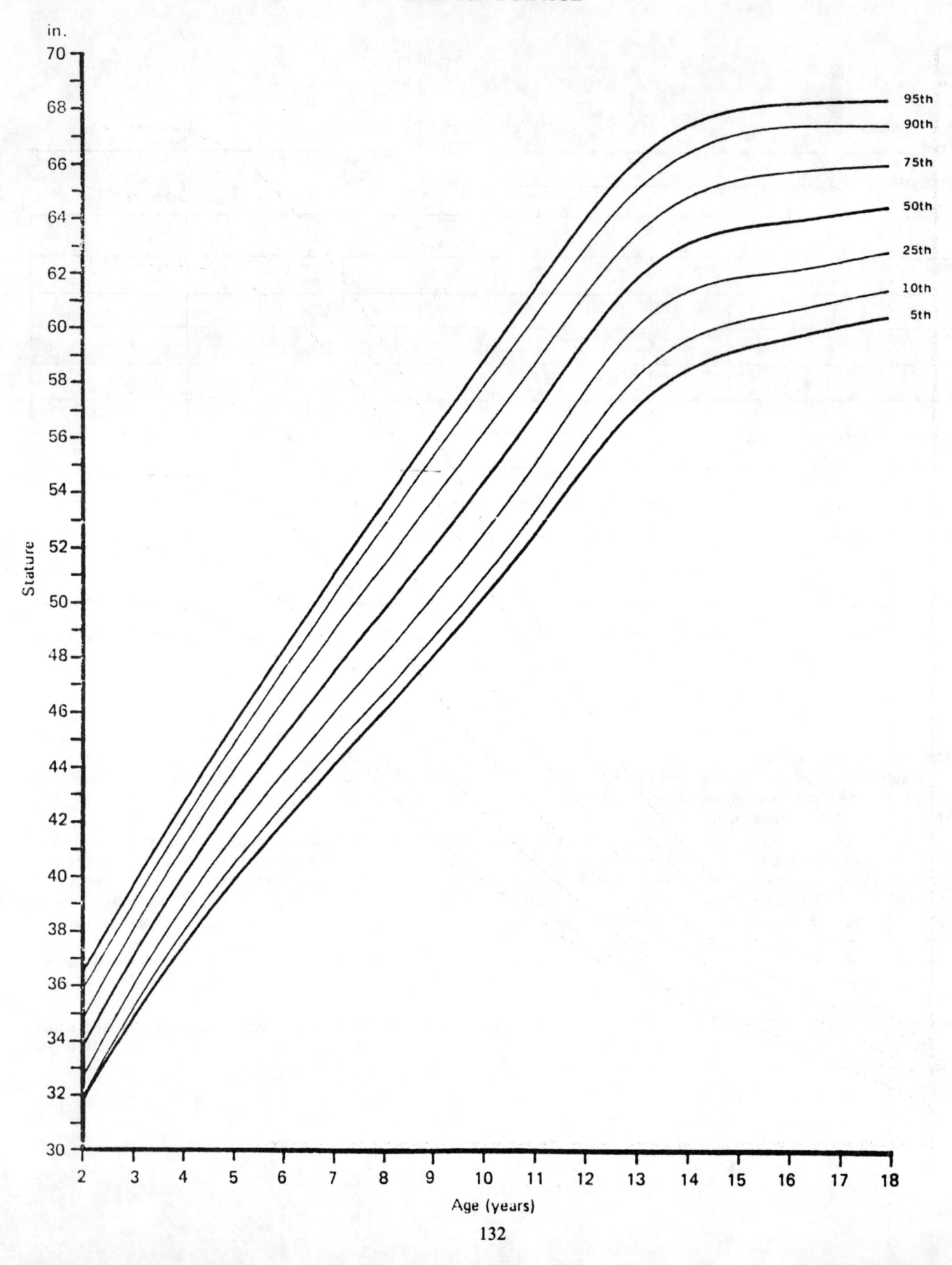

GIRLS FROM 2 TO 18 YEARS
WEIGHT FOR AGE

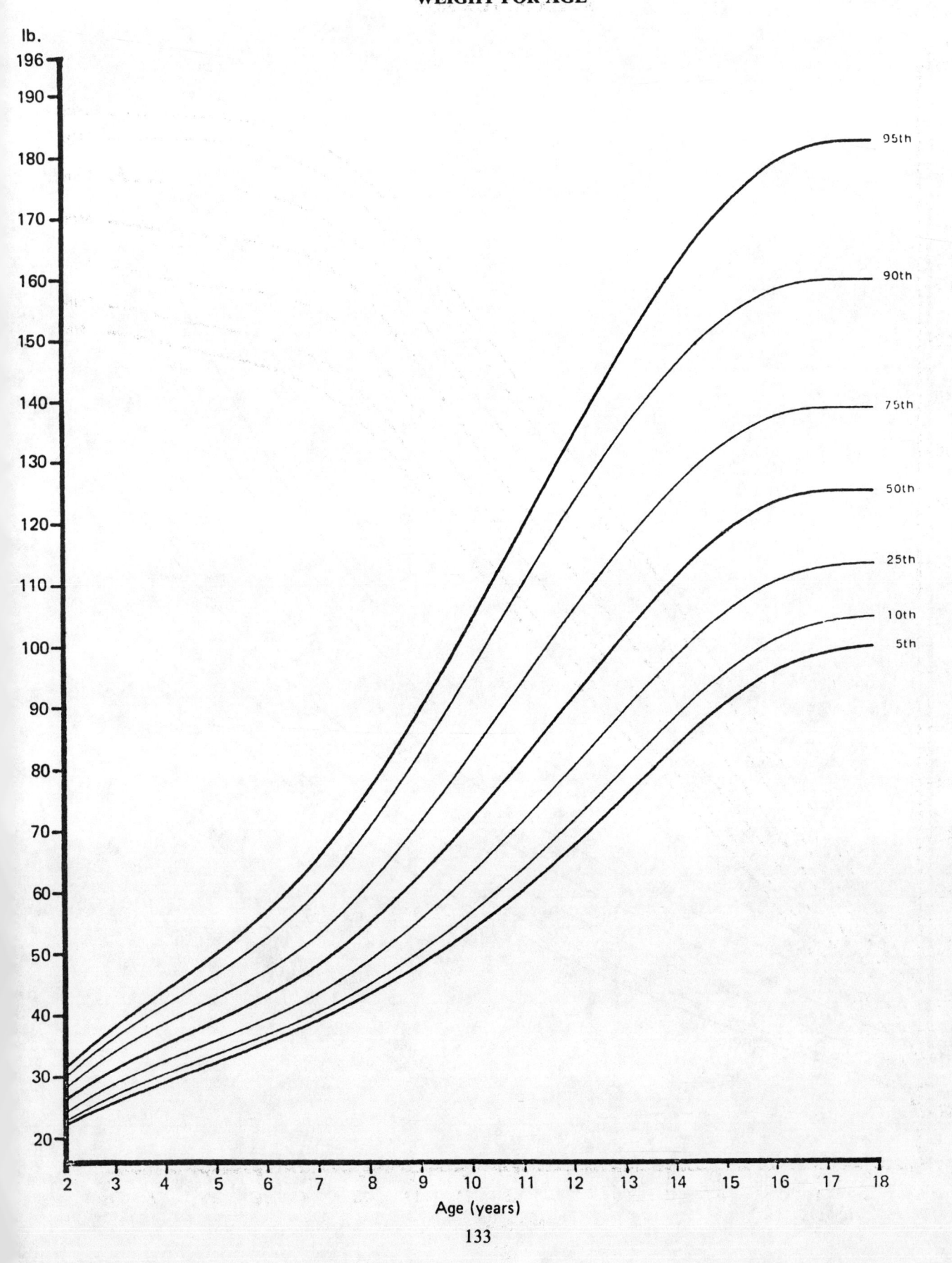

PRE-PUBERTAL GIRLS FROM 2 TO 11½ YEARS
WEIGHT FOR STATURE

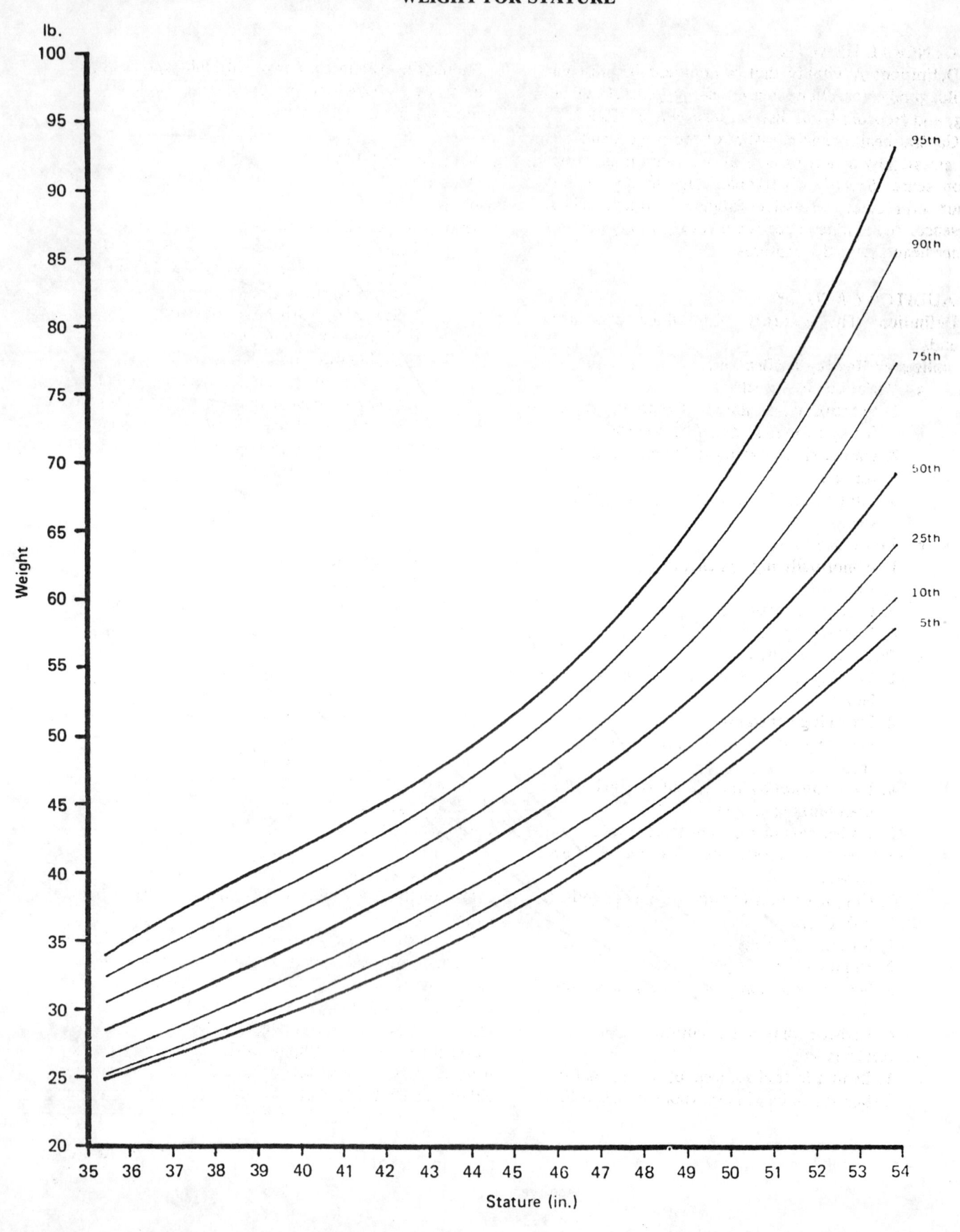

2. GENERAL HEALTH

Definition: A vitality that is apparent in muscular build, good color, abundance of energy, general well being, and freedom from disease, disorder, or illness.

General health characteristics of the subject can best be assessed by means of careful observation and common sense. Specific observable items might include: poor skin color; excessive fatigue; frequent school absences due to illness; persistent cough; runny nose; or other health related symptoms.

3. AUDITORY ACUITY

Definition: The accuracy with which one hears sounds.

Indices of Hearing Difficulties:
  a. Variations in Speech
     1. Substitution of sounds. Common errors: t for k; s for z; k for sk; and ts for s.
     2. Omission of sounds: often final consonants.
     3. Careless and inaccurate production of sounds.
  b. Voice Qualities
     1. Abnormally high pitched.
     2. Very soft.
     3. Dull and monotonous.
     4. Harsh, rasping, or metallic.
  c. Physical Mannerisms
     1. Turning the head to catch sounds with the better ear.
     2. Frowning constantly.
     3. Straining or leaning forward to hear speaker.
     4. Eyes constantly on lips of speaker rather than looking at eyes.
     5. Listlessness or frequent inattention.
     6. Unable to locate sound source with eyes closed.
     7. Cupping hands to ears to catch sounds.
  d. Health Factors
     1. Mouth breathing.
     2. Running ear.
     3. Severe and continued respiratory infections.
     4. Earache (may notice cotton in ear).
  e. Achievement
     1. Behind in tool-subjects of an oral nature.
     2. Sudden failure in oral tool-subjects following a severe illness.

Should the examiner note any difficulties, the subject should be referred to a competent otologist or audiologist for a complete ear/hearing evaluation.

4. VISUAL ACUITY

Definition: The accuracy with which one sees visual symbols.

Indices of Seeing Difficulties
  a. Behavior
     1. Attempts to brush away eye blurs; rubs eyes frequently; frowns.
     2. Stumbles or trips over objects.
     3. Blinks more than usual; cries often; is irritable when doing close work.
     4. Holds books or small objects close to eyes.
     5. Shuts or covers one eye; tilts or thrusts head forward when looking at objects.
     6. Has difficulty in reading or in other tool-subjects requiring close use of the eyes.
     7. Holds body tense, or contorts face for distant or close work.
     8. Is sensitive to light.
     9. Is unable to distinguish colors.
  b. Appearance
     1. Red rimmed, encrusted, or swollen eyelids.
     2. Repeated sties.
     3. Watery or red eyes.
     4. Crossed eyes.
  c. Complaints
     1. Dizziness, headaches, and/or nausea following close eye work.
     2. Blurred or double vision.

Should the examiner note any difficulties, the subject should be referred to a competent ophthalmologist or optometrist for a complete eye/visual examination.

5. COLOR VISION

Definition: The ability to distinguish between color variations.

Color vision is easily screened through the use of simple sorting and matching tasks. Provide the subject with various pairs of colored construction paper squares and have him match the pairs. Gross to fine color vision assessment may be accomplished by using increasingly closer shades of color. Should color vision problems appear to exist, a more formal evaluation by means of either the Ishihara or the Farnsworth tests for color blindness can be done (refer to Appendix B for a citation).

6. SUMMARY

Careful observation and assessment is necessary to rule out physical characteristics as contributory factors to presenting problems. Therefore, should difficulties be detected in any of the above areas, it is imperative that further evaluation be done by the appropriate specialist.

B. AUDITORY PROCESSING

Definition: The ability to accurately take in, understand, and use stimuli acquired auditorially.

Auditory processing involves the following components: auditory discrimination; sound location; auditory storage memory; auditory sequential memory; auditory recall memory; auditory meaning; sound blending; auditory closure; auditory figure-ground; and verbal output, each of which is thought to cntribute to the learning process, and as such is discussed in detail.

1. AUDITORY DISCRIMINATION

Definition: The ability to discriminate similarities and differences between stimuli presented auditorially.

Auditory discrimination can be evaulated through the use of a Wepman-like task (Wepman, 1973). With the subject's back to the examiner, the examiner pronounces various word pairs, and the subject is asked to determine whether the words of each pair are the same or different. The following list provides the examiner with word pairs which involve sounds in the initial, medial, and final word positions.

1. shine—sign
2. tin—thin
3. pine—pine
4. mop—mob
5. mud—mug
6. like—like
7. very—fairy
8. ship—ship
9. goal—coal
10. moon—noon
11. very—berry
12. buff—tuff
13. run—run
14. robe—rode
15. bus—buzz
16. bill—mill
17. brink—drink
18. fling—cling
19. lake—lake
20. scream—stream
21. and—end
22. mesh—mush
23. slid—sled
24. deck—dock

In addition to word pairs, auditory discrimination may be assessed through the use of rhyming words. First, have the subject select the word that rhymes with the target word from a list of words. E.g.: Which of these words rhymes with_____? (Examiner pronounces the first word in each series).

hit:	boy	man	fit
fun:	fat	sun	car
start:	cart	moon	barn
fast:	four	race	past
tail:	rail	chip	table

Next, have the subject supply a word that rhymes with the target word. E.g.:
What rhymes with:

cat? _____ pen? _____ chair? ____ book? _____

2. SOUND LOCATION

Definition: The ability to identify the direction from which sounds originate.

Sound location can be assessed by having the subject, with eyes closed, face the direction of a sound (e.g., bell ringing, snapping fingers, etc.). Or, start a metronome and hide it in the room; or hide an alarm clock set to go off. Have the subject find the object by its sound location. Failure to perform these tasks should alert the examiner to hearing and/or perceptual difficulties, both of which should be more thoroughly evaluated by the appropriate specialist.

3. AUDITORY STORAGE MEMORY

Definition: The ability to remember single concepts, facts, and/or data when presented verbally over a short period of time.

Short term auditory memory may be assessed by giving the subject a key word verbally and telling him that you will ask him to identify that word later. Allow 10 seconds to pass, then give the subject a series of five similar words including the target word and ask the subject to raise his hand when he hears the target word. Increase the complexity of the task by adding key words one at a time while simultaneously increasing the number of pool words.

An alternate method of assessment is to ask the subject to give you his birthdate, address, phone number, names of previous teachers, etc. Successful completion of this task indicates the subject is capable of remembering factual information over a period of time.

4. AUDITORY SEQUENTIAL MEMORY

Definition: The ability to remember, in the order given, a series of stimuli acquired auditorially.

Short term auditory sequential memory can be assessed by either of the following techniques (preferably both). Give the subject a series of single digits and have him immediately repeat them in the same order. Give two trials if necessary.

Examples:
2-6	6-8-5-9
3-7	4-5-8-4-1
6-4-9	9-4-7-0-6
7-2-6	9-6-3-2-7-1
4-7-9-1	1-3-8-6-5-2

Similarly, use unrelated words, giving two trials if necessary.

Examples:
book grass
chalk-shoe-paper
swing-bug-rope-hot-plant-road
rake-house-tall-lake-hill
rock-arm-shirt-fence

5. AUDITORY RECALL MEMORY (REAUDITORIZATION)

Definition: The ability to spontaneously recall the names of objects that are presented non-verbally, as evidenced by the subject correctly naming the objects.

A variety of techniques may be used to assess auditory recall memory. The first method involves the subject naming (recalling) the object which makes the sound the examiner makes (e.g., dog barking, train whistle, bell ringing, etc.).

Sentence completion can also be used to assess auditory recall memory. The subject completes the following sentences:

I read a _____.
I write with a _____.
We buy food at _____.
I throw a _____.
I live in a _____.
When I am sick, I go to a _____.

Another task involves the subject naming all the objects he can think of in a particular category (e.g., animals; things to eat; things you can ride on; etc.). Allow the subject 20 seconds for each category.

Also, the examiner may ask open ended questions, such as "how do you play hopscotch?", or "Describe what your car looks like", etc.

A possible indicator of an auditory recall problem is much better silent than oral reading ability (because oral reading requires the subject to recall how the names of the words read sound aloud).

6. AUDITORY MEANING

Definition: The ability to gain meaning from stimuli acquired auditorially.

Auditory meaning can be assessed by means of verbal analogies. This task is similar to the auditory association subtest of the ITPA (Kirk, 1968). The subject is asked to verbally complete the following statements:

Examples:
A mommy is big; a baby is _____ (little, small).
The sky is blue, salt is _____ (white).
Milk has a glass; soup has a _____ (bowl, cup).
A car has tires; people have _____ (legs, feet).

Another task involves the subject supplying a synonym for the word the examiner pronounces.

Examples: big; lady; thin; infant; etc.

A variation of this task involves the subject giving antonyms (opposites) for the word the examiner pronounces.

Examples: fat; night; slow; under; rich; etc.

The above tasks involve auditory recall memory ability. Therefore, the following task is offered as a pure assessment of auditory meaning. The examiner asks the subject to point to something made of cloth, wood, metal, glass, etc.

7. SOUND BLENDING

Definition: The ability to blend isolated sounds to make a word.

Sound blending can be assessed by tasks similar to the sound blending subtest task of the ITPA. The following word list is pronounced with 2-second pauses between each phoneme, as indicated by the dash. The subject then blends the sounds to pronounce the words correctly.

Sound Blending Examples:

1. m-e	9. g-oa-t
2. c-a-p	10. sh-i-p
3. t-ar	11. br-i-ck
4. p-ai-l	12. b-o-tt-le
5. s-u-n	13. t-el-e-v-i-sion
6. sl-a-p	14. r-e-f-r-i-g-er-a-tor
7. sp-o-t	15. a-l-ph-a-b-e-t
8. d-u-s-t	

8. AUDITORY CLOSURE

Definition: The ability to verbally identify the whole or complete word from a verbal presentation of that word with one or more phonemes omitted.

Auditory closure can be assessed by a task similar to that found in the ITPA. The following words are pronounced by the examiner, leaving out the phonemes indicated by the dashes. The subject then supplies the missing phonemes when pronouncing the words.

Examples:

cowb-- (cowboy)	-amburger (hamburger)
strawber-- (strawberry)	-ot-og (hotdog)
pu--y (puppy or putty)	-op-orn (popcorn)

9. AUDITORY FIGURE-GROUND

Definition: The ability to select an essential auditory stimulus among unessential and background auditory stimuli.

Auditory figure-ground can be assessed through the use of the Goldman-Fristoe Test of Auditory Discrimination. However, it is not necessary to administer the entire test. E.g.: Begin with plate number 89. Do not use the test pictures, but rather, tell the subject that the taped voice will say "point to" and then give a word. The subject is asked to read/supply the word. The task becomes increasingly difficult as the words are pronounced against a background of noise which gradually becomes louder. Only five or six items need be administered to determine the subject's auditory figure-ground ability (Goldman, 1970).

If the Goldman-Fristoe tape is not available, the examiner can create his own tape by using a tape recorder and a radio or television. Set the tape recorder in front of the radio or television and record the voices of the program; then superimpose key words over the radio or TV voices for the subject to identify. Increase the difficulty of the task by moving farther away from the microphone while continuing to superimpose key words. This tape can then be used in the same manner as the Goldman tape.

Finally, observe how the subject works in the classroom; note how he reacts to surrounding noise and activity. If he is able to remain on-task despite sound disruptions, one may assume his ability to select important auditory stimuli among extraneous auditory stimuli is adequate.

10. VERBAL OUTPUT

Definition: The encoding, responding, or output of stimuli by means of expressive language.

Throughout the SILI, the examiner should note the subject's verbal expressive ability. Should the examiner suspect verbal output problems, the following tasks might be considered in order to provide further evaluation of the subject's expressive language.

Engage the subject in conversation; note the subject's facility with words, semantics, syntax, rate, etc. The examiner may then compare this sample language with language samples of other subjects of similar age and background.

A method of eliciting verbal response involves the use of high interest pictures. Have the subject tell a story about the picture; again, note his facility with words, semantics, syntax, rate, etc.

C. VISUAL PROCESSING

Definition: The ability to accurately take in, understand, and use stimuli acquired visually.

Visual processing involves the following components: visual tracking; convergence; visual discrimination; visual storage memory; visual closure; visual figure-ground; visual-spatial relationship; and graphic output, each of which is thought to contribute to the learning process, and as such is discussed in detail.

1. VISUAL TRACKING

Definition: The ability to use both eyes in a coordinated and smooth manner when following a moving object.

A penlight flashlight is useful in observing the ability to visually track. In a darkened room, have the subject follow the light with his eyes without moving his head; move the light vertically, horizontally, and diagonally, about ten inches from the subject's eyes. Watch how the eyes work together, noting the following: do they jump at mid-point?; does one eye track while the other does not?; are the eye movements smooth or jerky?; does the subject seem to have trouble staying with the light?; etc.

2. CONVERGENCE

Definition: The point at which two separate images received from the eyes become one; generally about sixteen inches from the eyes.

A piece of string thirty-two inches long with a knot sixteen inches from each end is all that is necessary to check convergence. Have the subject hold one end of the string between his eyes on the bridge of his nose (without blocking his forward vision), while the examiner pulls the other end taut. The subject is then instructed to grasp the knot with his free hand. Should the subject's grasp be short of or beyond the knot by two or more inches, the subject should be referred for a visual examination.

3. VISUAL DISCRIMINATION

Definition: The ability to discriminate similarities and differences between stimuli presented visually.

Testing for visual discrimination can be done by using the following tasks from the spirit duplicator masters of the *Frostig Program for the Development of Visual Perception* (Frostig, 1972) (e.g., PS-15; PC-57; etc.); or by the tasks on the following pages (pp. 140-142). Evaluate the subject's ability to make gross then fine discrimination.

Find the matching picture.

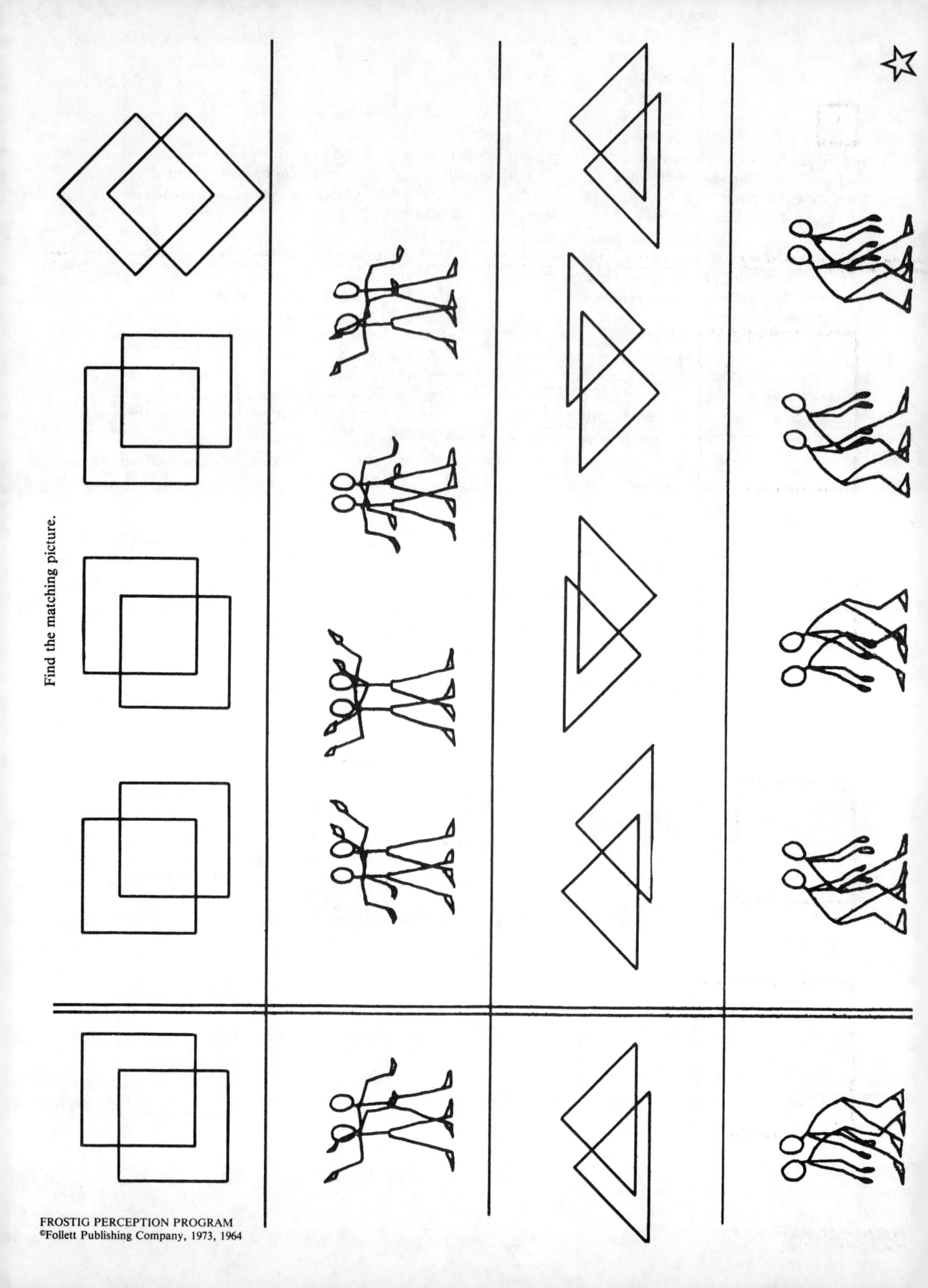

FROSTIG PERCEPTION PROGRAM
©Follett Publishing Company, 1973, 1964

1	2	3	4
Red	Blue	Green	Yellow

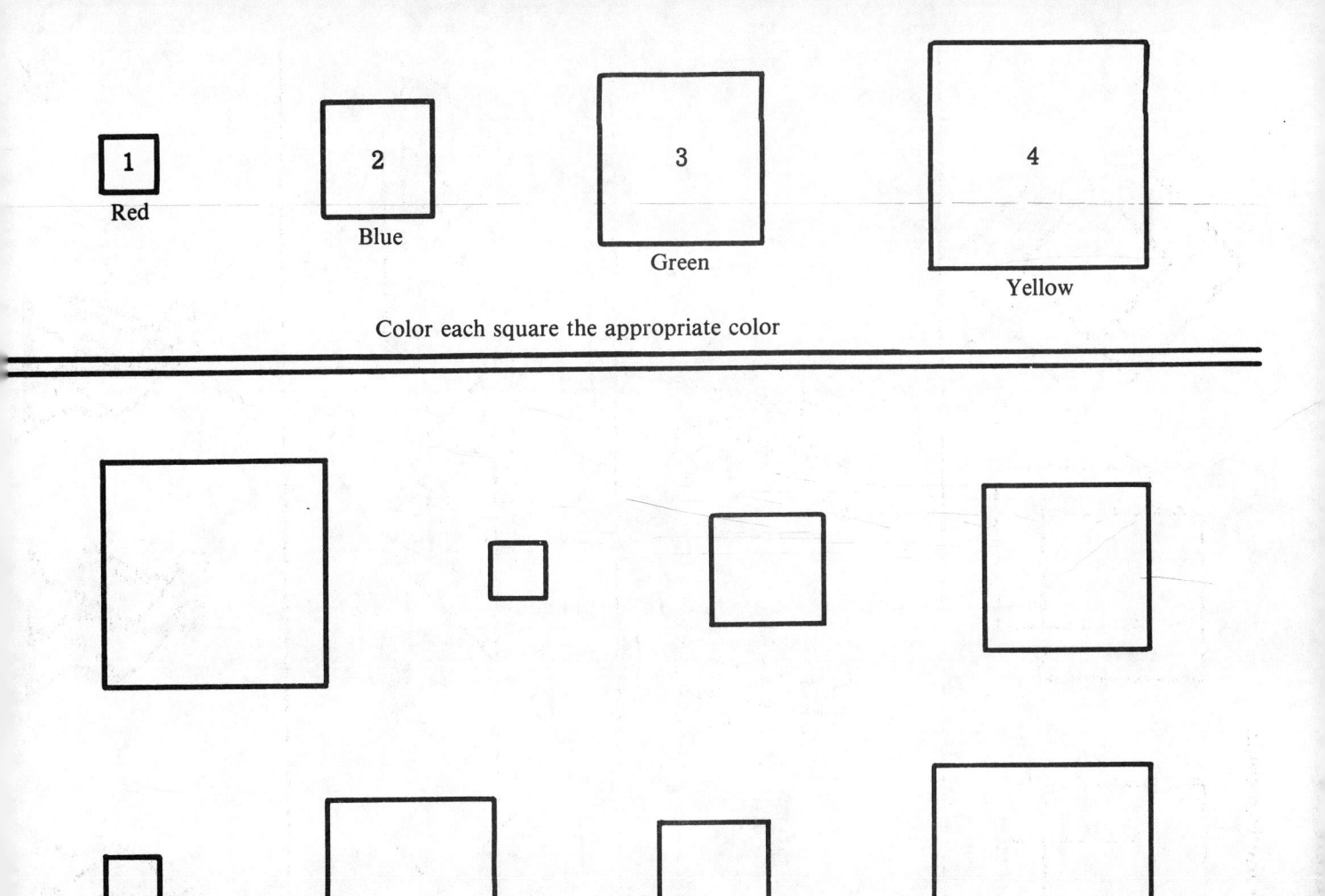

Color each square the appropriate color

PC: Exercise 56

FROSTIG PERCEPTION PROGRAM
©Follett Publishing Company, 1973, 1964

Find the missing part

Circle the one that is different

b b b b d b b b

n n n n n u n n

q q p q q q q q q q

Circle the one that is the same as the first one

saw   was   sav   wsa   saw   was

no   on   ou   uo   no   on

Circle the letters that are in the same order as the model

mild   milmdlimildldimidl

very   vervyrevrveryrevy

3. VISUAL STORAGE MEMORY

Definition: The ability to remember single concepts, facts, and/or data when presented visually over a short period of time.

Have twenty-four one inch cubes of various colors (e.g., 4 red, 4 blue, 4 orange, 4 yellow, 4 green, 4 purple, etc.). Select two cubes of any color from the whole group. Let the subject look at them briefly (5 seconds), while asking him to remember the colors he sees; then return the cubes to the main group. After mixing the cubes, have the subject select the same number and color of cubes as in the examiner's model. Sequential cube order is unimportant. Increase the difficulty of the task by increasing the number of cubes one at a time until the subject can no longer successfully perform the task. Give the subject two trials whenever necessary. Should the examiner suspect color blindness, the task can be easily modified. In place of the colored cubes, substitute a variety of small objects (e.g., keys, pennies, washers, bottle caps, etc.).

An alternate task involves the use of the following character cards. Prepare 3x5 cards with each set of characters sequenced on separate cards, as shown on page 143. Select one character card; present the first character on the card to the subject while keeping the remaining characters covered. After the subject has viewed the first character for about five seconds, cover it and reveal the remaining characters, asking the subject to find the one that matches the first one.

An alternate task involves the use of ordinary playing cards. Present the subject with one randomly selected card; expose for 10 seconds. Then remove the target card; place in a pool of five dissimilar cards; expose the six cards to the subject; ask him to identify the target card. Increase the complexity by gradually adding target and pool cards.

5. VISUAL SEQUENTIAL MEMORY

Definition: The ability to remember, in the order given, a series of stimuli acquired visually.

Visual sequential memory can be assessed by using the colored blocks, small objects, or the playing cards used for the visual storage memory tasks. The procedure is similar; however, for visual sequential memory tasks, remembering the cubes, objects, or cards in the precise order presented is necessary. Select two cubes (or cards) of any different color from the group of cubes and place them on the table in a horizontal row. Let the subject look at them briefly (5 seconds), while asking him to remember both the colors he sees and the order in which they are presented; then return the cubes to the main group. After mixing the cubes, have the subject select the same number, color, and sequence of cubes as in the model. Increase the number of cubes used by one until the subject can no longer successfully perform the task. Give the subject two trials whenever necessary. Once again, if the examiner suspects color blindness, substitute objects for the cubes.

An alternate task involves the use of the following character cards. Prepare 3x5 cards with each set of character sequences as shown on page 145. Select one character card. Present the first sequence on the card while keeping the remaining sequences covered. After the subject has viewed the first sequence for about five seconds, cover it and reveal the remaining sequences, asking the subject to find the one that matches the first sequence.

○ △   □ ○   ○ △   △ □

bpr   prb   pbr   dpr   bpr

MVXZ   ZXVM   MVXZ   MXVZ   MUZX

SVRMT   VSRMT   SVRMT   SVRMT

QSBFGZ   QSBFZG   QESBFZ   QSBFGZ

6. VISUAL RECALL MEMORY (REVISUALIZATION)

Definition: The ability to spontaneously recall how the names of words and/or objects presented verbally look in print, as evidenced by the subject graphically reproducing the target words or objects.

Visual recall memory can be assessed by comparing two different samples of the subject's handwriting. First, ask the subject to graphically copy several words presented visually (the words should be within the subject's reading vocabulary). Next, orally dictate several similar words (again within the subject's reading vocabulary), or the same words, and request the subject to graphically reproduce the words. Compare the two samples. Revisualization difficulty is expressed by the subject being unable to recall how words appear in writing when there is no visual model from which to copy. Thus, a subject with a revisualization problem will be able to graphically copy from a visual model, but will have difficulty writing words from dictation. If the subject has marked difficulty graphically copying from a visual model, the problem is not revisualization, but rather dysgraphia (graphic output problem). Regarding the two samples above, the subject with a revisualization problem would perform better regarding the first sample, and less well regarding the second sample.

With very young subjects, follow the above procedures, but use letters of the subject's name; or have the subject draw a square, triangle, cat, car, etc.

The following examples are included to aid the examiner in identifying visual recall difficulties.

Visual Recall Memory difficulty examples:

Examples of the way in which subjects with visual recall memory difficulty might copy words from a written visual model:		Examples of the way in which subjects with visual recall memory difficulty might write words from oral dictation:	
MODEL	SUBJECT'S RESPONSE	ORALLY DICTATED WORD	SUBJECT'S RESPONSE
rain	*rain*	chain	*chan*
		ran	*ruan*
		boat	*bote*
foot	*fot*	tame	*tam*
		pain	*pah*
chain	*chain*		
		float	*flot*

7. VISUAL MEANING

Definition: The ability to gain meaning from stimuli acquired visually.

Assessment of visual meaning can be accomplished by showing an interesting picture and asking the subject to describe what he sees, what he thinks is happening, and what he thinks will happen. This assessment also provides the examiner with an expressive language sample by which to evaluate verbal output.

An alternate task using non-verbal stimuli involves the subject matching pictures that go together, or matching parts of objects to whole objects. **Page 148** provides the examiner with several examples.

8. VISUAL CLOSURE

Definition: The ability to verbally identify (name) or graphically complete a visual stimulus (e.g., a word or picture), from a visual presentation of that stimulus, with one or more parts of the stimulus omitted.

Show the subject the following incomplete pictures and ask him to identify them. In addition, ask the subject to indicate what is missing from the picture. An alternate task involves the subject completing the incomplete pictures with a pencil.

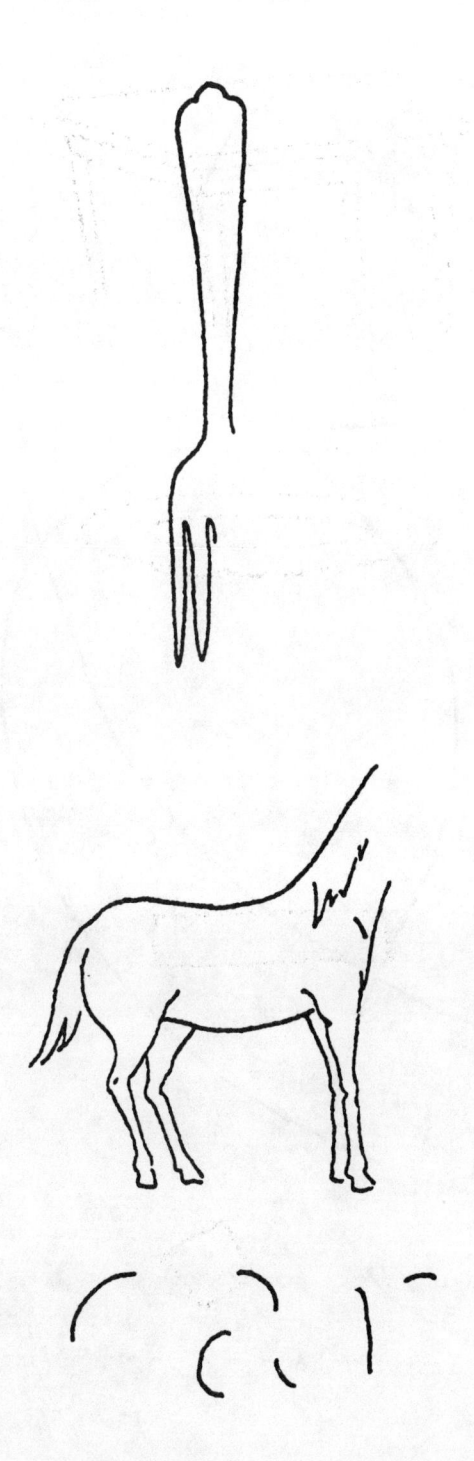

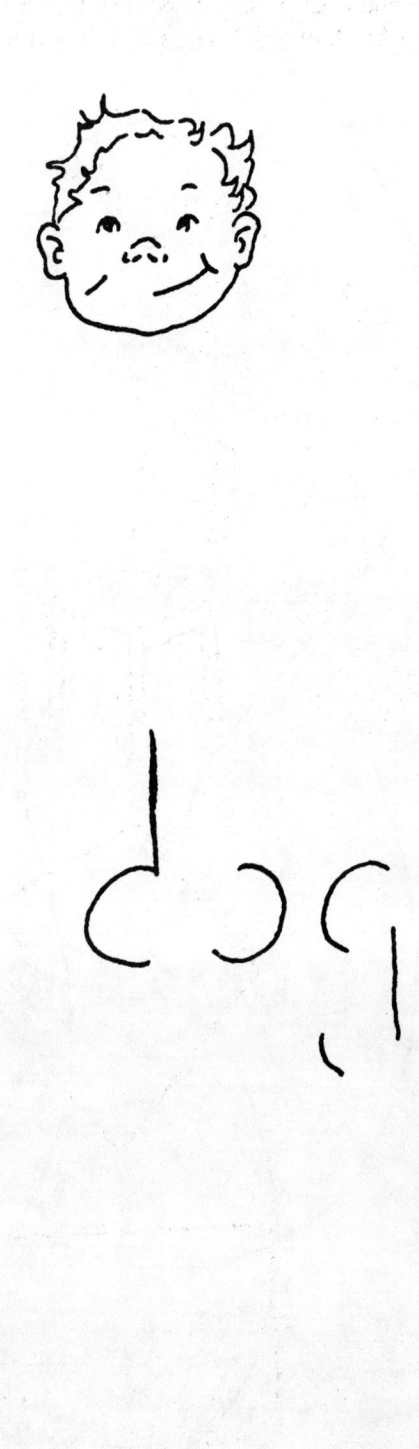

9. VISUAL FIGURE-GROUND

Definition: The ability to select an essential visual stimulus from unessential background visual stimuli.

Visual figure-ground can be evaluated by using the following tasks from the spirit duplicator masters of the *Frostig Program for the Development of Visual Perception* (Frostig, 1972) (e.g., FG-5; FG-27; FG-37; FG-14; etc.).

Another method involves the subject locating objects included in the hidden picture pages from "Child Highlights" magazine.

Still another method involves tasks represented by the following examples: Have the subject trace the letter or number within each matrix on page 154 with a brightly colored crayon.

Still another method involves lightly drawing a letter, number, word, or words on printed newspaper, thus obscuring somewhat the target symbol (letter, word, etc.). Have the subject pick out the target symbol.

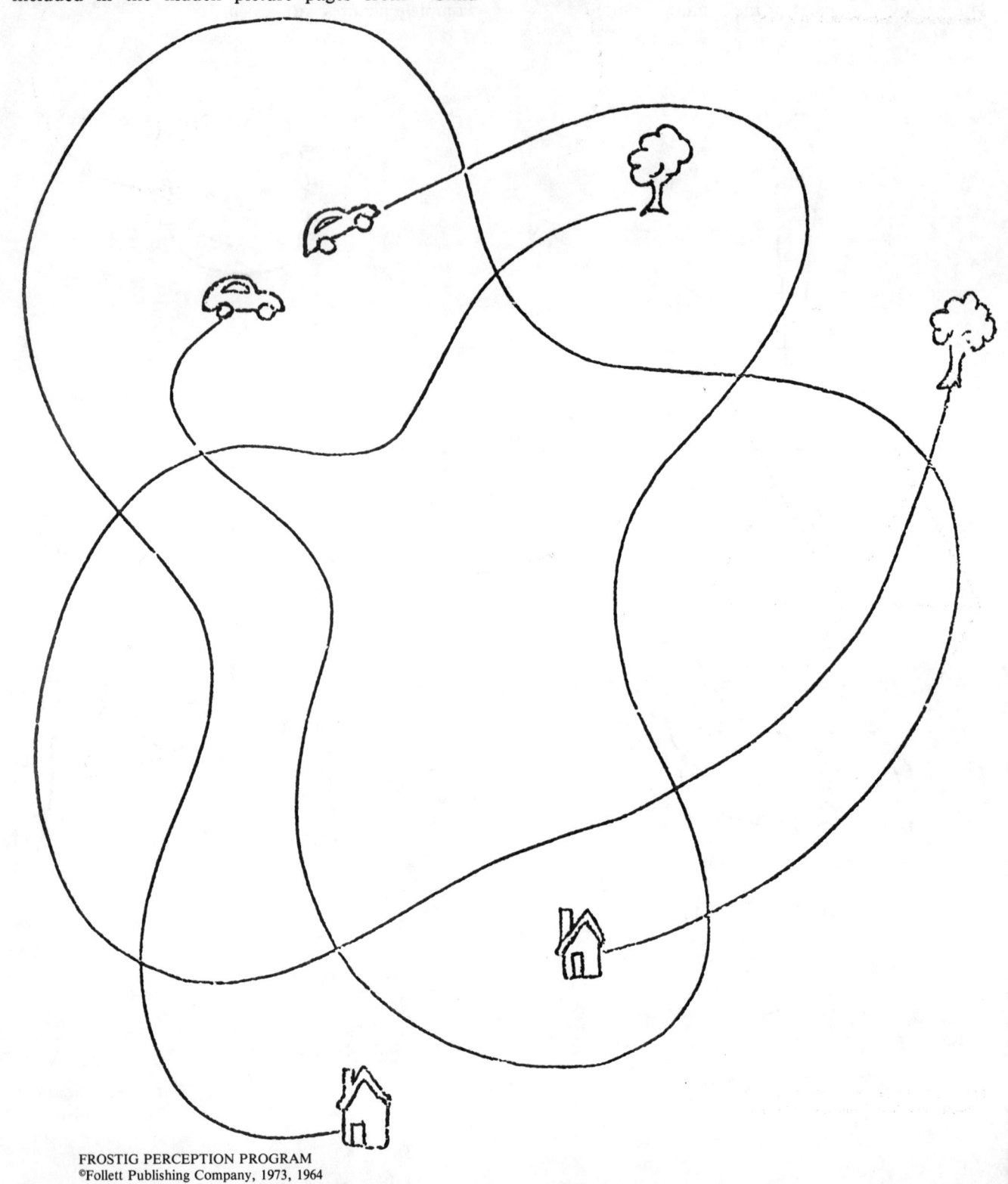

FROSTIG PERCEPTION PROGRAM
©Follett Publishing Company, 1973, 1964

With a crayon, trace the line from house to house, car to car, and tree to tree; use a different color for each line.

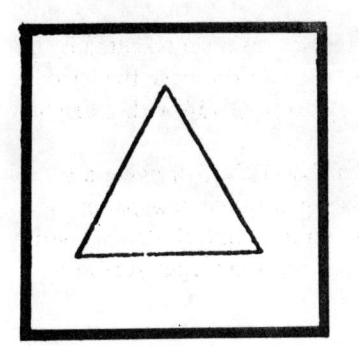

Outline with a crayon all the triangles hidden in the picture below.

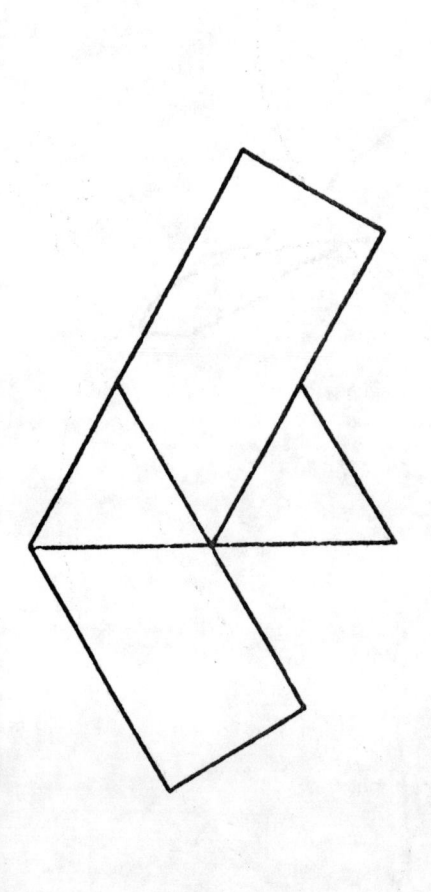

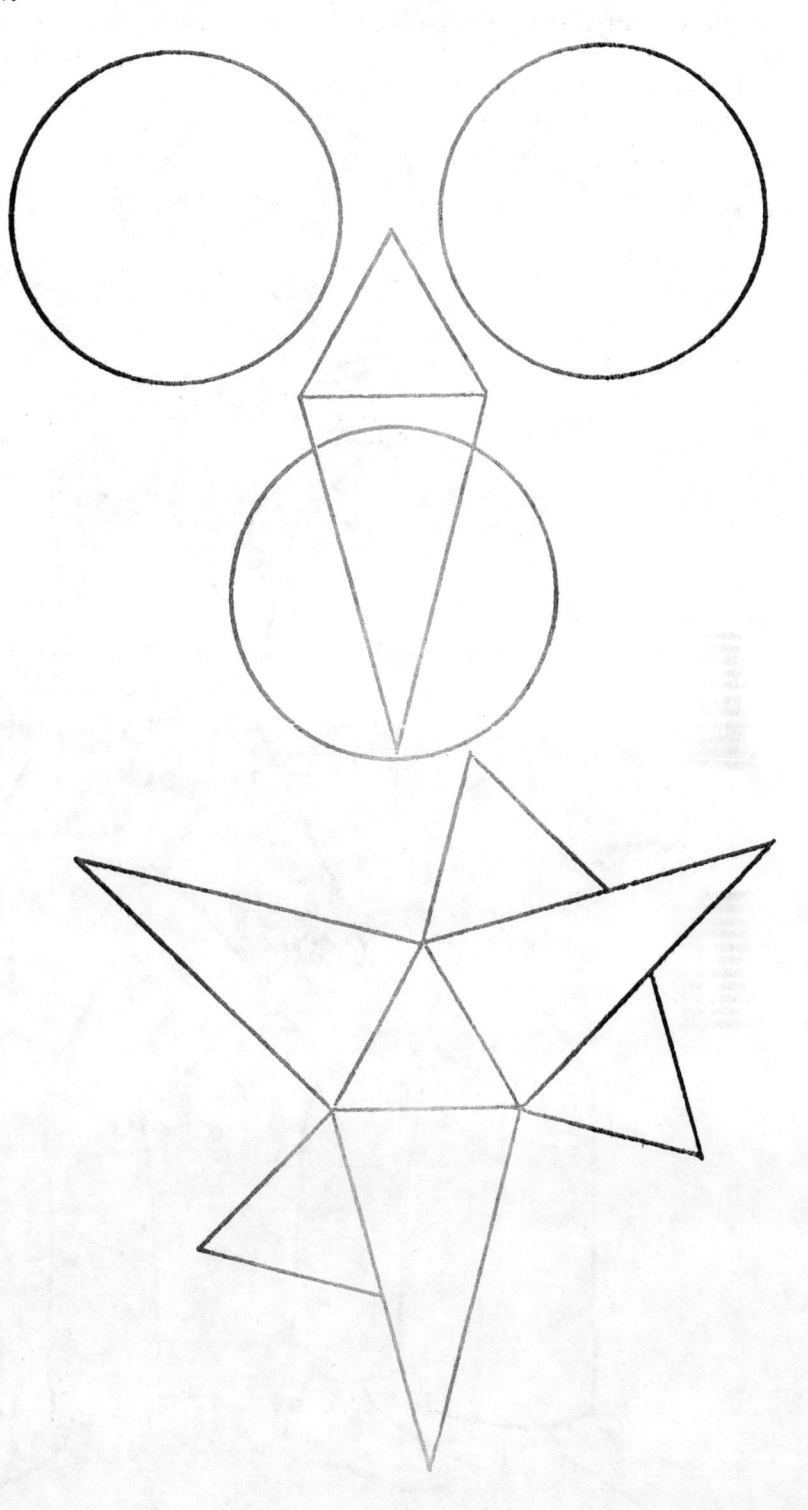

FROSTIG PERCEPTION PROGRAM
©Follett Publishing Company, 1973, 1964

Outline one boy with a blue crayon and the other with a red crayon.

Follow the lines by matching the numbers (one to one, etc.). Use a different color for each line.

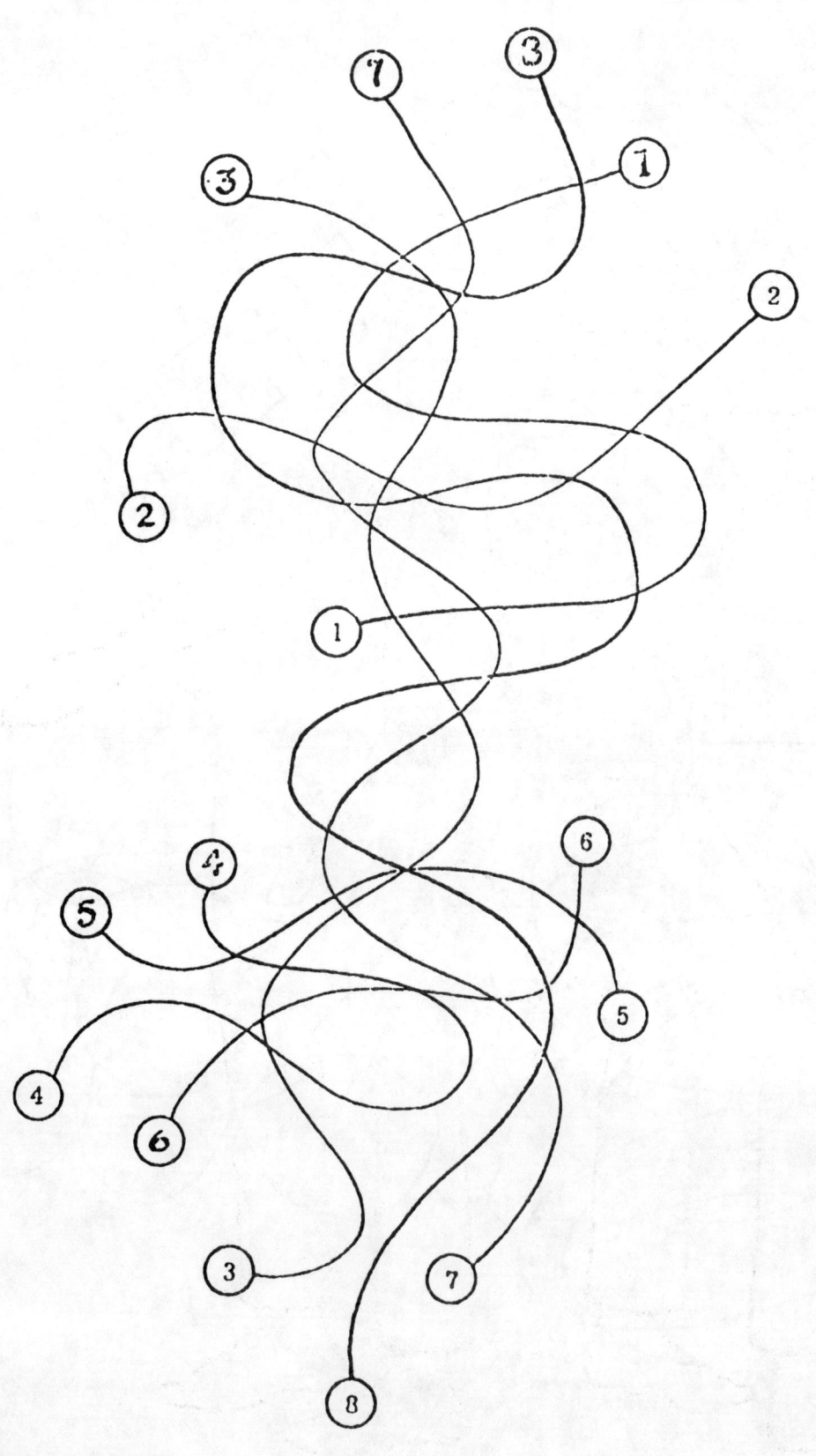

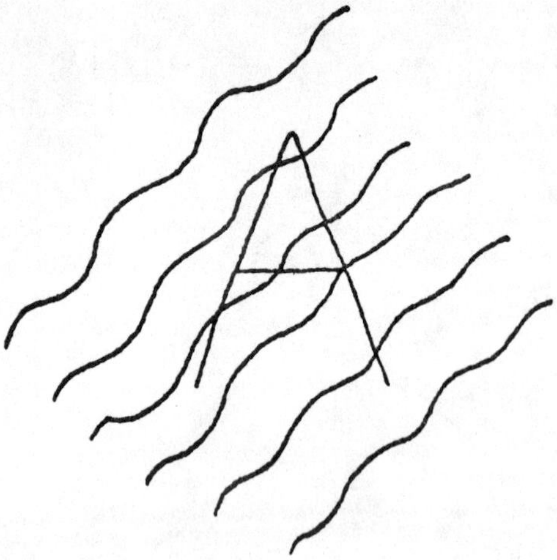

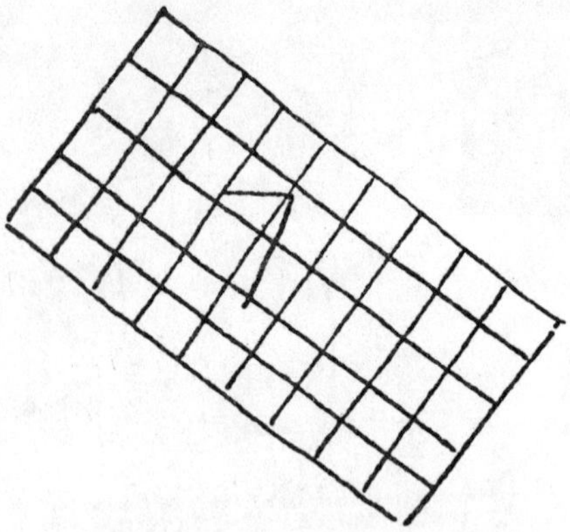

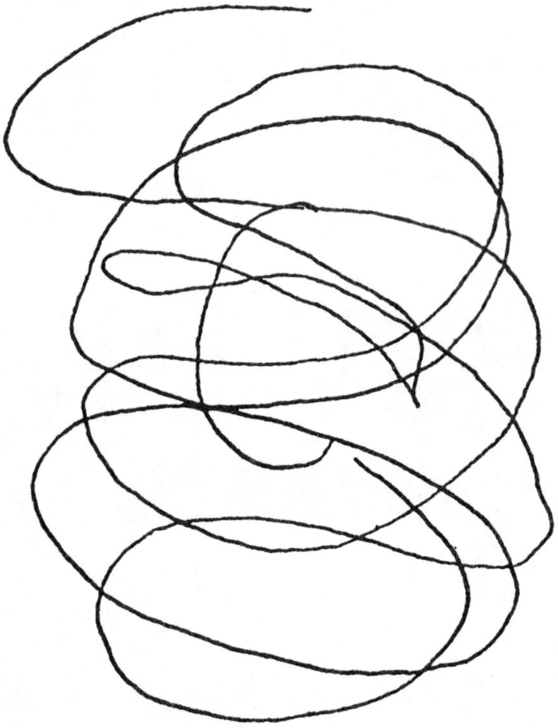

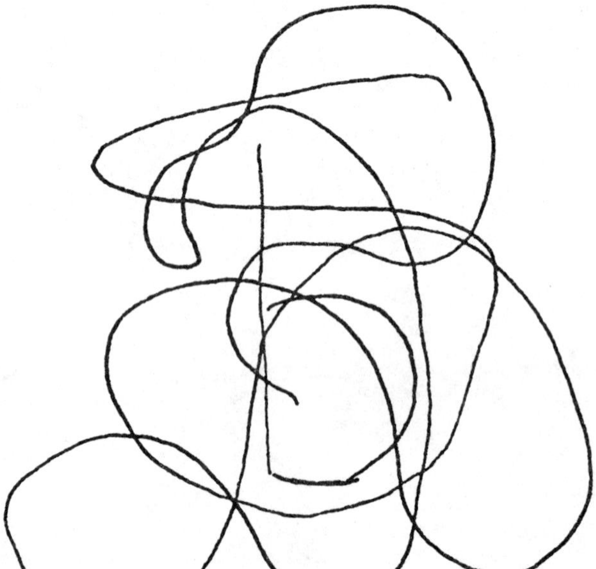

10 VISUAL SPATIAL RELATIONSHIP

Definition: The ability to visualize positions of objects in space, as evidenced by correctly matching and/or reproducing three dimensional designs.

Visual spatial relationship can be assessed by the examiner making increasingly complex designs on a geoboard, peg board, by means of design-blocks, etc. Then have the subject select from a pool of several pictures which approximate the target design, the one picture which is the same as the three dimensional target design. And/or, have the subject actually reproduce the designs using duplicate equipment.

11. GRAPHIC OUTPUT

Definition: The encoding, responding, or output of stimuli by means of paper-pencil activity.

a. The assessment of graphic output may reveal the possibility of a central nervous system dysfunction in the visual-motor area of the brain. Probably the best psycho-educational instrument for such assessment purpose is the Bender Gestalt Test (Bender, 1938). Indices of Bender revealed brain damage include design rotation, destruction of the design gestalt, and/or dog ears (illustrated below), which could result in a graphic output problem.

Examples of Bender Rotation

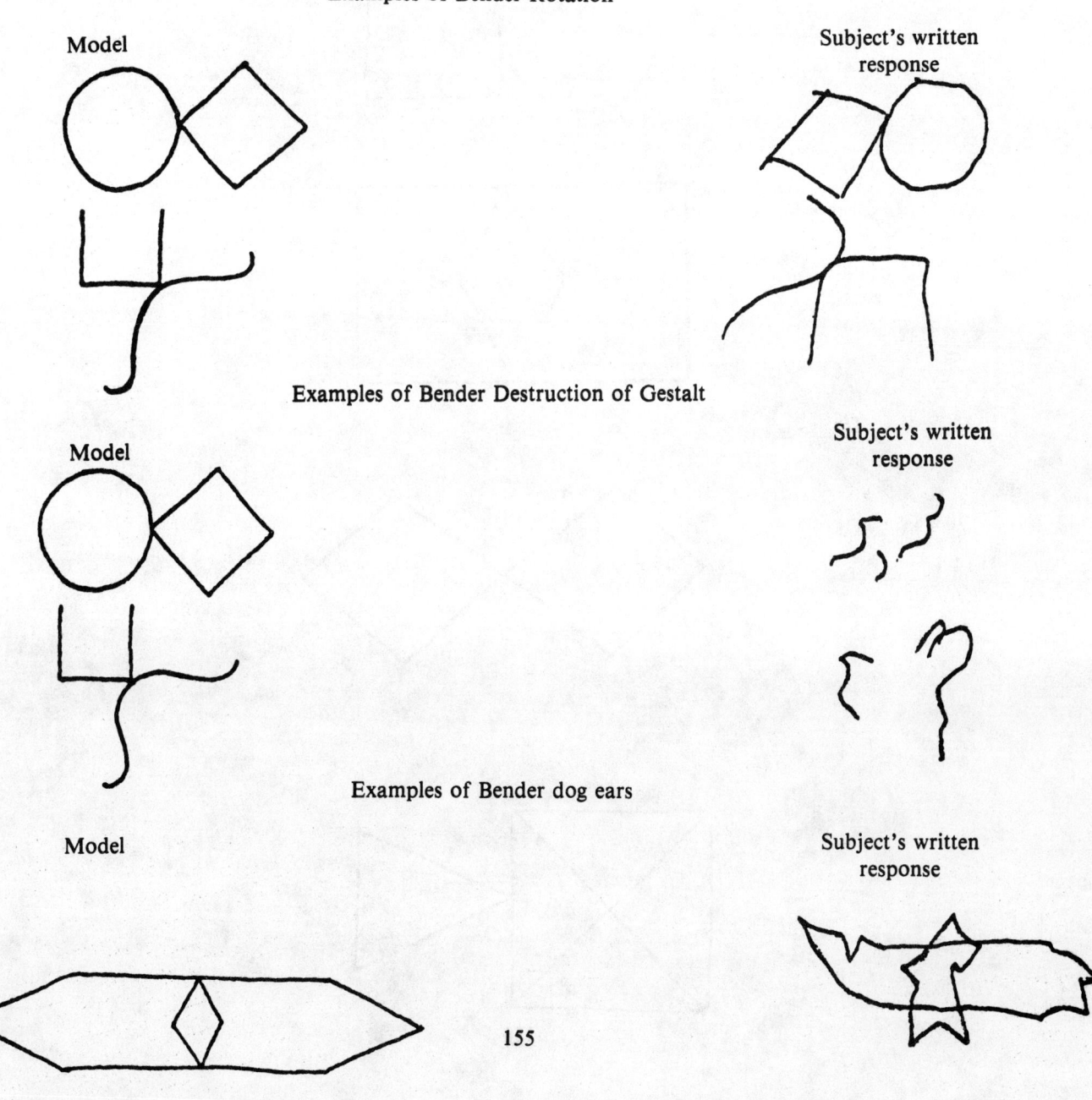

Model — Subject's written response

Examples of Bender Destruction of Gestalt

Model — Subject's written response

Examples of Bender dog ears

Model — Subject's written response

155

b. Should the Bender test not be available, the designs on page 156 are offered. As with the Bender designs, it is important to look for design rotation, destruction of the design gestalt, and/or dog ears, any of which could result in a graphic output problem. The examiner should also note the subject's pencil grasp, eye-hand coordination, and ease of graphic performance.

When presenting the designs to the subject, ask him to use a #2 pencil and the paper given, and "Copy them as he sees them," doing the best he can.

After the subject has copied the designs, it is important to determine if any existing difficulty is due to a graphic output problem or to an input/processing problem. This may be accomplished by asking the subject if his design is just like the model from which he copied. If he recognizes that his drawing is different but is unable to correct the difference, the problem is often one of graphic output. If however, he regards his imperfect reproduction to be the same as the model, the problem is often one of input rather than output.

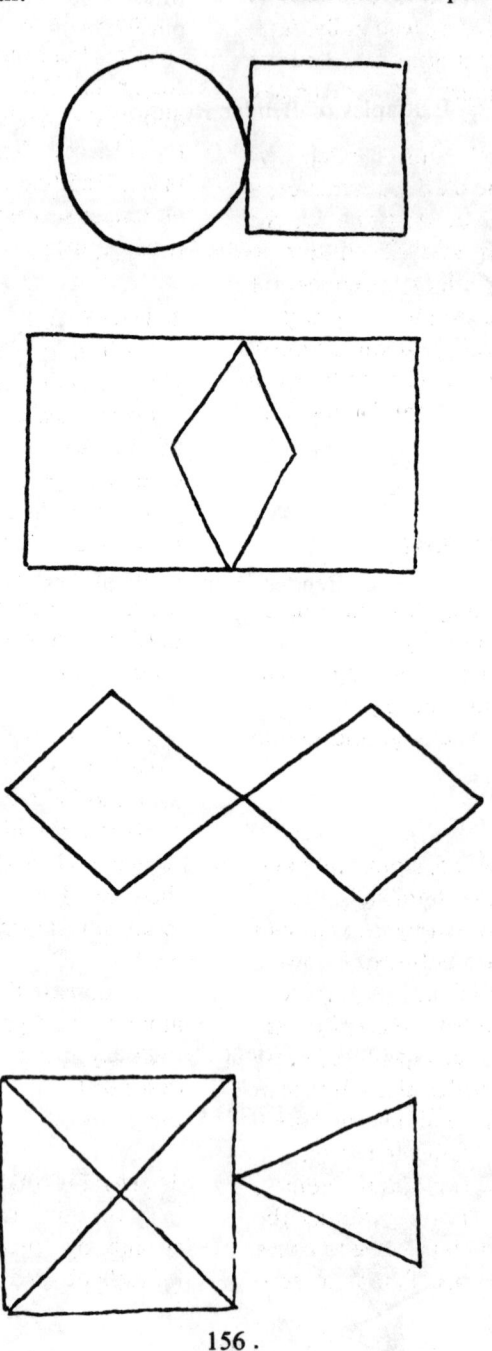

c. Another method of assessing graphic output involves obtaining a sample of the subject's written language. The examiner should have the subject graphically copy a written sentence, and then orally dictate a similar sentence for the subject to write. Handwriting, the ability to copy, and graphic output in general are maturational in nature. This means that the graphic output ability of the normal individual improves with age. Therefore, in order for the examiner to evaluate the graphic output ability of a given individual, he must be familiar with the normal graphic output of individuals the same age as the subject in order to make a comparison.

Should the quality of the subject's copied sentence be much better than the quality of the dictated sentence, a revisualization problem is suggested. If, however, the quality of both sentences is substandard relative to legibility, letter reversals or inversions, evenness of horizontal line, sloppiness, etc., a graphic output problem may be considered. The severity of the problem may be judged by the extent of the difference between the subject's product and what is normal for the subject's age.

D. HAPTIC PROCESSING

Definition: The ability to accurately take in, understand, and use stimuli acquired haptically.

Haptic processing involves the following components: haptic discrimination; haptic storage memory; haptic sequential memory; haptic meaning; and haptic output.

1. HAPTIC DISCRIMINATION

Definition: The ability to discriminate similarities and differences between stimuli presented haptically.

Haptic discrimination can be assessed by using a pool of cards on which various shapes are outlined by means of felt or other raised surface material (e.g., square, circle, triangle, rectangle, letters, numbers, etc.). Prepare two cards with each shape. Place a group of duplicate cards before the blindfolded subject; let him select then feel-trace one stimulus card; then have him immediately find the card with the same shape from the group.

To determine finer haptic discrimination ability, prepare cards with manuscript letters by outlining the letters with glue and sprinkling sand on the glue to give a raised letter effect. Use letters that are similar in configuration (e.g., b, d; p, q; m, n, u; etc.). Follow the procedure outlined above.

2. HAPTIC STORAGE MEMORY

Definition: The ability to remember single concepts, facts, and/or data when presented haptically over a short period of time.

Haptic storage memory can be assessed by using the cards from the Haptic Discrimination task above. Place a group of dissimilar letter-cards before the blindfolded subject; tell him you are going to select one card from the group. Allow the subject to feel-trace the card for about 10 seconds; return the card to the main group; ask the subject to find the card. Increase the difficulty of the task by adding one card at a time until the subject can no longer successfully complete the task. Card sequence is unimportant.

3. HAPTIC SEQUENTIAL MEMORY

Definition: The ability to remember, in the order given, a series of stimuli acquired haptically.

Haptic sequential memory can be assessed by using the previously described cards. Present two different cards in a prescribed order; allow the blindfolded subject to feel them, telling him to note the order in which they appear. After the subject has felt the cards, shuffle them and ask him to return the cards to their original order. Once again, increase the number of cards by one until the subject can no longer successfully perform the required task.

4. HAPTIC MEANING

Definition: The ability to gain meaning from stimuli acquired haptically.

Haptic meaning can be asessed by blindfolding the subject and then placing objects before him which he is then asked to identify by touching/feeling the objects (e.g., model airplane, model car, doll, chair, eggbeater, etc.).

To increase the difficulty of the meaning task, the examiner could present 8x10 cards with words written on them by means of the glue-sand technique previously described. The subject would then be asked to "read" the cards.

5. HAPTIC OUTPUT

Definition: The encoding, responding, or output of stimuli by means of a combination of tactual and kinesthetic activity (including visual-motor, gross-motor, and fine-motor activities.

Haptic output can be assessed by having the subject assemble a puzzle or small model, shoot a basket, throw and/or catch a ball, or any other visual-motor, gross-motor, and/or fine-motor activity. Note the ease with which the subject is able to perform the task, as well as his coordination and planning abilities.

APPENDIX A

THE SILI RECORD FORM

STELLERN-SHAW INFORMAL LEARNING INVENTORY

RECORD FORM

NAME_____ GRADE_____ EXAMINER_____

D.O.E. _____ D.O.B. _____ C.A. _____

PHYSICAL CHARACTERISTICS

1. Growth (circle one in relation to age norms)
   Height: short   average   tall
   Weight: under   average   over
   Frame: small   average   large

2. General Health (not any unusual conditions related to general health, strength, and endurance

   _____

   _____

   _____

3. Refer for further evaluation subjects who exhibit soft signs of vision or hearing difficulties.

4. Color Vision
   Materials: Various pairs of colored construction paper squares.
   Method: S matches pairs of squares

AUDITORY PROCESSING

1. Auditory Discrimination
   Method: Are the following words the same or different? (S is seated with back to examiner)

   1. shine - sign   13. run - run
   2. tin - thin   14. robe - rode
   3. pine - pine   15. bus - coal
   4. mop - mob   16. bill - mill
   5. mud - mug   17. brink - drink
   6. life - like   18. fling - cling
   7. very - fairy   19. lake - lake
   8. ship - ship   20. scream - stream
   9. goal - coal   21. and - end
   10. moon - noon   22. mesh - mush
   11. very - berry   23. slid - sled
   12. buff - tuff   24. deck - dock

EXAMINER NOTES

Alternate Method: Which word rhymes with:
(Examiner pronounces)

hit:	boy	man	fit
fun:	fat	sun	car
start:	cart	moon	barn
fast:	four	race	past
tail:	rail	chip	table

or

S supplies word to rhyme with:

cat _____ pen _____
chair_____ book _____

2. Sound Location
   Method: With eyes closed, S turns face in direction of sound (e.g., snap fingers, bell, etc.); or finds hidden metronome or alarm clock.

3. Auditory Storage Memory
   Method: Give S a key word verbally; wait 10 seconds; then say five similar words, among which is the key word; have S raise his hand when he hears the key word. Increase the complexity by adding key words as well as pool words.

   Alternate Method: Ask S his birthday, address, phone number, names of previous teachers, etc.

4. Auditory Sequential Memory
   Method: S repeats after E (give two trials if necessary).

   2-6   4-5-8-4-1
   3-7   9-4-7-0-6
   6-4-9   9-6-3-2-7-1
   4-7-9-1   9-3-8-6-5-2
   6-8-5-9

   Alternate Method: S repeats after E (give two trials.)
   book - grass   rake - house - tall -
   chalk - shoe - paper   lake - hill -
   rock - arm - shirt - fence   swing - bug - rope -
                                hot - plant - road

1. Auditory Recall Memory
   Method: S is asked to identify sounds E makes (e.g., dog barking, train, bell, etc.).

   Alternte Method: S completes the following:

   I read a _____. I throw a _____.
   I write with a _____. I live in a _____
   We buy food at _____. When I am sick, I go to
                                a _____.

   Alternate Method: In 20 seconds, S names all the: animals; things to eat; things to ride; toys, etc.; that he can think of.

Alternate Method: Show a picture and ask S to tell what is happening, what will happen etc.

Alternate Method: Ask S open-ended questions: How do you play hopscotch?, Describe what your car looks like?, etc.

6. Auditory Meaning
Method: S verbally completes the following:
E reads

A mommy is big; a baby is _____.
The sky is blue; salt is _____.
Milk has a glass; soup has a _____.
A car has tires; people have _____.

Alternate Method: S gives synonym for: big; lady; seat; thin; infant; etc.

Alternate Method: S gives opposite meaning for: fat; night; slow; under; rich; etc.

Alternate Method: S shows the examiner something made of: wood; metal; glass; etc.

7. Sound Blending
Method: What words am I trying to say (pause between phonemes as indicated by -).

m-e	g-oa-t
c-a-p	sh-i-p
t-ar	br-i-ck
p-ai-l	b-t-tt-le
s-u-n	t-el-e-v-i-sion
sl-a-p	re-fr-i-g-er-a-tor
sp-o-t	a-l-ph-a-b-e-t
d-u-s-t	

8. Auditory Closure
Method: What word am I trying to say? Tell me the right way to say:
cowb-- (cowboy)
strawber-- (strawberry)
pu--y (puppy)
--amburger (hamburger)
-ot -og (hot dog)
-op-orn (popcorn)

9. Auditory Figure-Ground
Method: Obseration: note how S reacts to surrounding noise and activity; does he remain on task despite minor auditory interruptions?

EXAMINER NOTES

Alternate Method: Goldman-Fristoe Test of Auditory Discrimination (noise subtest). Give the first four or five items without the test pictures; have S repeat the word the examiner uses.

Alternate Method: Examiner-prepared tape.

10. Verbal Output
Method: Observation throughout the evaluation, noting facility with words, semantics, and syntax.

Alternate Method: Elicit conversation from S.

Alternate Method: Use high-interest pictures; have S tell a story about the pictures.

VISUAL PROCESSING

1. Visual Tracking
Method: S follows penlight with eyes, vertically, horizontally, and diagonally.

Note how the eyes work together; do they jump at midpoint; does one eye track while the other doesn't; are the movements smooth or jerky; can S stay with the light?

2. Convergence
Materials: 32-inch string with knot 16 inches from the end.
Method: S holds one end of the string between his eyes on the bridge of his nose, while the examiner pulls the other end taut. S then is to reach out and grasp the knot. Record the distance between S's grasp and the actual location of the knot.

3. Visual Discrimination
Method: Use Frostig duplicator masters, PC 17, PS 8, PS 15, PC 57.

Alternate Method: Use examiner-constructed tasks similar to those on page 142 of the SILI.

4. Visual Storage Memory
Materials: one-inch cubes: 4 red; 4 blue; 4 green; 4 yellow; 4 purple.
Method: Randomly arrange blocks on the table; select 2 different color blocks from the group and allow S to view for 5 seconds; return blocks to pile and rearrange; have S select same color cmbination of blocks. Order is NOT important. Repeat procedure with 3, 4, etc. blocks until S cannot perform the task successfully. Give two trials if necessary.

EXAMINER NOTES

Alternate Task: Follow the above-outlined procedures, but replace colored cubes with a variety of small objects (e.g., keys, coins, bottle caps, etc.), or ordinary playing cards.

Alternate Task: Use examincer-constructed tasks similar to those on page 143 of the SILI.

5. Visual Sequential Memory
Method: Essentially the same as visual storage memory; however, order IS important. Again start with two blocks, or playing cards, and add on until S cannot successfully perform the task.

Alternate Task: Use examiner-constructed tasks similar to those on page 145 of the SILI.

6. Visual Recall Memory (Revisualization) Method: 1) have S graphically copy a series of words that are within his reading vocabulary; b) dictate a similar (or the same) word series and note any difference in the quality of handwriting and spelling of the two samples.

Alternate Method: With very young Ss, follow the above procedure, but use letters of his name; or have S draw a square, triangle, cat, car, etc.

7. Visual Meaning
Materials: Picture depicting real objects and actions.
Method: Have S describe picture: what is happening, and what he thinks will happen.

Alternate Method: S matches pictures that go together, or part of objects to whole objects, as illustrated on page 148 the SILI.

8. Visual Closure
Materials: See page 149 of the SILI.
Method: S identifies incomplete objects, and identifies what is missing.

Alternate Task: S completes incomplete pictures with pencil.

9. Visual Figure-Ground
Method: Use Frostig duplicator masters FG-5, FG-27, FG-37, FG-14.

Alternate Method: Hidden picture pages from "Child Highlights."

Alternate Method: Examiner-constructed tasks similar to those on page 154 of the SILI. Or, have the S pick out a letter or word superimposed on printed newspaper.

10. Visual Spatial Relationship
    Method: E builds increasingly complex designs on a geo-board, peg board, blocks, etc. S reproduces the designs using duplicate equipment.

    Alternate Method: S selects a picture from a picture-pool which is a copy of the three dimensional target design.

11. Graphic Output
    Method: Use the Bender design cards.

    Alternate Method: Use designs provided on page   of the SILI.

    Alternate Method: Obtain a sample of the S's written language, both from dictation and from copying a visual model.

HAPTIC PROCESSING

1. Haptic Discrimination
   Method: Using the materials described on page 157 of the SILI, S is asked to find matching cards while blindfoled.

2. Haptic Storage Memory
   Method: S, while blindfoled, feels a card, and then is asked to find the same card among a group of dissimilar cards; the task becomes more difficult as one card is added after each successful effort. (Use the same cards as in the haptic discrimination task).

3. Haptic Sequential Memory
   Method: Using the previously-decribed materials, the blindfolded S is asked to return the cards to the same order as the model. Begin with two different cards and add one for each trial until the S can no longer successfully perform the task.

4. Haptic Meaning
   Method: A blindfolded S is asked to identify objects placed before him (e.g., model airplane; model car; doll; chair; egg-beater, etc.).

   Alternate Method: Use 8x10 cards with words written on them by means of the sand and glue technique. Blindfolded S is asked to "read" the cards by feeling and tracing the cards.

5. Haptic Output
   Method: S assembles a puzzle or small model.

   Alternate Method: Any visual-motor, gross-motor, and/or fine-motor activity.

EXAMINER NOTES

STELLERN-SHAW INFORMAL LEARNING INVENTORY

PROFILE SHEET

	Strength	Acceptable	Weakness

A. Physical Characteristics
   1. Growth
   2. General Health
   3. Auditory Acuity
   4. Visual Acuity
   5. Color Vision

B. Auditory Processing
   1. Auditory Discrimination
   2. Sound Location
   3. Auditory Storage Memory
   4. Auditory Sequential Memory
   5. Auditory Recall Memory
   6. Auditory Meaning
   7. Sound Blending
   8. Auditory Closure
   9. Auditory Figure-Ground
   10. Verbal Output

C. Visual Processing
   1. Visual Tracking
   2. Convergence
   3. Visual Discrimination
   4. Visual Storage Memory
   5. Visual Sequential Memory
   6. Visual Recall Memory
   7. Visual Meaning
   8. Visual Closure
   9. Visual Figure-Ground
   10. Visual - Spatial Relationship
   11. Graphic Output

D. Haptic Processing
   1. Haptic Discrimination
   2. Haptic Storage Memory
   3. Haptic Sequential Memory
   4. Haptic Meaning
   5. Haptic Output

Formal Psychoeducational Tests Which Assess
the SILI Components

A. PHYSICAL CHARACTERISTICS

1. *Growth*
   a. Physical examination by physician.
2. *General Health*
   a. Physical examination by physician.
3. *Auditory Acuity*
   a. Audiometric Test.
4. *Visual Acuity*
   a. Keystone Visual Survey Telebinocular. Meadville, Pennsylvania: Keystone View Co., 1958.
   b. Snellen Chart. American Medical Association.
   c. Spache Binocular Vision Test. Meadville, Pennsylvania: Keystone View Co., 1961.
5. *Color Vision*
   a. The Farnsworth Dichotomus Test for Color Blindness. New York: The Psychological Corporation, 1947.
   b. Ishihara, Shinobu. Test for Colour-Blindness. Kenehara Shuppan Company, Ltd. U.S. Distributor: Graham-Field Surgical Co., Inc., 1917-67.

B. AUDITORY PROCESSING

1. *Auditory Discrimination*
   a. Wepman Auditory Discrimination Test. Chicago: Language Research Associates, 1973.
   b. Goldman-Fristoe-Woodcock Test of Auditory Discrimination. Circle Pines, Minnesota: American Guidance Services, Inc., 1970.
   c. Drake, C. PERC Auditory Discrimination Test. Sherborn, Massachusetts: Perceptual Education and Research Center, 1965.
2. *Sound Location*
   Formal measures of Sound Location are not currently available.
3. *Auditory Storage Memory*
   a. Environmental Sounds-Picture Identification Test. Institute for Developmental Studies, New York University.
   b. Goldman-Fristoe-Woodcock Memory Test (Recognition Memory Subtest). Circle Pines, Minnesota: American Guidance Services, Inc., 1974.
4. *Auditory Sequential Memory*
   a. Weschler Intelligence Scale for Children (Digit Span Subtest). New York: The Psychological Corporation, 1955.
   b. Illinois Test of Psycholinguistic Abilities (Auditory Sequential Memory Subtest). Urbana, Illinois: University of Illinois Press, 1968.
   c. Goldman-Fristoe-Woodcock Memory Test (Memory for Sequence Subtest). Circle Pines, Minnesota: American Guidance Services, Inc., 1974.
5. *Auditory Recall Memory*
   a. Environmental Sounds-Labelling. Institute for Developmental Studies, New York University.
   b. Fudala, Kunze, Ross. Auditory Pointing Test (Recognition Memory). Circle Pines, Minnesota: American Guidance Services, Inc., 1974.
   c. Goldman-Fristoe-Woodcock Auditory Memory Test (Recognition Memory). Circle Pines, Minnesota: American Guidance Services, Inc., 1974.
6. *Auditory Meaning*
   a. Illinois Test of Psycholinguistic Abilities (Auditory Association Subtest). Urbana, Illinois: University of Illinois Press, 1968.
   b. Environmental Sounds-Labelling. Institute for Developmental Studies, New York University.
7. *Sound Blending*
   a. Illinois Test of Psycholinguistic Abilities (Sound Blending Subtest). Urbana, Illinois: University of Illinois Press, 1968.
   b. Goldman-Fristoe-Woodcock Sound Symbol Test (Sound Blending Subtest). Circle Pines, Minnesota: American Guidance Services, Inc., 1974.
8. *Auditory Closure*
   a. Illinois Test of Psycholinguistic Abilities (Auditory Closure Subtest). Circle Pines, Minnesota: American Guidance Services, Inc., 1968.
   b. Rosewell-Chall Auditory Blending Test. New York: The Essay Press, 1963.
9. *Auditory Figure-Ground*
   a. Classroom Noise Making Test. Institute for Developmental Testing; New York University.

b. Goldman-Fristoe-Woodcock Auditory Selective Attention Test. Circle Pines, Minnesota: American Guidance Services, Inc., 1974.
10. *Verbal Output*
  a. Illinois Test of Psycholinguistic Abilities (Verbal Expression Subtest). Circle Pines, Minnesota: American Guidance Services, Inc., 1968.
  b. Yellow Brick Road (Vocal Encoding Subtest of Language Battery). Austin, Texas: Learning Concepts, 1975.

C. VISUAL PROCESSING

1. *Visual Tracking*
Formal measures of Visual Tracking are not currently available.
2. *Convergence*
Formal measures of Convergence are not currently available.
3. *Visual Discrimination*
  a. Marianne Frostig Developmental Test of Visual Perception. Palo Alto, California: Consulting Psychologists Press, Inc., 1972.
  b. Yellow Brick Road (Visual Discrimination Subtest). Austin, Texas: Learning Concepts, 1975.
  c. Metropolitan Readiness Test. New York: Harcourt-Brace-Jovanovich, 1966.
4. *Visual Storage Memory*
  a. McCarthy Scales of Chidren's Abilities (Pictorial Memory Subtest). New York: The Psychological Corporation, 1970.
  b. Weschler Intelligence Scale for Children (Coding Subtest). New York: The Psychological Corporation, 1955.
5. *Visual Sequential Memory*
  a. Illinois Test of Psycholinguistic Abilities (Visual Sequential Memory Subtest). Urbana, Illinois: University of Illinois Press, 1968.
  b. Benton Visual Retention Test. New York: Psychological Corporation, 1963.
6. *Visual Recall Memory*
Formal measures of Visual Recall Memory are not currently available.
7. *Visual Meaning*
  a. Illinois Test of Psycholinguistic Abilities (Visual Association Subtest). Urbana, Illinois: University of Illinois Press, 1968.
  b. Stanford-Binet Intelligence Scale. Boston: Houghton-Mifflin Co. , 1960 (Subtests YR II 5; III 2; IV 1).
8. *Visual Figure-Ground*
  a. Illinois Test of Psycholinguistic Abilities (Visual Closure Subtest). Urbana, Illinois: University of Illinois Press, 1968.
  b. Marianne Frostig Developmental Test of Visual Perception. Palo Alto, California: Consulting Psychologists Press, Inc., 1972.
  c. Strauss-Lehtinen Figure Background Cards. New York: Grune and Stratton, Inc., 1947.
9. *Visual Closure*
  a. Weschler Intelligence Scale for Children (Picture Completion Subtest). New York: The Psychological Corporation, 1955.
  b. McCarthy Scales of Children's Abilities (Puzzle Solving Subtest) New York: The Psychological Corporation, 1970.
10. *Visual-Spatial Relationship*
  a. Marianne Frostig Developmental Test of Visual Perception, Palo Alto, California: Consulting Psychologists Press, Inc., 1972.
  b. Wechsler Intelligence Tests (Block Design subtest), New York: The Psychological Corporation.
11. *Graphic Output*
  a. Bender Visual-Motor Gestalt Test. New York: American Orthopsychiatric Association, 1938.
  b. Beery Developmental Test of Visual-Motor Integration. Chicago: Follett Educational Corporation, 1967.

D. HAPTIC PROCESSING

Formal measures of Haptic Processing are not currently available.

Chapter 13

The Comprehensive History

Successful diagnostic-prescriptive teaching is dependent on the acquisition of information about the learner and presenting problem. Formal psychoeducational testing is one way to acquire that information. However, formal test results should not be interpreted in isolation. In order to meaningfully interpret test results, they should be considered in the context of antecedent information about the learner and presenting problem, a situation which can be achieved only by informal assessment. To provide an informal assessment instrument for the purpose of understanding the presenting problem and thus making sense out of test data, we developed the Comprehensive History.

The Comprehensive History represents a checklist of concepts that are important to the acquisition of necessary information about the learner and presenting problem. Each Comprehensive History concept has an interpretive hypothesis, and each concept and its interpretive hypothesis relate to a potential learning or behavior problem cause. It is our practice to meet with both parents of any minor subject for whom an intervention is being considered (or the individual himself if not a minor), in order to explore each Comprehensive History concept which seems germane to the presenting problem.

Table XV presents the Comprehensive History. A knowledgeably administered Comprehensive History can yield information as valuable as that yielded by formal testing. However, in terms of understanding the presenting problem, information acquired only through the Comprehensive History, or only through formal testing, is insufficient. Both kinds of information are necessary to complement the value of each other. Thus, we normally administer the Comprehensive History to an involved parent or subject prior to testing. Then on the basis of the presenting problem and the Comprehensive History information which illuminates the nature of that presenting problem, it becomes a relatively easy matter to select the appropriate battery of formal and informal tests for the purpose of greater presenting problem understanding and consequent resolution.

Table XV

The Comprehensive History

Each Comprehensive History concept and its interpretive hypothesis relate to a potential learning or behavior problem cause. By identifying the potential learning or behavior problem cause, a richer understanding of that problem is possible. By interpreting test data in relation to the potential problem-cause, it is possible to make more meaningful sense out of those test data. Lastly, by understanding the nature of the presenting problem, and by making sense out of the related test data, the likelihood of successful problem resolution is greatly increased.

Family Members

1. Subject's name and age.
2. Father's name, age, address, and education.
3. Mother's name, age, address, and education.

Parental age and education can be a potential source of subject stress and hence cause or influence the subject's learning or behavior problem. For example: young and immature parents can cause subject dependency frustration and instability. Old and rigid parents can cause subject rebellion, based upon authority resentment. Well-educated (but insecure) parents can create inappropriately high educational expectations for the subject, which in turn can cause subject failure, resentment, instability, etc. On the other hand, little parental education can create a home value system that is substantially different from the educational value system of the school, a situation that could cause subject frustration, conflict of interest, anxiety, and so on.

4. Number of siblings.

Having so many siblings that the parents are unable to provide sufficient subject security-need satisfaction and appropriate limit setting can cause subject resentment and instability. On the other hand, being an only child can create subject interpersonal problems in terms of being spoiled and demanding and thus unable to deal effectively with people. Either situation could contribute to the subject's presenting problem.

5. Number of marriages, divorces, separations, and the stability of the present marriage.

A high frequency of marriages, divorces, and separations, and/or an indication of chronic marital instability, suggest the possibility of unstable parents, and the possibility of consequent subject instability in terms of subject dependency frustration, inconsistent conscience development, control problems, etc., any or all of which could cause or influence the learning or behavior problem of the subject.

6. Whether the subject is the natural child of the parents with whom he lives.

Parental deprivation can cause serious subject stress and anxiety, depending on the age of the subject at the time of the parental deprivation, the emotional security of the subject at that time, and the suddenness with which the deprivation occurred. Generally, the degree to which any traumatic situation occurs suddenly and without subject preparation is the degree to which mastery of that situation is made difficult and the degree to which coping problems are likely to occur.

7. History of psychological, psychiatric, or neurological treatment, or special education.

A history of such professional treatment suggests the previous existence of a presenting problem. The relationship between that presenting problem and the current presenting problem of the subject should be explored.

8. History of suicide or suicide attempts, depression, and/or mood swings.

Suicide, suicide attempts, depression, and/or chronic and extreme mood swings all suggest a moderate-to-severe reaction to stress. Usually, a harsh conscience and resulting strict self-expectations contribute to the stress, with the individual's reaction to that stress being expressed by the self-punishment and worthless-gloom feelings that are respectively characteristic of the act of suicide and the condition of depression. The nature of the stress (and the family's reaction to that stress) should be explored relative to a possible relationship between the stress (and stress-reaction) and the presenting problem of the subject. Examples of the nature of such stress are: (a) Parents who are depressed because they cannot live up to the harsh expectations of their conscience often, in terms of normal parent-child interaction, inculcate the same harsh conscience values in their children, a situation which in turn could lead to subject depression due to the subject's inability to live up to his conscience expectations. (b) Parents who are severely depressed and/or suicidal during the early years of a subject's life may not be able to provide the subject with the necessary security-need satisfaction, appropriate controls, etc., thus causing subject stress, anxiety, and general vulnerability to learning or behavior problems.

9. History of psychiatric or general medication.

Medication is prescribed to combat a particular presenting problem. The possible relationship between the presenting problem for which the medicine was prescribed and the current problem of the subject should be explored.

10. History of alcoholism or narcotics.

A history of alcoholism or nonprescribed narcotics use suggests a reaction to stress. The nature of the family member's stress as well as the family's reaction to that stress should be explored in terms of any resulting impact on the presenting problem of the subject. For example, the withdrawing behavior of a young girl could be caused by the violent and frequent alcohol-induced punishment of the girl by her father.

11. History of difficulty with the law.

Chronic difficulty with the law and/or social value-norms suggest the possibility of a conscience defect and/or an atypical set of cultural-social values. In either case, parental problems of such a nature could directly relate to the learning or especially behavior problems of the subject.

12. Discipline: who administers; how administered; and with what severity.

The normal establishment of subject controls through healthy parental discipline is desirable. However, the degree to which punitive parental discipline, or an absence of parental discipline, is conducted is the degree to which unusual subject stress can occur. Chronic punitive parental discipline can cause intense subject fear of authority, a situation which can express itself in withdrawing and fearful behavior, or the opposite, destructive and revengeful behavior that is often directed toward authority figures or symbols. On the other hand, an absence of parental discipline can result in subject bewilderment, instability, and aimlessness, based on a defect in the conscience-value system. Such a subject could shallowly float around, from person to person and place to place, without a strong sense of commitment to right-wrong, work-play, love-hate, etc. Either circumstance could cause subject behavior or learning problems.

13. Religion: denomination; strength of belief; and how imposed on the subject.

Religious (or any other attitude) beliefs can become internalized as a way of life. The stronger the belief, the more influence that belief can have on the life process. If such a belief comes in conflict with normal biological impulses and/or normal social-peer pressure, intense stress can result. Therefore, any powerful attitude (either parental or that of the subject) should be examined in terms of the consequent development of harsh conscience values and the possible relationship between the harsh conscience, consequent subject stress, and the subject's learning or behavior problem. For example: a moderately depressed adolescent male with suicidal fantasies had been rigorously taught to avoid the opposite sex lest he be considered a sinner. The natural evolution of adolescent interaction resulted in social contact with the opposite sex, a situation which consequently resulted in seriously depressed subject behavior, which in turn negatively influenced the subject's learning ability and school work.

14. Number of bedrooms in the family home: which children sleep in each bedroom as well as each bed.

Children, and especially adolescents, of the opposite sex who are obliged to sleep in the same bed because of impoverished financial conditions or because of strange parental needs can, in so doing, be subject to undesirable stress. The possible relationship between such stress and the presenting problem of the subject should be explored.

15. History of mental retardation.

Mental retardation can be inherited. A history of mental retardation in a subject's family can give credence to, other variables being corroborative, the diagnosis of subject mental retardation.

16. History of epilepsy or convulsions.

A family history of epilepsy or convulsions might help explain subject seizurelike behavior and consequent behavior or learning problems. Any seizure is to be regarded as serious, especially after a head injury.

17. History of miscarriages.

A history of natural miscarriages suggests the possibility of a physiological anomaly. Such a possibility should be considered relative to understanding the nature of the subject's presenting problem.

18. Who works at what and when.

Since most behavior is not accidental but rather psychosocially determined, it is possible to make inferences about the personality characteristics of people in general, and parents of subjects in particular, based upon the nature of the occupation in which they freely engage. From an understanding of the personality characteristics of subject parents, it is possible to make inferences about the effect those parental characteristics might have on the subject and presenting problem. For example, it is not unreasonable to assume that a demolition expert possesses a great amount of aggression. It would be important to the understanding of the destructive and violent adolescent son of that demolition expert to explore the way in which the father's presumed aggression is expressed in the home and/or toward his son. Similarly, with a policewoman mother; conversely with a feminine hair-stylist father; etc.

A correlated issue is the time of day during which parents work. If, for example, the subject never sees his parents due to the work schedule of the parents, the impact of possible dependency frustration, lack of parental control, etc., should be explored relative to understanding the presenting problem of the subject.

19. Leisure time activities, including hobbies.

Just as the occupational choice of most people is psychosocially determined, so also is the choice of leisure-time activity. It is possible to make inferences about the personality characteristics of people in general, and parents of subjects in particular, based upon a knowledge of their chosen leisure-time activities. From such an inferred understanding of subject parents it is further possible to infer the effect those parental personality characteristics might have on the subject and presenting problem. For example, the personality characteristics expressed by a father's avocational interest in knitting doll clothes should be considered relative to understanding the nature of his son's passive behavior.

Subject Developmental History
Prenatal

20. RH incompatability factor.

There are several mother-fetus blood group incompatibilities, the best known of which is the Rh factor incompatibility. The Rh factor refers to a human blood factor, the possession of which is referred to as Rh-positive, and the absence of which is referred to as Rh-negative. The blood factor is inherited, and the existence of Rh incompatibility between mother and fetus occurs by means of an Rh-negative mother having an Rh-positive fetus because of a dominant Rh-positive gene inherited from the father. If any of the red blood cells from the Rh-positive fetus enter the Rh-negative mother's blood system, an antibody is produced by the mother to combat the foreign factor. This antibody can enter the bloodstream of the fetus and cause destruction of the red blood cells, a situation which can result in fetal anemia as well as brain damage and mental retardation due to anoxia (oxygen deprivation). The likelihood of anemia and anoxia is greater if the mother has already developed antibodies in her blood because of previous blood transfusions or previous pregnancies, hence first born children are less likely to be affected than subsequent children. One of the physical manifestations at birth of Rh incompatibility can be a jaundice or yellow-skin condition. Although Rh incompatibility is rare, and blood transfusions at birth can result in recovery from the jaundice condition (but not from previously incurred brain damage), Rh incompatibility should not be overlooked as a possible cause of a subject's learning problem (especially mental retardation) when it is discovered that the subject is an Rh-positive child of an Rh-negative mother, was jaundiced at birth, had early thriving problems, etc.

21. Extreme anxiety.

It is hypothesized that extreme and chronic maternal psychological-anxiety during pregnancy can cause maternal blood chemistry/hormonal change, which in turn can affect the biochemical system of the fetus so as to subsequently result in reduced subject ability to tolerate stress. This congenitally reduced tolerance for stress is thought to be independent of any postnatal learned reduction in stress tolerance, and thought to be capable of causing postnatal learning or behavior problems.

22. Depression.

Chronic and severe maternal depression during pregnancy could result in an abandonment of nutritional care, a situation which in turn could result in fetal damage and subsequent learning or behavior problems.

23. Maternal age.

Mothers at either extreme of the childbearing age run a higher risk of premature birth, and hence the possibility of subject brain damage. When the first child is born late in the life of a mother (45 years of age and up), there is a marked increase in the chance of that child being born mentally retarded.

24. Medication: type and amount.

Too much of any medicine during pregnancy could result in maternal body-chemistry damage and consequent fetal damage.

25. Poisonings (lead, alcohol, drugs, carbon monoxide, etc.), or bio-chemical intolerance (e.g., medication). Maternal poisoning during pregnancy can result in body-chemistry and/or oxygen deprivation damage, situations which could cause fetal damage and subsequent learning or behavior problems.

26. Rubella (German measles).

Rubella can be very damaging to the fetus, especially if contracted by the mother during the first trimester of pregnancy. Systemic fetal damage with severe mental retardation can result. Other viruses, such as the mumps virus, may have the same fetal damaging effect as Rubella.

27. Severe falls or blows to the abdomen.

A severe fall or blow to the abdomen of a pregnant woman could cause fetal brain damage and subsequent learning or behavior problems.

28. Hospitalization and/or surgeries.

The reason for pregnant mother hospitalization should be explored relative to a possible relationship between that reason and the subject's presenting problem.

29. Adequate medical attention.

A lack of adequate pregnant-mother medical care could result in fetal damage and subsequent subject problems.

30. X-rays.

Massive maternal radiation during the first trimester of pregnancy can result in termination of the pregnancy. Therapeutic maternal radiation can cause serious fetal abnormalities, the most common of which is microcephaly, often with consequent mental retardation.

31. Anoxia.

Maternal anoxia can cause fetal anoxia and consequent subject learning or behavior problems. Such maternal anoxia could result from maternal heart disorder, vaginal bleeding, blood disorder, convulsions, frequent and prolonged loss of consciousness, etc.

32. Infection.

Maternal infection (such as syphilis, toxoplasmosis, perhaps herpes simplex, etc.) can be transmitted to the fetus and cause serious fetal abnormalities, including brain damage, and mental retardation. Similarly, acute maternal febrile infection (especially associated with high fevers of long duration) during the first trimester of pregnancy can result in fetal abortion or fetal defect.

33. Nutrition.

Poor maternal nutrition in the early stages of fetal growth can result in fetal abnormality, with subsequent learning or behavior problems.

34. Any untoward accidents, illnesses, or incidents.

Perinatal

35. Very hard, long, and dry labor.
36. Precipitous delivery.

Unusually long, hard, and dry labor can cause neonatal brain damage. Similarly, precipitous delivery without sufficient pelvic dilation can also cause brain damage. Either situation can result in subsequent learning or behavior problems.

37. Unusual presentation (breech, transverse).

The usual neonatal delivery presentation is head first and face downward. In case of breech birth (buttocks first), or transverse presentation (fetus crosswise in uterus), the risk of brain injury is increased.

38. Prematurity.

Prematurity is defined as a birth weight of less than 5.5 pounds, and appears to be related to socioeconomic status, maternal age, and medical care. Although prematurity of a moderate degree (birth weight between 3 and 5.5 pounds) involves only a small risk of neonatal defect, severe prematurity (birth weight under 3 pounds) apparently can involve (although need not) a moderate risk of neonatal physical defects, with subsequent learning and behavior problems. It should be acknowledged that the survival rate of premature babies is much greater now than it was twenty years ago.

39. Instrument delivery.

Although rare, the pressure of instruments used during delivery can cause neonatal brain damage.

40. Anoxia at any time.

Insufficient oxygen supply to the brain at any time can cause cell death and irreparable brain damage. Perinatal anoxia can cause brain damage and subsequent learning and behavior problems. Perinatal anoxia can be caused by: the placenta being detached too soon; the umbilical cord kinking, or wrapped tightly around the neonate's neck, causing suffocation; or the infant failing to breathe and/or otherwise failing to receive oxygen for more than three minutes.

41. Discoloration of child (yellow, blue, or black).

Neonatal discoloration is not normal, and should be explored relative to the cause helping explain subsequent learning or behavior problems. Yellow coloration at or following birth suggests the possibility of jaundice. The yellow-skin color of jaundice suggests the presence of bilirubin in the bloodstream, which can be deposited in body organs, including the brain. When the bilirubin serum rises to a certain level, a condition known as kernicterus results, which, if untreated, can be fatal; survivors of kernicterus often suffer brain damage, mental retardation, and other defects. Below such a bilirubin level, the infant can recover without permanent damage.

Anomalous blue or black coloration at birth suggests the possibility of anoxia.

42. Incubation of child.

Prolonged incubation at birth suggests survival precautions and something atypical. Although incubation could be only a protective measure without implying damage, the cause for incubation should be explored relative to helping explain subsequent presenting problems.

43. Any other unusual factors at birth.

Postnatal

44. Was subject planned and wanted?

Babies are often unplanned, but subsequently wanted and loved, and consequently grow up normally. Those that are both unplanned and unwanted and as a result experience maternal rejection run a high risk of future emotional disturbance. It is our contention that the most typical cause of emotional disturbance is early and grim maternal deprivation (deprivation of early love, dependency, and security-need satisfaction). As a rule, the greater the early maternal deprivation, the greater the subsequent emotional disturbance, a situation which obviously can cause or influence learning or behavior problems.

45. Height and weight of subject at birth.

As previously discussed, birth size is related to prematurity and possible neonatal defect.

46. Breast or bottle fed.

As long as the mother-figure conducts the early feeding process with love and warmth, the emotional security benefits accruing from either breast or bottle feeding are positive and somewhat similar in nature. However, if bottle feeding is elected to avoid loving mother-child contact, and in particular, if a mechanical bottle-feeding prop is used to preclude mother-child contact, the implications are high for maternal deprivation and subsequent emotional disturbance and presenting problems.

47. Age of weaning.

Premature and enforced breast or bottle weaning (before six months of age) suggests the possibility of maternal rejection. On the other hand, unusually prolonged (and probably enforced) breast or bottle feeding (four and five years, for example), can suggest maternal attempts to keep the child at an infantile state of development, often for the dependency purposes of the mother. Both premature and prolonged breast or bottle feeding practices can cause subject stress and instability, and consequent behavior or learning problems.

48. Age of walking.

The normal age of first-step walking is around 12-14 months. Any significant deviation (for example, 7 months, or 36 months) suggests motor coordination and locomotion precocity or retardation.

49. Age of talking.

The normal age of first-word speech is around 12-14 months, and the normal age of two-word sentence use is around 18-20 months. Any significant deviation suggests verbal precocity or retardation.

50. Age of initial toilet training, and age at which toilet training was completed.

The nature of the toilet training process varies with the personality characteristics of the toilet trainers (usually parents), and therefore is not as developmentally predicatable as the walking and talking process. Nonetheless, toilet (bowel) training often begins around 15 months of age (although the optimal initiation age is slightly later), and is often completed by two and one-half years of age. Any gross deviation from such a beginning-completion pattern has implications for the future personal-social adjustment of the subject.

The toilet training process represents a major source of potential parent-child stress in that perhaps for the first time in the life of the child the biological urges of the child can come in direct conflict with the socialization requirements of the parents. If the parents demand a premature and inappropriate adherence to strict bowel movement standards, a great amount of subject resentment can generate, which, for example, could subsequently express itself in open defiance of authority figures, or in the more subtly defiant and passive-aggressive ways of school work underachievement, pouting, laziness, etc. On the other hand, if there is no parental control whatsoever regarding the toilet training process, the child could develop a grossly distorted sense of omnipotence, which could express itself in presumptuous and demanding behavior.

On a physiological basis, normal toilet habits are a function of sufficient sphincter-muscle maturity to permit voluntary muscle control, a sitation which normally does not occur prior to fifteen months of age. Thus, on a physiological basis alone, toilet training which is initiated before the acquisition of voluntary muscle control can lead to subjct frustration, resentment, and/or dejection.

51. Head injuries.

Accidents and beatings (battered child syndrome) which result in head injury, although rare, can cause brain damage, which in turn can cause learning or behavior problems. Similarly, brain tumors can cause learning or behavior problems.

52. Poisoning.

Lead, carbon monoxide, alcohol, drugs, perhaps hexachlorophene relative to infants, etc., poisoning or biochemical intolerance, can cause brain damage and consequent learning or behavior problems.

It is possible that food additives, such as artificial coloring, flavoring, preservatives, etc., can cause adverse bio-chemical reactions which could result in learning and/or behavior problems.

53. Anoxia.

Deprivation of oxygen to the brain cells can cause cell death and irreparable brain damage. Common causes of postnatal anoxia are: suffociation, blood disorders, heart disorders, etc.

54. Infection.

Infectious diseases, and high (105 degrees and up) and prolonged (more than 24 hours) fevers, can cause brain damage, with consequent learning or behavior problems. In particular, meningitis, which is an infectious inflammation of part of the brain, can result in a spectrum of brain damage related problems. Similarly, encephalitis, which is a form of brain inflammation due to a viral infection, often develops after an attack of childhood illness (measles, chicken pox, etc.), and can result in brain damage, often with a consequent change in the personality of the subject (e.g., from adaptive to nonadaptive behavior).

55. Seizures or convulsions.

Massive seizures can cause further brain damage, probably through cell degeneration or anoxia. Siezure control is thus important.

56. Eating and/or sleeping difficulties.

Chronic eating and/or sleeping problems are not normal and usually relate to a medical problem and/or emotional stress. Overeating and undereating often represent ways of coping with stress; usually, in this context, the more severe the stress, the more severe the eating problem symptom. Similarly, sleeping problems (usually the inability to get to sleep or stay asleep, but sometimes an escape into prolonged sleep) often reflect a high level of stress. Usually, in this context, the greater the stress, the more severe the sleeping problem symptom.

In an analogous way, stress can be reflected in the nature of the dream state. Generally, in this context, the more stress, the greater the frequency of dream activity, and the greater the frustration-nature of the dreams. Intense stress can be expressed in the form of nightmares, which if too symbolically intense, can result in the subject awakening.

57. Hyperactivity or Hypoactivity.

Chronic hyperactivity, or the opposite condition, hypoactivity, are not normal, and suggest a medical problem or an emotional reaction to stress. Hyperactivity is often associated with brain damage. Hypoactivity is often associated with a thyroid problem or with emotionally based depression. Either one can cause learning or behavior problems.

58. Head banging; colic; and restlessness.

Although seemingly unrelated, these three symptoms appear with great frequency, singly, or in combination, in the history of emotionally disturbed children. The presumption is that head banging, colic, and restlessness are voluntary or involuntary ways of coping with stress.

59. Motor coordination difficulty.

Chronic gross and/or fine muscle coordination problems suggest the possibility of physiological immaturity and the likelihood of paper-pencil learning problems.

60. Medication, hospitalization, and/or surgeries.

Prolonged parent-child separation by means of hospitalization, especially at an early age, can be stressful. The degree of security-need frustration involved may be reflected in the subject's later personal-social adjustment. Any surgery which results in organism change is worthy of note in terms of a possible relationship to subsequent learning or behavior problems.

61. Was subject affectionate, cuddly, and lovable?

Parents often report that their emotionally disturbed child is emotionally cold and not cuddly, and that the child rejects parental affection. Although this is often the case, in some instances we have found that the emotionally cold child merely reflects the emotional coldness of the parents, and/or, the emotionally cold parents project their own coldness onto the child and then attribute the coldness to the child. In any event, such a child is likely to subsequently have interpersonal problems.

62. Any untoward accidents, illnesses, or incidents.

Subject Emotional Factors

63. Bowel-bladder incontinence.

Nonmedically based bowel and/or bladder incontinence can be due to emotional stress. Most typically, emotionally based bowel incontinence (encopresis) represents an unconscious expression of aggression, a situation which can result in the subject rather effectively controlling the environment. However, bowel incontinence can also be due to anxiety. Similarly, emotionally based bladder incontinence (enuresis) typically represents either an unconscious expression of aggression, an anxiety equivalent, and/or, in rare instances, a sexualized emission. Nighttime enuresis is more common than daytime enuresis, and neither one is common beyond three to four years of age. Either the bowel or bladder incontinence condition could cause behavior or learning problems.

64. Thumbsucking.

Thumbsucking is not a normal developmental function of childhood, although it is not unusual or alarming for a child to thumbsuck up to the age of three to four years. Thumbsucking which persists into, or which is reactivated in, the school years, often is symptomatic of emotional stress and often of a dependency frustration nature. It is not atypical for a previous thumbsucker to resume temporary thumbsucking as a regressive coping measure with the advent of kindergarten. As the stress of the kindergarten experience dissipates, so often does the thumbsucking symptom.

65. Disturbance of eating and/or sleeping.

Chronic and nonmedically based eating and/or sleeping problems suggest the possibility of emotional stress. Because of the taking-in (and also refusing to take-in), and devouring (destroying), symbolism of eating, the process of eating can express many emotional conflicts. Two of the most common conflicts are: dependency frustration (e.g., eating huge amounts of food to compensate for lack of love, or the opposite, refusing to eat in order to symbolically prevent further rejection); and aggression (e.g., aggressively destroying food through the food chewing and swallowing process).

Similarly, because of the relaxed controls (or the fear of such relaxed controls) necessary for sleep, the process of sleep can symbolically represent the expression of emotional stress. Typically, anxious subjects have difficulty getting to sleep; depressed subjects often have difficulty remaining asleep. Often, nightmares represent the expression and working-through of threatening impulses by the disguised symbolism of dreams, with the subject awakening in a panic when the symbolic activity reaches a level of threat that is too high even for the sleep ego. Lastly, sleepwalking often represents emotional stress that is being expressed through the motor system without concurrent conscious awareness. Awakening the sleepwalker in the middle of the sleeptrip risks the danger of forcing the subject into a sudden and often traumatic mastery of why he is not where he went to sleep.

Eating and/or sleeping problems can reflect emotional stress, which could relate to the subject's learning or behavior problems.

66. How is anger expressed?

It is likely that most individuals in our complex society have some degree of conscious and/or unconscious anger. However, it is not the mere possession of anger that makes individuals unique but rather the way in which that anger is expressed. Basically, it is highly unusual for a subject never to express anger in any form; but it is also uncommon for the opposite situation to exist, namely, the chronic expression of anger by means of acting-out behavior. The former situation suggests the possibility of rigid control over the expression of anger, whereas the latter situation suggests an insufficient amount of control. Either way, subjects so involved could have consequent learning or behavior problems.

67. Masturbation.

Despite the fact that masturbation is common during early adolescence, high-frequency masturbation, public masturbation, or masturbation that is substituted for normal sexual relationships suggests atypical behavior. Such behavior is often a function of a combination of any of the following: poor sexual impulse control; anxiety regarding heterosexual (or homosexual) relationships; a highly eroticized individual; and/or a value system incompatible with delay of sexual gratification. In a significant amount, any of the above conditions could cause behavior problems.

68. Bizarre or out-of-context ideas.

Normal (conscious) ideation and thought processes are sequential in nature and subject to conventional laws of reality and logic. The degree to which ideation and thought processes are bizarre and unrelated to reality suggests the possibility of a psychotic condition. Such a condition can cause severe learning or behavior problems.

69. Can subject give and accept affection?

The normal individual can both give and accept meaningful affection. Often however, seriously emotionally hurt individuals are affectionally hard and callous, and thus cannot give affection at all, and have difficulty meaningfully accepting affection. On the other hand, some emotionally hurt individuals are affectionally very soft, and will sponge up any kind of affection, but will often have difficulty meaningfully giving affection. Either one of these conditions could cause behavior and learning problems.

70. Humor.

Natural and spontaneous humor is one sign of a healthy ego. An absence of humor often suggests emotional stress, which results in rigid control of feeling and expression, which manifests itself in emotional coldness and an absence of humor. Such a stress situation could cause a variety of presenting problems.

71. Rigid and perfectionistic behavior (or the opposite, sloppy behavior).

Persisting rigid and perfectionistic behavior suggests the likelihood of a harsh and demanding conscience, which results in high self-expectations, strict control over feeling, and rigid adherence to conscience-dictated patterns of behavior, all for the purpose of binding conscience-based stress. As a rule, the more demanding the conscience, the more rigid the personality and perfectionistic the behavior, until the breaking point is reached.

The converse of rigid and perfectionistic behavior is sloppy and untidy behavior. Such behavior is often due to rebellion against demanding and perfectionistic authority figures (parents usually), or a conscience system which is characterized by disorder and carelessness.

In either event, the nature of the conscience system could result in learning or behavior problems.

72. Mood.

The normal individual is relatively happy, and is neither persistently depressed nor persistently elated. Persistent depression or elation are usually caused by an overdeveloped conscience, which causes self-punishment (depression), or false pride (elation). The former condition can express itself in gloom, the spectrum of suicidal activities, and ideational-motor retardation. The latter condition, although rare, can express itself in accelerated ideational-motor processes to the extent that care and consideration may be abandoned. Either condition can result in school-based presenting problems.

73. Control.

Control refers to the ability of the organism to harmonize the various personality systems, through the delay of gratification capacity, and effect smooth and adaptive behavior. Essentially, persistent acting-out behavior (delinquent, impulsive, aggressive, etc. behavior) suggests underdevelopment and hence undercontrol of the conscience system, whereas persistent acting-in behavior (withdrawing, daydreaming, psychosomatic, etc. behavior) suggests overdevelopment hence overcontrol of the conscience system. As a rule, the more overcontrol, the more the organism is likely to be characterized by anxiety, guilt, the use of defense mechanisms, rigidity, and introversiveness. The more undercontrol, the more the organism is likely to be characterized by acting-out behavior, a relative absence of guilt and anxiety, little concern for others, and often, the seeming inability to learn from experience. Either condition can result in behavior and learning problems.

Within the context of identifying the nature of subject control, it is important to determine if there is a history of: (a) Nonmedically based fainting (overcontrol, designed to shut out threatening perceptions or expressions); (b) Psychosomatic complaints (overcontrol and due to the damming up of psychological energy which subsequently results in body function change); (c) Unusual fears of, for example, dirt, water, etc. (overcontrol, and often due to the displacement of threatening feelings onto neutral objects which subsequently are feared); (d) Absence of guilt subsequent to such acting-out behavior as lying, cheating, stealing, aggression, etc. (usually undercontrol, but the degree to which there is attendant guilt subsequent to acting-out mitigates the severity of the undercontrol implication); (e) Intense worry (overcontrol); and (f) Tics, stress-based stuttering, etc. (overcontrol).

74. Perseveration.

Perseveration refers to the inappropriate repetition of a response. Perseveration often manifests itself in ideational, verbal, visual-motor, and/or motor repetition. Perseveration is not normal, and although it can be caused by emotional stress, it usually is caused by brain damage, with a consequent inability to shift from the perseverated stimulus. Perseveration can cause marked learning problems.

75. Short attention span.

Like perseveration, short attention span can be caused by emotional stress as well as brain damage. Whatever the cause, it can seriously affect the learning process.

76. Memory problems.

Memory problems can be caused by emotional stress as well as brain damage. The memory function has many facets, any or all of which can cause marked learning and behavior problems. Some of those memory facets are: long-term memory; short-term memory; storage memory; sequential memory; retrieval memory; and/or auditory, visual, verbal, graphic, and/or haptic memory.

77. Relationship with authority.

Authority figures are individuals or symbols which represent positions of actual or symbolic authority over a subject. Developmentally, those authority figures or symbols are the parents; then extended family members; then teachers, policemen, the government; God; etc. Relationship with authority means the way in which a subject copes with the power and control that authority figures have over the subject. Normally, relationship with authority is learned, primarily by the way in which early authority figures (usually parents) execute their control over the subject. If the parents are punitive and dictatorial, the subject might be submissive to and/or fearful of authority, or just the opposite, rebellious and/or mean. If on the other hand, the parents are kind and democratic in their parent-child relationships, the subject might be respectful of authority and democratic in turn in dealing with people and issues. If the parents provide no controls whatsoever, the subject might have a confused regard for authority, which could express itself in little respect for but no rebellion against authority; a constant search for protective and control-giving authority; contempt for authority; etc.

A subject's relationship with authority can have a colossal impact on the learning and behavior processes that relate to our authority-based system of education.

78. Adequacy of senses (vision, hearing, touch, smell, etc.).

Sensory impairment can have a patent impact on the adequacy of the learning and behavior process.

79. Psychological, psychiatric, or neurological contact, medicine, or treatment.

A history of such professional contact, medicine, or treatment suggests the likelihood of a presenting problem the nature of which should be explored relative to a possible relationship with the subject's learning or behavior problem.

Subject School History

80. Subject's attitude toward school.

The attitude of a subject toward school is critical relative to educational success or failure.

81. Difficulty with reading, language, spelling, arithmetic, writing, etc.

A known history of tool-subject difficulty can help pinpoint the nature of a subject's learning (and behavior) problem.

82. Perceptual or visual-motor coordination problems.

A known history of perceptual and/or visual-motor coordination problems can further help pinpoint the nature of a subject's learning (and behavior) problem.

83. Grades, courses, and teachers liked and disliked

A knowledge of school-related likes and dislikes could reveal a pattern of performance that might be helpful relative to understanding a subject's presenting problem.

84. Peer problems.

Peer problems suggest the likelihood of interpersonal stress. Sometimes the nature of a peer problem reveals the kind of interpersonal stress, and if the kind of stress is known, problem resolution can be systematically goal directed and thus made easier. For example, the mechanics of problem resolution probably would be somewhat different relative to a subject who has peer problems of a bully nature, as opposed to a subject who has peer problems that involve persistent uncleanliness.

85. Discipline or daydreaming problems.

Although acting-out and daydreaming problems express themselves in opposite ways, they often are caused by the same personality factor, namely, the subject's control or conscience system. Basically, persisting discipline problems suggest the likelihood of undercontrol, whereas persisting daydreaming suggests the likelihood of overcontrol. Each kind of problem, in a different way, can cause learning or behavior problems.

86. Parents cooperative with school.

The likelihood of presenting problem resolution is greatly increased if the parents of the involved subject cooperate with the resolution process. Thus, a major effort should be expended to obtain parent cooperation with presenting problem resolution. Such cooperation could express itself in: continuing the school-based IEP activities at home; participating in parent group-counseling; serving as a volunteer classroom aide; simply being supportive of the school personnel and their professional resolution efforts; etc.

87. History of special education.

Impressions of Parents and Subject

88. Nature of parent roles.

A child, by modeling and identification, learns the primary social-sex role from the parent of the same sex. Thus, the boy-child learns how to behave as a male primarily from his father, and conversely with a girl-child. As such, for example, the passivity of a very passive father has implications for the social-sex role development of a boy-child (also daughter); similarly, the aggressiveness of a very aggressive mother has implications for the social-sex role development of a girl-child (also son). Any family dynamic that prevents or makes difficult the identification by a child with the same-sex parent (for example, the same-sex parent being absent from the home, a very punitive father, a cold and rejecting mother, etc.) can cause the child to model or identify with the opposite-sex parent, a situation that can result in social-sex role confusion and consequent behavior and learning problems. Whatever the separate as well as collective social-sex role nature of mother and father (male-female, passive-active, punitive-submissive, loving-rejecting, etc.), there will be a consequent developmental impact on the same-sex child, as well as, to a lesser extent, on the opposite-sex child. It is important to evaluate the nature of parent roles with respect to the possibility of a relationship between the parent roles, the resulting social-sex role of the subject, and the nature of the subject's presenting problem.

89. Nature of subject role.

The social-sex role of a subject is usually a function of having identified with the parent of the same sex. However, irrespective of the derivation of a subject's social-sex role, it is important to evaluate the possibility of a relationship between that role and the nature of the subject's behavior or learning problem. For example, the following social-sex role behaviors could directly cause behavior and/or learning problems: compensatory bully behavior; a young male subject associating only with younger females; an aggressive tomboy female; a frightened male; a haughty female, etc.

90. Parent-subject relationship.

The nature of the parent-subject relationship (including social-sex role identification) is probably the most important factor by which to understand an emotionally based presenting problem. Thus, it is important to arrange an observation of and pay close attention to parent-subject interaction, because the way in which the various family members relate to each other can dramatically cause and/or influence the learning or behavior problem of a subject. For example: harsh and rejecting parents can cause timid and fearful subject behavior, or the opposite, rebellious and defiant behavior; rigid and demanding parents can cause perfectionistic, overcontrolled, and unhappy subject behavior; weak, ineffective, and passive parents can cause, weak, ineffective, and passive kinds of behavior; emotionally cold parents can cause affectionally flat and unresponsive behavior; etc., any of which could cause learning and/or behavior problems.

91. Parent-subject personality variables.

The following parent-subject personality variables are important not only to an understanding of the individual involved but also to an understanding of any relationship between those personality variables and the nature of the subject's problem with learning or behavior.

    a. Character structure. The character structure (persisting attitudes, values, and mood) of parent or subject can influence the subject's learning or behavior problem. It is important to pay close attention to the possibility of a relationship between character structure and presenting problem. Examples of character structurek are: weakness and passivity; chronic depression; a rejecting and emotionally cold nature; callousness; a rebellious and defiant personality; impulsivity; a guiltless personality; identity confusion; a punitive nature; haughtiness; Pollyanna elation; rigidity and perfectionism; authoritative dominace; a shy and withdrawing personality.

    b. Reality testing. Reality testing is defined as the ability to interpret phenomena in a logical, accurate, and/or conventional way. The normal individual is capable of delaying the immediate gratification of basic impulse-related thoughts and behavior until acceptable, conventional, and logical thoughts and behavior can be identified and expressed. However, emotional stress can weaken the control involved with the delay of gratification process, a situation which could consequently result in thoughts and behavior becoming increasingly unconventional, illogical, out of context, and even bizarre. This kind of thought or behavior process typically involves poor reality testing, in that the individual misinterprets the meaning of reality. Any parent and/or subject demonstration of poor reality testing suggests the strong likelihood of emotional stress, a situation that could cause or influence the learning or behavior problem of the subject.

    c. Slips of speech. The normal thought and speech process involves the delay of gratification of basic impulse-related thought until logical and conventional speech can be identified with which to express as much of the impulse-related thought as is acceptably possible. However, stress, fatigue, and/or intoxication factors can weaken the control involved with the delay of gratification process, a situation which could manifest itself on a continuum from normal and minor slips of speech to psychotic-like bizarre speech. Since a speech slip represents a weakening of control relative to a more basic impulse-related idea or feeling, the slipped word probably represents what the individual really meant to say more than what the recovery word suggests. As such, it is important to pay close attention to slips of speech as possible indicators of the way in which the individual really feels. The meaning of a speech slip, as well as the possible emotional-stress derivation of speech slips, are important to the understanding of the parent and subject, the resulting parent-subject relationship, and the consequent possible impact on the nature of the subject's presenting problem.

    d. Anxiety. Anxiety can exist on a chronic basis or it can exist in relation to acute thoughts, feelings, or behaviors. Either way, parent or subject anxiety suggests stress, a situation that should be considered in terms of a possible causative or influential relationship with the subject's learning or behavior problem. Anxiety can be expressed in many ways: brow and/or palm perspiration; face flushing and paling; flitting eyes and/or avoidance of eye contact; twitching hands and feet; speech stammering; body tenseness or body shifting; dryness of mouth, and lip licking; a limp handshake; voice crackle; etc.

    e. Control. Control relates to the ability to delay the immediate gratification of basic impulse-related thoughts and behavior and is directly related to the developmental nature of the ego-conscience complex. As a rule, and up to a point, the more developed the conscience, the greater the control, the more extensive the delay, the less likely a particular thought or behavior will resemble its parent and originating impulse, and the more likely thoughts or behavior will be expressed in an organized and acceptable way. Conversely, the less developed the conscience, the less control and delay, and the more likely thoughts and behavior will be directly acted out. Since too much control or too little control can cause behavior or learning problems, it is important to be sensitive to parent and subject control indices, some of which follow. Strict control can express itself in the following ways: rigidity; perfectionism; threat; emotional coldness; affective flatness; lack of humor; tenseness; precise speech, handwriting, and behavior; strong moralism; anxiety and guilt; ceremoniousness; etc. Conversely, lax control can express itself in the following ways: impulsivity; acting out; little concern for others; opportunism; minimal anxiety or guilt; shallow interpersonal relationship; irresponsibility; fickle emotions; etc.

    f. Emotional honesty. This represents a positive, healthy self-regard based on the security of having become whatever one is. Emotional dishonesty represents the degree of pretense and ungenuine behavior in which an individual must engage in order to play the game of life. As a rule, the greater the sense of security, the healthier and more positive the self-regard, the less pretense, the more emotional honesty. In this context, it is a universal phenomenon, as it transcends the boundaries of race, religion, intelligence, culture, age, and sex. Fortunately, emotionally honest parents tend to provide a socialization atmosphere which fosters its development in their children. Unfortunately, the converse is also true, a situation that can cause emotional stress, which in turn can cause or influence behavior or learning problems.

    g. Humor. The natural and spontaneous ability to laugh at oneself and to find events humorous is, other variables being equal, one index of emotional health. The opposite situation, a persisting lack of humor, suggests a rigid, defensive, and threatened personality. Parent and/or subject relationships devoid of humor suggest emotional strain, which should be explored as a possible causative or influential factor relative to the nature of the subject's presenting problem.

    h. Bearing. Bearing is an index of pride, and pride directly relates to positive self-regard. It is expressed by, among other things, erect and proud posture, an alert and straightforward gaze, physical neatness, cleanliness, and good grooming. The opposite of bearing, slovenliness, can suggest a lack of pride, a situation which can influence the subject's presenting problem.

92. Parental willingness to cooperate with presenting problem resolution. This, in terms of a minor subject's presenting problem is one of the key ingredients of the successful resolution of that problem. Every effort should be made to enlist the genuine interest and cooperation of the parents because without it, success likelihood is dramatically decreased.

The Comprehensive History
Record Form

Family Members

1. Subject's name and age. _____

2. Father's name, age, address, and education. _____

3. Mother's name, age, address, and education. _____

4. Number of siblings. _____

5. Number of marriages, divorces, separations, and the stability of the present marriage. _____

6. Whether the subject is the natural child of the parents with whom he lives. _____

7. History of psychological, psychiatric, or neurological treatment, or special education. _____

8. History of suicide or suicide attempts, depression, or mood swings. _____

9. History of psychiatric or general medication. _____

10. History of alcoholism or narcotics. _____

11. History of difficulty with the law. _____

12. Discipline: who administers; how administered; and with what severity. _____

13. Religion: denomination; strength of belief; and how imposed on the subject. _____

14. Number of bedrooms in the family home; which children sleep in each bedroom as well as each bed. _____

15. History of mental retardation. _____
_____

16. History of epilepsy or convulsions. _____

17. History of miscarriages. _____

18. Who works at what and when. _____

19. Leisure time activities, including hobbies. _____
_____

Subject Developmental History
Prenatal

20. Rh incompatibility factor. _____

21. Extreme anxiety. _____

22. Depression. _____

23. Maternal age. _____

24. Medication: type and amount. _____
_____

25. Poisonings or bio-chemical intolerance. _____

26. Rubella (German measles). _____

27. Severe falls or blows to the abdomen. _____

28. Hospitalization and/or surgeries. _____
_____

29. Adequate medical attention. _____

30. X-rays. _____

31. Anoxia. _____

32. Infection. _____

33. Nutrition. _____

34. Any untoward accidents, illnesses, or incidents. _____

Perinatal

35. Very hard, long, and dry labor. _____

36. Precipitous delivery. _____

37. Unusual presentation (breech, transverse). _____

38. Prematurity. _____

39. Instrument delivery. _____

40. Anoxia at any time. _____

41. Discoloration of child (yellow, blue, or black). _____

42. Incubation of child. _____

43. Any other unusual factors at birth. _____

Postnatal

44. Was subject planned and wanted? _____

45. Height and weight of subject at birth. _____

46. Breast or bottle fed. _____

47. Age of weaning. _____

48. Age of walking. _____

49. Age of talking. _____

50. Age of initial toilet training, and age at which toilet training was completed. _____

51. Head injuries. _____

52. Poisoning or bio-chemical intolerance. _____

53. Anoxia. _____

54. Infection. _____

55. Seizures or convulsions. _____

56. Eating and/or sleeping difficulties. _____

57. Hyperactivity or hypoactivity. _____

58. Head banging; colic; and restlessness. _____

59. Motor coordination difficulty. _____

60. Medication, hospitalization, and/or surgeries. _____
_____

61. Was subject affectionate, cuddly and lovable? _____
_____

62. Any untoward accidents, illnesses, or incidents. _____

Subject Emotional Factors

63. Bowel-bladder incontinence. _____

64. Thumbsucking. _____

65. Disturbance of eating and/or sleeping. _____

66. How is anger expressed? _____
_____

67. Masturbation. _____

68. Bizarre or out-of-context ideas. _____
_____

69. Can subject give and accept affection? _____

70. Humor. _____

71. Rigid and perfectionistic behavior (or the opposite, sloppy behavior). _____
_____

72. Mood. _____

73. Control. _____
_____

74. Perseveration. _____

75. Short attention span. _____

76. Memory problems. _____

77. Relationship with authority. _____
_____

78. Adequacy of senses (vision, hearing, touch, smell, etc.). ____
_____

79. Psychological, psychiatric, or neurological contact, medicine, or treatment. _____
_____

Subject School History

80. Subject's attitude toward school. _____
_____

81. Difficulty with reading, language, spelling, arithmetic, writing, etc. _____
_____

82. Perceptual or visual-motor coordination problems. _____
_____

83. Grades, courses, and teachers liked and disliked. _____
_____

84. Peer problems. _____

85. Discipline or daydreaming problems. _____
_____

86. Parents cooperative with school. _____
_____

87. History of special education. _____

Impressions of Parents and Subject

88. Nature of parent roles. _____
_____

89. Nature of subject role. _____
_____

90. Parent-subject relationship. _____
_____

91. Parent-subject personality variables. _____
_____

92. Parental willingness to cooperate with presenting problem resolution. _____
_____

Chapter 14

The Reinforcement Inventory

The last informal psychoeducational assessment instrument that is discussed in this section is the Reinforcement Inventory. As with the other informal assessment instruments discussed, the Reinforcement Inventory is designed to facilitate the acquisition of necessary learner information that cannot be obtained through the use of formal assessment instruments.

The Reinforcement Inventory relates to the learner and the application of the last management model component, behavior modification and change agents. The Reinforcement Inventory is designed to help identify what the learner regards as rewarding (reinforcing) and aversive (unpleasant). This information is critical to the successful execution of IEPs, since systematic behavior modification is crucial to effective programming, and the execution of systematic behavior modification is often a function of whether appropriate rewards and aversive stimuli have been correctly identified and used by the practitioner. In order to provide a standardized way of identifying those appropriate rewards and aversive stimuli, the Reinforcement Inventory was developed.

The Inventory appears in Table XVI. The Inventory is simple to administer, either directly to an older subject or to the parents of a younger subject about that subject, for the purpose of finding out what that subject likes and dislikes. Based on the appropriate use of those likes and dislikes relative to the application of meaningful behavior modification strategy, the practitioner can increase the likelihood of prescriptive intervention success.

Table XVI

Reinforcement Inventory

Client name_____Date_____

1. Name three things you would like to have at home that you do not have now.

    a._____
    b._____
    c._____

2. Name one or more things you would like to be able to take home from school.

    a._____
    b._____
    c._____

3. The best reward anyone can give me is _____

4. What are your hobbies, or favorite activities?

    a._____
    b._____
    b._____

5. Name three games you like to play.

    a._____
    b._____
    c._____

6. If you had the opportunity, what would you like to do more often at home than you do now? Write your favorite activity first.

   a. _____
   b. _____
   c. _____

7. When you have free time outside of school, what do you like to do most?

                 Fall   Summer   Winter

   a. _____
   b. _____
   c. _____

8. What do you like to read?

   a. _____
   b. _____
   c. _____

9. When I grow up, I want to be _____

10. My favorite adult at school is _____

11. I feel terrific when _____

12. Something I really want is _____

13. If I had a chance, I sure would like to _____

14. I will do almost anything to avoid _____

15. The thing I like to do best with my mother is _____

16. The activity or entertainment I enjoy most is _____

17. When I do well at school, I wish my teacher would _____

18. I will do almost anything to get _____

19. It sure makes me mad when I cannot _____

20. I wish my teacher would not _____

21. The thing I like to do best with my father is _____

22. The things I like to do with my friends are _____

Chapter 15

The Five Kinds of Necessary Learner Information

As was previously mentioned, the operation of diagnostic-prescriptive teaching and programming is dependent on the acquisition of five kinds of information about the learner. A discussion of the five kinds of information follows.

Obtained and potential problem-solving ability

Obtained problem-solving ability refers to a subject's typical level of problem solving, which can be identified by the subject's verbal, performance, or composite IQs as derived from the Wechsler tests, the Binet, Peabody, Columbia, and so on. Potential problem-solving ability refers to a subject's best predicted verbal or performance level of problem solving, which can be identified by the subject's highest Wechsler Scaled Scores, the subject's best concept-performance on the Binet, the highest IQ of several IQs obtained from tests measuring different problem-solving ability, differential strengths as revealed by the SILI, etc.

The theoretical average individual would have a flat profile of Verbal, Performance, and Full Scale IQs and Scaled Scores. It is our contention that subjects with problems do not represent the theoretical average and that because of their problems, they often manifest a difference between obtained and potential problem-solving ability. We further contend that unless special recognition is given to that potential problem-solving ability, only the obtained IQ will be acknowledged, with a consequent loss of practitioner aspiration for the subject, and a resulting self-fulfilling prophecy wherein both the practitioner and the subject become lulled into the stagnating assumption that the subject is nothing more than the subject appears to be by means of the obtained IQ. We argue that this stagnation is wrong, and contend that if the subject's potential ability were fully acknowledged and then used as a level of problem-solving aspiration, the subject, practitioner, and society would benefit from any accrued higher level coping ability.

Learning Characteristics, including channel strengths and weaknesses

We recognize five primary learning channels (auditory, visual, verbal, graphic and haptic), and four primary learning processes (input, memory, meaning, and output). The identification of subject learning characteristics (input, memory, meaning, output, attention span, physical factors, self structuring ability, obtained vs. potential IQ, personality factors, reinforcers, etc.) relative to an instructional presenting problem permits teaching to the subject's learning strength, identifying the subject's learning weaknesses and then conducting the necessary learning-weakness remediation. For example, Clyde is nine yars old and is in the third grade. The teacher reported that Clyde was unable to read orally. Without attempting to identify the nature of the presenting problem the teacher began remediation by reducing Clyde to the lowest reading group; then by changing Clyde's workbook; then by giving Clyde additional phonic help; then becoming frustrated and seating Clyde by himself during the reading sessions; then remanding Clyde to the second-grade clas during the reading session, subsequent to which the second-grade teacher repeated all the above steps; after which, Clyde was recommended for retention in the third grade. However, if the necessary learner information had been collected, the teacher would have realized that Clyde's Verbal IQ was low (82); that his Performance IQ was high (128); that his Bender Test and DAP were precocious for a nine-year old; that the ITPA and SILI revealed good auditory and visual input processes, good meaning processes, good motor output, good visual memory, but poor auditory sequential memory; and that Clyde developed an encephaletic fever subsequent to chicken pox at the age of four years and since that time has had difficulty carrying out verbally expressed direction. Had the teacher been aware of this information, rather than using a random remedial approach, the teacher might have used Clyde's superior visual and performance abilities for the purpose of teaching him to read visually and might have attempted to remediate the reading problem (which was not a reading problem at all but an auditory sequential memory problem) by providing Clyde with specific auditory sequential memory training exercises.

Learning characteristic strengths and weaknesses can be identified by the high and low Scaled Scores or test parts of the ITPA, Wechsler tests, the Binet, SILI, the Bender Test, the DAP, and the Peabody when contrasted with the Columbia (or any other two tests which purport to measure different learning channels or factors), the Comprehensive History, or any other formal or informal assessment instrument which is designed to measure components of the learning process.

Tool-subject achievement level and resulting learning quotients

Tool-subject refers to academic subjects, such as reading, language, arithmetic, writing, etc. Achievement level refers to a learner's academic ability relative to a particular tool subject, a situation which is usually reported in grade level form. When combined, the two concepts become tool-subject achievement level, which is easily obtained by means of the Wide Range Achievement Test, the Peabody Individual Achievement Test, or any other standardized achievement test.

The acquisition of tool-subject achievement level information increases IEP-IIP precision. For example, Florence is eight years old and is in the third grade. She has an oral-reading grade level score of 3.1, a silent-reading grade level score of 3.3, an oral-arithmetic grade level score of 3.0, an oral-spelling grade level score of 2.9, but a written-spelling grade level score of 1.5 (due to the inability to revisualize what a word looks like in writing). Such differential tool-subject strength and weakness information not only has diagnostic implications but also remedial implications.

The learning quotient (Johnson & Mykelbust, 1967) concept is similar to the concept of achievement level. The LQ is a number score, similar to the IQ in value, which represents tool-subject achievement in relation to ability. The LQ is determined by the following formula:

$$LQ = \frac{TSGL + 5}{MA} \times 100$$

Regarding the formula:

TSGL is the subject's tool-subject grade level for any tool-subject which the examiner wishes expressed in the form of an LQ; 5 is a constant value and represents five years, which is the length of time between birth and the time the normal student enters school; and, MA represents the subject's mental age. Mental age can be determined from a given IQ by the formula, IQ x CA (chronological age) ÷ 100.

The learning quotient has an approximate average score of 100. Any tool-subject can be converted into a learning quotient as long as it is possible to express that tool-subject in grade level achievement form. Thus, a learner could have a reading LQ, spelling LQ, arithmetic LQ, etc. Furthermore, that learner could have an oral reading LQ, silent reading LQ, oral spelling LQ, written spelling LQ, etc. The advantage of the LQ concept over the conventional grade level achievement score is that the LQ describes tool-subject achievement in relation to the subject's problem-solving ability (mental age). This makes the LQ concept relative to the subject, as opposed to being relative to a standardization sample.

An LQ under 90 is suggestive of a learning problem as that problem relates to the tool-subject which is represented by the TSGL. By using 90 as an LQ cutoff score, it is easy to obtain a profile of the learner's tool-subject strengths and weaknesses. However, it is important to recognize that an LQ under 90 refers to a learning problem, not a learning disability.

The LQ is helpful in identifying a profile of the learner's tool-subject learning strengths and weaknesses, which in turn should identify a priority of intervention procedure. Since learning problems can be caused by a variety of conditions (emotional disturbance, learning disabilities, mental retardation, cultural difference, improper instruction, sensory impairment, malingering, etc.), it is possible for a learner with average intelligence to have, for example, an above-average reading LQ, but a below-average arithmetic LQ. These differential scores suggest that that learner, for his ability, is overachieving in reading and underachieving in arithmetic. In terms of a priority of intervention procedure, the teacher probably would want to concentrate more on that learner's arithmetic difficulty than on his reading skills. Similarly, a teacher probably would want to concentrate more remedial time on the learner whose LQ scores are all below 90 than on the learner whose LQ scores are all above 100.

Regarding the LQ, a seeming paradox can occur: the theoretical average learner will have LQ scores of 100. Similarly, the average mental retardate will also have LQ scores of 100, despite the mental retardation, and despite the fact that that mental retardate is below grade level in achievement. This seeming paradox exists because the average mental retardate who is below grade level in achievement is also below average in problem-solving ability. As such, the below grade level achievement is where the mental retardate should be in relation to his below-average ability, a situation which is expressed by average LQs (100). Once again, the LQ concept reflects individual achievement in relation to individual ability.

To calculate the LQ, the subject's mental age is used. That mental age is usually the subject's obtained mental age but can be the subject's potential mental age (highest Scaled Score, translated into an IQ then MA value). However, the use of the potential mental age results in a comparatively larger denominator in the LQ formula, which, when calculated, expresses itself in a lower LQ. To avoid any confusion, we recommend either calculating the LQ by means of only the obtained mental age, or calculating the LQ both ways and using the two LQ scores as an indication of the potential growth available to the learner.

The LQ may be used as the basis for an instructional objective. Since a given individual should be able to achieve commensurate with his ability, and since the LQ of 100 expresses that commensurateness, it would be meaningful to help a learner with a tool-subject problem achieve a learning quotient of 100 in that tool-subject. This could easily be converted into an instructional objective.

Important learner personality characterics

In order to justify intervening in the life of a human being, as many variables as possible involved with that intervention should be controlled. Thus it is important to identify those personality characteristics of the learner and learner's family which are essential to know in order to smoothly effect the environmental manipulation which is often a necessary adjunct of IEPs.

The acquisition of the following kinds of information about the personality of the learner and family are desirable in order to effect successful intervention:

(1) the stability and intactness of the family; (2) the adequacy of the relationship of the subject to father, mother, and siblings; (3) the degree to which the parental expectations of the subject are realistic; (4) which of the parents is the family authority, and the adequacy with which that authority is exercised relative to the subject; (5) the general security level of the subject as well as of other family members; (6) the level of care that the family members have for each other; (7) the subject's comfort with his aggression, dependency needs, and sex-role identification, and the same for the relevant other family members; (8) the level of general family openness or defensiveness; (9) the perception of relevant family members regarding the nature of the subject's presenting problem and what must be done to correct it; and (10) the willingness of the subject and family members to cooperate regarding the resolution of the presenting problem.

With the above knowledge, it is possible to more systematically intervene with a presenting problem and feel reasonably comfortable about rendering the necessary intervention recommendations (including the least restrictive educational environment), some of which might include: (1) Behavior modification for the subject, in terms of the specific kinds of rewards, the specific reinforcing conditions, the specific reinforcing family members, all in relation to precise, psychologically sound, and feasible objectives for the subject. (2) School environmental manipulation, in terms of the sex and personality of the teacher, specific teacher-counselor-principal behavioral/instructional objectives and prescriptions, and, practitioner encouragement of school officials during times of learner-frustration, based on the practitioner's confidence in the IEP. (3) Counseling or psychotherapy, in terms of the sex and age of the therapist, the theoretical orientation of the counselor or therapist that would be most compatible with the subject's psychodynamics, the frequency and expected duration of the counseling or therapy, whether the subject needs counseling rather than psychotherapy (or the converse), a projected outcome of counseling or psychotherapy, and therefore some overall therapeutic plan regarding the subject, etc. (4) Residential treatment, in terms of the kind, location, and projected duration, all in relation to precise and theoretically sound objectives for the subject. (5) Nonschool environmental manipulation, in terms of a certain kind of club activity, hobby, etc., based on a sound theoretical assumption that the recommended activity would be remedial for the subject. (6) Agency involvement with the subject and/or family, including probation, welfare, health services, etc.

All of the above kinds of learner information can be acquired by the trained examiner, especially if that person is willing to visit the family and administer the Comprehensive History which is the best instrument discussed in this book for obtaining this kind of information. However, the mere mechanical administration of the Comprehensive History will not be productive; on the other hand, a perceptive examiner who understands the interpretative hypotheses of the various Comprehensive History concepts and who has a sound theoretical orientation with which to understand personality-behavior in relation to the Comprehensive History information will be richly rewarded with helpful information.

In addition to the Comprehensive History, other formal and informal assessment instruments that are effective relative to the acquisition of information about the personality characteristics of the learner and family are, in the order that they are effective: the DAP, the Bender Test, the DAF, the precisely defined presenting problem, the Wechsler tests, and the Precision Referral Form (to be discussed later).

Many of the above-discussed remedial recommendations are often essential to presenting problem resolution. However, making those recommendations without sufficient information about the personality characteristics of the learner and family is, in our opinion, unprofessional.

Identifying what the learner regards as rewarding and aversive

Effective IEP-IIP programming is dependent on the systematic application of behavior modification and change agents, which in turn is dependent on the correct identification and appropriate use of rewards and aversive stimuli. Thus, it is important to the meaningful operation of the management model to identify those things that the learner regards as rewarding and aversive.

Unfortunately, this identification task is harder than it seems. It would be simple if the task involved only the casual identification of a few reinforcers and aversive stimuli. But that is not the case. As will be discussed under behavior modification and change agents, in order for reinforcers and aversive stimuli to have their most productive modification effect they must be need-satisfying. Thus, in part, the goal of the practitioner is to identify need-satisfying reinforcers and aversive stimuli (need-satisfying aversive stimuli means things that are unpleasant to the subject). In order to accomplish this goal, it is usually necessary to spend time with the subject's parents, friends, and teachers. In order to make the job of collecting this kind of information easier, we use the Reinforcement Inventory, to which the preceding chapter is devoted, and which appears in Table XVI. Despite the standardized way in which the Inventory is designed to operate, the practitioner still might find it necessary to talk to the subject's parents and/or friends in order to gain knowledge about the particular rewards and aversive stimuli that are need-satisfying to the subject.

The reader should be cautioned that the use of rewards and aversive stimuli pursuant to behavior modification is a powerful tool of change and must be used wisely. Similarly, the reader should understand that the inappropriate use of rewards and aversive stimuli results in a great deal of wasted time. This is so because many practitioners use what they think should be appropriate reinforcers and aversive stimuli rather than what the subject regards as reinforcing and aversive. For example, the M & M's fail because the subject does not like candy, yet no one bothered to ask the subject. As a result, the teacher becomes frustrated with the failure, the student regresses, the parents become agitated, the principal becomes resistant to the future use of behavior modification strategies, and unfortunately, behavior modification gets a bad name.

SELECTED REFERENCES

Johnson, D., and Myklebust, H. *Learning Disabilities. Educational Principles and Practices*. New York: Grune & Stratton, 1967.

Section III

A Theoretical Orientation to the Understanding of Personality

Chapter 16

A Theoretical Orientation to the Understanding of Personality

The interpretation of the IEP information necessary for effective intervention with learning and behavior problems is a function of not only test interpretation skill, keen observation ability, and perceptive parent and subject interviewing skill, but also the integration of that mass of information into an internally consistent and theoretically sound understanding of subject personality and behavior. In order for this integration and interpretation to occur, the examiner should have developed a system of hypotheses which serve to make possible the explanation of subject personality and behavior. This system of hypotheses is not easy to develop. However, we argue that each examiner should attempt to develop his own system, so that behavior becomes explicable, so that the examiner can make correct predictions about a subject's behavior, so that the examiner can make theoretically sound predictions about the impact of certain behavior upon the subject (for example, counseling, residential treatment, etc.), and so that effective problem resolution can take place.

The following discussion represents one theoretical orientation to the understanding of human personality. This orientation is a derivative of Freudian psychology and represents an adaptation of ego psychology (Hartman, 1973). This orientation is only one of many and is presented only for the purpose of illustrating that a certain set of assembled hypotheses can explain personality and behavior, a situation which is necessary in order for effective diagnostic-prescriptive teaching to occur.

Basis of Personality

Our interpretation of ego psychology pictorially regards the human personality structured as in Figure II.

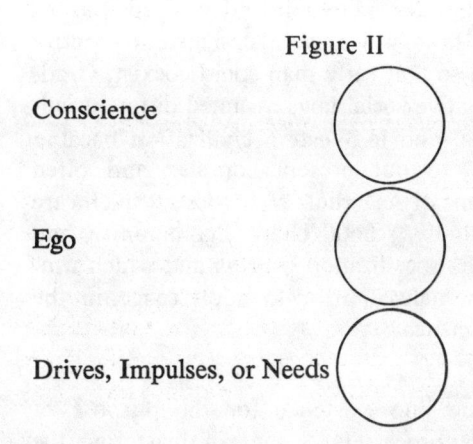

Figure II

Conscience ◯

Ego ◯

Drives, Impulses, or Needs ◯

Drives

A drive is defined as a biological or physiological (somatic) source of tension, which originates and exists in the form of metabolic energy, and which strives for discharge in order to reduce the tension-level (pain) of the organism. Drives are most often expressed in the form of aggression, sexuality, love-security-dependency, hunger, thirst, and the need for safety, protection, and shelter. Drives are genetic in nature, although the amount of tension varies with the body chemistry of the individual. Since they are genetic, drives are universal, representing a common denominator of man. Drives, in and by themselves, are not lawful, and strive only for immediate discharge gratification; as such, drives represent the animal part of the human personality. Since drives are a function of somatic tension-energy and strive for discharge, they form the origin of behavior motivation.

Conscience

The conscience represents the human system of morality. Unlike drives which are genetic and universal, the conscience is learned and culturally determined, from infancy, by means of the gradual yet powerful reward-punishment component of the culturally-based socialization process. Thus, the conscience represents the familial-cultural attitudes and values that have been formally and informally learned during the never-ending socialization process. The conscience manifests itself in the individual's system of right-wrong, good-bad, morality-immorality, etc., and operates to dispense praise (pride) when behavior is compatible with good conscience values, and to dispense punishment (guilt) when behavior is incompatible with good conscience values. Originally, the conscience developed out of primitive social laws which were designed to control the drive system so that early man could coexist. Gradually, those primitive social laws assumed different cultural dimensions, and in Western civilization became more "refined," to our present complex and often confusing system of external regulations which are taught by the family, school, church, community, and culture during the socialization process and which usually become internalized prior to adolescence in the form of the conscience.

Ego

The ego came into existence for the purpose of ensuring the life process by means of mastering the powerful drive system seeking immediate expression and the often equally powerful conscience-control system seeking an inhibition of that drive expression. Without such ego mastery, the human organism would be rendered helpless by the powerful internal psychological struggle.

The ego's mastery function operates by delaying the immediate expression of drives until behavior can be identified which would serve as an acceptable compromise to both the drive and the conscience systems. The compromise behavior discharges enough tension to sufficiently lower the drive-level of the organism, yet is also acceptable in kind and force to the conscience. Smooth, efficient, and adaptive behavior results, a situation which we, in this culture, call normal behavior.

In the context of normal behavior, it is important to understand that the mastery purpose of the ego represents more than just a mediation of the drive and conscience systems but an adaptive purpose as well. This adaptive purpose operates to select and effect whatever compromise behavior will be the most enhancing to the life process of the organism, thereby permitting that organism to cope effectively with the demands of the situation. Thus, all behavior, even psychopathological behavior, can be regarded as coping and adaptive behavior.

Psychodynamics

The ego's mastery ability is, in part, a function of how well the ego can delay the gratification of the drive system seeking immediate tension reduction. In turn, the ability of the ego to delay gratification is a function of ego strength, and ego strength is a function of the love and security satisfaction, as well as the appropriate frustration, to which the organism has been exposed by the major socialization agents, primarily the parents. Basically, the stronger the ego, the more delay of gratification capacity the ego has, the more likely the ego will be able to successfully perform its mastery function, thus enhancing the life process. As delay of gratification involves damming up the tension energy of the drives, and as putting off the conscience until acceptable behavior can be identified also means damming up energy, the ego's mastery function is in essence a mastery of energy systems. The way in which the ego masters the energy systems becomes the psychology of energy dynamics or psychodynamics. The study of psychodynamics and the resulting adaptive processes of the ego represents our conception of ego psychology.

Psychodeterminism

The energy used by the ego, drive, and conscience systems comes from the same source — the metabolic-physiological processes of the body. The stronger the body chemistry, the more potential energy there is for the life-process.

The drive system is directly energized by the metabolic processes. The drive system seeks to directly express that energy in the form of immediate behavioral discharge.

The conscience system is also directly energized. The human organism has the longest period of socialization-dependency of any mammal; in addition, it is estimated that one-half of a normal individual's total knowledge is acquired before the age of six years; and it is hypothesized that love, dependency, and security-need satisfaction are among the most powerful, if not the most powerful, needs of the human organism. The sum of this is that for a lengthy attitude-forming period of life the human organism is dependent on the mother and father figures for the receipt of life-needed love and dependency satisfaction, a situation which makes authority figures powerful reinforcers and behavior modifiers. The conscience is learned by the organism introjecting and thus behaving in ways compatible with the values of mother and father, and then the culture, in order to earn praise (love-pleasure), and to avoid punishment (rejection-pain). This conscience-developing praise-punishment proclivity facilitates the life-process and is directly energized by the metabolic or life-building system of the body.

Similarly, the ego is energized as well as learned. The source of energy that permits ego development is body metabolism, but the process by which the ego is learned is initially a function of the parents, then the extended family, then the community, etc., providing an appropriate praise-punishment atmosphere in which a strong and healthy ego can develop. Healthy and secure parents usually provide the appropriate amount of love, security, and dependency satisfaction, as well as the right amount of need frustration, in order for an organism to develop a realistic sense of being loved, wanted, and secure. This state of security is known as ego strength. The stronger the ego, the more adequate the ego will be with respect to delaying immediate drive expression, the more likely easy and smooth coping behavior will result, the more the life-process is enhanced, and the more energy the ego has for its mastery and adaptive functions.

Except for reflex response, behavior is energized and thus originates by means of the tension-energy of the drives seeking expression. However, the process, as well as the behavior by which those drives are ultimately expressed is learned, due to: (1) the learned attitudes and values of the conscience, which determine which particular drives, and the amount of energy associated with those drives, will be expressed; and (2) the learned strength of the ego, which serves to delay the expression of the drives, in relation to the attitudes and values of the conscience, until compromise behavior can be effected. Most behavior is psychosocially determined by a complex process of energy dynamics, a situation which is known as psychodeterminism.

The mechanics of psychodeterminism involve the ego delaying immediate drive expression, searching the memory-experience bank for behavior that will serve as an acceptable compromise to the drive and conscience systems, and then permitting the organism to behave in that compromising but coping way. This compromise behavior is almost never of the same force or kind that was originally determined by the drive system because the conscience-control system of most civilized individuals (and lawful societies) will not permit the direct expression of drive behavior. To arrive at the compromise behavior, the ego employs the concept of energy displacement, which makes possible the channeling of energy from a given drive or group of drives into a related but substitute form of behavior. Thus, the individual who is basically destructively angry but whose conscience will not permit the direct discharge of that destructiveness into behavior could effect the more socially acceptable compromise behavior of, for example, playing (or even just watching) football, working as a demolition expert for a salvage company, etc. In this context, the operation of the energy displacement concept likely is responsible for many of man's major life-process choices, such as choice of mate, vocational choice, choice of hobby, etc. However, since substitute behavior is never as tension-energy reducing as the original drive expression, civilized man has gradually accumulated a pool of undischarged tension, which serves as a permanent motivating force for behavior, and also tends to account for man's basic state of restlessness.

Emotional disturbance

We define emotional disturbance as acting-out or acting-in behavior which is symptomatic of the inability of the ego to master the drive system and/or conscience system. Emotional disturbance is a form of behavior and therefore follows the hypothetical laws that have been established for behavior in general. Specifically, emotional disturbance, as with most behavior, originates with, and is energized by, the metabolic processes of the body. As such, emotional disturbance is genetic and universal because metabolic processes are genetic and universal. However, irrespective of origin, the way in which emotional disturbance is expressed is learned and culturally determined because the acting-out or acting-in behavior, which by definition is characteristic of emotional disturbance, is caused by the culturally determined conscience system in relation to the strength of the ego system, both of which are learned. Thus, the origin of emotional disturbance is genetic and universal, but the way in which emotional disturbance is expressed is learned and culturally determined, for if man were not governed by the learned and culturally determined conscience system of right-wrong behavior, there could be no emotional disturbance.

As emotional disturbance is characterized by acting-out or acting-in behavior, that acting-out or acting-in behavior is caused by an underdeveloped or overdeveloped conscience in relation to the strength of the ego and with respect to the force of the drives seeking expression. Emotional disturbance can be classified in two ways: (1) acting-out (externalization), which is usually due to an underdeveloped conscience and weak ego, and thus not enough control or (2) acting-in (internalization), which is usually due to an overdeveloped conscience and weak ego, and too much control. Not enough control often manifests itself in impulsive, acting-out, and/or delinquent behavior, which is characterized by little concern for the feelings and rights of others. Too much control often results in a damming up of the energy associated with unacceptable feelings or behavior, which in turn manifests itself in increasingly rigid and defensive behavior, and which often is characterized by psychosomatic complaints, neurosis, psychosis, etc.

The development of the conscious and unconscious parts of the personality is directly related to the developmental state of the conscience. Conscious is defined as the existence and awareness of a situation or feeling. Unconscious is defined as the existence but lack of awareness of a situation or feeling. Normally, the more overdeveloped the conscience, the more developed (larger) the unconscious; similarly, the less developed the conscience, the more developed the conscious. This exists because the overdeveloped conscience has learned to regard many basic impulses and expressions of behavior as undesirable and it operates to keep those undesirable impulses and expressions of behavior out of conscious awareness. If those undesirable impulses and expressions of behavior were to become conscious, the conscience would exert self-punishment (guilt), which is painful and contrary to the life-process enhancing rationale of the ego, and hence to be avoided. Thus, the individual with an overdeveloped conscience often has a large unconscious and, conversely, the individual with an underdeveloped conscience usually is much more conscious of feelings and emotions.

Treatment implications

The individual with the overdeveloped conscience and dammed-up drive system pictorially looks like Figure III.

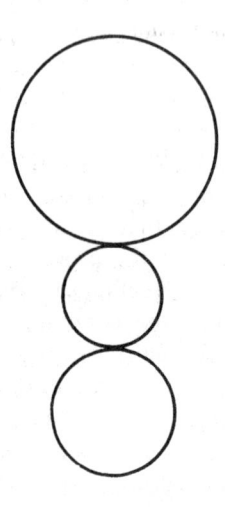

Figure III

The individual with an underdeveloped conscience pictorially looks like Figure IV.

Figure IV

The treatment objective for the overcontrolled individual is to reduce the harshness of the conscience and to build ego strength, thus increasing the conscious state, and thereby making previously psychologically bound energy available to the individual for constructive life-process activities. This treatment objective is most effectively carried out by counseling, behavior modification strategies, and to some extent, medication. Particularly when the subject is a minor, it is essential to involve the parents as well as the subject in the treatment process, thereby intending to change the parental attitudes and values with respect to the subject and his behavior, and thus change the conscience (attitudes and values) and ego structures of the subject.

The treatment objective of reducing the harsh conscience and building ego strength can be conducted both by counseling as well as behavior modification. Counseling, relative to such a treatment objective, involves creating a nonthreatening professional atmosphere in which, over a period of time (there is no substitute for time), the subject (and parents) can slowly and gradually become aware (conscious) of previously unacceptable and unconscious feelings and/or behavior, by means of the accepting, understanding, and clarifying nature of the counselor, and thereby ultimately release the previously bound energy associated with the unacceptable feelings and behavior into constructive life-process activities. Behavior modification, relative to such a treatment objective, and optimally in conjunction with counseling, would involve the reinforcement (over a period of time) of flexible, open, and insightful behavior, and the extinction of defensive, rigid, and psychologically resistive behavior. Lastly, at times, and with respect to counseling or behavior modification, the use of prescribed medicine for an anxious, depressed, or fragile subject can facilitate the treatment process.

Relative to the undercontrolled individual a different treatment objective should be employed. The undercontrolled individual is often in external difficulty because of acting-out behavior. Such behavior is often caused not so much by an overactive drive system as by an underdeveloped conscience-control system in relation to perhaps just a normal drive system. The two best treatment strategies with respect to this kind of individual are: (1) behavior modification, for the purpose of building ego strength, as well as for the purpose of attempting to develop a more socially appropriate conscience structure, both of which would have the effect of greater behavior-control; and (2) the possibility of medication, for the purpose of controlling acting-out behavior until a sufficient conscience and ego structure can be developed.

Of the two kinds of emotional disturbance, the latter probably is least susceptible to long-term change for two reasons: (1) since the conscience structure is basically established in childhood, the reshaping of the conscience is increasingly difficult to the degree that subject chronological age exceeds mid-adolescence. As a rule, the best counseling or psychotherapy prognosis is afforded the individual whose pathology begins late and whose treatment begins early. (2) the second reason that the undercontrolled individual has a less favorable prognosis for change is that lawful medication is about the only way of working directly with the drive system, which in this case would involve reducing the force of the drives and thus reducing acting-out behavior through the application of medicine. Since medication is not a desirable method of effecting long-term personality change, treatment attention needs to focus on the reshaping of the conscience which, as has been expressed, is difficult.

Ego functions

Emotionally healthy parents usually nurture children

with healthy and strong egos. The stronger the ego, the more likely the three major ego functions of delay of gratification, energy displacement, and coping-adaptive ability will be smooth and efficient. However, in our complex society, even the normal individual operates under stress. Too much stress can cause a breakdown in the ego functions, a situation which can result in acting-out or acting-in behavior, which is symptomatic of the increase in stress and characteristic of emotional disturbance. Between the normal ego functions and ego breakdown due to unmanageable stress, there are some personality mechanisms which are in the service of the ego and which are designed to assist the ego with its mastery function. Anxiety and guilt are two of those mechanisms. Anxiety is intangible, inexplicable, psychological fear. Guilt is conscience-based self-punishment. Both anxiety and guilt serve the ego as a warning or danger signal regarding an imminent internal or external threat to the stability of the organism. In this context of a danger signal, anxiety and guilt are very necessary, and thus serve a major constructive ego-mastery purpose. However, too much anxiety or guilt can flood and overwhelm the ego, in which case the anxiety-guilt mechanism can be destructive. In either case, when confronted with stress-based anxiety or guilt, the ego (organism) can: (1) attempt to understand the nature of the situation by means of direct confrontation, (2) elect to literally and physically leave in an attempt to avoid the unknown source of stress, and/or (3) erect defense mechanisms.

The first ego-alternative is probably the healthiest, although it takes a strong and secure ego to face moderately stressful and anxiety-provoking circumstances. The second alternative is a weaker solution, and usually not effective, in that the escaping ego is always accompanied by the stress-producing conscience; as such, it is difficult to escape from one's self. The third ego-alternative (defense mechanisms) is one to which even the normal ego resorts in its attempt to maintain mastery and adaptive stability. However, the degree to which the ego must continue to resort to long-term defense mechansims is the degree to which the ego and personality in general become increasingly weak, vulnerable, less and less efficient, and subject to behavior that is symptomatic of stress and characteristic of emotional disturbance.

There are many defense mechanisms, all of which are designed to assist the ego with its mastery and coping function by binding and/or removing threatening and unacceptable feelings, memories, thoughts, behaviors, etc., from consciousness, and by means of those mechanisms, to permit the organism to cope with stress. In this context, emotional disturbance can be considered a defense mechanism, in terms of the disturbed behavior, of whatever symptomatic nature, being designed to permit the organism to cope with stress. Thus, rather than regarding the emotionally disturbed individual as nothing but ill, it is possible to regard that individual as having made personality adjustments necessary to cope with intense stress.

The typical defense mechanisms used by the ego to maintain coping and adaptive behavior are: repression of thoughts and memories into the unconscious; denial of thoughts; projection of unacceptable feelings or thoughts onto a person, or external object (as in school phobia); reaction formation, involving a total personality change from, for example, unacceptable anger to acceptable passivity (usually, any extreme behavior is thought to be a psychological protection from the opposite kind of behavior); displacement of emotions from a threatening object to a nonthreatening object; intellectualization, involving the separation of words from their threatening feelings, and then often talking a good game but not feeling it; regression to a less threatening emotional level of adjustment; withdrawal from threatening situations to the quiet of one's own world; internalization of energy, which locates in a body organ, and which can thus cause body-function change or loss; anxiety and guilt, in the sense that they represent a warning and danger signal to the ego; emotional blocking of threatening thoughts and memories, which can result in behavior ranging from a momentary blank, through fainting, to severe amnesia; acting-out of impulses; and sublimation, which involves the expression of basic drives in culturally acceptable ways. As a rule, most normal as well as many non-normal individuals sublimate. However, with that one exception, the degree to which the ego must rely on the increasing and prolonged use of defense mechanisms for ego-mastery assistance is the degree to which that ego is weak and potentially fragile.

Like any other activity, the operation of defense mechanisms takes energy. The more defense mechanisms are used, the more total personality and life-process energy is consumed. The more such energy is consumed, the weaker and hence the more vulnerable the ego (and thus the entire personality). Specifically, some indications of a weak and vulnerable ego are: emotional rigidity; unexplained irritability; chronic emotional threat; defensiveness; oversensitivity (touchiness); unexplained fatigue; loss of humor; emotional coldness; a flattening of mood; and, decreasing problem-solving efficiency.

Unfortunately, the stress-defense mechanism cycle is vicious. For, often, the greater the stress, the more need for defense mechanisms, the more energy is consumed, the weaker the ego, the less efficient the ego is with respect to its mastery functions, the greater the stress, the greater the need for defense mechanisms, etc., until much of the life-process energy is consumed by the defensive struggle. This cycle results in markedly decreased coping ability and behavior that is characteristic of emotional disturbance.

On the other hand, indications of a healthy and strong ego are: easy, smooth, and efficient behavior; culturally acceptable behavior; creativity; flexibility; openness; humor; a constant source of energy, with many outlets of a constructive nature; security; emotional honesty; genuineness; objective (impartial) perceptual discrimination; and, minimal anxiety and guilt.

Conclusion

We stress the importance of models (parents, teachers, etc.) to the development of the healthy personality. Specifically, the attitudes and values of models are important to the development of the conscience. The ability of models to appropriately dispense praise and rewards is important to the development of the ego and the conscience. The values of the particular culture in which models choose to live are important to the development of the conscience. The ability of models to provide meaningful success experiences is important to the development of the ego. The ability of models to maturely express love as well as anger is important to the development of the conscience. And the ability of models to sublimate is important to the development of the personality as well as the social system. For, as models and their children go, so goes society.

SELECTED REFERENCES

Freud, A. *The Ego and the Mechanisms of Defense.* New York: International Universities Press, 1946.

Freud, S. *The Interpretation of Dreams.* In J. Strachey (Ed.), *The Standard Edition of the Complete Psychological Works.* Vols. IV and V. London: Hogarth Press, 1953.

Freud, S. *Psychopathology of Everyday Life.* In *The Basic Writings of Sigmond Freud.* New York: Random House, 1938.

Freud, S. *Three Essays on Sexuality.* In J. Strachey (Ed.), *The Standard Edition of the Complete Psychological Works.* Vol. VII. London: Hogarth Press, 1953.

Hartman, H. *Ego Psychology and the Problem of Adaptation.* New York: International Universities Press, 1973.

Hartman, H. *Essays on Ego Psychology.* New York: International Universities Press, 1973.

Rapaport, D. *Organization and Pathology of Thought.* New York: Columbia University Press, 1951.

PART III

THE SECOND COMPONENT OF THE EDUCATION INTERVENTION AND MANAGEMENT MODEL:

Behavioral-Instructional Objectives

Diagnostic-prescriptive teaching operates by means of the management model for the purpose of effecting systematic intervention with learning or behavior problems. Behavioral-instructional objectives represent one of the major management model strategies by which the systematic nature of an IEP intervention is possible. A behavioral-instructional objective is a behaviorally defined indication of the intended outcome of an IEP intervention, including the criteria by which the intervention success is to be measured. As such, behavioral-instructional objectives represent one of the accountability bases of the management model.

Chapter 17

An Orientation to Behavioral-Instructional Objectives

The management model emphasizes a systematic approach to problem resolution, not only by means of the acquisition of the previously discussed necessary learner information but also by means of the second management model component, behavioral-instructional objectives.

A behavioral-instructional objective (Mager, 1975) is a prescriptive teaching plan of action and is somewhat like a lesson plan. A behavioral-instructional objective is defined as a written statement that behaviorally describes the intended outcome of an IEP intervention in relation to the terminal behavior expected of the learner. Terminal behavior involves the identification of the following criteria:

1. The identification, in behavioral terms, of what the learner will be physically doing when demonstrating the achievement of the objective. This identification should be in behavioral terms so as to permit objective measurement.
2. The identification of the important conditions under which the terminal behavior must occur. If a condition such as in-seat behavior or the use of flash cards is important to the objective, that condition should be included under this terminal behavior criterion.
3. The identification of the criteria of acceptable performance which will be used to evaluate the success of the intervention. Criteria of acceptable performance maximally involves three concepts, any or all of which form one of the accountability bases of the management model: time (for example, within 5 minutes), accuracy (for example, with 90% comprehension), and difficulty level (for example, from a second grade reader).

The terms behavioral objective and instructional objective are often used interchangeably. However, we prefer to relate the term behavioral objective to non-academic behavior and the term instructional objective to academic behavior. Despite the slight semantic difference, a good objective involves up to five essential ingredients: (1) performance-based terms, (2) the important conditions, (3) the criteria of acceptable performance, which include time, (4) accuracy, and (5) difficulty level.

The concept of behavioral-instructional objectives is one of the most important of the management model components. This exists because: 1. An objective identifies a specific direction for each intervention, a situation which keeps the practitioner alert to where he is going, which reduces intervention trial and error, and which increases the systematic nature of the intervention process. Without an objective, the practitioner would not know where he is going, how to get there, or when he has arrived. 2. An objective identifies the criteria of acceptable performance which serve as evidence of the successful achievement of the objective. The criteria permit a continuing evaluation of the intervention progress, a situation which serves to increase the likelihood of problem resolution. 3. The terminal behavior of each objective is identified in performance-based terms. In conjunction with criteria of acceptable performance, such performance-based terminal behavior permits an evaluation of the success of the intervention in terms of whether the related objective was successfully achieved. Because of the importance of objectives, the management model is designed to operate in terms of establishing an objective for each major intervention with a learning or behavior problem.

Although it is initially difficult to easily generate good behavioral-instructional objectives, the necessary skill can be acquired with only a moderate amount of practice. One means of evaluating the adequacy of an objective is to determine whether that objective contains the ingredients essential to its operation. Another evaluation criterion is whether the particular objective is stated with sufficient clarity so as to permit another practitioner to deliver it.

Examples of good objectives

1. Roxie will orally read any five page section of any third grade reader within 20 minutes with 95% comprehension at the verbal request of the teacher.
2. While looking at 5 different geometric shapes, Linda will match the shapes by means of a duplicate set, within one minute, with no errors.
3. After observing the arrangement of five toy ranch animals for 5 seconds, the animals will be removed and Lois will replace the animals in the same sequential order within 30 seconds with 100% accuracy.
4. Given 50 four-word sets, three words in each set beginning with the same consonant, Bertha will identify the odd word in 45 out of 50 cases within five minutes.
5. Ann will arrange in alphabetical order twenty-six 3 x 5 cards, each with a different lower-case manuscript letter on it, within 5 minutes with 100% accuracy.
6. Jody will correctly solve, in writing, any 25 single-digit multiplication problems in the form ($a \times b = ?$) within 5 minutes with 60% accuracy.
7. Cindy will read at grade level by the end of the school year, as judged by the Wide Range Achievement Test.
8. Cheryl will be seated at her desk for any randomly selected 10-minute period during any randomly selected day for the rest of the school year.

Examples of poor objectives

1. At the end of six months Joel will be able to read.
2. After using behavior modification techniques Harlan will not talk so loudly in class.
3. After four hours of instruction Stan will be able to make change.
4. By the end of the school year John will be able to write better.
5. Because of parent-child counseling Velma will have good social manners.

The only purpose of an objective is to increase the systematic nature of an intervention and thus increase the likelihood of intervention success. Therefore, objectives should serve the intervention process, and should be simple, clear, and streamlined. In essence, an objective should be helpful to the practitioner because of its common sense and clarity, rather than a hindrance because of its complexity.

SELECTED REFERENCES

Mager, R., *Preparing Instructional Objectives,* (2nd ed.) California: Fearon, 1975.

Chapter 18

Analysis of the Ingredients of a Good Objective

A good objective involves up to five essential ingredients: (1) performance-based terms, (2) the important conditions, (3) the criteria of acceptable performance, which include time, (4) accuracy, and (5) difficulty level. This chapter presents an analysis and explanation of these ingredients.

Performance-based terms

A good behavioral-instructional objective identifies in performance-based terms what the subject will be doing when demonstrating the achievement of the objective. The key to the successful use of this ingredient is the careful identification of the performance basis of the terminal behavior, a situation which should result in the terminal behavior being directly observable and thus measurable. This usually means rendering a physical description of the terminal behavior by action-observable verbs, as opposed to action-ambiguous verbs. As an illustration, the following two lists contain examples of action verbs which are directly observable and action verbs which are ambiguous and therefore not directly observable.

Action verbs: observable
To underline	To repeat orally
To circle	To point to
To draw a line through	To list
To walk	

Action verbs: ambiguous
To understand	To know
To appreciate	To enjoy
To have faith in	To find out

Examples

The first example identified below represents an objective which employs clear, observable, and measurable performance-based terms. The second example represents an objective which employs ambiguous performance-based terms.

Good objective:
Upon request, Norm *will verbalize his telephone number in correct sequential order* within 30 seconds.
Poor objective:
Upon request, Norm *will demonstrate* his understanding of his telephone number within 30 seconds.

Important conditions

A good behavioral-instructional objective identifies the important conditions associated with the way the subject must meet the objective. The key to the successful use of this ingredient is the identification of the who, where, and what of the terminal behavior. The practitioner should determine who will present the stimulus which is designed to evoke the desired behavior; where the objective will be met; and what materials will be used by the learner. Nevertheless, it is important not to clog an objective with unnecessary important conditions.

Examples

Who	Where
teacher given cue	in the order center
cue from the chalkboard	in Terry's seat
cue from a recording	in a group setting
cue from flash cards	

What
from the text book
using pencil and paper
using felt numbers

Examples
Good objective:
Given a traffic light model, and upon *teacher request*, Linda will correctly point to and name the three colors of the light within one minute.
Poor objective:
Linda will know the colors of a traffic light.

Criteria of acceptable performance: time

A good behavioral-instructional objective identifies the criteria that are to serve as evidence of the successful achievement of the objective. These criteria are usually expressed in the form of time, accuracy, and/or difficulty level, and are identified as criteria of acceptable performance. These criteria serve to evaluate the success of an intervention and form one of the major accountability bases of the management model.

Although it is essential to include criteria of acceptable performance in behavioral-instructional objectives, it is equally essential to include only those criteria that are relevant to the objective. Thus, it is not necessary to always use all three of the criteria, but rather only those that are important to the objective.

The first criteria of acceptable performance is that of time. The time criterion identifies the length of time after a stimulus has been presented within which the subject must perform the objective (for example, within 5 minutes after the presentation of the worksheet). The reader should distinguish this time criterion from the length of time necessary to learn the behavior in order to perform the objective (for example, "By the end of the semester, Ann will..."). Although the second kind of time requirement may be used in an objective, it is not essential to the criteria of acceptable performance concept and we do not recommend its use. The first kind of time criterion is essential, and should be used whenever relevant to the objective.

Examples
    Stevie will solve the arithmetic problem within 10 minutes of presentation.
    Audrey will be quiet for 15 minutes.
    Tony will run the 40-yard dash in 5 seconds.

Criteria of acceptable performance: accuracy

The second criteria of acceptable performance is that of accuracy. The accuracy criterion identifies the number or percentage of correct responses which will be accepted as evidence of having achieved the objective.

When using the accuracy criterion with instructional objectives, it is meaningful to represent that accuracy by a percentage rather than a frequency figure. For example, "John was able to answer 50% of the questions correctly," rather than "John was able to answer 5 of the 10 questions correctly." The use of a percent figure makes it unnecessary to control the number of task-items presented; for example, if 50% correct were the accuracy criterion, that criterion could be achieved by 5 correct out of 10, 10 correct out of 20, etc. The use of a percent figure makes it possible to directly compare the accuracy results of different objectives; for example, an 80% correct figure can be directly compared with the accuracy results of any other percentage-based objective.

It is equally desirable to use the percent method of reporting accuracy relative to behavioral objectives. However, many behavioral objectives are not compatible with a percentage computation and thus a frequency method for reporting accuracy becomes necessary. For example, rather than saying "Lois will remain in her seat 50% of the time," it would be better to state, "Lois will be out of her seat only three times without permission during any randomly selected 30-minute period of time." And, rather than, "Peg will not speak out with 75% accuracy," it would be better to state, "Peg will not speak without permission more than two times during a given reading class."

Objectives should be streamlined by using only those ingredients that are essential to the clear execution of those objectives. Thus, the accuracy criterion should not be used unless it is relevant to the objective. As an example, the following accuracy criterion, as represented by the percent figure, is not meaningful to the objective, and therefore should not have been included: "Carol will not strike any of her classmates within one week with 100% accuracy."

The accuracy criterion of an objective should be in relation to the problem-solving ability of the subject. This is to say that a 100% accuracy figure may not be realistic for a given subject, whereas a 30% or 60% accuracy figure might be. In such a case, the realistic rather than the maximal figure should be used.

Criteria of acceptable performance: difficulty level

The difficulty level criterion is more appropriate for use with instructional objectives than behavioral objectives. This criterion usually refers to the difficulty level of the instructional materials that are identified in the objective. This criterion represents another means of pinpointing terminal behavior, which in turn increases the success likelihood of the intervention. As with all ingredients, the difficulty level criterion should be used only when it is relevant to the objective.

Examples
> from a second grade basal reader
> the following list of first grade words
> using the Dolch word list
> by means of two-digit addition problems

As an illustration of the appropriate use of the difficulty level criterion, the following objective is presented twice, once with the difficulty level appropriately included, and then again with the difficulty level inappropriately excluded.

Good objective:
Sue will orally read the first 15 pages of the *third grade basal reader* within 10 minutes with 80% comprehension.

Poor objective:
Sue will orally read a 15-page passage within 10 minutes with 80% comprehension.

Summary

Behavioral-instructional objectives are designed to facilitate an intervention by identifying the direction of that intervention. Objectives should work for, not against, the practitioner. Objectives should be as clear, simple, and streamlined as possible, and ingredients should be used only when their inclusion is relevant to the particular objective.

Exercises

The following section is devoted to behavioral-instructional objective exercises in which the reader is encouraged to engage for the purpose of developing skills relative to the mechanics of using objectives.

A-1: Upon verbal request from the teacher, Jennie will correctly name the two colors of a stop sign.

The essential criterion that is missing is time. The objective does not state how long Jennie will be given to name the two colors.

If you were able to identify the missing criterion, go to B-1; if not, reread the previous time criterion section, then read A-2.

A-2: Upon verbal request from the teacher, Emy Lu will correctly orally spell the words house, cart, and bear.

The essential criterion that is missing is time. The objective does not state how long Emy Lu will be given to spell the three words.

If you were able to identify the missing criterion, go to B-1; if not, reread the previous time section, then read B-1.

B-1: After listening to the record at the listening center, Eileen will understand each word on the record within 20 seconds with 100% acucracy.

The essential criterion that is missing is performance-based terms. The word understand is an ambiguous word which is subject to a variety of interpretations. A better way to express the terminal behavior might be:...Eileen will repeat each word outloud...

If you were able to identify the missing criterion, go to C-1; if not, reread the previous performance-based terms section, then read B-2.

B-2: Dan will participate during the Wednesday morning class discussion.

The essential criterion that is missing is performance-based terms. The word participate is ambiguous and could have several meanings, from body movement to verbal response.

If you were able to identify the missing criterion, go to C-1; if not, reread the previous performance-based terms section, then read C-1.

C-1: Upon verbal request from the teacher, Jane will assemble a puzzle within 3 minutes with 100% accuracy.

The essential criterion that is missing is difficulty level. The objective does not state the size or number of pieces, and thus there is no indication of the terminal behavior difficulty level.

If you were able to identify the missing criterion, go to D-1; if not, reread the previous difficulty level section, then read C-2.

C-2: Upon request, Marilyn will read aloud the first paragraph of a book within 3 minutes with no pronunciation errors.

The essential criterion that is missing is difficulty level. The objective does not state the grade level and type of book.

If you were able to identify the missing criterion, go to D-1; if not, reread the previous difficulty level section, then read D-1.

D-1: Upon request, Janice will write the numbers 1 through 10 with a black crayon on wide-lined paper within 2 minutes.

The essential criterion that is missing is accuracy. The objective does not state the level of acceptable performance (e.g., legibility, within the lines, etc.).

If you were able to identify the missing criterion,

go to E-1; if not, reread the previous accuracy section, then read D-2.

D-2: Given a traffic light model, Emily will name the colors within two minutes.

The essential criterion that is missing is accuracy. The objective does not state the level of acceptable performance (e.g., assuming there are three colors, all three colors named correctly, two out of three, etc.).

If you were able to identify the missing criterion, go to E-1; if not, reread the previous accuracy section, then read E-1.

E-1: Judy will name the Dolch words within 5 minutes with no pronunciation errors.

The essential criterion that is missing is important conditons. The objective does not state which Dolch words are to be used, and how they are to be presented.

If you were able to identify the missing criterion, then you have successfully completed this section on behavioral-instructional objectives. If you were unable to identify the missing criterion, then reread the previous important conditions section, then read E-2.

E-2: Janet will not verbally swear during a given week, with 100% accuracy.

The essential criterion that is missing is important conditions. The objective does not state the location or area to which the objective is confined (i.e., home, school, classroom, etc.).

We hope you were able to identify the missing criterion; if not, reread the previous important conditions section.

Conclusion

Of the five essential ingredients, we regard important conditions as typically being the least valuable. Nevertheless, no ingredient should be included in an objective unless it is necessary to the easy understanding and deliverability of the objective. As an example, the use of 100% accuracy in the preceding Exercise E-2 is meaningless, serves only to clog the objective, and should not have been included.

Chapter 19

Behavioral-Instructional Objectives; 94-142; and IEPs

P.L. 94-142 requires an individualized education program for each handicapped child who is receiving special education. The IEP must include "a statement of annual goals, including short term instructional objectives," and appropriate objective criteria to determine "on at least an annual basis whether the short term objectives are being achieved."

Clearly, IEPs must contain short term instructional objectives, and they must be measurable. It is unclear whether the "annual goals" must be in objective form and measurable. We think they should be.

It is our interpretation of P.L. 94-142 that "annual goals" refers to a time period of 12 months, and that "short term instructional objectives" refers to the concept of monthly enabling objectives as well as the expectation of daily objectives. We further presume that "behavioral objectives" is included in the concept "instructional objectives." And, we argue that any and all IEP objectives should be in the style discussed in this part of the book, and above all, streamlined and measurable.

The three kinds of IEP objectives (annual, short term, and daily) can be systematically developed in the following two ways:

a. Based on the learning characteristic information acquired about the student (IQ, input, output, achievement, etc., discussed in Part II of this book), the student's educational progress during a preceding time period, and the progress the student *could* have made had programming been optimal, project forward the student's proficiency for each tool-subject involved by 12 months, and translate that proficiency into instructional-behavioral objective form; allow each projected objective to represent the annual goal for each tool subject to which it relates. Break down each annual objective into 12 roughly equal skill segments, and translate each into objective form; allow each of these 12 objectives to represent monthly short term objectives for each related tool subject. Lastly, break down the last monthly short term objective into 20 roughly equal skill segments and translate each into objective form; allow each of these 20 objectives to represent daily objectives.

b. Begin with the knowledge of the student's existing proficiency for each tool-subject involved. Translate each tool-subject proficiency into instructional-behavioral objective form; allow each objective to represent a daily objective for each tool-subject to which it relates. Project each daily objective forward by 20 days into a proficiency, and translate that proficiency into objective form; allow that objective to represent a monthly short term objective for each tool-subject involved. Lastly, project each tool-subject monthly objective forward by 12 months into a proficiency, and translate that proficiency into objective form; allow that objective to represent an annual goal for each tool-subject involved.

As mentioned above, objectives should be streamlined. In addition to developing original objectives as discussed in Chapter 18, several ways to streamline objectives are:

a. Use the coding system of a skill continua, such as the System Fore, to identify instructional objectives. The System Fore uses SLI numbers. If a student currently functions at SLI number 4.7.1, project where he reasonably should be in a month (e.g., 4.7.9) and use that figure as a monthly objective: e.g., within one month Ace will perform the 4.7.9 System Fore task within five minutes with less than three errors.

In addition to using the coding system to identify objectives, that same system may also be used to identify a meaningful and sequential task analysis, by allowing the numbered tasks between the student's current skill and the terminal skill to represent the sequential steps of the task analysis. Thus, the task analysis steps of the 4.7.9 objective for Ace would be: 4.7.2, 4.7.3, 4.7.4,—4.7.9

b. Use the coding system of the publisher's Scope and Sequence chart that relates to the textbook used for the paricular tool-subject: e.g., within one month Jane will accomplish task H-10 in the Houghton-Mifflin basic math series, within 10 minutes with no more than three errors.

c. Use achievement test grade-level scores: e.g., within a year Shannon will achieve a spelling grade level score of 4.1 on the Wide Range Achievement Test.

The above form of objective presumes that the student has been tested on the same instrument prior to the development of the objective.

d. Use the same teacher-made or commercial tool-subject test to measure pre-objective as well as post-objective proficiency: e.g., within one month, Jim will improve by 25% on Mrs. Jacobs' grooming test.

PART IV

THE THIRD COMPONENT OF THE
EDUCATION INTERVENTION AND MANAGEMENT MODEL:
Task Analysis

The management model operates to permit systematic presenting problem resolution. In addition to the acquisition of the necessary learner information and the establishment of behavioral-instructional objectives, problem resolution is facilitated by the application of the third model component, task analysis. A task analysis is developed for each behavioral-instructional objective, and represents the sequential steps through which a learner must progress to get from the observed behavior to the terminal behavior. A task analysis permits precision IEP intervention, and forms one of the three management model accountability bases.

Chapter 20

Task Analysis

Task analysis (Bateman, 1967) is defined as the identification of the sequential steps through which an individual must progress in order to get from the observed behavior (presenting problem) to the terminal behavior that is exprssed by the behavioral-instructional objective. Task analysis represents the process of breaking down an objective into its component parts and then arranging those component parts in a developmental sequence of first to last. Thus, task analysis is a process of breaking down into sequential steps what an individual must do to achieve an objective.

The management model operates by establishing a behavioral-instructional objective for each major intervention with a learning or behavior problem. For every objective, a task analysis is established. As with objectives, it is essential that a task analysis serve as an intervention asset rather than a liability. Thus, a task analysis, like an objective, should be as clear and simple as possible, and should not represent a theoretical exercise in deductive logic but rather a commonsense approach to the identification of the major sequential steps through which a subject must progress in order to get from where he is to where it is desirable for him to be.

Objectives and task analyses should serve the purpose of efficient intervention. The sequential steps of a task analysis are:

1. A task analysis should be simply and clearly stated.
2. It should relate only to the important steps through which the subject must progress.
3. It should be stated in such a commonsense way that another person could understand the task analysis sequence and actually deliver that sequence.
4. It should not be clogged with unnecessary words.
5. It should be sequentially arranged from beginning steps to terminal steps.
6. The sequential steps should not only be arranged from beginning to terminal steps but also there should be no major gaps in the arrangement of the sequenced steps. Many gaps or large gaps represent missing conceptual information without which the subject might not be able to sequentially progress from the observed to the terminal behavior.

Behavioral-instructional objectives form the basis of task analyses. As such, the two concepts complement each other. This usually means that a simple objective will involve a simple task analysis. On the other hand, a complex objective will usually involve a complex and often confusing task analysis. As a rule, we recommend the use of simple objectives in order to permit noncomplicated task analyses.

Behavioral-instructional objectives and task analyses are operationally similar in many respects: (1) They both provide systematic direction for an intervention. Whereas an objective identifies an overall intervention goal, the task analysis represents a breakdown of that goal into its important component parts and an arrangement of those parts into a beginning-to-end sequenced order. The adherence to that sequenced order provides the basis for intervention direction. (2) Objectives and task analyses provide the diagnostic-prescriptive teaching process with a foundation for precision intervention. Objectives provide the basic intervention-direction information as well as the criteria which will be accepted as evidence of intervention success. Task analyses provide a sequenced order of the component parts of the terminal behavior which, in conjunction with the necessary learner information, permit an identification of the intervention entry level. By means of the task analysis arrangement, the practitioner may select the component step at which the subject functions and begin the intervention process at that point, rather than fumble by trial and error to find that entry point. (3) Objectives and task analyses, along with baseline measurement, provide the diagnostic-prescriptive teaching process as well as IEPs with a built-in accountability system. Objectives should specify the criteria of acceptable performance.

These criteria indicate the point at which intervention success is achieved. By means of baseline measurement, and in relation to the sequenced task analysis steps and the objective-based criteria of acceptable performance, intervention progress may be measured either on a task analysis step-by-step basis or on an overall objective basis. Whichever method is elected, the result will provide an accounting of the intervention process which can be used to document IEP success and/or intervention effort.

Objectives and task analyses are dissimilar in many ways: (1) Although an objective can operate by itself, a task analysis is dependent on an objective for its origin and meaning and thus never exists independently of an objective. (2) Unlike an objective which has up to five specific ingredients that are essential for effective operation, a task analysis has no such specific ingredients. The only operational requirements of a task analysis are that the component steps be sequential and that the component part breakdown be sufficiently comprehensive so that no major conceptual gaps exist which could impede learning progress. (3) Unlike an objective, there is no absolute right or wrong way associated with the task analysis concept, except that the task analysis should naturally evolve from its objective, be sequential without major gaps, and commonsense in nature. There is, however, one qualification. Relative to theoretical task analyses, the first three sequential steps should probably involve: (1) the acuity adequacy of the various senses, particularly hearing and vision; (2) subject attention (for example, Mary Lou looking at the teacher); and (3) subject response (for example, Janis verbally responding to the teacher). Although these three task analysis steps are usually taken for granted, the reader should recognize that the learning process will be impeded if acuity, attention, and/or response functions are defective. However, objectives and task analyses should be practical in nature and should serve rather than hinder the intervention process. The first three steps of the theoretical task analysis sequence should be acknowledged only when the nature of the presenting problem involves acuity, attention, and/or response difficulty.

We have found the task analysis concept so important to intervention success that the following statement has evolved as a diagnostic-prescriptive teaching axiom: prescriptive teaching failure is most often due to: (1) gaps in the sequential task analysis steps; and/or (2) an inappropriate reinforcement schedule (which will be discussed in the chapters on behavior modification).

Although it is initially difficult to develop sequential task analyses, the necessary skill can be acquired with only a moderate amount of practice. In fact, we contend that master teachers intuitively engage in the process of objectives and task analyses. Diagnostic-prescriptive teaching involves the same intuitive process, only with greater systematization.

Enabling objectives

An enabling objective is a task analysis sequential step that has been upgraded to the status of a behavioral or instructional objective. Enabling objectives are usually appropriate only for complex task analyses and are designed to reduce the task analysis complexity by substituting behaviorally defined objectives for two or three appropriately spaced task analysis steps. By means of enabling objectives, it is possible to increase the specificity of the intervention direction.

Enabling objectives serve only to help with the task analysis process and their use is optional. If enabling objectives are used, they should be expressed in the form of behavioral or instructional objectives, and should therefore contain the ingredients essential to the operation of the objectives. Enabling objectives would be of little value, and therefore should not be used, with two kinds of task analyses: (1) simple task analyses, and (2) complex task analyses, each sequential step of which is associated with criteria of acceptable performance, with the expectation that the progress of each step will be measured. Nevertheless, enabling objectives provide a greater opportunity for intervention progress measurement and hence accountability.

The following instructional objective and task analysis represent an illustration of the enabling objective concept.

Debbie is nine years old, in the second grade, has a WISC Verbal IQ of 83 and Performance IQ of 42, and has moderate to severe visual discrimination and visual memory problems. Until recently, Debbie had been misdiagnosed as a trainable mental retardate.

Objective

Debbie will correctly name the words MAT, CAT,

and RAT within 15 seconds each after they are presented in upper-case form on separate flash cards.

Task analysis
1. Teacher points to the letter M. Teacher says the M sound several times.
2. Have Debbie point to the letter and say the M sound.
3. Have Debbie trace the letter M with her finger as she says the sound.
4. Enabling objective: Debbie will correctly identify the M letter and say the M sound within 15 seconds after being presented with five flash cards, each with a different upper-case letter on it, one of which contains the letter M
5. Repeat task analysis steps 1-4 for the letter A, then T.
6. Teacher says and writes the word MAT very slowly, sound by sound.
7. Have Debbie trace the MAT letters, saying the letter sounds as she does so.
8. Use a Language Master with a prepared MAT card. Let Debbie see and hear the word, and have her write the word while seeing and hearing it.
9. Give Debbie three flash cards, with M on one, A on another, and T on the third. Jumble the order, have Debbie arrange the flash cards to spell MAT, and say the word as she arranges the flash cards in the correct order.
10. Enabling objective: From a pool of ten scrambled flash cards with different upper-case letters, including the letters MAT, and within 15 seconds after presentation, Debbie will correctly arrange the letters to spell MAT and will correctly say the word.
11. Repeat the entire process for the word CAT, then RAT.
12. Objective.

SELECTED REFERENCES

Bateman, B. "Three Approaches to Diagnosis and Educational Planning for Children with Learning Disabilities." *Academic Therapy Quarterly*, 1967, *11*, 215–222.

Chapter 21

Sample Task Analysis

This chapter contains sample task analyses. The major ingredients of a task analysis are: (1) the inclusion of the important component parts of the objective, (2) the appropriate sequentialization of those component parts, and (3) simplicity and common sense. Other than the satisfaction of these three task analysis ingredients there is no right or wrong way to develop a task analysis. Thus, the character of task analyses will vary with the nature of the learner, the kind of presenting problem, and the complexity of the objective, and will be just as mechanical or humanistic, creative or rigid, and sophisticated or naive as the practitioner. For these reasons, the following task analysis samples do not represent right (as opposed to wrong) task analyses, but rather task analyses that reflect the character of the total environment in which they were developed.

Task analysis 1

The following task analysis represents one way of conceptualizing the sequenced component parts of auditory reading ability.

1. Adequacy of auditory acuity.
2. Awareness of sound versus no sound.
3. Direction of sound.
4. Auditory discrimination of sounds, from gross sounds to fine sounds.
5. Auditory storage memory.
6. Auditory sequential memory.
7. Rhythm and cadence of sounds.
8. Matching letter sounds.
9. Matching the real sounds of objects (e.g., car, train, etc.) with the pictures of those objects.
10. Sound-symbol association: i.e., matching the m, t, s, short i, and short a sound with their visual symbols.
11. Match words that begin with previously studied sounds with the picture of the object that the words represent.
12. Blending the studied sounds into words.
13. Develop word families (e.g., mat, pat, sat; map, man, mat; etc.).
14. Combining two vowels into one sound (e.g., b*oa*t, fl*ee*, etc.).
15. Consonant blends (e.g., *st*and, *pl*ace, etc.).
16. Use of experience chart.
17. Necessary phonic rules.
18. Simple sentences and paragraphs based on studied words and the above processes.
19. Basal reader.

Task analysis 2

The following task analysis represents one way of conceptualizing the sequenced component parts of visual reading ability.

1. Adequacy of visual acuity.
2. Visual storage memory.
3. Visual sequential memory.
4. Visual discrimination of gross objects (eg., ○, ⌂, △, +, □, etc.).
5. Visual discrimination of fine objects (e.g., ⊕, ⊕, ⊕, ⊕, ⊖, etc.).
6. Discrimination of objects, then words, then letters and numbers, on the basis of external outline (e.g., ship . . . shape; etc.).
7. Discrimination of objects, then words, then letters and numbers, on the basis of internal configuration (e.g., peg . . . pig; etc.).
8. Relationship between the printed symbol or word and the spoken symbol or word.
9. Match the printed word with the real object that the word describes.
10. Match the printed word with a picture of the object that the word describes.
11. Sight alphabet, initially with corresponding pictures.
12. Sight vocabulary, initially with corresponding pictures.
13. Blending letters into familiar words.
14. Syllabication, using familiar words.
15. Simple sentences and paragraphs based on the sight words studied.
16. Experience chart based on the sight words studied.
17. Basal reader.

Task analysis 3

The following task analysis represents one way of conceptualizing the sequenced component parts of pre-arithmetic ability.

1. Visual discrimination of geometric shapes and forms, then numbers.
2. Visual and auditory memory.
3. Visual-motor coordination.
4. Understanding the concepts of size (volume, height, and length).
5. Understanding the concept of one-to-one relationship.
6. Rote auditory counting (not comprehension).
7. Association between the auditory number-symbol and the related visual number-symbol.
8. Relationship between auditory and visual number-symbols and the experience of those number-symbols (meaning).
9. Alignment of numbers (e.g., top to bottom, right to left, etc.).
10. Visualizing then counting objects in a group; then counting objects in various groups.
11. Computation signs ($+$, $-$, $\times$, $\div$).
12. Actual arithmetic computation.

Task analysis 4

The following task analysis represents one way of conceptualizing the sequenced component parts of handwriting ability.

1. Gross, then fine, motor coordination training (jumping, throwing, calisthenics, eye-tracking exercises, pegboard and puzzle activities, cutting, bead stringing, etc.).
2. Random scribbling with chalk on blackboard.
3. Scribbling, but with increasingly reduced blackboard space available for scribbling (make gradually decreasing blackboard boundaries).
4. Teach directionality (up-down, left-right) with chalk on blackboard.
5. Teach eye-hand coordination imitation by means of large then small, random then controlled, chalk-blackboard and finger paint activity.
6. Regarding No. 5, vary speed of activity and imitation, from slow at first to fast.
7. Using stencils, make various letter-related and number-related geometric forms. Name the forms (triangle, square, etc.).
8. Using a stencil, make a straight line. Examine the line. Have subject reproduce the line with finger in the air. Guide subject's hand if necessary.
9. Using a raised-surface (sandpaper, crayon, felt, etc.), cut out a straight line. Trace it slowly with finger.
10. Make a straight line with pencil on paper. Guide subject's hand if necessary. Trace with finger. Continue until subject can make straight line with pencil on paper.
11. Ditto 8, 9, and 10 for a circle, using tracing and raised-surface techniques when needed.
12. Use arrows and/or verbal directions to help with the movement patterns (i.e., up, down, ↑ , ↓ , ↙ , etc.).
13. Use exercises to reinforce line and circle drawing ability (e.g., dot-to-dot figures, tracing over onion-skin paper, etc.).
14. Identify simple one or two-part lower-case manuscript letters (b, d, p, o, c, h, i, t, etc.). Break down each letter into its basic line and circle components. Teach each letter by making the line and circle components separately, then blend them into the letter (e.g., the b is composed of a line, | , and a half-circle,)).
15. Repeat No. 14 for numbers.
16. Use learned letters to make written words, then sentences and paragraphs.
17. Teach the subject to read the letters, numbers, and words that he is learning to write.
18. Present simple oral words, then sentences, and have the subject write the words.

Task analysis 5

The following is an example of a long-term instructional objective and task analysis relative to a third grade student without prereading (or prespelling) skills. Until recently, Chris had been hidden from the outside world by seclusive parents.

Objective

Chris will orally read any five-page section of a second grade reader within 20 minutes with 65% comprehension.

Task Analysis
1. Attention.
2. Response.
3. Auditory and visual acuity.
4. Gross visual discrimination; use large objects of different shapes and sizes: □ , △ , ○ .
5. Fine visual discrimination; use shapes and symbols common in the alphabet: o|, |o, ō, o̱ .
6. Sound discrimination (gross environmental sounds).
7. Sound discrimination (fine verbal differences).
8. Explain and practice left-right sequencing, using symbols in Nos. 4 and 5.
9. Teach letter names.
10. Teach the main sound associated with each letter.
11. Combine sounds into familiar words (blending).
12. Introduce word families that variously have the same initial, middle, and terminal sound.
13. Sight word vocabulary, with the Dolch List as a guide.
14. Use experience chart words to enhance sight word vocabulary.
15. Introduce capital letters.
16. Explain and practice use of capitals with words from experience chart and sight word vocabulary.
17. Group words into phrases; use experience chart.
18. Group phrases into sentences, then paragraphs.
19. Start reading in first grade reader; then second grade.
20. Objective

Task analysis 6

This is an example of a long-term instructional objective and task analysis relative to a fourth grade nonreader.

Objective

Jocelyn will orally read a 500-word story from a third grade book of her choice with 80% comprehension within ten minutes.

Task Analysis
1. Attending.
2. Responding.
3. Auditory and visual acuity.
4. Auditory and visual memory.
5. Discriminating dissimilar then similar geometric objects.
6. Discriminating dissimilar then similar digits, then letters.
7. Visually finding identical letters at the beginning of written words.
8. Visually finding identical letters at the end of written words.
9. Gross sound discrimination.
10. Fine sound discrimination, including letter sounds.
11. Teach a few letter names (for example, m, t, s, i, a, p).
12. Letter-sound association.
13. Concept of left-to-right sequence.
14. Sound blending.
15. Word families.
16. Identifying small printed words.
17. Finding given letters in words.
18. Word-picture association.
19. Sight word vocabulary.
20. Experience charts.
21. Building and reading short sentences.
22. Reading short stories and answering simple questions about them.
23. First, then second grade stories and questions.
24. Third grade stories for enjoyment and practice.
25. Test for objective.

Task analysis 7

The following is an example of a short but deceptively complex instructional objective and task analysis relative to a second grade student with a moderate-to-severe visual discrimination problem.

Objective

Kathy will correctly order and repeat the letter sounds of the alphabet within five minutes when given twenty-six scrambled 3 x 5 cards each with a different lower-case manuscript letter on it.

Task Analysis
1. Sensory acuity.
2. Gross visual discrimination: e.g., discriminate between curved and straight lines; point to the one that is different: ○ ○ — ○ ; etc.
3. Fine visual discrimination: e.g., discriminate between variations of circles and lines; find the two that are alike: ⊂ , ⊃ , ○ , ⊃ , — , ∪ , | ; etc.
4. Visually discriminate between different letters of the alphabet that are dissimilar in shape.
5. Visually discriminate between letters that are similar in shape.

6. Learn the letter names in sequence of three (A-C, D-F, etc.).
7. Learn the sound-symbol relationships.
8. Test for objective.

Task analysis 8

This is an example of a long-term behavioral objective and task analysis. Velma is six years old and has a moderate-to-severe auditory discrimination problem.

Objective

Velma will correctly comply with a two-word spoken direction within one minute.

Task analysis
1. Attention.
2. Response.
3. Sensory acuity.
4. Sound versus no sound.
5. Localization of sound.
6. Discrimination of gross, then fine, nonverbal sounds.
7. Discrimination of gross, then fine, verbal nonword sounds; then words.
8. Relationship between selected action verbs and their experience.
9. Perform one-word direction (e.g., "look").
10. Perform two-word direction (e.g., "sit down").
11. Objective.

Task analysis 9

This is an example of a thorough instructional objective and task analysis. Dianne is nine years old, has an IQ of 95, is in the third grade, and has preschool tool-subject skills. The reader will recognize the long-term nature of the objective and the tremendous amount of detailed work involved with the execution of the task analysis. Some enabling objectives would have been helpful. This is an ambitious objective and task analysis.

Objective

Dianne will demonstrate a sight word vocabulary of 100 words by naming each word within three seconds per card when successively shown a set of 100 3 x 5 flash cards each containing a different word selected from second grade basal readers. Dianne will achieve the objective with 75% accuracy in a one-to-one relationship with the teacher.

Task analysis
1. Attention.
2. Response.
3. Sensory acuity (auditory and visual).
4. Memory (visual storage, and visual sequential).
5. Visual discrimination of gross, then fine, objects.
6. Discriminate objects, then words, using external outline; gross, then fine.
7. Discriminate objects, then words, using internal outline; gross, then fine.
8. Relationship between printed symbol and spoken word.
9. Match concrete nouns with actual objects and/or experience; then verbs; then adjectives; then prepositions.
10. Match nouns, then verbs, then adjectives, then prepositions, with corresponding pictures.
11. Teach sight-alphabet with pictures.
12. Teach sight-word vocabulary with pictures.
13. Sight word vocabulary without pictures.
14. Test for objective.

Task analysis 10

The following is an example of a behavioral objective and a task analysis that are clearly stated, but the execution of which will take a great deal of time, and will depend on the appropriate use of behavior modification strategies.

Randy is eight years old and habitually refuses to leave home and attend school. He says he is scared.

Objective

Randy will attend school and sit at his desk for 30 minutes without attempting to leave.

Task analysis
1. Stepping outside the home upon a particular cue.
2. Walking halfway to school with the practitioner.
3. Entering the main school door with the practitioner.
4. Standing outside the classroom door with the practitioner.
5. Speaking to a friend who is inside the classroom, with the practitioner.
6. Taking one step into the classroom with the friend.

7. Randy standing by his desk with the friend standing alongside.
8. Randy sitting at his desk with the friend standing alongside.
9. Sitting at the desk for 5 minutes without the friend.
10. Increase the desk-sitting behavior until the 30 minute objective is met.

Task analysis 11

The following provides an example of a deceptively involved behavioral objective and task analysis. Joe is seven years old and is unable to identify body parts (and even himself in a mirror) due to body-image problems.

Objective

Joe will correctly assemble a jig-saw puzzle of a man within three minutes during any class period.

Task Analysis
1. Adequate auditory and visual acuity.
2. Attending (Joe looks at the teacher when teacher speaks).
3. Responding (Joe answers questions).
4. Visual-motor coordination ability sufficient to visually imitate, then independently manipulate, puzzle pieces.
5. Teacher points to and names parts of own body; Joe imitates.
6. Teacher names parts of Joe's body reflected in full length mirror; Joe imitates.
7. Joe names the parts of his body touched by the teacher while Joe is blindfolded.
8. Teacher traces Joe's body outline on paper; Joe draws in and names the parts.
9. Teacher cuts body outline into two parts and Joe puts the parts together; teacher cuts body outline into thirds, fourths, etc., after which Joe puts parts together.
10. Repeat No. 9 using a puzzle.
11. Objective.

Task analysis 12

The following task analysis illustrates the use of reverse chaining. The objective involves teaching Donna to correctly complete a six-piece body-part puzzle.

Task analysis
1. Show Donna the completed puzzle.
2. Remove one piece of the puzzle (head), and have Donna replace that piece.
3. Remove two pieces of the puzzle (head and torso), and have Donna replace those pieces.
4. Remove three pieces of the puzzle (head, torso, and one arm), and have Donna replace those pieces.
5. Remove four pieces of the puzzle (head, torso, and two arms), and have Donna replace those pieces.
6. Remove five pieces of the puzzle (head, torso, two arms, and one leg), and have Donna replace those pieces.
7. Remove all six pieces of the puzzle, and have Donna replace those pieces, at which time the puzzle has been correctly assembled by means of reverse chaining.

Task analysis 13

The following task analysis illustrates another use of reverse chaining. The objective involves teaching Jud to print his name.

Task analysis
1. Present a raised-surface manuscript model of the name Jud.
2. Have Jud trace the model with his fingers.
3. Have Jud copy the model by means of pencil-paper.
4. Present the model, and below it also present the manuscript letters Jud . Have Jud write his name by copying the letters with pencil-paper, completing the dotted line in so doing.
5. Present the incomplete manuscript name in the following sequence, and in each case have Jud write his full name, completing the dotted line in so doing.
   a. Ju l
   b. Ju ¦
   c. Ju
   d. J u
   e. J
   f. J
   g. J
   h. J
   i. Print the entire name.

PART V

THE FOURTH COMPONENT OF THE EDUCATION INTERVENTION AND MANAGEMENT MODEL:
Individualization and Success

This management model component provides information necessary for the mechanical operation of the diagnostic-prescriptive teaching classroom, all of which is designed to increase the likelihood of IEP-IIP success.

Chapter 22

Prescriptive Teaching and Classroom Mechanics

Diagnostic-prescriptive teaching represents a self-contained system of learning and behavior-problem intervention strategies. The system is appropriate for anyone who chooses to master the strategies involved, and is applicable to any learning or behavior problem irrespective of where it occurs. But since the system is self-contained, it would be difficult for an individual not trained in that system to carry out the mechanics that are uniquely applicable to the education classroom. This section presents those mechanics.

1. Special education philosophy

Philosophically, special education should not exist in a vacuum. We contend there is no reason for special education unless, by means of that special education, the student is better equipped to survive, both during as well as after the school years, in our socially complex and work-oriented society. We further contend that whatever educationally happens to the special education student should result in greater coping skills, as those skills relate to practical kinds of survival ability. We see no justification for the teaching of tool subjects in isolation. Rather, we see an immense justification for teaching tool subjects as coping skills relative to equipping the student by means of those skills for economic efficiency, civic responsibility, social competence, and self realization.

2. The Sequential Steps of Diagnostic-Prescriptive Teaching and Programming

The sequence of D-PT activities is the same for any student, irrespective of educational placement or special education category. That sequence involves:
1. Determine the age and school grade-level placement of the students, and the presenting problems.
2. Conduct formal and/or informal psycho-educational assessment of the students relative to learning-behavior strengths and weaknesses.
3. Identify a learning contract-schedule system.
4. Based on the psycho-educational assessment, and in relation to the daily class schedule, determine a curriculum match for each subject.
5. For each subject, develop long and short term behavioral/instructional objectives and task analyses, including curriculum materials based on #4 above.
6. Select X-work and independent student activities.
7. Select a classroom engineering design, and student grouping procedure.
8. Select a systematic as well as random behavior management program.
9. Identify the baseline measurement system.
10. Develop an overall behavioral and instructional accountability system.
11. Using the above and other germane information, develop and execute an IEP and IIP for each special education student.

3. Individualized Education Program (IEP)

P.L. 94-142 requires that an IEP be developed for each handicapped student. What follows is a sequential D-PT format regarding the development of IEPs.
   a. Student's name, chronological age, and grade in school.
   b. Precise presenting problem of the student.
   c. Summary, in grid form, of learning characteristics: (physical characteristics; attention factors; input, memory, meaning, output strengths and weaknesses; obtained and potential IQ; tool-subject achievement levels; emotional factors; reinforcers; and self structuring capability).
   d. Curriculum match statement (CA, IQ, achievement level relative to each tool subject, learning modalities, self structuring, etc.)
   e. Long/short term instructional/behavioral ob-

jectives for each tool-subject and target behavior.
f. Learning contract/schedule, to include curriculum materials and X-work relative to #e above.
g. Grouping and classroom engineering.
h. Systematic behavior management program:
   a. Management strategies
   b. Reinforcers
   c. Punishers
   d. Schedule
   e. Behavior grid
i. Graphic representation of daily baseline measurement, and monthly accountability system, relative to e, f, and h above.
j. Least restrictive educational environment recommendation.
k. Beginning and ending dates.
l. Related services.
m. Environmental considerations.
n. Criteria for annual evaluation of objectives in #e above.
   a. Time
   b. Method of evaluation
o. Signatures of parents and committee members indicating approval or dissent.

4. Curriculum Match

Successful IEP development and prescriptive programming involve matching curriculum materials to the student's learning-behavior strengths and weaknesses. Curriculum match criteria are:
a. The student's chronological age and interest level.
b. The student's significant physical characteristics.
c. Attention span strengths and weaknesses.
d. Input, memory, meaning, and output strengths and weaknesses.
e. Tool-subject grade level.
f. The difference between the student's obtained and potential IQ.
g. The student's self-structuring capability.
h. The tool-subjects for which curriculum materials are needed.

The curriculum match concept should translate into a brief written statement for each student, which should be part of each IEP, and which should serve as a specific guide to the efficient selection of the best curriculum materials for each tool-subject for each student.

The curriculum match statement does not include reference to specific curriculum materials; rather, only to the information necessary to match the student's learning strengths and weaknesses with the curriculum material modalities of input, output, grade level, IQ, etc.

A good curriculum match statement should permit the teacher, a curriculum materials librarian, an ERC facilitator, etc., to quickly select the specific curriculum materials which match the student's learning strengths and weaknesses.

Regarding the curriculum match criteria:

1. The probability of eductional success is increased if a student's *chronological age* and *interest level* are matched with those same characteristics of prospective curriculum materials.
2. Some physical characteristics which need to be matched to the specifications of curriculum materials are: hyperactivity; poor fine and/or gross motor coordination; poor pincer grasp; seizures; bi-lateral problem; fatigue level; allergies; needs medicine at noon; etc.
3. Many handicapped students have differential *attention span* capability. Some students attend better and/or longer to auditory stimuli, or visual stimuli, or haptic stimuli, or a combination. In order to increase the success factor, it is important to match the student's attention span strengths and weaknesses with the attention span requirements of available or prospective curriculum materials.
4. Most handicapped students have differential *input, memory, meaning,* and output strengths and weaknesses. A student may have good auditory input, poor visual input, good verbal output, and poor graphic output. Or, a group of students may have good visual processing and poor auditory processing abilities. Or a student might have normal learning processes except for a moderate visual sequential memory problem. Whatever the situation, it is important to match each student's input, memory, meaning, and output strengths and weaknesses with those same modality requirements of available or prospective curriculum materials.
5. It is obviously critical to match a student's *grade level* ability with the grade level requirement of prospective curriculum materials.

6. A match of a student's *IQ* with the intellectual level of prospective materials increases the likelihood of educational success. Similarly, by distinguishing between a student's obtained IQ (e.g., 79) and potential IQ (e.g., 112), and matching the intellectual level of prospective materials with an IQ somewhere between the two (i.e., 79 and 112), the forecast of success is increased.
7. *Self structuring* means capable of independent work. It is important to educational success to match a non-self structuring student with curriculum materials which involve built-in structure (either people and/or environment), as well as the converse.
8. It is obvious that prospective curriculum materials must be matched to the tool subjects being taught: i.e., reading, language, career education, body image, etc.

An example of a curriculum match statement is: Ken (CA 10) needs materials which emphasize auditory input and graphic output, minimize reliance on visual memory, minimize visual attention span (no more than five minutes), average IQ, self structuring, which relate to a 10 year old interest level but beginning second grade reading and math, and beginning third grade language skills, and which have a career education component.

5. Learning Contract-Schedule

A learning contract-schedule is a prominent D-PT strategy which can be used irrespective of the kind of student or educational placement. Contracts are written, define the Daily Class Schedule (left column of Table XVII), identify the student grouping (fourth column from left of Table XVII), identify the daily objectives for each subject taught (fifth column from left Table XVII), and provide baseline measurement as to whether the daily objectives for each tool-subject taught were successfully completed (far right column Table XVII).

Learning contracts are the daily vehicle by which to conduct IEPs (IIPs), and as such form one of the most important components of the Diagnostic-Prescriptive Teaching and Programming System. We recommend that each student receive a new learning contract daily, at the beginning of the school day; that each learning contract evolve from the parent IEP; that the teacher or aide make a checkmark in the completion column for each objective successfully completed at the end of each tool-subject period; that the number of instructional checkmarks be added each day and transferred daily to a monthly accountability grid, and thereby serve as an easy but reliable baseline measurement indication of instructional progress; and that the daily learning contracts for each student be saved for the entire school year, in order to provide a specific reference for parents, administrators, etc., regarding previous instructional objectives, progress, etc.

The concept of baseline measurement is presented in Part VI of this book. The strategies discussed are very detailed, and are excellent for the measurement of highly specific behavior. But they also take a lot of time. We think the baseline measurement system provided by the completion column of the learning contract represents an easy and practical compromise between the detailed and precise measurement of highly specific behavior (e.g., symbol reversals), and no measurement at all. Although the contract completion and monthly accountability grid form of baseline measurement lose information in the sense that specific instances of, for example, symbol reversals are not recorded, it is easy to find that information by returning to the particular daily learning contract and examining the daily objective(s) which related to, for example, symbol reversals. Since all objectives should be measurable by means of success criteria (time, accuracy, and/or difficulty level), the necessary frequency and/or response-quality information should be thereby available.

Table XVII presents two sample learning contract-schedules; the first relates to elementary education, and the second to secondary education.

Name _____

Date _____

Table XVII

LEARNING CONTRACT/SCHEDULE

TIME	TASK NO.	SUBJECT	CENTER	ASSIGNMENT	COMPLETED
8:30	1	Pow Wow			
8:45	2	Reading			
9:30	3	alternate Career Ed/Body Image			
10:00	4	Spelling-Handwriting			
10:30	5	Recess			
10:40	6	Language			
11:25	7	alternate Art/Music			
12:00	8	Lunch			
1:00	9	Order Task			
1:10	10	Math			
1:50	11	alternate Auditory Remediation/ Visual Remediation			
2:20	12	Recess			
2:30	13	Life Experience			
3:00	14	Charting/Dismissal			

Name _____

Date _____

Table XVII

LEARNING CONTRACT/SCHEDULE

TIME	TASK NO.	SUBJECT	CENTER	ASSIGNMENT	COMPLETED
8:30	1	Goal Conference			
8:45-9:25	2	Consumer Math (life survival skills			
9:30-9:55	3	Body Image			
10:00-10:40	4	Consumer Reading (life survival skills)			
10:45-11:25	5	PE			
11:30-12:00	6	Consumer Language (life survival skills)			
12:00-1:00	7	Lunch			
** 1:00-1:40	8	Career Education			
1:45-2:20	9	Alternate Science/Music/Art/Social Studies			
2:25-3:00	10	Life Survival Skills (Citizenship, getting along, health, etc.)			
3:00	11	Goal Conference			
3:15	12	Dismissal			

**On-the-job training for 10th-12th graders.

231

6. Skill Continua

The concept of skill continua represents a recent innovation regarding commercial curriculum materials. The concept is similar to that of "scope and sequence", and involves targeting on a major tool-subject (so far, primarily reading, mathematics, language, and self-help skills), identifying the major components of each target tool-subject, breaking down each component into its various detailed parts, and then sequencing those parts from first to last into a task analysis of steps necessary for individuals to get from non-performance regarding the target tool-subject to the terminal skill.

The D-PT process makes heavy use of skill continua, primarily because they represent highly refined task analyses of tool-subjects, and therefore it is unnecessary to reinvent the wheel relative to deciding what precise tool-subject skill comes next for a particular student, student entry level, etc. Also, since the sequential steps of most skill continua are numbered, it is easy and convenient to use the skill continua numbers as long and short term objectives for IEPs or general prescriptive programs, assuming that success criteria are added to the numbers, and the student's entry level or current performance level regarding the skill contiua is known.

Two of the skill continua which we most frequently use are:

a. *System FORE*. FOREWORKS, P.O. Box 9747, North Hollywood, California 91609. System FORE includes Skill Continua in language, reading, and math for ages 2-18. This is a developmental, sequenced, criterion based, individualized, diagnostic and support system in reading, math, and language, with cross references to specific teaching materials relative to basic skill tasks in these disciplines.

b. *Fountain Valley Teacher Support System in Reading and Math*. Richard L. Zweig, Associates, Inc., 1711 McGaw Ave., Irvine, California 92714. This is a K-6, criterion based, individualized, sequenced, diagnostic and support system in reading and math, with cross references to specific instructional materials for each skill in the developmental sequence.

7. Accountability Grid

Educational accountability is a concept which not only is highly desirable, but which is now required by P.L. 94-142 (IEPs must include "Appropriate objective criteria and evaluation procedures and schedules for determining, on at least an annual basis, whether the short term instructional objectives are being achieved."

The D-PT accountability system involves the use of the monthly accountability grid (Table XVIII), in relation to instructional baseline measurement information from the "completion" column of the learning contracts (P. 230), and in relation to behavioral baseline measurement information from the checkmark grid (Table XXX, P. 321).

Daily instructional baseline measurement information is collected by means of the learning contract "completion" column. Also, daily behavioral baseline measurement information is collected by means of the checkmark grid. Both sets of information are in the form of checkmarks or tallies. At the end of each school day, the teacher, aide, and/or involved student counts the number of instructional and behavioral checkmarks, and separately enters them on the accountability grid, by means of dots, in the appropriate day column.

An accountability grid should be available for each student for every month. It is easy and simple to count checkmarks and enter the data into the grid. The grids for all students for the current month should be visually displayed in the classroom, for immediate feedback purposes as well as peer reinforcement. A completed grid quickly reveals the instructional and behavioral progress achieved by each student during that month.

It is possible to combine instructional and behavioral checkmarks in the same grid day—column by color coding: red for instructional and blue for behavioral. By connecting the dots with straight lines, a profile will result. Should the profile reveal lack of progress, or regression, a reassessment of the behavior management program and/or the task analysis difficulty level is necessary.

In conjunction with learning contracts, the monthly accountability grids should be saved, and included in the student's folder for future parent, administrator, IEP, staffing committee, etc., accountability needs.

Table XVIII

Accountability Grid

8. Contingency Contracts

Contingency contracts are a behavior management technique, and represent a humorous way by which to increase student motivation while at the same time specifying behavioral contingencies. The contracts should be signed by the people involved, and may be used whenever a high-interest formal motivation technique is needed relative to target behavior.

Table XIX presents sample contingency contracts.

9. Learning Circuit Model

The learning circuit model identifies the essential learning characteristics by which information is received, processed, and expressed. The model is applicable to anyone, without regard to educational label or placement. Should a mild through severe problem with one or more of the model concepts exist, a learning difficulty could result (for example, an auditory sequential memory problem could cause phonic reading difficulty). Should the problem be caused by a central nervous system dysfunction, a learning disability could result.

The learning circuit model is a prominent D-PT concept. A basic D-PT assumption is that most behavior is caused. As such, the efficient remediation of behavior or learning problems is contingent on identifying the cause of those problems. When the cause is known, the treatment becomes apparent. When the specific treatment for a particular cause is known, the success prognosis is dramatically increased.

To illustrate: a child has a severe reading problem, which is caused by father-child stress; the stress creates auditory and visual recall memory difficulty, which results in the reading problem. The cause is stress; the memory and reading problems are symptoms of the stress. Efficient remediation involves treating the cause, not the symptoms. Thus, the father-child stress should be treated, by means of counseling and/or behavior modification techniques, as opposed to the improper and inefficient treatment of the symptoms, by means of remedial reading, auditory and visual memory exercises, changing reading workbooks, etc., which do not change the cause of the problem, and therefore do not change the problem. When the cause of a problem is successfully treated, however, the problem and the symptoms usually abate.

Part II of this book is devoted to psychoeducational assessment techniques, which are designed to identify the cause of learning and behavior problems. The remainder of the book is devoted to a system by which to treat cause, as opposed to symptoms.

Back to the learning circuit model: if a problem exists with one or more model concepts, a learning and/or behavior difficulty could result. Efficient remediation involves an assessment of the problem in order to determine the cause. Instruments like the SILI and the Comprehensive History provide the psycho-educational assessment, and the Learning Circuit Model provides the theoretical basis by which to help understand the cause. Thus, if one or more of the learning processes or circuits are defective, a learning difficulty could result. Efficient remediation involves identifying the defective circuits causing the problem, and then providing specific remediation, as opposed to ignoring the cause and treating the symptom of, for example, written spelling difficulty.

Table XX presents the Learning Circuit Model.

Table XIX

You have really been speeding along.

Enjoy _____ minutes of free

time at the _____

Center.

C O N G R A T U L A T I O N S !!!

Date _____ Driver _____

It's in the bag!!!!!!!

_____ has earned the

right to _____

_____

_____

Date _____

YOU CAN "HOLE UP" AT THE

_____ CENTER

FOR _____ Minutes.

Date _____ Witness _____

You have landed yourself a big one!!

Enjoy _____ minutes to _____

_____

Invite a friend to go with you.

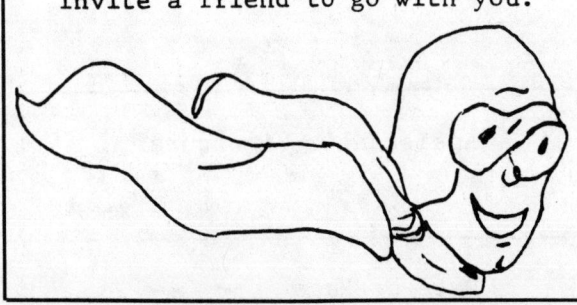

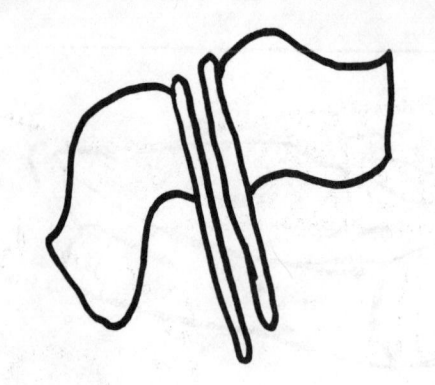

Beat your own record

By _____. _____ agrees to

_____

_____.

_____ agrees to help by _____

_____.

When they win they can celebrate by _____

_____.

_____
Driver's Signature

_____
Assistant's Signature

_____
Date of Race

Take a long look at our agreement

I will try to _____

_____

_____

by _____.

When I do I would like to be able to

_____

_____

_____

Student's Signature

I will try to help by _____

_____

_____

_____

_____.

When you finish you may:

__ have 10 minutes free time

__ talk to a friend for 5 minutes

__ go to a center for 15 minutes

__ read a book

_____

Teacher's Signature

An unbeatable team

_____ and _____ want to get over these humps.

They have agreed to help one another. _____ will help _____ by _____.

_____ will help _____ by _____. When they reach their goals they will be able to _____

_____.

_____   _____   _____
Date   Student Signature   Student Signature

Table XX

Learning Circuit Model

We regard the Learning Circuit Model in the following fashion:

A. There are five major channels of learning: auditory, visual, verbal, graphic (visual-motor and/or paper-pencil coordination), and haptic (a combination of tactual and kinesthesia).

B. There are four major learning processes: input, memory, meaning, and output.

C. Combining the preceding learning channel and learning process concepts, many learning systems result, each of which is identified by an X in the grid below:

CHANNELS

	Auditory	Visual	Verbal	Graphic	Haptic
Input	X	X			X
Memory	X	X	X	X	X
Meaning	X	X	X	X	X
Output			X	X	X

PROCESSES

D. Combining the previous three concepts, the important learning circuits can be identified as:

	Input	Memory	Meaning	Output
1.	Auditory	Auditory	Auditory	Verbal
2.	Auditory	Auditory	Auditory	Graphic
3.	Visual	Visual	Visual	Verbal
4.	Visual	Visual	Visual	Graphic
5.	Haptic	Haptic	Haptic	Verbal
6.	VAKT	VAKT	VAKT	Verbal or graphic
7.	Etc.	Etc.	Etc.	Etc.

LEARNING CIRCUITS

---

10. Teach to the Student's Strength

A basic D-PT principle is teach primarily to student learning/behavior strengths, and secondarily attempt to remediate the weaknesses. We recommend that about 75% of each class period be devoted to teaching the instructional program by means of student learning/behavior strengths, and only about 25% of each class period be devoted to the attempt to remediate student weaknesses. This strength/weakness ratio is recommended because there is no consistent evidence that presenting problem resolution can be achieved by an exclusive effort to remediate the learning/behavior weaknesses. In addition, and of equal importance, there is evidence to suggest that problem solving strengths can atrophy on the basis of nonuse. As such, it makes sense to teach primarily to learning/behavior strengths, and only secondarily to attempt to remediate the weaknesses (which may never entirely be accomplished).

The learning circuit model is useful in terms of understanding learning strengths and weaknesses. "Strengths" refers to model concepts which are at least of normal ability; "weaknesses" refers to model concepts which are characterized by mild, moderate, or severe defects in problem solving.

If, for example, a student has normal auditory processing (input, memory, and meaning) but moderate problems with visual discrimination and graphic output, it is essential to educational success to match the instructional program, including curriculum materials, to the student's auditory strengths. It would make no sense, and would invite failure, to educationally program such a student in relation to his weaknesses (visual input and graphic output). However, it is equally essential to provide a remedial program relative to the student's weaknesses. We recommend an instructional strength/weakness ratio of 75%/25%.

Specifically, and relative to the above student, we recommend that each tool-subject time period (reading, math, language, science, handwriting, etc.) be divided 75%/25%; teach each tool-subject during the 75% time period according to the student's strength (auditory or phonic, and avoiding visual stimuli as much as possible); and, during the 25% tool-subject time period, attempt to remediate the student's learning weaknesses (visual discrimination and graphic output), as they relate to the particular tool-subject being taught at that time.

11. Body Image

Body image is a prominent D-PT concept. We define body image as the adequacy with which one regards one's physical appearance, physical structure, and physical ability. In essence, body image is the motor component of the self concept.

Most special education students have body image problems, and therefore need body image remediation activities. Such activities are more than just physical education exercises, although the body image activities should relate to the development of gross and fine motor coordination, graphic output, and self concept improvement through adaptive physical education concepts. In addition, the U.S. Congress may have had reference to body image in the physical education section of P.L. 94-142, as it is now required that "if specially designed physical education is prescribed in a child's individualized education program, the public agency responsible for the education of that child shall provide the services directly, or make arrangements for it to be provided through other public or private programs."

We recommend that special education instructional programs routinely include a 15 minute morning and a 15 minute afternoon body image activity time period, either conducted by the teacher or by an occupational/physical therapist, and that a body image center within the classroom be the location of the body image activities. Such a center might include: a balance beam; full-length mirror; exercise mats; exercise equipment, such as weights, jump rope, punching bag; grooming activities for females; etc.

Some good commercial body image programs are:

I Can. Hubbard Co., P.O. Box 104, Northbrook, Illinois 60062. This is a structured sequenced, individualized, pre-school to high school physical education program. The strategies of this program are based on individual needs and learning styles so that feelings of confidence and self-worth are fostered. The primary skills program and instructional materials are organized into four major skills areas: Fundamental Skills, Body Management, Health and Fitness, and Aquatics.

Frostig Move-Grow-Learn. Follett Publishing Co., 1000 West Washington Blvd., Chicago, Illinois 60607. This kit provides a variety of classroom activities designed to develop agility, strength, body awareness; flexibility, speed, balance, and endurance.

Project Me, Body Image Program, Levels I and II. Bowmar, 622 Rodien Drive, Glendale, California 91201. This program deals with early learning concepts in body image, visual perception, feelings, cause and effect, size discrimination, and form perception.

Body Management Activities. MWZ Associates, P.O. Box 144, Dayton, Ohio 45306 (a book).

The Fairbanks-Robinson Program. Teaching Resources, Inc., 100 Boylston Street, Boston, Massachusetts 02116. This is a training program in the development of basic motor skills, providing a transition from gross motor to fine motor skills.

Dubnoff School Program. Teaching Resources Inc., 100 Boylston St., Boston, Massachusetts 02116. This is a developmental program designed to teach motor-perceptual skills.

Transition. American Guidance Service, Publishers Building, Circle Pines, Minnesota 55014 (a kit). Transition explores the needs, goals, expectations, feelings, values, and conflicts of secondary students. It is a teacher directed program which specifically addresses the student's social and emotional needs. The program helps to develop empathy and personal responsibility.

Two excellent resources for body image activities are: Kephart, N. and Chaney, C. *Motoric Aids in Perceptual Training*. Charles E. Merrill Publishing Co., Columbus, Ohio, 1968; and Cratty, B. *Active Learning*. Prentice-Hall, Inc., Englewood Cliffs, New Jersey, 1971.

Some informal body image activities follow:

a. Arm walk: Have the subject lie flat on the floor and push his body up with his arms, keeping his knees straight; have him walk forward with his arms while his feet drag behind.
b. Walking beam: Use a long two-by-four placed flat on the floor for forward, backward, and sideways walking in stocking feet. Raise walking beam between blocks for advanced skills, moving on the two-inch side.
c. Use above exercise, including walking beam, while blindfolded.
d. Running in place: Assume relaxed stance. Begins slow run in place. Gradually increase pace to hard run, bringing knees high. Return to original slow pace.
e. Maze run: Lay out obstacle course in yard or classroom for timed running.
f. Foot races: Teach sprint positions, and organize races covering 25, 50, and 75 yards.
g. Football run: Mark out running area for catching football while in stride.
h. Beanbag toss: Practice throwing, using large holes, such as in tires, as targets. Use beanbag for pitching games to see who can come closest to a line or floor marker.
i. Sponge ball basketball: Use shoe box with the bottom removed. Tape to wall for indoor basketball.
j. Jump rope: Alternate one foot forward and backward, holding one rope. Also, have subject run in and jump while others turn rope; jump for time and speed.
k. Bounce skip: While bouncing a basketball, have subject skip to a goal and return.
l. Draws self: Have subject draw a picture of himself; have him describe himself and picture into tape recorder and play back (for use by teacher).
m. Have subject assemble body-part plastic models and describe body functions.
n. Body concept: Have subject discuss personal characteristics, including interests, feelings, strengths, etc. Tape description of himself for feedback discussions (for use by teacher).
o. Self concept development: Extend the above ("n") activity to include discussion of: "The person I am"; "What I want to be"; "My heroes"; "The person I hope to become"; etc. (for use by teacher).
p. Trampoline activity.
q. Swimming.
r. Fine motor coordination activities such as tracing-books, Etch-a-Sketch, puzzles, clay, fingerpainting, paddle ball, marbles, tiddley winks, pick up sticks, etc.
s. Frequent parent, teacher, and other significant adult compliments about personal appearance are appropriate and should be encouraged (e.g., "You're looking sharp today"; or "That's really a good looking shirt you are wearing.").
t. Foot races, informal games; or other unstructured physical activities such as "I'll race you back to the house," or Simon Says activities involving imitating physical movements, might be helpful.

12. Career Education

We define career education as the assessment of, and instruction in, those body image, interpersonal, occupational aptitude and interest, and pre-vocational technical skills, which will result in job acquisition, efficiency, and happiness.

One guiding D-PT philosophy is that by means of special education (and career education), handicapped students should be equipped with life-survival and coping skills by which to constructively adjust and contribute to the post-school interpersonal and work world.

Career education is an important component of D-PT pilosophy. We recommend that career education be an essential and daily ingredient of all special education programming on a K-12th grade basis.

A task analyses of career education follows:

a. A life survival instructional program is recommended, which should blend instruction in academics with life-survival skills (e.g., personality traits necessary to get along with people and hold a job; use of money; safety skills; etc.). Some of the specific skill areas necessary for life-survival include:

1) Health
2) Safety
3) Effective communication
4) Homemaking and family living
5) Learning to understand oneself and to get along with others
6) Learning to understand the physical environment
7) Learning to use leisure time wisely
8) Earning a living
9) Citizenship
10) Learning to manage money
11) Learning to travel and move about

b. Develop body image, and gross and fine motor coordination, by means of body image activities (K-12th grades).
c. Continuously conduct career awareness activities (1-12th grades).
d. Continuously assess the student's occupational aptitude and interests (3-12th grades).
e. Assess the local community occupations suitable for the individual if and when he enters the work world.
f. Assess the occupation and personality skills involved in "e" that are necessary for job success.
g. Provide specific classroom training relative to those skills (3-12th grades).
h. Allow on-the-job observation and exploration of careers and occupations during junior high school.
i. It is recommended that a complete assessment of the student's occupational interests and pre-vocational skills be made prior to his fifteenth birthday, or on entrance to high school.
j. High school experience should include salaried but supervised half a day on-the-job training.

Some good career education references follow:

a. An excellent K-12, performance based, sequenced, life-experience oriented, diagnostic and related teaching materials program in career education/vocational education for special education students is: *The Vocational Education/Special Education Project I and II* (VESEP). Central Michigan University, Sloan 208, Mt. Pleasant, Michigan 48859.

b. An excellent curriculum guide for the slow learner relative to life survival skills is: *The Slow Learning Program in the Elementary and Secondary Schools.* Cincinnati Public Schools: Ohio, 1964.

c. A good occupational-interest assessment instrument with purported sixth grade reading ability and a high school orientation is: Kuder E, *General Interest Survey.* Chicago, Illinois: Science Research Associates, 1976.

d. *Reading Skills Program, Real People at Work.* Changing Times Education Service, 1729 H Street, N.W., Washington, D.C. 20006. This is a multisensory and developmentally sequenced reading program that uses teacher and student-directed lessons. Basic decoding and comprehension skills are taught through career education related stories.

e. *Pacemaker Vocational Readers.* Fearon-Pittman Publishers, Inc., 6 Davis Drive, Belmont, California 94002. This kit of high-interest low-vocabulary books and cassette tapes introduces the student to 10 different careers in which handicapped students have demonstrated success.

f. *Expo 10: Exploring Career Interests.* Science Research Associates, 759 East Erie St., Chicago, Illinois 60622. This career exploration program for intermediate through secondary age students uses games to develop occupational awareness. A comprehensive set of teacher directed and reinforcement plans are included.

g. *Janus Job Interview Guide.*
Janus Job Planner.
Job Application File.
Janus Job Interview Kit.
Using the Want Ads.
People Working Today.
Changing Times Education Services, 1729 H Street, N.W., Washington, D.C. 20006. These six kits of high-interest low-vocabulary pre-vocational materials are self structured, and relate to the world of work.

h. *Listen to Career Cassettes.* Eye Gate House, 146-01 Archer Avenue, Jamaica, New York 11435. This high-interest self-structured career awareness program represents 116 jobs arranged according to career clusters. This information is retrieved from cassette tapes.

i. *Getting A Job.* Fearon Publishing Inc., 6 Davis Drive, Belmont, California 94002. Reading grade level: 3. Interest grade level: junior high-high school.

j. *Work for Everyone.* Frank E. Richards Publishing Co., Phoenix, New York 13135. Reading grade level: 2.5/3.3. Interest grade level: junior high-high school.

k. *All About the Hall Family.* Same address as above. Reading grade level: 2.0 Interest grade level: junior high-high school.

m. *Looking Into the Future.* Same address as above. Reading grade level: 2.0. Interest level: junior high school.

n. *Finding Your Job.* Finney Company, 3350 Gorham Avenue, Minneapolis, Minnesota 55426. Reading grade level: 2.5/5.0. Interest level: junior high-high school.

o. *Application Forms.* Frank E. Richards Publishing Co., Phoenix, New York 13135. Reading grade level: 3.0. Interest level: junior high-high school.

13. Sex Education

We regard sex education as an important component of D-PT and K-12 special education programming. However, some parents and school administrators do not. Therefore, it is wise to obtain written parent/administrator permission before conducting sex education. We suggest that sex education, especially in secondary special education, be conducted twice a week, for at least 45 minutes, using audio-visual aids whenever possible, and encouraging student group discussion.

A task analysis of sex education follows:
1. Body image development, including activities in front of a full length mirror.
2. Self concept development, by means of DUSO, TAD, role playing, behavior modification, etc.
3. Awareness of body parts.
4. Anatomical differences between male and female.
5. Manners, social grace, and respect for others.
6. Getting along with oneself and others.
7. Male and female social roles.
8. Male and female personal hygiene.
9. Biological functions of male and female reproductive organs.
10. Menstruation.
11. Love.
12. Petting.
13. Human and animal sexual intercourse.
14. Venereal disease.
15. Marriage and family planning.
16. Birth control.
17. Child birth.
18. Child care and responsibility.
19. Abortion.
20. Consideration of parent and social values relative to sexual behavior.
21. Dating.
22. Masturbation, wet dreams, etc.
23. Pre-marital sex.
24. Not necessary to engage in sexual behavior to feel wanted.
25. Legal rights of minors, regarding marriage, birth control, competence, etc.
26. Career education relative to child responsibility.
27. Acceptance of sexual feelings.
28. Ways of sublimating sexual feelings.
29. Homosexuality.
30. Sexual deviance.
31. Being picked-up.
32. Sexual exploitation: instances; what to do, how to avoid; etc.
33. Prostitution.
34. Pornography; dirty words.
35. Proper places for sexual expression; and also proper places to discuss sexuality.
36. Responsible and right sex habits vs. irresponsible and wrong sex habits (e.g., public masturbation).
37. Philosophical issues: sterilization; right to have children; etc.
38. Myths: e.g., masturbation will not result in damage, kissing will not cause pregnancy; etc.
39. Public agencies: public health nurse; family planning agency; etc.

Two good sex education references are: Burt, J. and Meeks, L., *Education for Sexuality. Concepts and Programs for Teaching,* (2nd Ed.) Philadelphia: W.B. Saunders Company, 1975.

Social and Sexual Development. A Guide for Teachers of the Handicapped. Des Moines, Iowa: Special Education Curriculum Development Center.

The Iowa State Department of Public Instruction, 1972. (Mailing address: Campus Stores, University of Iowa, IMLL Room #30, Iowa City, Iowa 52772.

14. X-Work

X-work refers to high-interest educational materials which provide students with constructive activity during dead times of the school day. X-work is usually of a visual input and graphic output nature; is usually teacher made; should relate to the content of one or more tool-subjects currently being studied; and is most efficient in packets of 25 or 30 pages, with each page representing a different task.

Each student should have a noncompleted X-work packet every day; the packets should be used during dead times, such as after successfully completing an objective but before the end of the tool-subject time period; and each X-work page, or series of pages that represent a single concept, should be coded on the page in a way that refers to equivalent material in a skill continua, in order to defend the use of X-work should the teacher be challenged by a parent, administrator, etc.

The scope and sequence of X-work are limited only by the intelligence and imagination of the teacher.

Table XXI presents examples of X-work.

15. Least Restrictive Educational Environment; and Mainstreaming

P.L. 94-142 requires "(1) that to the maximum extent appropriate, handicapped children, including children in public or private institutions or other care facilities, are educated with children who are not handicapped, and (2) that special classes, separate schooling or other removal of handicapped children from the regular educational environment occurs only when the nature or severity of the handicap is such that education in regular clases with the use of supplementary aids and services cannot be achieved satisfactorily."

"Each public agency shall ensure that a continuum of alternative placements is available to meet the needs of handicapped children for special education and related services." The continuum must include the alternative placements of "instruction in regular classes, special classes, special schools, home instruction, and instruction in hospitals and institutions,' and "make provision for supplementary services (such as resource room or itinerant instruction) to be provided in conjunction with regular class placement."

The least restrictive educational environment concept simply means that special education students must be educated in regular classes to the extent they can achieve success and feel good about themselves. If the student presenting problems are of such a nature that success is not possible in regular classes, then other educational environments may be considered, but only to the extent that the other environments do not restrict contact with non-handicapped students more than necessary to ensure success for the handicapped students.

As indicated above, P.L. 94-142 defines a continuum of least restrictive educational environment. An expanded continuum of least restrictive environment follows:

a. Regular class placement.
b. Regular class, with modified curriculum/behavior management.
c. Regular class, with consultation to teacher.
d. Regular class, with direct assistance to student from consultant (special education teacher, tutor, etc.)
e. Regular class—resource room combination.
f. Regular class—self contained special class combination.
g. Self contained special class—regular class combination.
h. Self contained special class.
i. Self contained special class—diagnostic/treatment center.
j. Self contained special class—homebound combination.
k. Special day school.
l. Homebound program.
m. Residential school.
n. Institutionalization.

For example, the least restrictive educational environment concept means that a handicapped student who is unsuccessful in regular class reading and math but who could be successful in regular class with resource room help regarding reading and math may not be placed in the "more restrictive" educational environment of, for example, a "self contained special class."

The use of the concept mainstreaming preceded in time the least restrictive educational environment concept. When initially used, mainstreaming was widely but incorrrectly interpreted to mean that all handicapped students would be educated in regular classes (mainstreamed), the thought of which caused concern among teachers. Now, the concept of mainstreaming has been replaced by the better understood least restrictive educational environment concept. The two concepts have the same meaning.

Table XXI

Color the picture that Rhymes with hat red.

What shape am I?

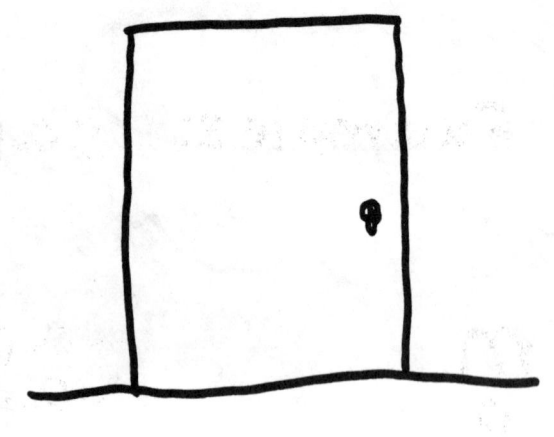

triangle

square

circle

rectangle

Choose letters to make new words

Examples: cap   make   fine

m
p   -ap   _ake   -ine
t   -ap   -ake   -ine
f
d
b
h

6.9.1

Name_____ Date_____
Order Task   No. 41

Make one   ☐ the same   ☐ upside down ☐ larger

⊙			
⌡			
🐦			
✂			

☐ Follow ☐1 ☐2 to the finish using a crayon

Name_____ Date_____

Fill in the missing numbers

7831642	7_3164_	_8_16_2	7___1__2
9548307	954_3_7	9__83_7	9__8_0_
2710546	2_10_46	__1054_	_7_05__
6849510	684_5_0	6_49__0	6_4_5__
1231896	12_189_	123__9_	1__1__6
7956483	7_5_4_3	___64_3	7___4__
8796411	_79_4_1	8__6__1	__9__1_

Name_____ Date_____

Copy the designs below
in the squares next to them

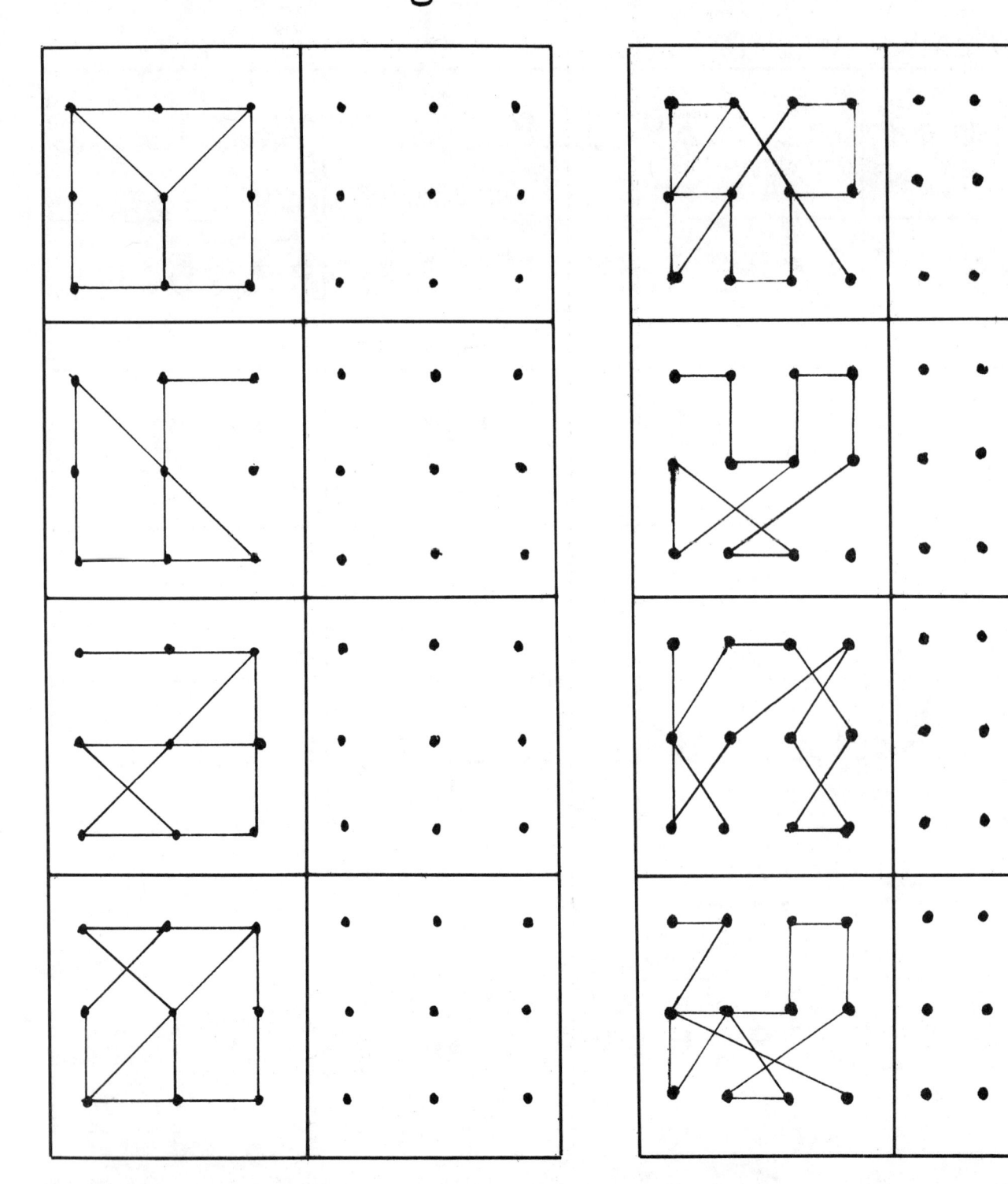

16. Resources

From time to time, it becomes necessary for teachers to seek outside resource help relative to student learning or behavior problems. The following resources are available to teachers:

1. The Federal government subsidizes a nationwide network of thirteen Regional Resource Centers. The workscope of the RRC is to provide assistance to states regarding the implementation of the IEP process. In addition, RRC personnel can assist state education agencies with the establishment of local resource centers (LRC or ERC), the workscope of which could involve the direct provision of educational materials and services to teachers.

2. The Council for Exceptional Children Information Services/ERIC Clearinghouse on Handicapped and Gifted Children maintains a comprehensive data base of professional literature as well as print and non-print information products that relate to the following aspects of the education and training of handicapped and gifted students: classroom instruction, pre- and in-service training of professional and para-professional personnel, counseling and guidance, program administration, research, Federal and state laws, litigation, statistic and incidence data, and information for parents. A fee is charged for such information in order to insure the continuation and growth of the system. A list of services, products, and fees is available upon request from the CEC Information Services, 1920 Association Drive, Reston, Virginia 22091.

An excellent service is provided by Closer Look, P.O. Box 1492, Washington, D.C., 20013. Upon written request, and without charge, information will be sent regarding the kind and/or location of special education services in a given region within a given state. This service is particularly useful for parents of special education children who are contemplating moving and wish information about the special education facilities in the receiving area.

Within the context of teacher resources and materials, we wish to express a caution: The special education community is rapidly developing a sophisticated system of material and information retrieval so that a requesting teacher should be able to receive necessary materials within a matter of weeks. However, there is a danger inherent in this procedure. There are many good educational materials; on the other hand, there are probably more poor educational materials. Although usually conscientious, a teacher may fall into the trap of using materials as a substitute for systematic and appropriate intervention. As such, it is easy to get into the habit of requesting materials only for the sake of materials. We contend that this is not good educational practice, and that the only legitimate value of any commercial or teacher-made material is when the material has been carefully matched with the needs of the teacher in relation to the specific problem of the subject. Therefore, we advise that teachers not avail themselves of materials unless a careful match has been made between what the materials purport to do, and the particular nature of the subject's presenting problem, the teacher's psychoeducational hypotheses about the presenting problem and the IEP. The ERC faculty and/or good school-district curriculum coordinators should be able to help with that match.

17. Teacher qualities

We regard the following teacher qualities as essential to good diagnostic-prescriptive teaching: personal security, patience, humor, the ability to employ classroom structure, personal objectivity, the ability to be firm, the ability to reward, good rapport qualities, genuineness, a sincere interest in working with people, personal and professional enthusiasm, and the possession of appropriate technical knowledge.

18. Professional identity

Many of the newly emerging special education roles involve innovative learning and behavior management strategies. A contemporary special educator should be proud to belong to a profession that is seeking new ways of solving old problems. When seeking a job, the special educator should feel secure in identifying the strengths that person can offer the job despite the fact that those strengths might relate to untraditional special education practices. The job candidate should also feel secure in requesting from the prospective administrator the special education objectives of the employing administration in order to determine if the candidate and job match. The candidate should further feel secure in attempting to obtain a commitment from the administrator relative to the special education manner in which the candidate wishes to professionally operate.

19. Public relations

It is important for a special education teacher to maintain good faculty and community public relations if for no other purpose than to dissipate some of the misunderstanding that often characterizes special education. This PR can often be accomplished by: offering an occasional open house; providing an open invitation to faculty to visit the special education classroom; special education student sponsored assemblies; making contact with community and business leaders for the purpose of inviting them to the classroom, and the converse; integrating special education students with regular classes as often as possible, but only when there is reason to believe that the special education students will succeed in the regular classes; etc.

20. Written parent permission

We advise, and P.L. 94-142 now requires, written parent permission be obtained prior to the testing and/or placement in a special education class of a minor handicapped subject. Table XXII presents a Request for Service form and a Parent Approval for Enrollment in Special Class form. We advise using the written permission concept, although the reader is urged to employ the procedure that is best suited for his purpose.

Table XXII

Request for Service

Date _____

I give my permission for initial and continuing interviewing/psycho-educational assessment/-counseling in order to assist my (son-daughter) _____ in the educational program at (his-her) school.

_____   _____
        (School)   (Parent-Guardian)

Parent Approval for Enrollment in Special Class

TO: _____   DATE: _____

I understand that a careful study of my child's school achievement and placement has been made. I have been informed that he has the opportunity to attend a special class where he will receive help for his learning or behavior problems.

I approve of the enrollment of _____
                                      (child's name)
in the special class, and agree to cooperate with the remedial program.

_____
Signature of Parent or Guardian

21. Referral forms and procedures

We recommend, and P.L. 94-142 now ensures that special education not be used as a student dumping ground. This can be avoided by developing a strong special education identity, which can partially be facilitated by the development of professional procedures that have a usefulness unique to the purpose for which they are designed. The following discussion presents two such procedures.

a. We contend that special education services should be last-resort services, and that the regular teacher should own primary responsibility for the education of assigned students. We argue that the regular teacher, and the battery of pupil-personnel workers employed to assist the regular teacher, should exhaust whatever resources are available to them with respect to resolving a presenting problem prior to referring a student to special education. We contend there should be a definite referral procedure established for each school district which would control the way in which a student is referred out of regular education to special education. We suggest the following chain of referral: from the regular teacher, to the principal, to the counselor or psychologist (if there is one), to the nurse (if necessary), to a screening committee, and then if warranted, to special education. The individuals involved in this referral procedure should be obliged to exhaust (and account for what they have done) their resources before referring the presenting problem to the next person in the referral chain. Table XXIII presents the Student Referral Form, and Table XXIV presents a Health History form, which we have used for the purpose of school referral and information. We urge the use of these professional concepts, but the reader should develop his own mechanics. Whatever the mechanics, we suggest if a request for services form of some nature is used, the form should have a specially designated place where each person in the referral chain may indicate what was done to resolve the presenting problem.

Table XXIII

Student Referral Form

Name_____ Birth date_____ School_____

Address_____ Emergency phone_____ Grade_____

Specific reason for referral_____

_____

_____

Home Information

Mother's name_____ Phone_____ Phone_____
                          Business   Home
    Address_____

Father's name_____ Phone_____ Phone_____
                          Business   Home
    Address_____

If student not living with natural parents, give necessary information _____

_____

_____

Siblings — names and ages _____

_____

Health Information

Vision _____

_____

Hearing _____

_____

General health _____

_____

Specific health problems _____

_____

_____

_____

_____

_____

_____

_____

_____

School Information

Classwork — specific _____

_____

_____

General behavior (discipline needs, personality factors, emotional stability, authority and group relations, and other significant behavior): _____

Test Information

Aptitude _____

_____

_____

Achievement _____

_____

_____

Specific efforts made by school personnel to resolve the difficulty (e.g., student conferences, parent conferences, school environment manipulation, counseling, discipline action, guidance room, etc.) _____

_____

_____

_____

Service requested by _____
Teacher/Counselor/Principal

Date submitted _____

Date received _____ Approved _____

Table XXIV

Health History

Family History

	AGE	HEALTH Good	Fair	Poor
Father's name _____	____	____	____	____
Mother's name _____	____	____	____	____

Children:
1. _____   _____   _____   _____   _____

2. _____   _____   _____   _____   _____

3. _____   _____   _____   _____   _____

4. _____   _____   _____   _____   _____

Circle if the following diseases or conditions have been present in any family member or relative:

    Epilepsy   Seizures   Mental Retardation   Emotional Illness

    Cerebral Palsy   Diabetes   Brain Dysfunction   Blood Disorder

Any psychiatric, psychological, or neurological contacts?

Special Education?

Prenatal or Obstetric History

Father's age at time of subject's birth _____

Mother's age at time of subject's birth _____

Was this mother's 1st _____ 2nd _____ 3rd _____ 4th (or more) pregnancy? _____

Any history of miscarriages, premature birth, stillbirths, etc.? _____

_____

_____

Circle any of the following conditions mother may have had during pregnancy with subject. Indicate the month during which each condition occurred.

Viruses	Seizures	Poisoning
Bleeding or Spotting	Loss of Consciousness	Anxiety
X-Rays	Depression	Medicine
Illness	Anemia	Loss of Oxygen
High Fever	Excessive Nausea or Vomiting	

Other _____

Where was subject born? _____ Mother's RH blood factor _____

Was subject a 9-month (full-term) baby? _____ If not, explain _____
_____

Hours in labor _____ Medication? _____ Anesthesia? _____

Complications of labor or delivery _____

Any known birth injuries or defects? _____

Did baby breathe promptly? _____

Incubator needed? _____ How long? _____

Birth weight? _____ Oxygen given to baby after birth? _____

After birth, was baby discolored (yellow, blue, black)? _____

Feeding History _____

Breast? _____ When weaned? _____

Bottle? _____ When weaned? _____

When did subject begin eating solid food? _____

Feeding difficulties? _____

Subject's Medical History

Name and addresses of doctors (clinics) who have cared and are caring for subject.

1. _____
2. _____
3. _____

Circle any of the following conditions subject has had, and indicate age when each condition occurred.

Convulsions (seizures)	Asthma	Anoxia	High fevers
Measles	Chicken pox	Mumps	Serious infection
Head Injuries	Diabetes	Head banging	Heart condition
Motor coordination problems		Mental retardation	

Brain dysfunction   Emotional Illness

Operations _____

Serious accidents_____

Serious illnesses _____

Special tests (EEG, etc.)_____
_____

Any psychiatric, psychological, or neurological contacts? Special Education?

Developmental History

At what age did subject:

Walk _____ Say sentences _____

Say first word _____ Age bladder-trained _____

                                 Age bowel-trained _____

General Information

Does subject have a hearing problem? _____

Does subject have a vision problem, or wear glasses?_____

Does subject take any medication? _____

Does subject tire easily? _____

Does subject have good appetite? _____

Does subject require a special diet? _____

Is subject unusually active or restless (hyperactive)? _____

Does subject have any sleep problem, including nightmares? _____

Is subject right or left-handed? _____

How is subject's motor coordination? _____

Does subject have any unusual behavior problems? _____

What concerns you the most about your child? _____

_____

What pleases you the most about your child? _____

_____

b. Efficient programming is dependent on certain learner information. One important type of learner information is the presenting problem. We contend there should be no testing, counseling, or special education consideration without a well-defined presenting problem. If the presenting problem is well defined, then appropriate assessment procedures, counseling techniques, and/or special education opportunities may be identified and made available. The more behavioral precision with which the presenting problem is defined, the better the practitioner will be able to decide upon the appropriate intervention strategies. In this context, the Precision Referral Form was developed, and is presented in Table XXV. The reader is urged to study this form and to employ the concept but to develop whatever mechanics are meaningful to the reader.

An example may help: if a subject is referred to special education with the vague presenting problem of reading difficulties, the receiving teacher would not have much information with which to begin an intervention strategy. On the other hand, if the subject is referred with the presenting problem of: "eight years old, Binet IQ 103, cannot verbally express himself, can follow verbal directions, can match visual letters and forms, can match at least grade-level visual words with pictures, but cannot orally read," the receiving teacher would have a better grasp of the situation and could begin to develop appropriate intervention strategies based on the precision with which the presenting problem was defined. We argue that the ability to define precisely a presenting problem is not the exclusive province of special education but rather any good educator should be able to do so.

Table XXV

Precision Referral Form

I. Student_____ Sex_____ Date of Birth_____ Age_____

Grade_____ School _____ Teacher _____

Parent/Guardian _____ Address _____

Name of Person Completing Form _____ Position _____

Please check the following behaviors which are descriptive of the subject:

_____ 1. Attendance problems (absent or tardy)
_____ 2. Leaves room without permission
_____ 3. Leaves seat without permission
_____ 4. Disobeys authority
_____ 5. Physically violent toward peers by kicking, hitting, etc.) _____
_____ 6. Distracts classmates by _____
_____ 7. Cries

____ 8. Curses
____ 9. Makes derogatory remarks about
   _____ (self or others)
____ 10. Is a loner
____ 11. Shy
____ 12. Withdraws
____ 13. Daydreams
____ 14. Odd or out-of-context ideas
____ 15. Destroys property
____ 16. Talks-out inappropriately
____ 17. Copies work of others
____ 18. Does not contribute to discussion
____ 19. Clumsy _____
   (falls, runs into, drops, etc.)
____ 20. Asks for verbal directions to be repeated
____ 21. Limited attention span
____ 22. Does not complete assignments
____ 23. Miscopies from_____
   (chalkboard, books, etc.)
____ 24. Reading grade level
____ 25. Specific reading problems
   _____
____ 26. Math grade level

____ 27. Specific math difficulty
____ 28. Language grade level
____ 29. Specific language problems
   _____
____ 30. Oral reading errors of _____
   _____
   (omission, substitution, mispronunciation, pauses, etc.)
____ 31. Uses incorrect verb forms in conversation
____ 32. Uses incorrect noun or pronoun forms in conversation
____ 33. Illegible handwriting (attach sample)
____ 34. Misspells words
____ 35. Misarticulates the_____ sounds
____ 36. Has unusual voice quality
____ 37. Stutters
____ 38. Paper-pencil coordination problems
____ 39. Fine motor coordination problems
____ 40. Gross motor coordination problems
____ 41. Body image problems
____ 42. Others _____
   (Specify)

---

22. Testing and assessment

Effective IEP-IIP intervention is dependent on the meaningful analysis of the necessary learner information in relation to a subject's presenting problem. We recommend that the learner information be collected by a battery of carefully selected formal and/or informal assessment instruments.

23. Student Study Committee

In order to protect the professional identity of special education, and to wisely regulate the flow of special education students relative to the least restrictive educational environment, we recommend, and P.L. 94-142 now requires, that each school district operate a student study committee, for the purpose of admitting students into special education classes, developing and monitoring IEPs, screening students out of special education classes, and advocating for the special education student and parents. The recommended committee should be composed of: the receiving and losing teachers and principals, a psychologist, the school or public health nurse, the student and his parents, and any other person connected with the case who could make a contribution to the committee purpose, such as the probation officer, welfare worker, etc. The committee should meet at regular intervals, and be charged with the responsibility of evaluating all the learner information relevant to the presenting problem, developing and monitoring IEPs, and making the best possible disposition of the student with respect to the least restrictive educational environment. We argue that it is as important to screen a special education student out of special education into regular education as the converse. Thus, it is important for the special education teacher and student study committee to make recommendations to the regular teacher relative to important intervention strategies for the special education student.

24. Ethics

Educators are professional people with awesome responsibility. The private information which they acquire about students and families is confidential and should not be discussed with individuals who are not professionally involved with the subject or case.

A major professional responsibility of the educator is that of respecting the educational chain of command. Everyone in public education has a supervisor or someone to whom he is responsible. Job-related complaints and problems should normally be addressed to the immediate supervisor.

25. Maximum number of students

We recommend there be not more than ten special education students in a self-contained class that operates without an aide, and not more than thirteen special education students in a self-contained class that operates with an aide. This is to admit that the special education teacher is human and has a frustration tolerance point beyond which job efficiency dramatically decreases. We consider the maximum classroom student number of ten and thirteen to approach that frustration tolerance point.

26. Entry of new students

We suggest that at the beginning of the school year, or any other time when many special education students are destined to enter the same class at the same time, the entry of those students be staggered three at a time, with the next group of three entering two days later. Such a procedure may necessitate the teacher beginning class a few days before school normally opens. The rationale for this recommendation is that the staggered entry gives the teacher and students the opportunity to adjust to one another on a gradual basis.

27. Student age range

We contend that the optimal student chronological age (and mental age) range in a given class is three years. This means that the oldest student in the class should not be more than three years older than the youngest student in the class. It also means that the most intelligent student in the class should not be more than three years more advanced in mental age than the least intelligent student in the class. It should be emphasized that this is an optimal range, and many times such an optimal situation is not possible. Yet, the degree to which student age range stretches significntly beyond three years is the degree to which the teacher's talents and frustration tolerance may also be stretched.

28. Student reevaluation

We recommend that learning disabled and emotionally disturbed students be reevaluated every year, and that mentally retarded students (assuming the diagnosis of MR is accurate) be reevaluated every two year. The reevaluation should consist of whatever formal and informal psychoeducational testing procedures are necessary relative to the nature of the presenting problem, the subject's personality and learning characteristics, and the objectives for the subject. A good reevaluation formal test battery relative to instructional problems is: the Comprehensive History, which necessairy involves a parent interview, the SILI, the appropriate Wechsler test, the ITPA, WRAT, Bender Test, and DAP. This battery can be shortened in relation to the nature of the presenting problem, the objectives regarding the subject, etc. However, we recommend that the parent interview not be eliminated, and that the practitioner maintain contact with the parents in terms of updating information about the subject, and also updating information relative to how the parents can continue the school intervention program at home.

P.L. 94-142 requires that IEPs be evaluated at least annually, to decide whether the short term objectives are being achieved; and that a reevaluation of each handicapped child occur every three years.

29. Professional agencies

The dedicated special educator will probably elect to belong to those professional organizations which represent his professional needs. Some important special education organizations are: the Council for Exceptional Children, which has several categorical divisions (MR, ED, LD, etc.); the American Association on Mental Deficiency; the Association for Children with Learning Disabilities; the Association for Retarded Children; the local, state, and national psychological associations, including the American Psychological Association; the local, state, and national education associations; and the local Parent-Teacher-Association.

Three generic journals of interest to special educators are: *Exceptional Children* (published by the Council for Exceptional Children), and the *Journal of Special Education,* and the *Journal of Learning Disabilities.*

Federal legislation is important to the viability of special education. In 1970, President Nixon signed into law an important enactment for special education. The enactment is Public Law 91-230. Title VI of P.L. 91-230 is known as the Education of the Handicapped Act. In 1974, P.L. 93-180, the Education of the Handicapped

Amendments of 1974, was enacted. In 1975, P.L. 94-142, the Education for all Handicapped Children Act, was enacted. And in 1974, P.L. 93-516 was passed, amending Section 504 of the Rehabilitation Act of 1973. The nature of these legislations is discussed in Part VIII of this book.

30. Kinds of special education teachers

There are three basic kinds of special education teachers.

The self-contained teacher

The most traditional kind of special education teacher is the self-contained teacher. This involves a teacher who is permanently assigned to a classroom and then assigned a certain number of special education students for whom that teacher has full-time educational responsibility. As such, that teacher provides all the educational experiences for those students.

The resource teacher

The resource teacher is becoming popular, particularly in rural America. This involves a special education teacher who is assigned full-time to a classroom but who is responsible for students only to the degree that students are referred, through appropriate channels, to that teacher for special attention. As such, the resource teacher has only limited educational responsibility for the students, since the regular teacher has the major responsibility. The resource teacher is frequently used in rural America where sufficient funds and/or students with problems are not available for the purpose of maintaining a full-time special education program. In such a case, the resource teacher often serves the entire school, relative to not only special education but also remedial regular education. In general, the resource teacher should operate on a highly structured referral basis in order to know the exact nature of the presenting problem and then what to do about it; should not have more than ten students in the resource classroom at the same time; should attempt to remediate the presenting problem rather than teach developmental education which is the province of the regular teacher; should not be regarded as a disciplinarian or a place to send students for punishment purposes; should have as a prime objective the quick return of the student to the regular class; and thus should accommodate students on a daily or weekly basis, but probably not on a permanent basis.

The itinerant teacher

The least frequent of the three kinds of special education teachers is the itinerant teacher. This kind of teacher also is becoming popular in rural America. The itinerant teacher has no classroom, is not expected to offer extensive direct service to students, and has no full-time student responsibility. Rather, the itinerant teacher serves as a consultant to teachers who request special help relative to student presenting problems. The itinerant teacher needs to have a flexible schedule, and often serves as a consultant to not only many teachers within a given school building but also to many schools within a given district. Recently, this concept has been expanded to the itinerant teacher serving many school districts, particularly as an employee of a multidistrict board of cooperative educational services.

As discussed in Part VIII of this book, P.L. 94-142 requires that handicapped students be educated in the least restrictive educational environment. As such, a handicapped student could be scheduled into a variety of classrooms, including any combination of regular class, itinerant teacher help, resource room, self contained class, etc.

31. Generalist or specialist

Traditional special education has operated on the basis of self-contained classrooms to which students are assigned who are representative of only one special education category (MR, LD, ED, etc.), and who are taught by teachers who have been trained in only that one special education category. These teachers are specialists. However, a new trend in national special education is emerging, in terms of noncategorical or crosscategorical special education, which manifests itself in a generalist teacher who is capable of systematic intervention with many kinds of learning or behavior problems irrespective of the traditional label attached to those problems. The specialist teacher seems to be prevalent in urban education, and the generalist teacher more prevalant in rural education. Irrespective of the specialist or generalist issue, it is our contention that special educators should be experts with basic developmental education techniques prior to teaching special education. This means that a special educator should also be a good regular educator, and therefore be expected to apply basic developmental education concepts along with special education concepts to the resolution of learning and behavior problems.

SELECTED REFERENCES

Exceptional Children, Council for Exceptional Children, 1920 Association Drive, Reston, Virginia 22091

Journal of Learning Disabilities, 101 E. Ontario Avenue, Chicago, Illinois, 60611

Journal of Special Education, 3515 Woodhaven Road, Philadelphia, Pennsylvania 19154

American Association on Mental Deficiency, 5101 Wisconsin Avenue, N.W., Washington, D.C. 20016

American Psychological Association, 1200 Seventeenth Street, N.W., Washington, D.C. 20036

Association for Children with Learning Disabilities, 4156 Library Road, Pittsburgh, Pennsylvania 15234

Association for Retarded Children, 2709 Avenue E East, P.O. Box 6109, Arlington, Texas 76011.

Chapter 23

Direct Instruction
Jim Jacobs, Ph.D.

New skills and technologies are continuously accruing from the growing knowledge of events that influence learning. It is the purpose of this chapter to present a set of principles that underly some of these skills and technologies, and thereby facilitate the teaching/learning process.

Direct instruction is defined as a pre-determined and systematic method of instructional delivery which is designed to maximize the efficiency of the teaching/learning process. The teaching part of this process is both pre-determined and precise. The efficiency of the teaching/learning interaction is measured by the rate and accuracy of student responses.

It is recommended that direct instruction be employed when teaching outcomes are clear and behaviorally stated, and the measurable responses of the students are the criteria for determining the level of successful teaching/learning. It is not suggested that the entire school day be spent in the direct instructional process; rather, when the goal is to teach precise responses in the most efficient way, DI techniques are recommended.

Before engineering a direct instruction sequence, a tremendous amount of prior planning and rehearsal is necessary, for each step in the direct instruction process occurs quite rapidly, and it is typical to elicit eight to ten responses per minute form each student within the instructional group. DI prerequisites include: a determination of the necessary learner information through psycho-educational assessment; a curriculum match statement; learning contracts (including behavioral/instructional objectives and related curriculum materials); behavioral management systems; student grouping; classroom engineering; and accountability strategies.

The suggested student grouping procedure involves three separate groups of five to six students each, with the classroom engineered into a minimum of three centers (refer to Chapter 24, Table XXIX, for a graphic description of the DI classroom arrangement). Center one is the direct instruction center from which the teacher presents all direct instruction. Center two is supervised by an aide and provides an opportunity for the repetition of concepts taught in Center one. Center three is the mastery center in which students work independently on concepts previously acquired in Centers one and two. It is the purpose of each direct instruction activity to introduce new concepts at a rate which will provide the slowest member of the group with functional mastery of the concepts presented.

A typical direct instruction presentation is designed for fifteen minute time periods. Thus, during a typical fifty minute class period, all three instructional groups rotate through the direct instruction centers. By the time students have rotated through the three centers, a tremendous amount of concept repetition has occurred. It is this teacher specified repetition that facilitates long term mastery of the concepts taught.

Direct instruction consists of the following 18 skills. Most of these skills will be used in every direct instruction presentation. However, due to the uniqueness of objectives and materials to be used, some presentations will not use all the direct instruction techniques discussed. Nonetheless, the objective is for the teacher to master all 18 direct instruction techniques and incorporate as many as possible into every direct instruction presentation.

Direct Instruction Skills
1. Attention Signals.

The basic principle is that before a teacher can efficiently teach a student anything, the teacher must have the student's attention. Most teachers however were never taught how to obtain student attention and dismiss the idea as impossible. Obtaining the attention of all students in a small group is a relatively simple process. However, this feat requires some planning and teaching. Students frequently learn that it is unnecessary to attend in order to obtain reinforcement. Students learn quickly from the teacher and each other that when they do not attend they come up winners more often than losers.

Rules:
1. Train student attention early. Ideally the training of student attention would be consistent throughout school from kindergarten through 12th grade.
2. Develop a variety of attention signals or cues.
3. Teach the desired student response(s) to selected signal(s).
4. Never begin instruction until all students are attending.

5. Immediately reinforce those students who respond to the attention signal.
6. Never accidentally reinforce the non-attending student with attention that could be interpreted as positive.
7. Ensure that the stimulus that follows each attention signal is reinforcing to the students. If what follows the attention signal is consistently boring or irrelevant, the attention signal will soon lose its effectiveness.

Examples of attention signals include: visual: teacher raises one hand; teacher turns light off and on rapidly; etc. Auditory: teacher says "listen," or "look"; or sounds a buzzer or bell; etc. Attention signals should be practiced several times before using.

Example:

Teacher: "I have something new to share with you today. When I hold my hand up like this (teacher models), it means stop what you're doing, sit up in your chiars, and listen to me."

2. Instances and Non-Instances.

Whenever the concept being taught allows, it is advisable to teach that concept in a two-step operation. First, teach what the concept is. For example, if the teacher is attempting to teach the color red, the logical first step would be to select some red object and present it to the group and say "This is red!" Most teachers do this well. The problem is that most teachers stop here; but this is teaching only instances of the concept. It is equally important to teach what red is not. This process forces the teacher to teach cleanly; that is, one concept at a time. It also facilitates student learning.

Rules:

1. Teach what the concept is. Give several examples (instances) of the concept.
2. Teach what the concept is not. Give several non-examples (non-instances) of the concept.

A suggested format for an instance/non-instance presentation is shown below. The sound being taught is "s".

```
        d           y
              ⓢ
        j           x
```

Example:

Teacher: Pointing to the s in the center of the group of letters, teacher says, "This is 'ssssss'." After repeating the above several times:
Teacher: "Group, what is this; it is _____?"
Student: "ssssss"
Teacher: "Good." Then pointing to another letter, teacher says, "Is this 's'?"
Student: "No."
Teacher: "Good, you are right!"

3. Response Signals.

To facilitate teacher control of the student group it is necessary to program which students will respond at what time to a given stimulus. To do this, the teacher must develop and use signals which elicit responses from students. The general rule is: wait until you see the student response signal before responding.

Rules:

1. Develop a variety of response signals.
2. Develop signals which elicit both individual and group responses.
3. Teach what the signal means through modeling, reinforcement, and CONSISTENCY.
4. Never accept a response from a student to whom a signal was not presented. Do not be guilty of accidentally reinforcing inappropriate behavior, even occasionally.
5. Immediately reinforce students who have responded on cue for:
   a. waiting for the cue; and b. the accuracy of the response.

Example of response signals include: visual: pointing to a student with a finger or hand; using a pointer; using an exaggerated sweeping hand motion for group response; etc. Auditory: calling a student by name; giving such cues as "everyone," "group," etc.

By controlling student responses the teacher can easily individualize response rate, increase or decrease reinforcement, and control the amount of student repetition and general rate of instruction.

Examples:

Teacher: "When I want you to respond, I will call your name and point to you" (teacher

Teacher: models). "If I want everyone to answer I will say 'everyone' and point like this" (teacher makes a sweeping motion toward the group).
Teacher: Repeats the response signals instructions; then:
Teacher: "Bobby, what does this mean?" (pointing to Bobby).
Bobby: "I can talk."
Teacher: "Super, you remembered the rule."

4. Feedback.

The concept of providing feedback to learners is universally accepted. To effectively use the feedback process the teacher must: a. elicit a high rate of student response, and b. react to each student response in a way the student is able to judge the adequacy of his or her response.

Some teachers feel that correcting a student's response will cause psychological harm to the student. This is a false assumption. To respond to a student's incorrect response with a simple "no", especially if followed immediately by the desired response, is effective and without harm. The principle is, when a response is given by the student, the teacher reinforces the response if it is acceptable or immediately corrects the response if it is unacceptable.

Rules:

1. Provide feedback immediately. If a response needs correcting, do so with a simple "no".
2. Provide props or cues to elicit a correct response, or model the correct response for the student.
3. Use a variety of reinforcers for correct responses.
4. Praise specific behavior rather than non-specific behavior. Example: "Good counting!" rather than "Good job!"
5. Ensure that a positive to negative feedback ratio is never less than three-to-one.
6. Ensure that reinforcers are reinforcing to the recipient.

Examples of feedback include: visual: displaying an accepted manual sign which conveys the intended meaning; body language to convey the intended meaning; etc. Auditory: presenting selected verbal reinforcers for appropriate responses; saying "no", and model the correct response; etc.

Examples:

Teacher: "Who has the answer to this problem?" (4 + ? = 5) Teacher gives response signal (points to Bill), and says "Bill."
Student: "Nine."
Teacher: "No, the answer is '1'. What is the correct answer?"
Student: "It's '1'."

5. Pacing

Learning occurs when one reacts to the stimuli being presented. Effective pacing of instructional delivery can be a tremendous aide in eliciting reactions and maintaining attention to concepts presented. Instructional pacing is defined as variance in the rate of instruction. By preplanned and continuous variance of the rate of instruction, the teacher can facilitate increased student attention and reaction to what is being presented.

Rules:

1. Teach fast: Direct instruction should proceed at a faster rate than non-direct instruction.
2. Vary the pace of instruction. When a particular point is to be made, either increase or decrease the rate of instruction. Students will predictably respond with increased attention and learning.

6. Pauses.

The effective use of planned pauses (actual stops) during instruction can be effective at recapturing the wandering attention of students or emphasizing a particular point. Pauses are effective almost any time, but are particularly valuable: 1. after attention signals are presented; 2. after a question has been asked and before a response signal is given; 3. immediately before a major point is made; or 4. immediately after a major point has been made.

Rules:

1. Plan pauses into the content of instruction.
2. Pair pauses with other methods of instructional control.
3. Use body language to emphasize the effect of pauses.

Pauses, especially when coupled with proper pacing, can be an effective measure of attention control.

7. Volume.

No single direct instruction concept is more effective at holding attention and eliciting student response than the effective varying of volume or loudness with which an oral lesson is presented. Increase and decrease volume as appropriate when emphasizing a point of instruction. Alternating from LOUD to soft (voice inflection) is DYNAMITE!

Rules:

1. Plan variance of volume as part of instructional content.
2. Pair with other methods of instructional control, especially pacing and pauses.
3. Use appropriate body language to accompany volume variance.
4. Practice.

8. Rhythm.

Rhythm is defined as the cadence or flow of the instructional delivery. Instructional rhythm is distinguished from pacing in that rhythm involves the cadence of instruction, whereas pacing involves the rate of instruction. Rhythm, in conjunction with pacing, pauses, and volume, are three of the four basic tools of the actor. Thus the process of designing and delivering a good direct instruction presentation closely approximates the dsigning and acting out of a good one-act play. In order to establish an acceptable instructional rhythm, the teacher should vary the cadence of the instruction: loud, soft, fast, slow, stop, etc.

Rules:

1. Use a variety of pacing, volume, and intentional pauses in order to construct the desired instructional rhythm.
2. Practice.

9. Body Language.

Body language is defined as the planned use of body-part movements for the purpose of increasing teaching effectiveness. Body language can be used to accentuate a point, reinforce a student, facilitate the correction of a student response, etc. Body language involves but is not limited to: planned motion of the hands and/or feet; proximity of the body relative to the student; facial gestures; etc.

To this point nine fundamental skills of direct instruction have been identified. Mastery of these nine skills constitutes the most work for the beginning student of direct instruction. If one is successful at mastering these first nine skills, those skills that follow can be easily accommodated into teaching methodology. As such the remaining nine direct instruction skills will be discussed more briefly than the preceding skills.

10. Attention Span.

Students, even those with short attention spans, attend to various stimuli with varying degrees of attention for varying periods of time. Student attention span is therefore relative to the concept being taught, the stimulus materials being used, and the skill of the teacher. Nonetheless, when student attention is less than 80%, direct intervention is called for.

Rules:

1. Prior to the beginning of instruction, select some method of continuously assessing student attention level.
2. During instruction, monitor the attention level of each student.
3. When any student attends less than 80% of the time, intervene.
4. Attention problems are problems with instruction, not the students.

11. Stimulus Change.

Stimulus change is defined as the teacher presentation of new stimuli to which students are expected to respond with a frequency equal to that of the student with the shortest attention span in the group. Too frequently one stimulus is presented to which all students are expected to attend for the duration of the planned instruction. The stimulus change idea is to present new and changing stimuli at a frequency which maintains a high degree of student attention.

Plan to change stimuli frequently, and plan a variety of stimuli. When a student's attention begins to wander, present a new stimulus to which the student is expected to respond. A variety of reinforcing and well-used stimuli relate directly to attention span.

Rules:

1. Plan every presentation in such a way that the primary stimulus changes at least every five

minutes (or more frequently with problem students).
2. Use a variety of stimuli that are known to be reinforcing to the students.
3. Plan at least three different activities for each fifteen minutes of instruction.
4. When any attention level in the group fails to reach 80%, change the stimulus.

12. Surprises.

Students, from kindergarten through secondary level, enjoy surprises. Most teachers, however, fail to utilize this effective method of maintinging or reobtaining student attention. Examples of surprises could include: dropping a book; breaking a pencil; slapping the desk or table; etc. The point is, when attention begins to fall below 80%, do something different, such as create a surprise.

Rules:

1. Plan at least one surprise for every fifteen minute presentation.
2. Practice surprises before instruction.
3. Develop a list of surprises that have proven successful for various student ages.

13. Intentional Mistakes.

By making intentional mistakes during a direct instruction presentation, the teacher can accomplish at least two things. First, the teacher can teach, through modeling, that the consequences of making a mistake are not disastrous. Second, students appear overjoyed at discovering teacher errors. Such mistakes, especially if the students have been alerted to deliberate teacher mistakes, will increase student motivation and attention span.

Rules:

1. Make a minimum of two intentional mistakes during each presentation.
2. Once the mistake is made, continue instruction as if the mistake had not been made unless students discover the error.
3. Once the mistake is discovered by students, act surprised. Praise the student or students responsible for "catching" the mistake.
4. Encourage the students to continue to look for errors.

Examples of intentional mistakes include: putting a letter on the felt board upside down; misspelling a word on the chalkboard; leaving a word out of a sentence; an incorrect answer to a math problem; etc.

14. Game Format.

Students enjoy games from which they receive reinforcement. By incorporating games into instruction, the teacher may elicit increased student attention or recapture lost attention. Commercial competitive games are readily available. The teacher may also design a variety of competitive or noncompetitive games. As some students are not emotionally ready for competition, extensive work must be done relative to self concept development before some students are ready for competitive games.

Rules:

1. Use at least one game for each instructional period.
2. For competitive games where students are playing against the teacher: a. the teacher should initially take the lead in scoring; b. as the game progresses, the students should catch the teacher; c. approximately 3/4 of the time the students should win a closely contested game. Conversely the teacher should win approximately 1/4 of the contests; and, d. occasionally a game should end in a tie.
3. For competitive games where students are competing against students: a. the teacher must always be in control; b. the game should allow one group (or individual) to initially take a reasonable lead in scoring; c. as the game progresses, other groups or individuals should obtain the lead; and, d. each group or individual should win on the basis of teacher control.
4. For non-competitive games, the only rule is for the teacher to be in control. Ensure that the student who needs the reinforcement of scoring scores frequently.

Games are especially functional if introduced at the end of a direct instruction presentation and completed with the aide as part of follow-up exercises.

15. Reinforcers.

Positive reinforcement is one of the basic tools of behavior change, and as such is the premier change agent available to teachers. Every teacher should program the activities of each school day in such a way that every student in the classroom receives a tremendous amount of reinforcement. It is essential to the direct instructrion process that students receive both primary and secondary reinforcement as necessary (see Chapter 28 for primary and secondary reinforcers).

Rules:

1. Use a variety of reinforcers during each direct instruction presentation.
2. Use a tremendous amount of verbal reinforcement.
3. Use physical reinforcement. Touch students.
4. Ensure that each student receives at least three positive reinforcers to each instance of negative feedback.

16. Response Rate.

Response rate is defined as the frequency of student responses. Just as student attention is a necessary part of the instructional process, so is a high rate of student response.

Rules:

1. Plan a presentation which requires a minimum of 30 verbal or graphic responses per student for each fifteen minute direct instruction session.
2. Provide feedback for student responses.
3. Monitor responses to ensure a minimum of 80% accuracy.

When the accuracy of response falls below 80%, consider it a signal that instruction is inadequate. Give honest feedback relative to the accuracy of student responses.

17. Enthusiasm.

Teacher enthusiasm is contagious, and inspires student attention, motivation, and learning. Enthusiasm can be conveyed by voice volume, inflection, and rate; body language; mood; responsiveness; active listening; facial expression; etc.

Rules:

1. Be genuine and natural with your use of enthusiasm signals.
2. Use a combination of enthusiasm signals whenever possible, such as smile, body gestures, and voice inflection.
3. Combine positive reinforcement with enthusiasm signals.
4. Do not reinforce non-target behavior with enthusiasm signals.

18. Mastery.

Ensure that those concepts elected for teaching are worthy of being taught. Briefly, teach only necessary concepts. Then ensure mastery of all concepts taught.

Rules:

1. Select and teach only necessary concepts.
2. Require mastery before proceeding with additional instruction.

DI Format

The following is presented as a sample DI small-group format. It is intended to acquaint the beginning DI practitioner with the basic format, content, and rhythm of a DI presentation.

After assembling the group in the Direct Instruction Center:

Teacher:
1) Gives attention signal.
2) Reinforces group for attending.
3) Presents stimulus item (instance of concept).
4) Asks students for a response.
5) Presents response signal.

Students:
6) Respond.

Teacher:
7) Reinforces student for correct response, or corrects incorrect response (feedback).
8) Repeats items 3,4,5,6, and 7 for each member of the group one or more times (programmed repetition).
9) Presents a new stimulus to group (non-instance of concept).
10) Asks for student response.
11) Presents group response signal.

Students:
12) Response.

Teacher:
13) Reinforces students for correct responses, or corrects incorrect responses.
14) Requires necessary repetition to ensure student mastery.
15) Presents a stimulus change: a surprise, mistake, new concept, game, etc.
16) Repeats steps 1-15 as appropriate.

Chapter 24

The Physical Arrangement of the Classroom

The management model is designed to permit systematic intervention with learning or behavior problems irrespective of whether the intervention involves a single individual or a group of individuals. The model is designed for diversity of application and, therefore, the setting in which the model is conducted should complement that diversity. It is possible to use the traditional education classroom physical arrangement for the purpose of delivering the management model, but such an arrangement restricts the delivery diversity of the model and thus is not recommended. We suggest that prudent innovation be used relative to the creation of classroom physical arrangements that are designed to enhance the delivery of effective intervention strategies.

We have found four classroom physical arrangements to be particularly effective relative to the delivery of the management model. Those four arrangements are presented in Tables XXVI, XXVII, XXVIII, and XXIX. The arrangements are analyzed in the discussion that follows.

Table XXVI presents a classroom arrangement design the diversity of which matches the diversity potential of the management model delivery system. It is a variation of Hewett's engineered classroom (Hewett, 1968) and is designed to be used with a teacher-aide. The classroom design operates on an interest center theory and has sufficient variety potential to meet the needs of most students with learning or behavior problems. Yet the classroom arrangement is such that a maximum of control is possible, thus making this particular design effective for acting-out as well as benign students.

Beginning the analysis of Table XXVI, in the upper left corner, the order center operates to help acting-out subjects control their emotions by means of controlling the environment. For that purpose, the order center provides structured tasks that have fixed starting points and definite conclusions. Such tasks might be: puzzles, pegboards, model building, paper-pencil direction following exercises, etc. A subject may be referred to the order center whenever such external control is necessary.

Moving clockwise, the checkmark card holder is for the purpose of maintaining student checkmark cards when not in use. The checkmark system is explained in greater detail in the chapters devoted to behavior modification and change agents. However, each student is given a fresh checkmark card daily, and checks are made by an aide on a routine interval basis as a means of rewarding desirable behavior. At the end of the day or week, the subject totals the number of checkmarks awarded and surrenders that total for an equivalently valued object of interest.

The time-out area will be more thoroughly discussed in the behavior modification chapters. However, the time-out area is designed to remove a disturbing subject from the stimulation of the classroom, isolate that subject as a means of punishment, and if desired, to use negative reinforcement by permitting the subject to return to the classroom whenever the subject decides he is capable of acceptable behavior. The time-out area should be devoid of all stimuli except a chair. The time-out area functions best if it is external to the classroom, although such an area can operate inside the classroom if it is screened and sturdy. The time-out subject loses the privilege of receiving checkmarks while in the time-out area.

The exploratory center exists to provide students with multisensory experiences of a hands-on nature. The center is divided into three sections, with the science section providing such things as telescopes, microscopes, live animals, listening posts, gardens, science experiment activities, etc. The art section should include such things as paints, crayons, paper, clay, sandbox, music, a variety of sorting objects, etc. The communication section should include such things as tape recorders, walkie-talkies, code games, tachistoscopes, mail-order catalogs and store activities to foster one-to-one communication, games such as Battleship to foster one-to-one communication, etc.

This classroom design is most effective when a

teacher-aide is available. The aide should receive inservice training in terms of educational philosophy, intervention strategies, and classroom management techniques.

The free-time area serves as a reinforcement for desirable behavior. It should contain objects of high interest to the students in the classroom. It is possible to identify such high interest objects by means of the Reinforcement Inventory as well as other strategies discussed in Part II. The free time area is most effectively used in conjunction with contingency contracts (discussed in Chapter 22). The reader is cautioned that the free-time area will not operate in the desired reinforcing way unless the objects included are of need-satisfying value to the subjects using them.

Body image is defined as the adequacy with which one regards one's physical appearance, and in essence is the motor equivalent of the self concept. It is our contention that most special education subjects have body-image problems, and that such problems can cause low esteem, compensatory behavior, apathy, and learning problems. A body-image center is included in this classroom arrangement design for the purpose of attempting body-image problem resolution. Such resolution can be attempted by the following kinds of body-image tasks and equipment: tumbling mats, mirrors, a balance beam, punching bag, jump rope, a small weight set, grooming activities, a vanity and cosmetic equipment for the girls, etc.

A carrel is a study booth. Carrels operate to reduce extraneous classroom stimuli for those subjects who have attending problems. Carrels are used for study purposes only and never for punishment purposes. On the other hand, the time-out area is always used for punishment purposes and never for study purposes. A student who is having attending problems due to extraneous classroom stimuli (noise, light, vibration, etc.), can often benefit from assignment to a carrel, in which case that student should not lose the privilege of receiving checkmarks. Unlike the time-out area where there is a time limit to a student's punishment, a student conceivably could use a carrel indefinitely, as long as the controlled environment serves to resolve the attending problem.

In the middle of the classroom is the mastery center. This center exists to permit tool-subject mastery work for those students who can independently problem solve. For reasons discussed in the preceding chapter, the mastery center should have no more than thirteen desks, one desk for each student (we recommend that whatever the nature of the classroom design, and for emotional-security purposes, each special education student be assigned to, and permitted to own, a desk). The desks can be arranged either in the traditional rows or in a circle. We favor a circle, with the desks facing inward, which permits the teacher and aide to monitor student tool-subject progress by walking around the back of the circle and looking over the shoulders of the students. The application of contingency contracts is excellent here, and as an additional reinforcer, the teacher may arrange for the student to turn the chair around after having successfully completed the contract.

Table XXVII presents a classroom arrangement design that is a variation of the preceding design. Whereas the former design is good for acting-out as well as benign students, the currently considered classroom design is good for students with instructional problems, including learning disabilities. This classroom design operates on the basis of learning centers, which are primarily defined by the major learning channels, as discussed in Part II.

This classroom arrangement can operate in the more traditional way of assigning students to the mastery center for independent tool-subjet work and then, if necessary, assigning students to appropriate learning centers for remedial work. Or in a less traditional way of operating, this classroom arrangement permits the grouping of students into auditory, visual, and haptic learning strengths and weaknesses; assigning students to appropriate learning centers for tool-subject instruction in the area of strength; and then regrouping the students into appropriate centers for learning weakness remediation. Regarding the second way of operating, mastery center assignment could be employed as a reward for students who successfully complete their assignments.

The auditory learning center should be supplied with auditory input, memory, meaning, and language output materials. Such materials might include: listening posts, walkie-talkies, the Peabody Language Development Kits (Dunn, L., and Smith, J., 1967), the Distar Language materials (Engleman, S., and Osborn, J., 1973), Language Masters, matching sound activities, tape recorders, the Auditory Discrimination in Depth program (Lindamood, C., and Lindamood, P., 1975), the GOAL Language program, (Karnes, M., 1977), the Goldman-Lynch Sounds and Symbols program (Goldman, R., and Lynch, M., 1971), etc.

The time-out area for this clasroom design is the same as that for the preceding classroom design.

The visual learning center should be supplied with visual input, memory, meaning, and graphic output materials. Such materials might include: the Frostig visual-perception materials (Frostig, M., and Horne, D., 1972), pegboards, puzzles, dot-to-dot exercises, etch-a-sketch, clay, sand, finger paints, sandpaper, tachistoscopes, felt material, crayons, the Fairbanks-Robinson materials (Fairbanks, J., and Robinson, J., 1977), the Dubnoff program (Dubnoff, B., et al., 1968), the Ann Arbor Tracking materials (Geake, R., and Smith, D., 1975), etc.

The body-image center and free-time area are the same as those for the preceding classroom design.

The VAKT center is designed for those subjects who have general learning-channel deficiency. We have found the VAKT remedial technique (Fernald, 1943) to be effective with these kinds of subjects, and have therefore included a VAKT center within the learning center classroom design. The VAKT center should be supplied with multisensory kinds of materials, and the primary remedial emphasis should be on tracing, saying, seeing, and feeling. Those materials might include: raised-surface materials (sandpaper or felt letters and numbers), experience chart materials, clay, sand, finger paints, the crumbly kind of crayons, etc.

The carrel concept is the same as that for the preceding classroom design. However, carrels might be even more important for the learning center than the interest center classroom in that many learning disabled students are very distractable, a situation which carrels are designed to help.

The mastery center operates the same way as for the preceding classroom design.

Table XXVIII presents a modified version of Homme's menu concept (Homme, 1970). This classroom arrangement operates on the basis of interest centers as well as a free time/menu area. This classroom design is most appropriate for acting-out students when operating without a teacher-aide.

The order center, time-out area, body-image center, carrels, and mastery center operate in much the same way with this classroom design as they do with the preceding two classroom designs.

We have found that this classroom design works best by employing the strategy of contingency contracts. The contracts may be written or oral, and involve identifying what a student must do in order to earn a high-probability privilege from the teacher. That privilege is usually expressed in the form of free time in the free-time area. For example, for having completed a particular contract, the student is permitted ten minutes of free time in the free-time area.

Upon completing a contract, the student turns his chair around to face the outside of the mastery center and brings the completed contract to the teacher's desk for checking. If the contract is successfully completed, the student may select from the menu bulletin board that activity in which he would like to engage in the free-time area. The student receives a watch-fob timer, sets it for ten minutes, and engages in the activity. At the expiration of the time, the student returns to the teacher's desk, obtains a new contract, returns to the mastery center, turns the chair inward, and begins a new contract cycle. If the stuent begins to develop unacceptable behavior, and/or if nontool-subject problem-solving tasks are needed, the student may be refrerred to the order center, body-image center, X-work, or time-out area. Except for the time-out area, a student should not be punished by checkmark deprivation for needing to experience nontool-subject tasks.

The menu bulletin board should be a partition of above-head height which extends the width of the classroom, with the exception of the entry area at which the teacher's desk is located. On the menu board should be pictorial descriptions of the free-time activities located inside the free-time area. Those pictorial descriptions may be of several fashions, such as pictures drawn by the students, pictures obtained from magazines, pictures taken with a camera by the students, etc. It should be stressed that a free-time area will not operate effectively as a reinforcer unless the activities included have a need-satisfying and high-probability value to the students using those activities.

As with any application of contingency contracts, the teacher may use reinforcers in addition to the free-time area. Such reinforcers could include: field-trips, nonschool experiences with the teacher, movies, in-school experiences with the teacher, tokens, etc.

Table XXIX presents the DI classroom arrangement. The function of the DI center (#1) is for the teacher to present new concepts to students, using Direct Instruction techniques. All materials to be used are stored adjacent to the center to facilitate storage and retrieval relative to changes in student groups. The Follow-Up center (#2) exists to provide students leaving the Direct Instruction center with supervised repetition relative to concepts taught in the Direct Instruction Center. Center #2 is supervised by an aide, who is available to students for the purpose of providing immediate instructional feedback. The Mastery Center (#3) exists in order to provide students leaving the Follow-Up Center with an opportunity to practice independently those skills learned in the two previous centers. The Mastery Center is also supervised by an aide. The Goal Center (#4) provides the teacher and aide with a specified place within the classroom where: 1) Students can be encouraged to set daily behavioral and academic goals; and 2) students receive feedback relative to goal achievement.

SELECTED REFERENCES

Dubnoff, B., Chambers, I., and Schaefer, F. *Dubnoff School Program.* Boston: Teaching Resources, 1968.

Dunn, L., and Smith, J. *Peabody Language Development Kits.* Circle Pines, Minnesota: American Guidance Service, 1967.

Engleman, S., and Osborn, J. *Distar Language, I, II, & III.* Chicago: Science Research Associates, 1973.

Fairbanks, J., and Robinson, J. *Fairbanks-Robinson Program.* Boston: Teaching Resources, 1977.

Fernald, G. *Remedial Techniques in Basic School Subjects.* New York: McGraw-Hill, 1943.

Frostig, M., and Horne, D. *Frostig Program for the Development of Visual Perception.* Chicago: Follett Publishing Company, 1972.

Frostig, M., and Maslow, P. *Move-Grow-Learn.* Chicago: Follett Publishing Company, 1973.

Geake, R., and Smith, D. *Ann Arbor Tracking Program.* Worthington, Ohio: Ann Arbor Publishers, 1975.

Goldman, R., and Lynch, M. *Goldman-Lynch Sounds Development Kit. Circle Pines, Minnesota: American Guidance Service, 1971.*

Hewett, F. *The Emotionally Disturbed Child in the Classroom.* Boston: Allyn and Bacon, 1968.

Homme, L. et al. *How to Use Contingency Contracting in the Classroom. Illinois: Research Press, 1970.*

Karnes, M. *GOAL and GOAL II Programs: Language Development. Springfield, Massachusetts: Milton Bradley, 1977.*

Lindamood, C., and Lindamood, P. *The A.D.D. Program—Auditory Discrimination in Depth.* Boston: Teaching Resources, 1975.

Table XXVI
Interest Center Classroom Arrangement

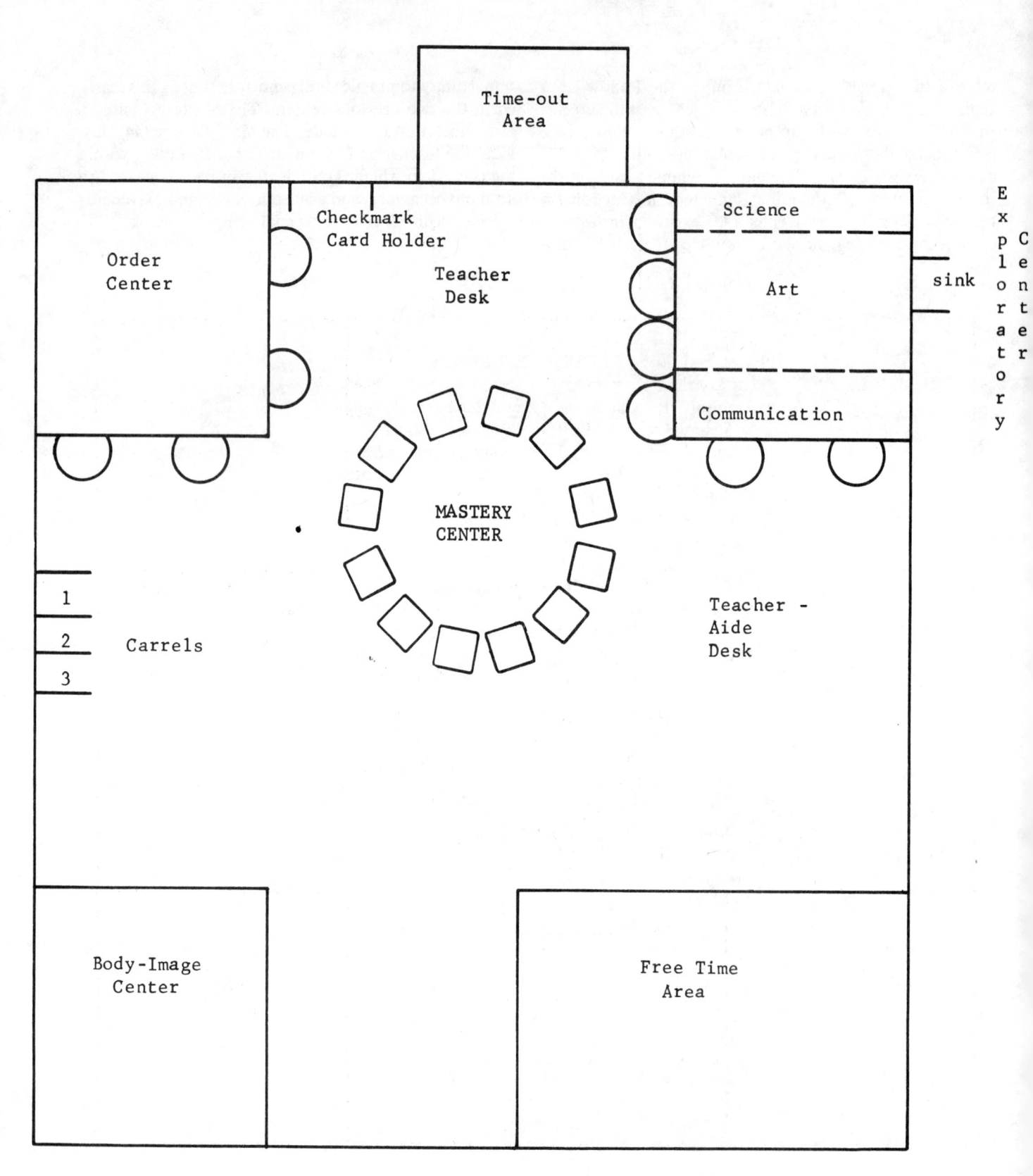

Table XXVII
Learning Center Classroom Arrangement

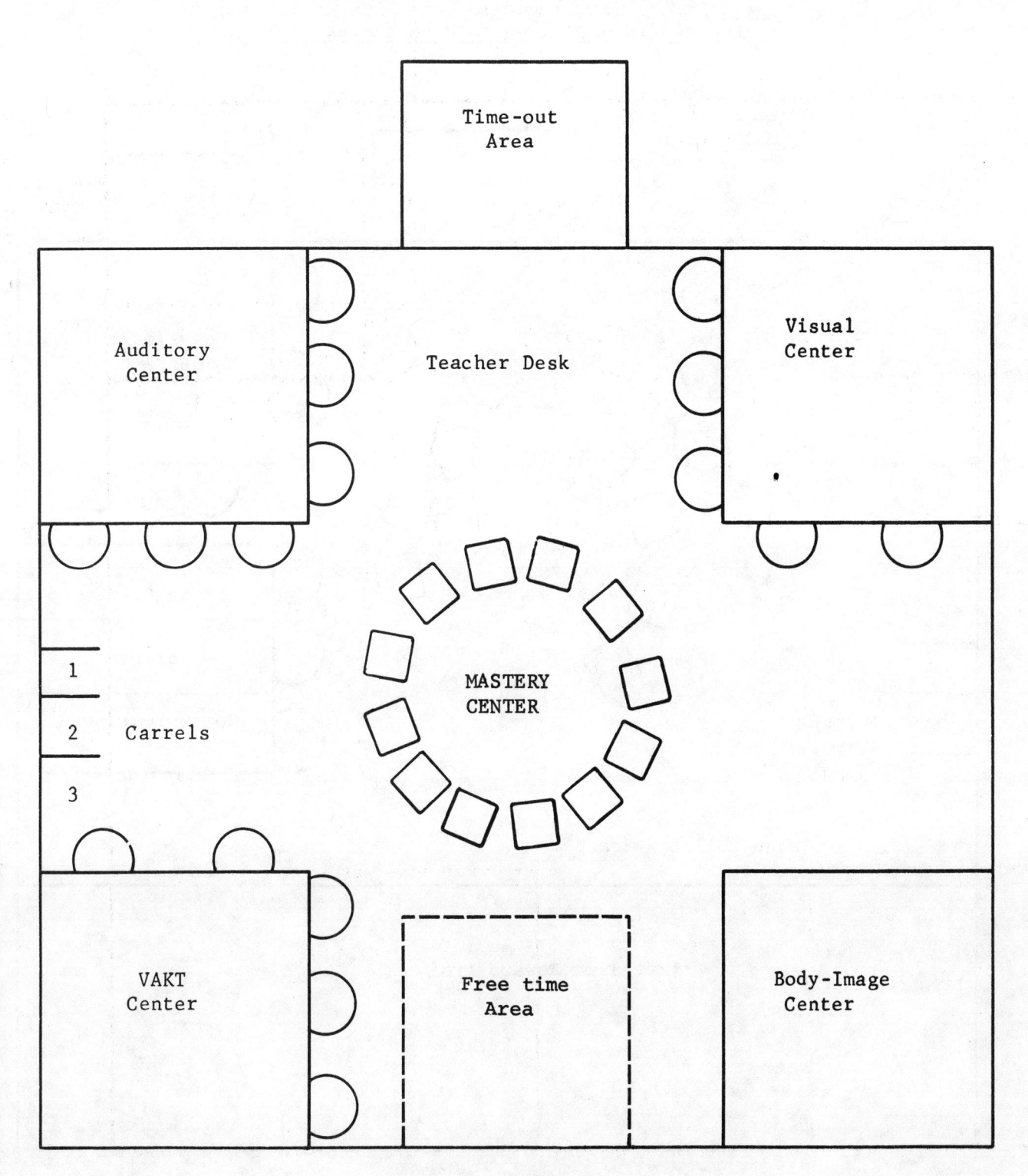

Time-out Area

Auditory Center

Teacher Desk

Visual Center

1
2 Carrels
3

MASTERY CENTER

VAKT Center

Free time Area

Body-Image Center

Table XXVIII

Learning Menu Classroom Arrangement

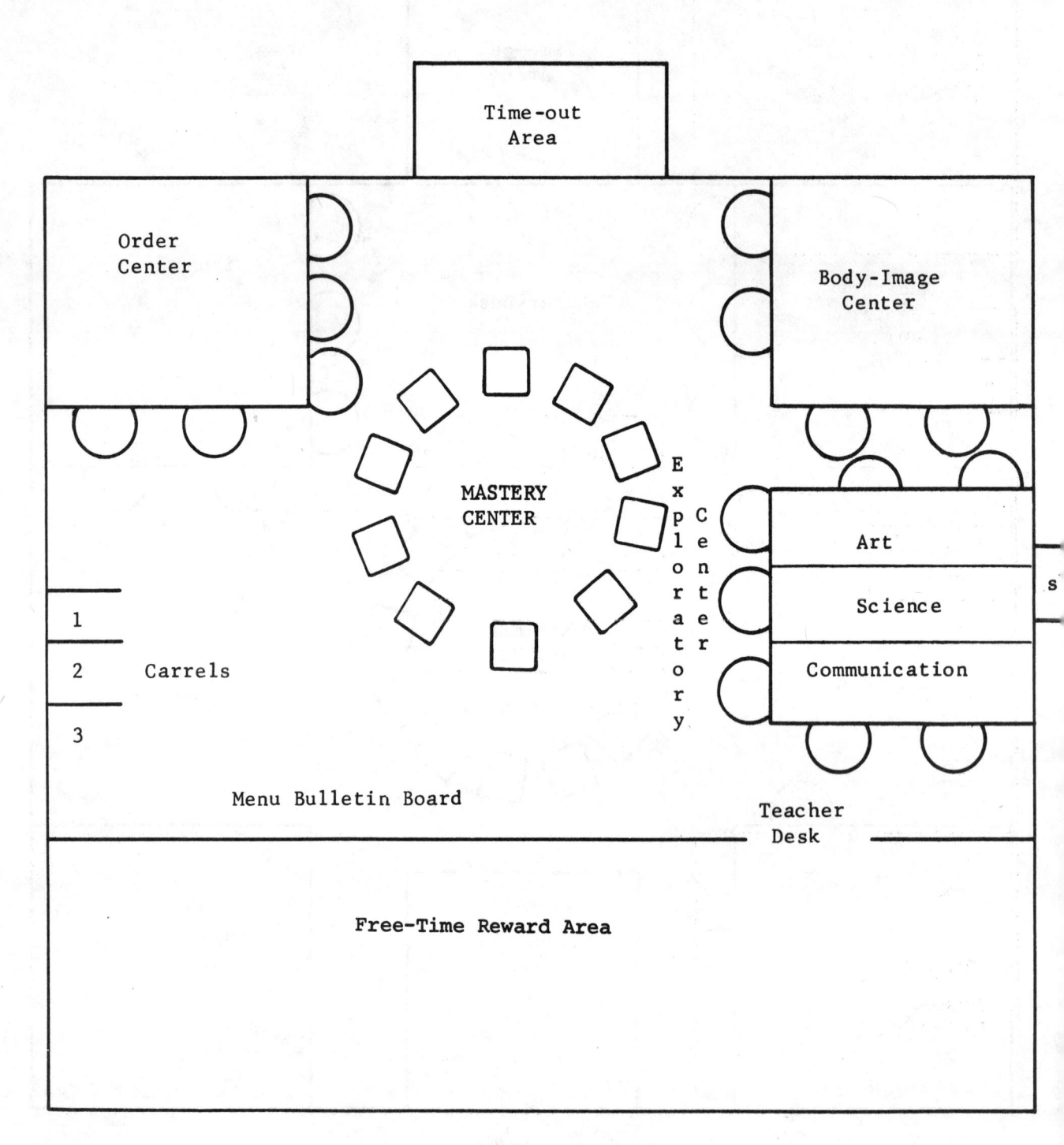

Table XXIX

Direct Instruction Classroom Arrangement

- Goal Center (#4)
- Materials
- Direct Instruction Center (#1)
- Storage
- Carrels
- Time-Out Area
- Teacher Desk
- Mastery Center (#3)
- Follow-up Center
- Body Image Center
- Free Time Area

Chapter 25

Classroom Grouping Arrangements

The management model is applicable to individual as well as group prescriptive programming. However, the more students there are, the more difficult it is to individualize instruction for each student. Therefore, student grouping procedures become necessary.

The present chapter presents various arrangements by which student grouping can be achieved. As with the selection of educational materials, the selection of a classroom grouping arrangement should be made on the basis of a match between the nature of the student presenting problem and the assets of the various grouping arrangements. But, student grouping should be arranged on the basis of the largest possible common denominator: i.e., 2 groups of seven students each are easier to teach than 7 groups of two students each.

The following discussion, in conjunction with Table XXX, presents the various classroom grouping arrangements.

1. Group according to student grade level ability for each tool-subject. For reading, the students would be grouped according to their reading grade level ability. The same for spelling, arithmetic, etc. This is a traditional grouping arrangement, and if there are no students with learning disabilities in the class, it is a sound grouping arrangement (Refer to Table XXX, No. 1, for an illustration).

2. Group across all tool-subjects according to IQ. For example, for reading, language, arithmetic, etc., students with IQs between 70-85 would be grouped together, students with IQs between 85-100 would be grouped together, students with IQs between 100-115 would be grouped together, etc. We regard this grouping arrangement as primitive and without much to recommend it (Table XXX, No. 2).

3. Group according to learning channel weakness, with primary student assignment to mastery center desks. Basic problem solving would occur at the mastery center, but students would be identified in terms of auditory, visual, or haptic learning strengths and weaknesses; when learning problems of a channel-weakness nature occurred, the students would be referred to the appropriate center for remedial activity. We regard this grouping arrangement as acceptable, especially if the range of student ability is wide and the students have learning as opposed to behavior problems (Table XXX, No. 3).

4. Group by assigning students to learning centers, for each tool-subject, according to student learning strengths and weaknesses. Unlike number 3 above, this grouping arrangement does not involve a mastery center; rather, students would be assigned to learning centers, based on their learning strengths and weaknesses, for each tool subject. For "reading: learning strength", students with auditory strength would be assigned to the auditory center; students with visual strength would be assigned to the visual center; and students with no strength would be assigned to the VAKT center. Reading, for example, would be taught by student learning strength for approximately 75% of the total reading period time. The other 25% of the reading period would involve re-grouping the students according to their learning channel weakness, and attempting to remediate the particular tool-subject problem by remediating the learning weakness (Table XXX, No. 4).

We regard this classroom grouping arrangement as good, but only if the student presenting problems are learning and not behavioral in nature. A major reservation we have about this classroom arrangement is that students are not assigned a permanent desk. We contend that students should be assigned a desk which becomes private territory for the duration of the time the student is in the class. The resulting sense of ownership helps provide school identity and pride.

5. Group across all tool-subjects according to chronological age. For example, where the student chronological age range is wide, five- and six-year-old students would be grouped together, seven and eight together, nine-year-olds together, etc. We do not recommend this

grouping arrangement as it is too crude to have many advantages (Table XXX, No. 5).

6. Group across all tool-subjects according to special education category. Mentally retarded students would be grouped together, learning disability students would be grouped together, emotionally disturbed students would be grouped together, etc. This grouping arrangement is possible only when there is a wide variety of subject presenting problems, and only when the special education categories are definite enough to be distinguishable. Nevertheless, we do not recommend this grouping arrangement as it is too crude to have many advantages (Table XXX, No.6).

7. Group across all tool-subjects according to student ITPA Composite Psycholinguistic Age (CPLA). For example, students with CPLA scores of 4-5 would be grouped together, 6-7 would be grouped together, etc. This grouping arrangement is effective only if the presenting problems are learning and not behavioral in nature, and even then it is too crude to provide many advantages (Table XXX, No. 7).

8. Group across all tool-subjects according to grade in school. For example, first grade students would be grouped together, second-third grade students grouped together, etc. Again, this grouping arrangement is crude, and we do not recommend it (Table XXX, No.8).

9. Group for each tool-subject according to student learning quotients for each tool-subject. For reading, for example (or spelling, or arithmetic, etc.), students with learning quotients below 80 would be grouped together; students with learning quotients from 80-90 would be grouped together; students with LQs from 90-110 would be grouped together; etc. We regard this grouping arrangement as having potential merit, and if combined with an interest center arrangement, could be effective for students with either learning or behavior problems (Table XXX, No. 9).

10. Group by means of interest centers (Hewett, 1968), with primary student assignment to mastery center desks. The classroom arrangement should include an order center, exploratory center (science-art-communication), body-image center, free time area, a time-out room, carrels, and a mastery center. This classroom arrangement is excellent for students with behavior problems; it is not as good for students with learning disabilities (Table XXX, No. 10).

11. Group by means of activity centers. Students would be assigned mastery center desks but would have access to the various activity centers should the instructional-behavioral need arise. The operation of the classroom would be coordinated by use of learning contracts in relation to a token economy system and store. We regard this classroom grouping arrangement as very good, especially when operating without an aide and with students who represent a variety of learning and behavior problems (Table XXX, No.11).

12. This classroom grouping arrangement involves the use of the learning menu (Homme, 1970) classroom design, and has three different variations, all of which effectively operate by means of the learning contracts and free time strategies.

   a. Group according to student grade level ability for each tool-subject. One-third of the physical classroom would be devoted to the menu oriented free time area, and the other two-thirds would be devoted to the grouping arrangement. The grouping would be different for each tool-subject. For reading, for example, students with first grade reading ability would be grouped together; students with second and third grade reading ability would be grouped together; etc. Optimally, this classroom design would involve a time-out area and a body-image center (Table XXX, No. 12a).

   b. Again, the learning menu classroom design is used, but students would be grouped into learning centers, for each tool-subject, according to learning strengths and weaknesses. Thus, for "arithmetic: strength," students would be grouped into the auditory center or the visual center according to their learning strength. Most of the total arithmetic period time would be spent teaching arithmetic by means of the learning channel strength. Students who have no learning channel strength would be grouped into the VAKT center. For "arithmetic: weakness," students would be grouped into learning centers according to their learning weaknesses in an attempt to remediate the arithmetic difficulty by remediating the learning weakness. Optimally, this classroom design would involve a time-out area and a body-image center (Table XXX, No. 12b).

   c. Still using the learning menu classroom design, students would be grouped according to learning strengths and weakness for each tool-subject, into learning centers, which are subdivided by means of tool-subject grade level ability. As in (b) above, there would be auditory, visual, and

VAKT centers for each tool-subject. However, within each of those centers would be grade level subcenters. For example, for "spelling: strength," students with first grade spelling ability who also have auditory strength would be grouped into the first grade auditory subcenter; students with second grade spelling ability with auditory strength would be in that particular subgroup; students with first grade spelling ability but with visual strength would be in that particular subgroup; etc. Most of the tool-subject period would be devoted to teaching that tool-subject by means of the learning strength, although approximately 25% of the tool-subject period would be devoted to an attempt to remediate the tool-subject problem by attempting to remediate the learning channel weakness (Table XXX, No. 12c).

The advantage of (a), (b), and (c) above is that the learning menu classroom design is good when operating without an aide. Arrangement (a) is particularly good when the student presenting problems are not of a learning disability nature. Arrangements (b) and (c) are good when the student presenting problems are of a learning disability nature. Arrangement (c) is good when there are a large number of students in the class, a wide range of student ability, and a variety of learning problems.

13. Group by means of interest centers in relation to the learning menu classroom design. Students would be assigned mastery center desks but would have access to order center, exploratory center, and body-image center activities should the instructional or behavioral need arise. The operation of the centers would be coordinated by the use of contingency management in relation to the menu-based free time area. In addition, this grouping arrangement involves the use of carrels for the purpose of reducing extraneous environmental stimuli for students who are hyperactive and/or have attention problems. We regard this classroom grouping arrangement as very good, especially when operating without an aide and with students who have behavior problems (Table XXX, No. 13).

14. Group into learning centers according to grade level ability for each tool-subject. In addition, each student is permanently assigned a mastery center desk, not only for academic achievement purposes but also to increase student identification with school. Learning center regrouping would occur for each tool-subject according to student learning strengths and weaknesses. In addition: carrels are provided for students who have attending problems; a time-out area is provided for the purpose of extinguishing undesirable student behavior; and a free time area is provided for contingency management purposes. We regard this classroom grouping arrangement as very good, especially when working with an aide, when there is a wide variety of student learning problems, and when there is a moderate to large number of students in the class (Table XXX, No. 14).

15. A useful classroom grouping arrangement for trainable mental retardates is that of grouping according to the mental age interest of, and the survival experiences necessary for, the students in the class. With respect to a primary TMR class, the mental age interests of the students should be equivalent to the interests of 3-5 year old children. Thus, the survival experiences necessary for such primary TMR students might include home activities, safety activities, cleanliness activities, and social activities. Those survival experience activities should be represented by classroom interest centers in which appropriate problem solving activities that are related to the mental age of the students would be conducted. In addition, there should be a mastery center, a body-image center, and depending on the nature of the students, a time-out area. We regard this grouping arrangement as desirable for moderately retarded students who need a life-experience approach to learning necessary coping skills (Table XXX, No. 15).

SELECTED REFERENCES

Hewett, F. *The Emotionally Disturbed Child in the Classroom.* Boston: Allyn & Bacon, 1968,

Homme, L. et al. *How to Use Contingency Contracting in the Classroom.* Illinois: Research Press, 1970.

Table XXX

Classroom Grouping Arrangements

1. Group by tool-subject grade level ability.

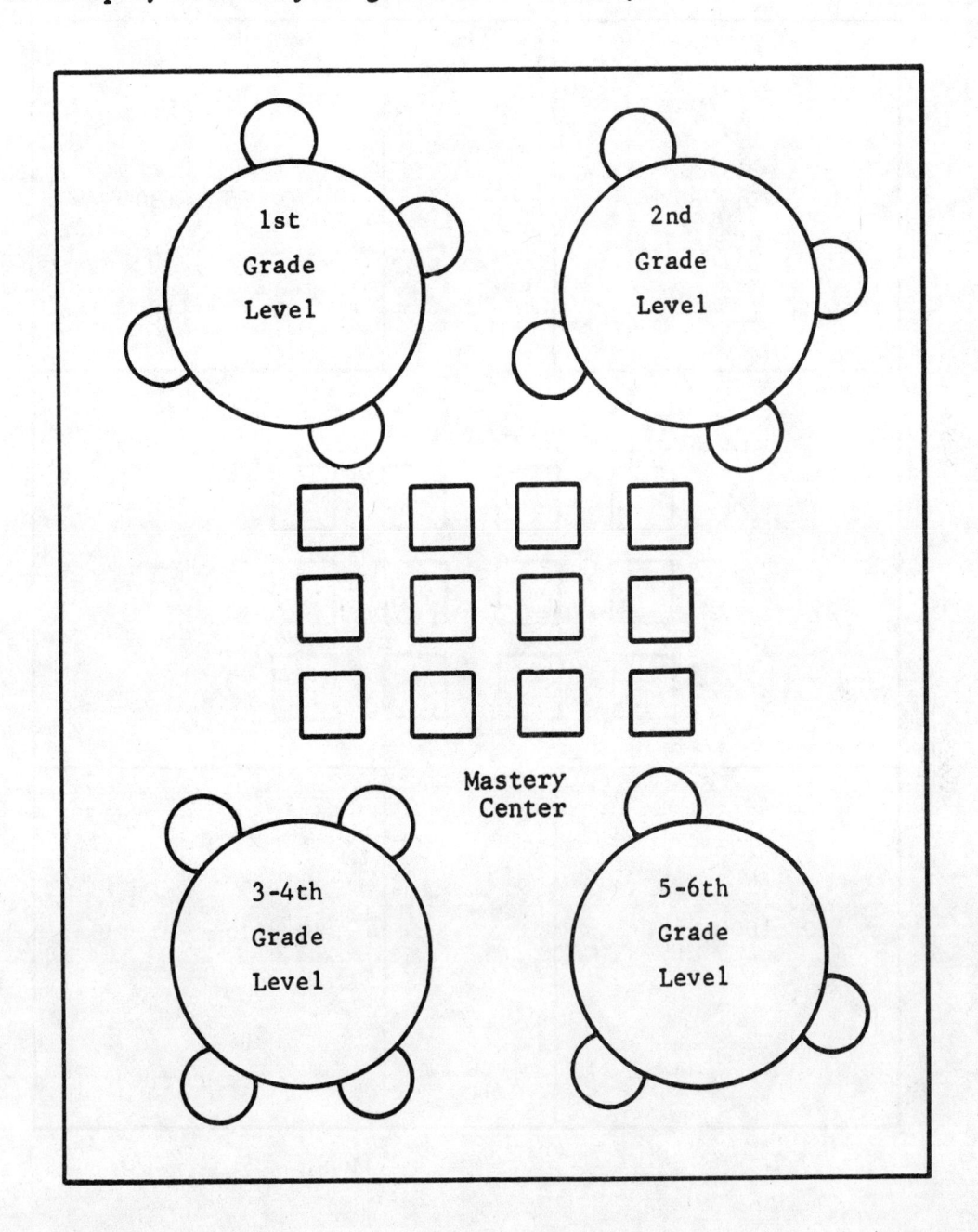

2. Group by IQ

```
┌─────────────────┐  ┌─────────────────┐
│                 │  │                 │
│   IQ  70 - 85   │  │  IQ  85 - 100   │
│                 │  │                 │
└─────────────────┘  └─────────────────┘
     Mastery Center
        □ □ □ □
        □ □ □ □
        □ □ □ □
┌─────────────────┐  ┌─────────────────┐
│                 │  │                 │
│  IQ  100 - 115  │  │    IQ  115+     │
│                 │  │                 │
└─────────────────┘  └─────────────────┘
```

3. Group by learning weakness and learning centers,
   with mastery center assignment.

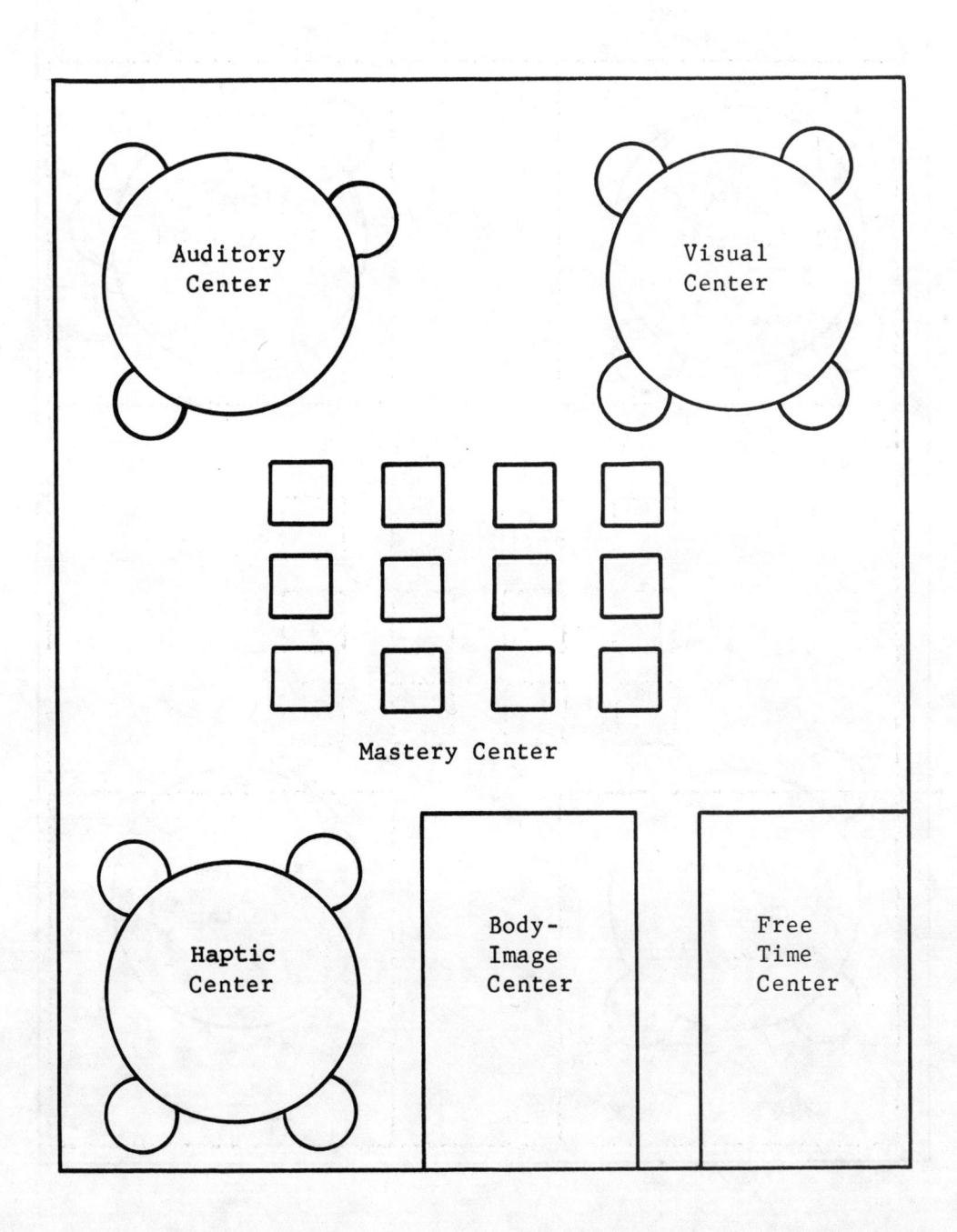

Auditory Center

Visual Center

Mastery Center

Haptic Center

Body-Image Center

Free Time Center

4. Group by learning strengths and weakness, and learning centers for each tool subject.

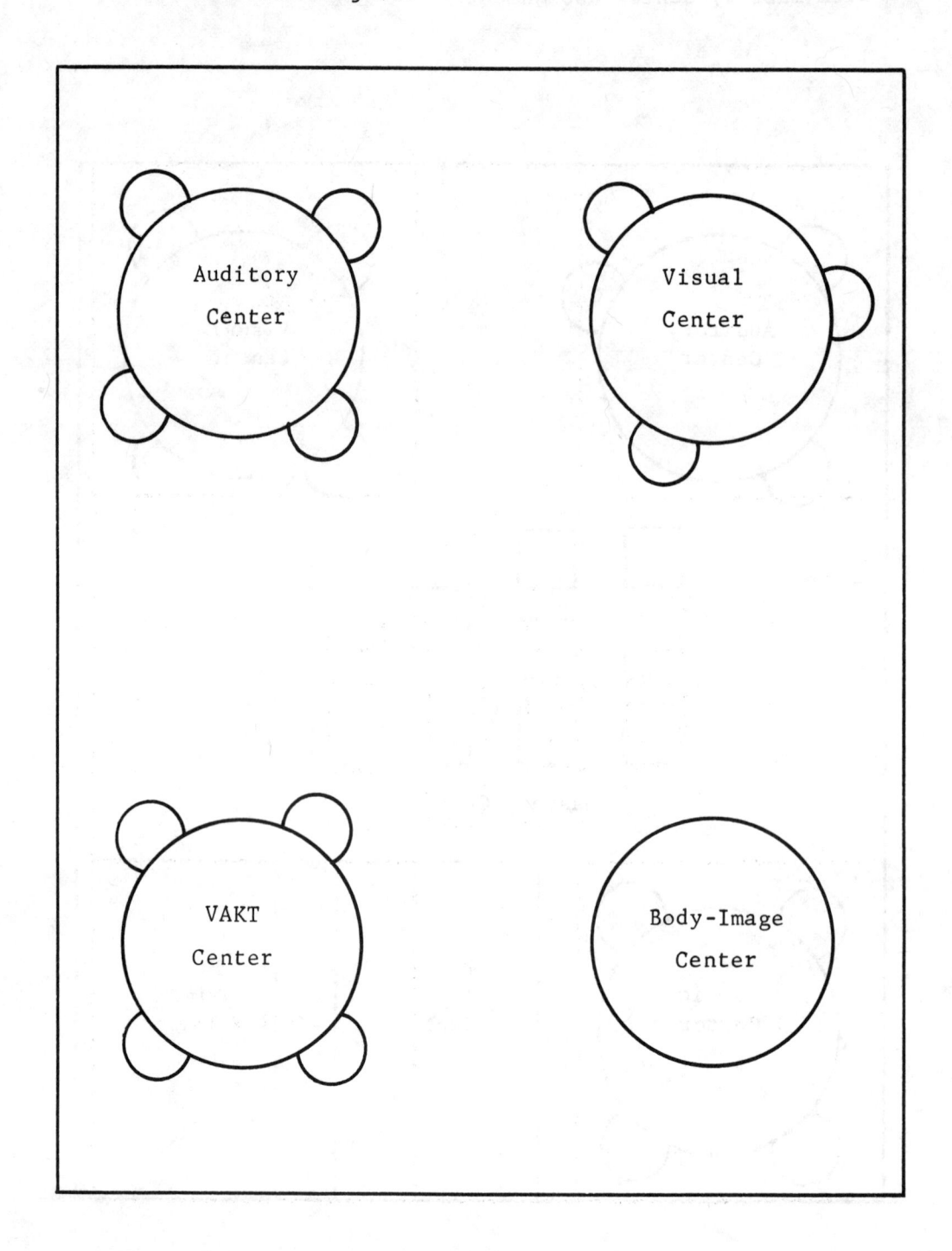

Auditory Center

Visual Center

VAKT Center

Body-Image Center

5. Group by chronological age.

```
┌─────────────┐     ┌─────────────┐
│             │     │             │
│  5-6 years  │     │  7-8 years  │
│             │     │             │
└─────────────┘     └─────────────┘
         Mastery Center
        □  □  □  □
        □  □  □  □
        □  □  □  □
┌─────────────┐     ┌─────────────┐
│             │     │             │
│   9 years   │     │ 10-11 years │
│             │     │             │
└─────────────┘     └─────────────┘
```

6. Group by special education category.

ED	LD

Mastery Center

MR	Regular (Normal)

7. Group by ITPA composite psycholinguistic age.

```
┌─────────────┐   ┌─────────────┐
│             │   │             │
│  CPLA 4-5   │   │  CPLA 6-7   │
│             │   │             │
└─────────────┘   └─────────────┘
┌───────────────────────────────┐
│        Mastery Center         │
│      □   □   □   □            │
│      □   □   □   □            │
│      □   □   □   □            │
└───────────────────────────────┘
┌─────────────┐   ┌─────────────┐
│             │   │             │
│  CPLA 8-9   │   │  CPLA 9+    │
│             │   │             │
└─────────────┘   └─────────────┘
```

8. Group by Grade in School

```
┌─────────────────┐   ┌─────────────────┐
│                 │   │                 │
│                 │   │                 │
│    1st Grade    │   │   2-3rd Grade   │
│                 │   │                 │
│                 │   │                 │
└─────────────────┘   └─────────────────┘
         Mastery Center
           □  □  □  □
           □  □  □  □
           □  □  □  □
┌─────────────────┐   ┌─────────────────┐
│                 │   │                 │
│                 │   │                 │
│   4-5th Grade   │   │   6-7th Grade   │
│                 │   │                 │
│                 │   │                 │
└─────────────────┘   └─────────────────┘
```

9. Group by learning quotient for each tool subject.

LQ 80 <		LQ 80 - 90
	Mastery Center	
LQ 90 - 110		LQ 110 >

10. Group by interest centers

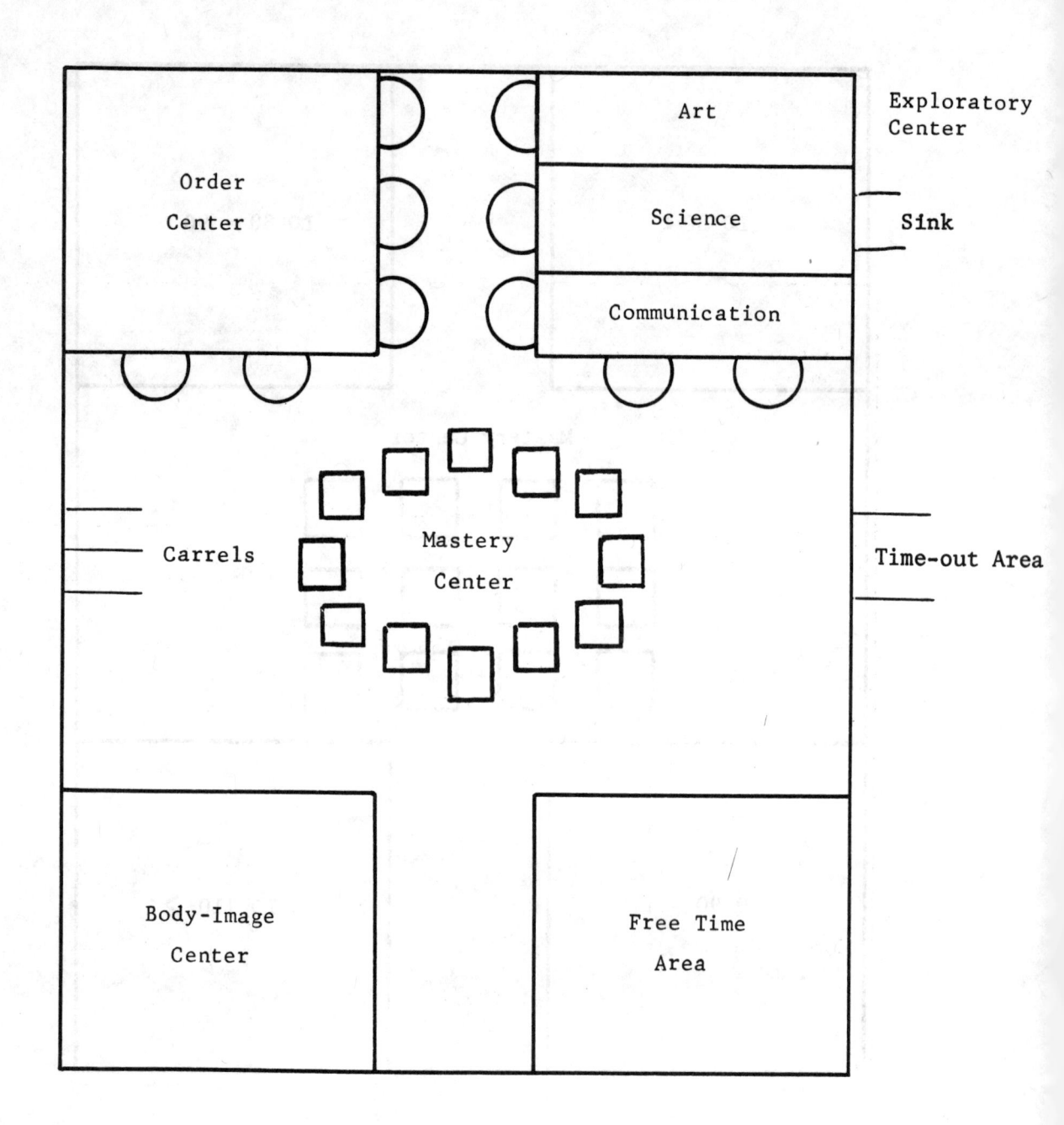

- Order Center
- Art
- Science
- Communication
- Exploratory Center
- Sink
- Carrels
- Mastery Center
- Time-out Area
- Body-Image Center
- Free Time Area

11. Group by activity centers

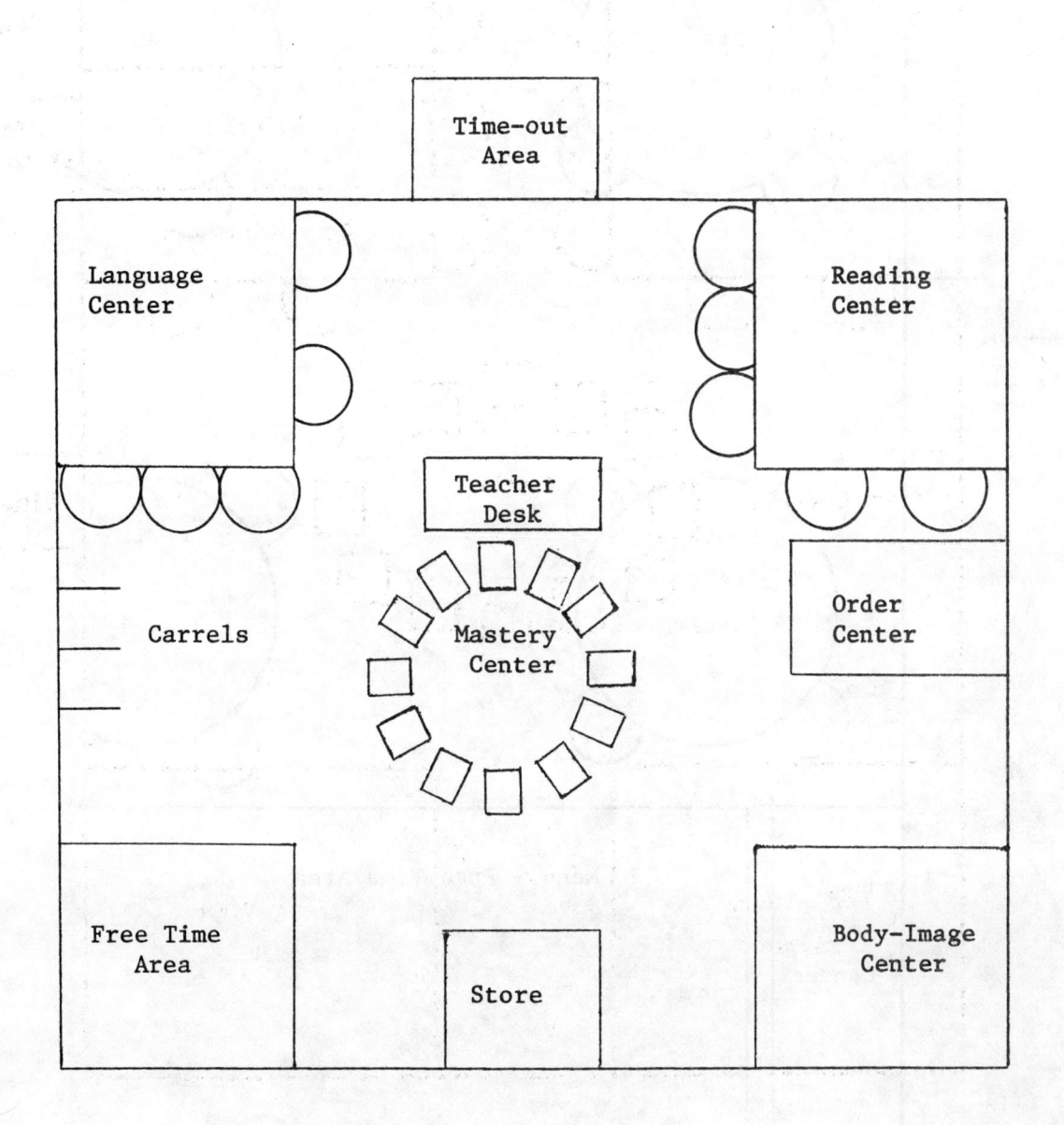

```
                    ┌──────────┐
                    │ Time-out │
                    │   Area   │
                    └──────────┘
┌─────────────┬──────────────────────┬─────────────┐
│  Language   │                      │   Reading   │
│   Center    │                      │   Center    │
│             │   ┌──────────┐       │             │
│             │   │ Teacher  │       ├─────────────┤
├─────────────┤   │   Desk   │       │    Order    │
│             │   └──────────┘       │   Center    │
│   Carrels   │      Mastery         │             │
│             │      Center          ├─────────────┤
│             │                      │             │
├─────────────┤                      │ Body-Image  │
│  Free Time  │      ┌───────┐       │   Center    │
│    Area     │      │ Store │       │             │
└─────────────┴──────┴───────┴───────┴─────────────┘
```

12a. Three variations of the learning menu classroom arrangement. Group by tool-subject grade level ability.

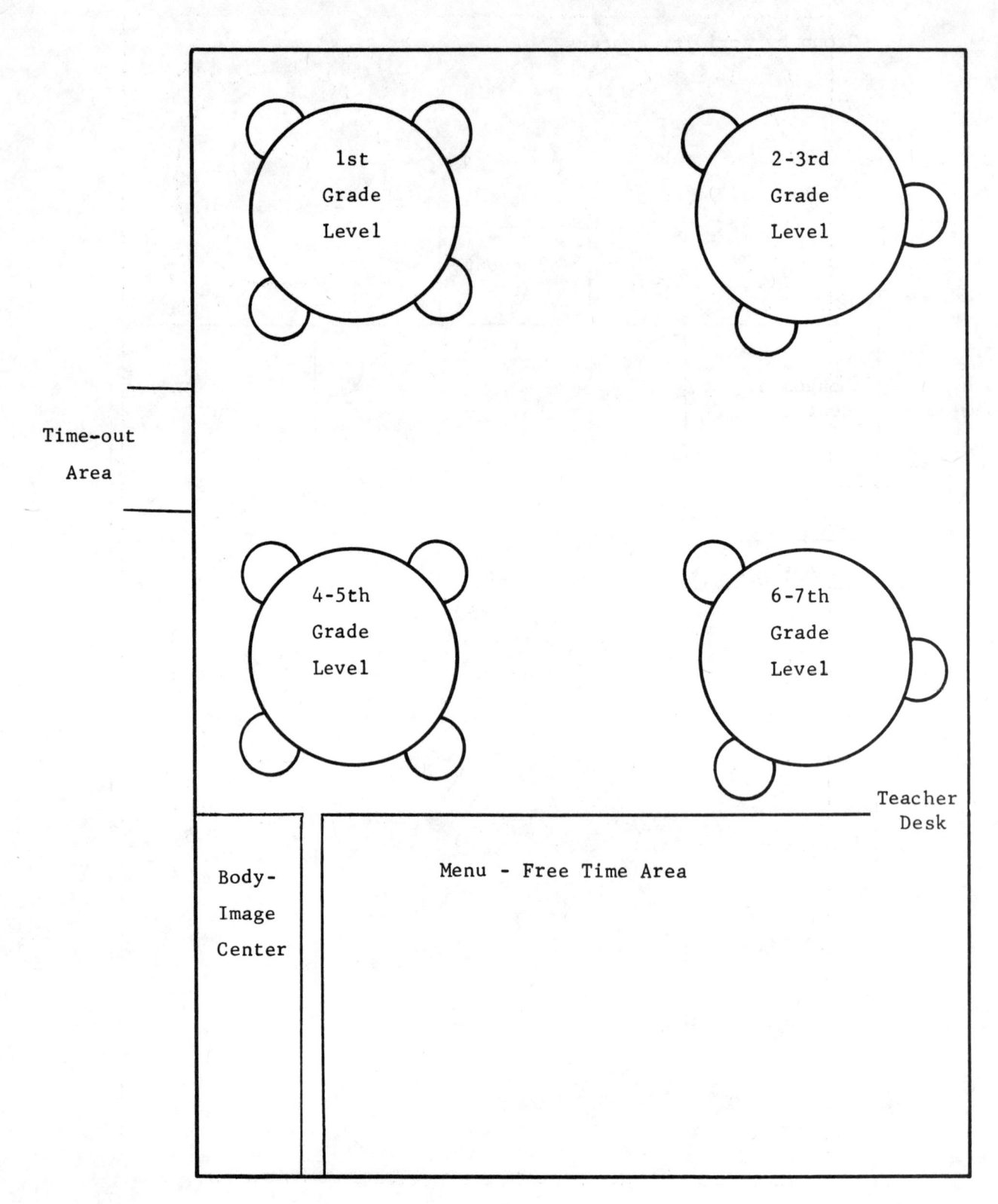

1st Grade Level

2-3rd Grade Level

Time-out Area

4-5th Grade Level

6-7th Grade Level

Teacher Desk

Body-Image Center

Menu - Free Time Area

12b. Group by learning strengths and weakness, and learning centers for each tool-subject.

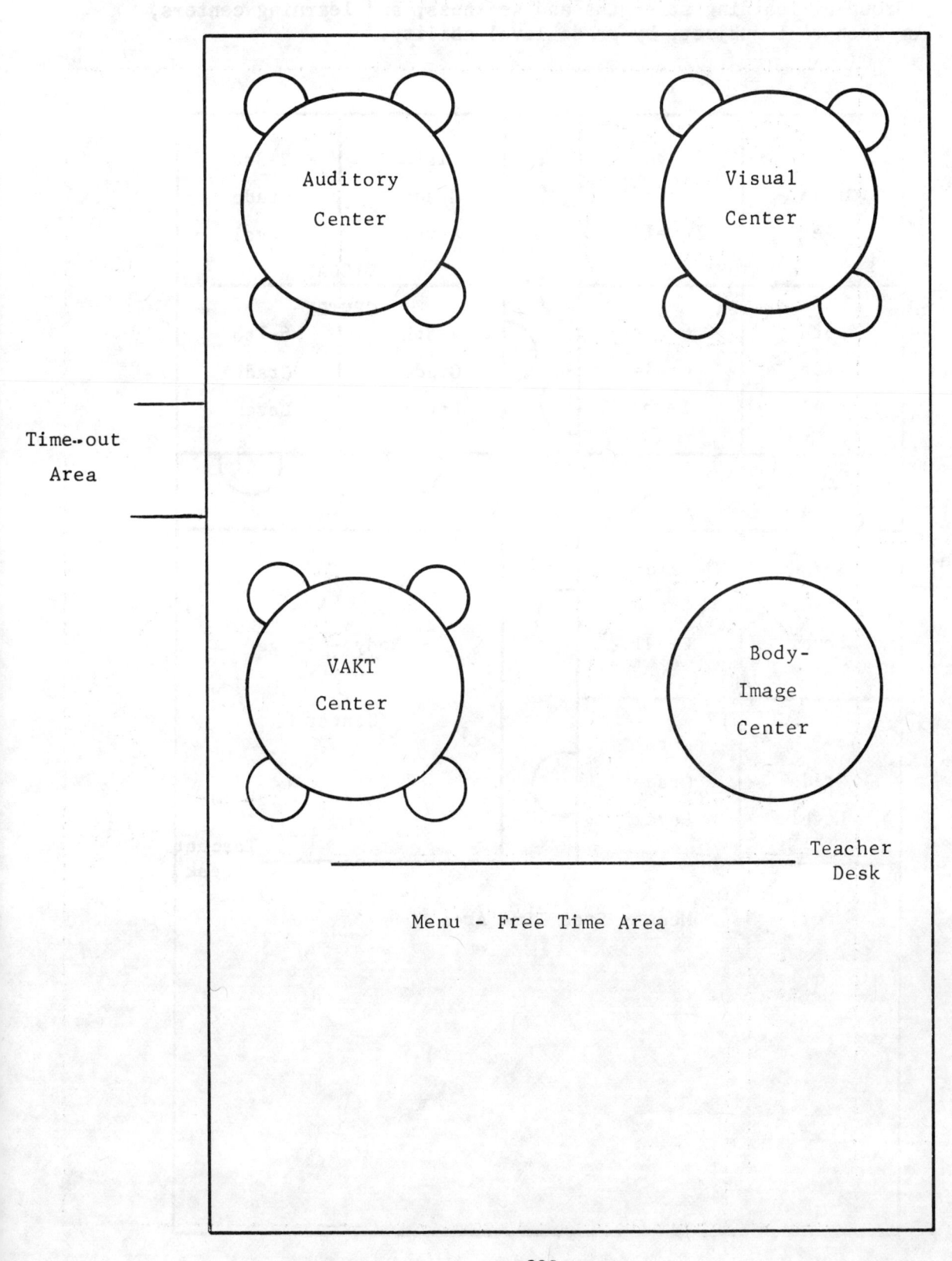

Auditory Center

Visual Center

Time-out Area

VAKT Center

Body-Image Center

Teacher Desk

Menu - Free Time Area

12c Group by learning strengths and weakness, and learning centers,
     for each tool-subject, by grade level ability.

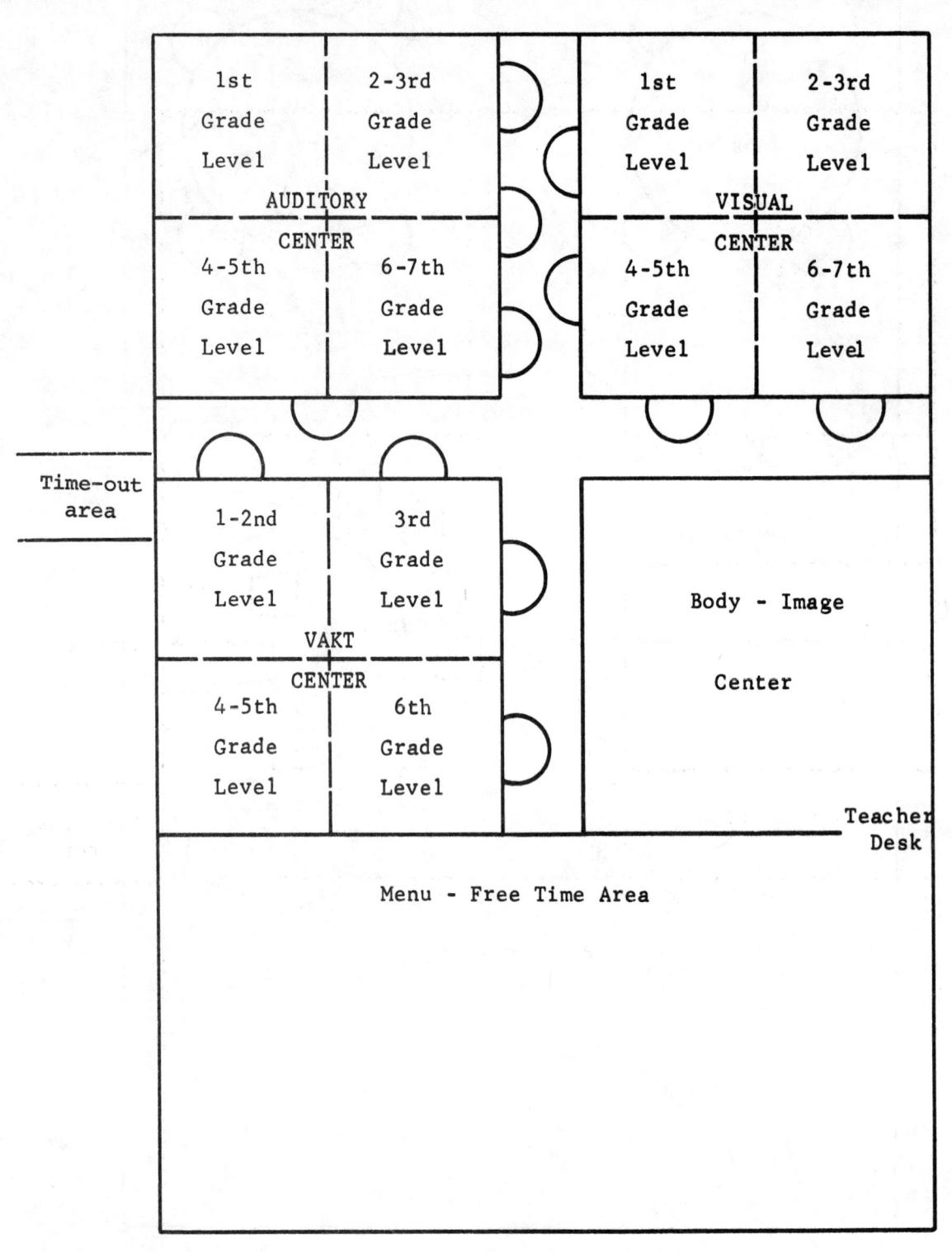

```
┌─────────────────────────┐      ┌─────────────────────────┐
│   1st    │   2-3rd      │      │   1st    │   2-3rd      │
│  Grade   │   Grade      │      │  Grade   │   Grade      │
│  Level   │   Level      │      │  Level   │   Level      │
│─ ─ ─AUDITORY─ ─ ─ ─ ─ ─ │      │─ ─ ─ VISUAL─ ─ ─ ─ ─ ─ ─│
│         CENTER          │      │         CENTER          │
│  4-5th   │   6-7th      │      │  4-5th   │   6-7th      │
│  Grade   │   Grade      │      │  Grade   │   Grade      │
│  Level   │   Level      │      │  Level   │   Level      │
└─────────────────────────┘      └─────────────────────────┘

Time-out
 area
         ┌─────────────────────────┐  ┌──────────────────────┐
         │  1-2nd   │   3rd        │  │                      │
         │  Grade   │   Grade      │  │                      │
         │  Level   │   Level      │  │    Body - Image      │
         │─ ─ ─ VAKT─ ─ ─ ─ ─ ─ ─ ─│  │                      │
         │         CENTER          │  │       Center         │
         │  4-5th   │   6th        │  │                      │
         │  Grade   │   Grade      │  │                      │
         │  Level   │   Level      │  │                      │
         └─────────────────────────┘  └──────────────────────┘
                                                       Teacher
                                                        Desk
              Menu - Free Time Area
```

13. Group by interest centers within the learning menu classroom arrangement

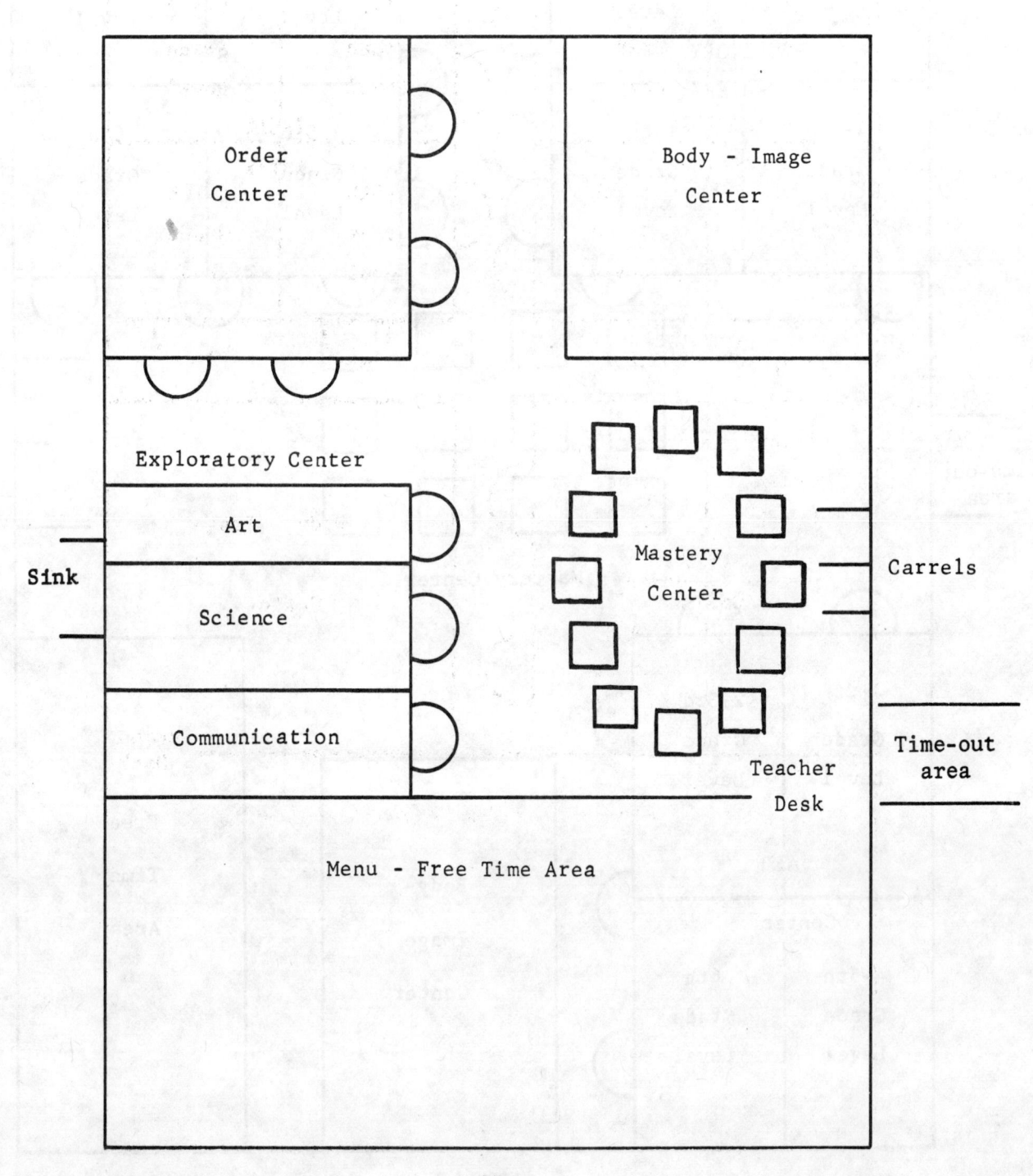

14. Group by learning strengths and weakness, and learning centers, for each tool subject, by grade level ability, with Mastery center assignment.

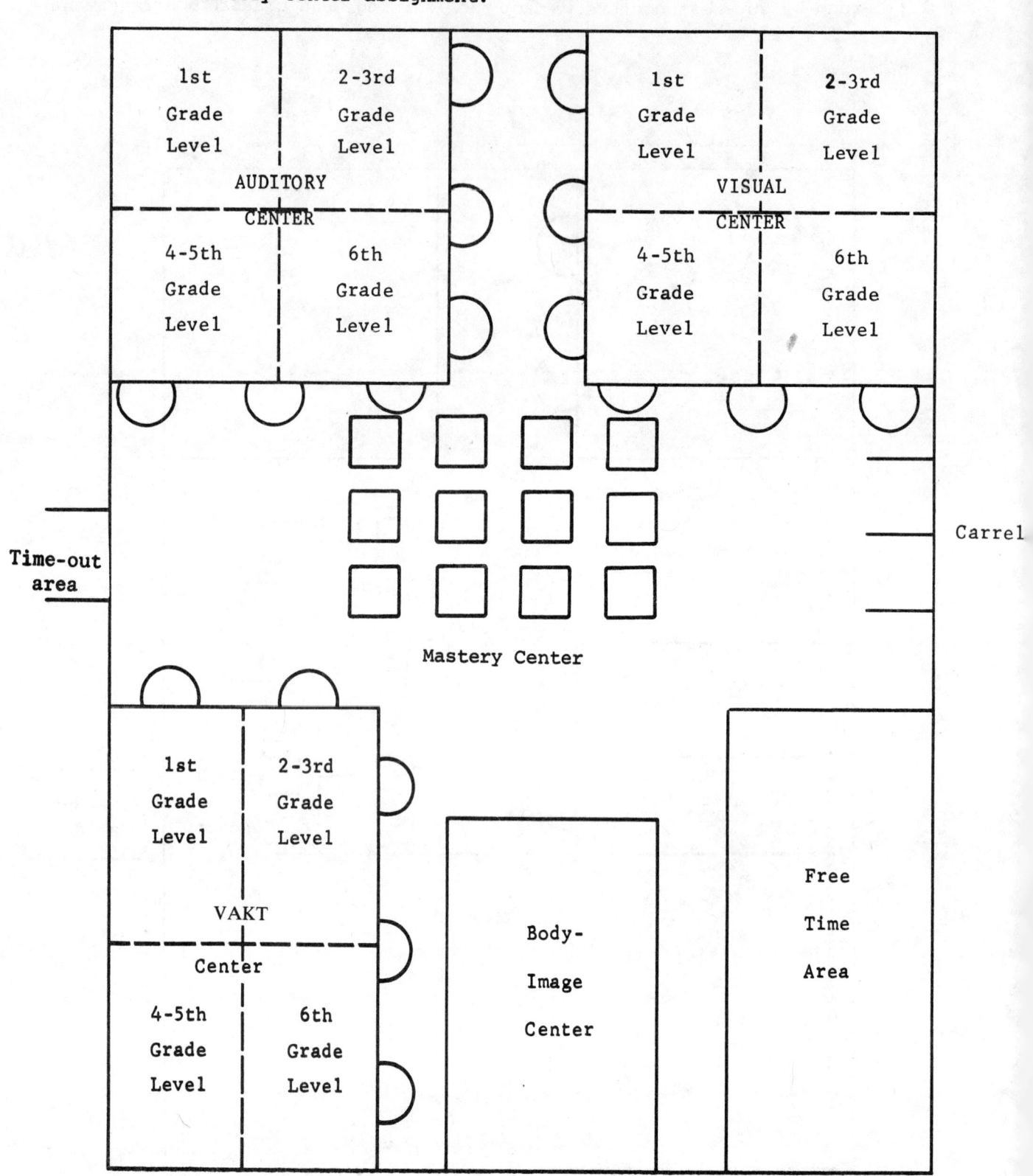

AUDITORY CENTER		VISUAL CENTER	
1st Grade Level	2-3rd Grade Level	1st Grade Level	2-3rd Grade Level
4-5th Grade Level	6th Grade Level	4-5th Grade Level	6th Grade Level

Time-out area

Mastery Center

Carrel

VAKT Center	
1st Grade Level	2-3rd Grade Level
4-5th Grade Level	6th Grade Level

Body-Image Center

Free Time Area

15. Group mental Retardates by mental age interest-based survival centers

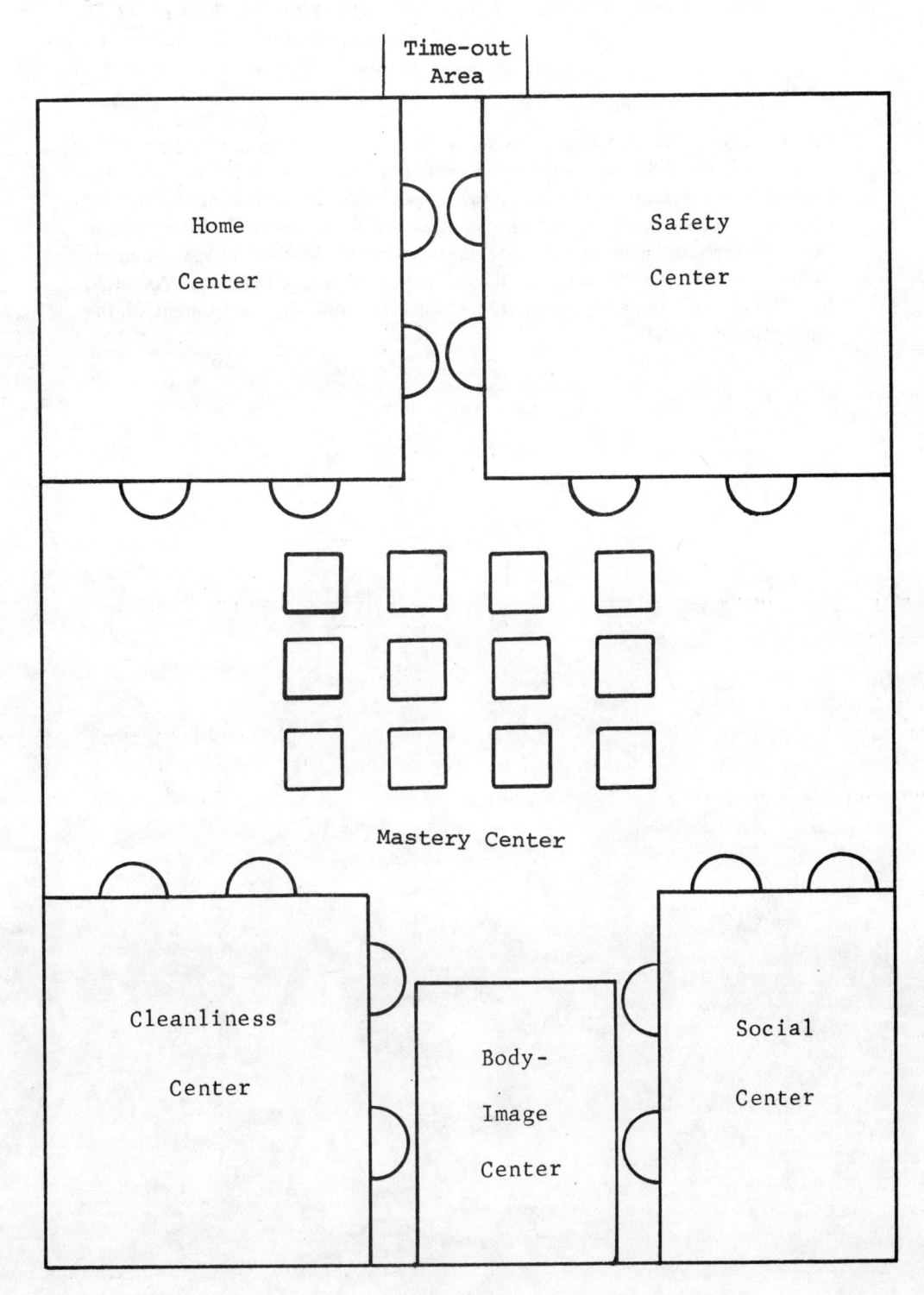

	Time-out Area	
Home Center		Safety Center

Mastery Center

| Cleanliness Center | Body-Image Center | Social Center |

PART VI

THE FIFTH COMPONENT OF THE EDUCATION INTERVENTION AND MANAGEMENT MODEL:
Baseline Measurement

The purpose of the management model is to permit successful intervention with learning or behavior problems. In order to conduct such intervention it is necessary to pinpoint and measure the target behavior. This pinpointing and measuring is accomplished not only by behavioral-instructional objectives and task analyses but also by baseline measurement. Baseline measurement is defined as the identification of the frequency of target behavior. As such, baseline measurement represents the main accountability component of the management model.

Chapter 26

The Theoretical Aspects of Baseline Measurement

Contemporary public education is facing a professional identity crisis. Unlike the disciplines of medicine, psychology, and private industry, the discipline of education is insufficiently developed to be represented by a conceptual system that serves as a theoretical rationale for professional objectives. The discipline of education is not yet able to operate on the basis of an integrated system of philosophy and practice, and thus assumes its professional form on an ever-changing trial-and-error basis. This has led to professional successes and failures, and public criticism. In addition, until recently, educators have not made effective use of behavior measurement techniques by which to evaluate the success of their professional responsibilities. As a result, the discipline of education has little accountability evidence as to its operational effectiveness.

In order to help bring some accountability structure to the discipline of education, and especially special education, we developed the management model. The model represents a measurable systems approach to educational intervention. The systems approach operates by the application of the six model components. Of the six, the one component necessary for intervention accountability which has not yet been discussed is baseline measurement.

Baseline measurement is defined as the identification of the frequency of target behavior. Baseline measurement is necessary in order to pinpoint target behavior and then measure the degree of target behavior change which occurs due to the intervention. By serving to pinpoint target behavior, baseline measurement provides systematic direction to the intervention process. By permitting the measurement of target behavior change, baseline measurement not only increases the success likelihood of the intervention, but also serves as the accountability referent of the management model as well as IEP-IIP procedures.

Baseline measurement operates by counting and recording specific behavior. However, just as a task analysis is dependent on a behavioral-instructional objective for its origin and meaning, baseline measurement is dependent on an objective and/or related task analysis for its origin and meaning. Thus, for each major intervention relative to a learning or behavior problem, an objective and task analysis should be developed, as well as a baseline measurement indication of the degree to which target behavior changes due to the intervention. The target behavior that baseline measurement serves to count and record is the behavior identified in the objective and/or related task analysis.

We contend that any concept worth teaching should be capable of being expressed in the form of behavior. Since any external behavior can be observed and therefore measured, it follows that any concept worth teaching should be capable of being observed and measured. The identification of the frequency of target behavior by baseline measurement should be applicable to all concepts that are taught. For example, the concepts of love, dignity, and faith are all philosophically desirable and necessary for survival in the human world. However, it is not worth teaching such concepts unless they can be expressed, hence communicated, in the form of external behavior. That is, there is no value in the concept of love unless it can be communicated. If such concepts can be expressed, then they can be observed and hence measured by baseline measurement techniques. If all concepts worth teaching can be observed and measured, they can also be defined, and therefore the entire teaching process is subject to accountability laws.

The mechanics of baseline measurement involve the counting and recording of the frequency with which target behavior occurs. The best way to facilitate the counting of target behavior is by a wristband mechanical counter or a tally sheet. Recording of target behavior can be facilitated by using graph paper and constructing a two-axis measurement grid which employs the vertical axis for the purpose of recording the frequency of target behavior and the horizontal axis for recording the time periods during which that behavior frequency is measured.

(For example: Frequency of oral-reading errors)

FREQUENCY
50
45
40
35
30
25
20
15
10
5

TIME

Figure V

(For example: Five minute time-periods)

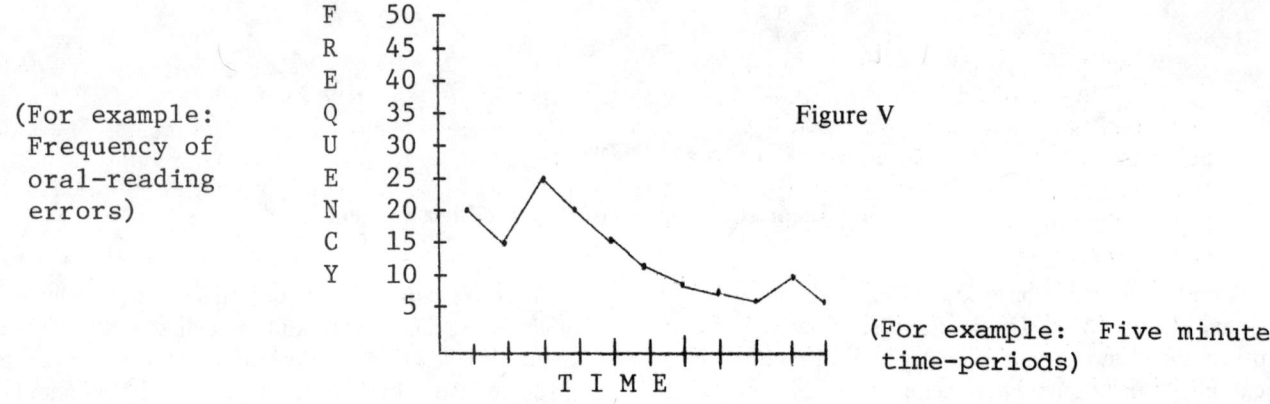

The vertical axis of the measurement grid is used exclusively for the purpose of recording the number of times target behavior occurs. The horizontal axis of the measurement grid is used exclusively for the purpose of indicating the time period within which the target behavior is to be counted. The procedure used to count the number of times target behavior occurs should be selected on the basis of the nature of that target behavior. Similarly, the length of the time period within which the target behavior is to be counted should be in relation to the nature of the target behavior and the procedure selected to count that target behavior. Thus, baseline measurement is a flexible concept, the process of which exists only in relation to a particular learner, target behavior, and intervention program. (See Figure V).

The operation of baseline measurement is simply a matter of the following procedure. (1) Counting the frequency of target behavior that occurs in a given time period; (2) plotting that frequency on the vertical axis of the measurement grid in relation to the target behavior counting time period which is expressed on the horizontal axis; and (3) connecting the various grid plots. That connection will provide a baseline profile of the frequency with which the target behavior occurred.

Most target behavior should be sampled several times a day for several days prior to initiating an intervention. Such preintervention baseline measurement will provide an indication of the frequency with which the target behavior occurred prior to initiating the intervention. After beginning the intervention, baseline measurement should be continued on the same preintervention measurement basis until the intervention is terminated, at which time a postintervention baseline measurement should be obtained. Thus, baseline measurement involves three phases of target behavior measurement: preintervention measurement, continuing-intervention measurement, and postintervention measurement. If the continuing-intervention baseline measurement indicates the target behavior is improving, it can be assumed that something positive is happening and the intervention strategies in use should be continued. If the continuing-intervention baseline measurement indicates the target behavior is not improving, or is getting worse, then the intervention strategies should be changed.

Baseline measurement involves counting the frequency with which target behavior occurs. However, it would be impossible to count each frequency with which some target behavior occurs, especially high-frequency behavior such as speech lisp, reading omissions, out-of-seat behavior, etc. In order to facilitate the target behavior counting process, four shortcut time-sampling methods are presented, from which a practitioner may choose.

1. Random time-sampling: If the target behavior occurs on a high-frequency and regular basis, the practitioner may randomly (without deliberation) select a certain period of time (e.g., one minute) and count the frequency with which the target behavior occurs during that time period. The practitioner should select several of these random time periods throughout the day, all of which should be of the same length, in order to get an average frequency with which the target behavior occurs during that day. By means of the random time-sampling procedure, it is unnecessary to count each expression of the target behavior; only the expression that occurs during the selected time periods.

2. Fixed time-sampling: If the target behavior occurs with high and regular frequency, it is possible to

select several fixed time periods during the day (e.g., 10:00-10:05, 1:15-1:20, 2:05-2:10, etc.) and count the frequency with which the target behavior occurs during those fixed time periods. It is necessary to select several such time periods throughout the day in order to obtain an average target behavior frequency.

3. Random within fixed time-sampling: If target behavior occurs with high and regular frequency, it is possible to select several fixed time periods throughout the day and then randomly select a counting period (e.g., one minute) within those fixed time periods for the purpose of determining the frequency with which target behavior occurs (for example, 10:00-10:01 out of the fixed time period 9:55-10:15). As usual, there should be several behavior counting periods a day in order to obtain an average target behavior frequency.

4. Tally sampling: If target behavior occurs with low-frequency and/or on an irregular basis, the best target behavior counting procedure is the recording of a tally in a notebook, on the chalkboard, etc., each time the target behavior occurs. This technique is especially useful for infrequent fighting behavior, irregular undesirable language expression, etc. With the tally procedure, there is no need to obtain an average frequency with which target behavior occurs as the tallies can be counted each day or week and the resulting tally sum will represent the total frequency with which the target behavior occurred during the time period.

There are a few more baseline measurement concepts which need to be discussed. (1) If possible, it is effective to express the information plotted on the vertical axis of the measurement grid in percentage form. The vertical axis would thus range from zero percent at the bottom to 100% at the top, the use of which would permit the comparison of target behavior that has a different measurement basis. (2) It is important that the pre-, continuous-, and post-intervention target behavior be counted and recorded in the same way; that is, the baseline measurement procedure should be the same throughout the intervention program. This sameness of baseline measurement permits the interpretation as to whether target behavior change is a result of the intervention process. If baseline measurement procedures changed during the intervention process, there could be a resulting change in the frequency with which target behavior is counted and recorded without any change in the actual frequency of the target behavior itself. This would preclude an accurate interpretation of change in the actual target behavior. (3) As with objectives and task analyses, baseline measurement is designed to assist the practitioner with an intervention. Therefore, the baseline procedure should be as simple as possible, and if it is determined that a particular method of counting and recording target behavior is consuming too much time, the practitioner should consider alternate baseline measurement strategies in order to make the process an asset rather than a liability. (4) We regard the adequacy of a particular baseline measurement procedure not only in terms of whether that procedure is capable of counting and recording target behavior, but also in terms of whether that procedure is sufficiently clear and practical to permit another person to understand it. (5) The two most common reasons for prescriptive intervention failure are that the sequential steps of the task analysis are too large and/or the reinforcement schedule is inappropriate. In either case, it is the baseline measurement procedure which permits identification of the failure. (6) Before baseline measurement procedures can be effectively applied they must relate to something. Baseline measurement always relates to behaviorally defined objectives or sequenced task analysis steps. As such, the use of baseline measurement is not as easy as it might initially appear. However, the justification for using baseline measurement is in the ability of the procedure to increase the success likelihood of an intervention and to provide an effective IEP accountability mechanism.

Baseline measurement exists only in relation to target behavior which has been identified by an objective and/or task analysis. This means that whatever baseline counting and recording procedure is used, it probably will be applied to one of three kinds of possible target behavior: (1) The target behavior identified by the behavioral or instructional objective. Although a task analysis for that objective would be developed, the sequential steps of the task analysis would not be baselined, and only the terminal behavior identified by the objective would be counted and recorded. This particular baseline measurement application is appropriate for relatively simply objectives which do not involve long and complex task analyses. (2) The target behavior identified by the overall objective and enabling objectives. Only the target behavior which is identified by the overall objective and enabling objectives would be counted and recorded. This application is appropriate for moderately complex objectives and task analyses which are accompanied by enabling objectives. (3) The target behavior identified by the task analysis steps. This baseline measurement application requires that each task analysis step be behaviorally defined and associated with criteria of acceptable performance, and that the baseline counting and recording be in relation to the target behavior identified by each of the sequenced task analysis steps. This baseline measurement application is the most comprehensive, and also the most work, and is appropriate primarily for long-term objectives and complex task analyses.

Although each intervention should involve one of the three kinds of baseline measurement applications, the application selected should be a function of the complexity of the objective and task analysis as well as the detail with which the practitioner wishes to count and record the target behavior.

Chapter 27

The Mechanical Aspects of Baseline Measurement

Baseline measurement involves the counting and recording of the frequency with which target behavior occurs. That target behavior is identified either by the overall objective, the overall objective and enabling objectives, or by the task analysis steps. And, there are four basic methods of time sampling: random, fixed, random within fixed, and tally sampling.

In addition to the above baseline measurement concepts, there are also four basic target behavior counting procedures: frequency, rate, percentage, and duration. The following discussion presents an analysis of each of these four procedures.

Frequency

The frequency target behavior counting procedure is appropriate when the target behavior is discrete (not continuous). This procedure operates by the following steps. (1) Selecting an appropriate time-sampling method (usually tally sampling for low-frequency behavior, and random sampling for high-frequency behavior). (2) Selecting an appropriate time period within which the target behavior is to be counted. (3) Counting the number of times the target behavior occurs within that time period. (4) Recording the target behavior frequency on the baseline measurement grid. Examples of discrete target behavior that are appropriate for the frequency baseline procedure are: out-of-seat behavior, biting, kicking, fighting, and symbol reversal.

The following example illustrates the use of the frequency baseline measurement procedure, (See Figure VI).

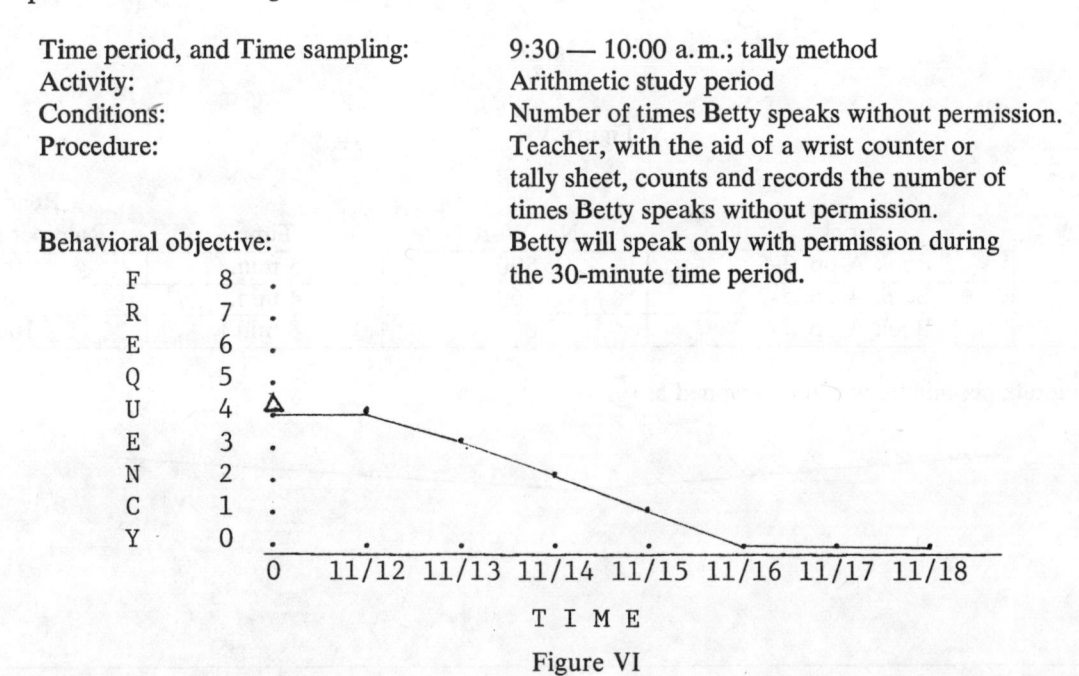

Time period, and Time sampling: 9:30 — 10:00 a.m.; tally method
Activity: Arithmetic study period
Conditions: Number of times Betty speaks without permission.
Procedure: Teacher, with the aid of a wrist counter or tally sheet, counts and records the number of times Betty speaks without permission.
Behavioral objective: Betty will speak only with permission during the 30-minute time period.

```
F  8 .
R  7 .
E  6 .
Q  5 .
U  4 △
E  3 .
N  2 .
C  1 .
Y  0 .    .      .      .      .      .      .      .
   0   11/12  11/13  11/14  11/15  11/16  11/17  11/18
                         T I M E
```
Figure VI

Prior to actually beginning an intervention, the preintervention target behavior frequency should be obtained. It is common to baseline the preintervention target behavior several times a day for several days in order to obtain the average preintervention target-behavior frequency (a triangle △ is used to indicate the average preintervention target behavior frequency). After the preintervention baseline has been established, the actual intervention may begin, during which time the target behavior should be continuously counted

305

and recorded by the same procedure as used for the preintervention baseline measurement. At the conclusion of the intervention, a postintervention target-behavior frequency should be obtained for the purpose of comparing preintervention and postintervention behavior change. It is this baseline measurement revealed pre–post intervention target behavior change that forms the evaluation and accountability basis of the management model. By examining the above-presented baseline measurement grid, it can be observed that the objective of not speaking out was met on November 16, and to that extent, the intervention was successful and the teacher accountable.

Rate

The rate of target behavior counting procedure is similar to the frequency procedure. The rate of target behavior is determined by dividing the target behavior frequency by the elapsed time (the length of the time period). Since the computation of the rate of target behavior involves both frequency and time, the rate of behavior is an average figure and is a stronger baseline measurement procedure than the frequency procedure which utilizes only the dimension of frequency.

The rate procedure is appropriate only when the target behavior can be timed. It is effective when the time periods are short (e.g., one minute, five minutes, one hour, etc.), and thus is often useful for baselining classroom learning activities. The operation of the rate procedure involves several steps: (1) The selection of an appropriate time-sampling method (usually fixed time). (2) The selection of an appropriate time period during which target behavior is to be counted. (3) Counting the frequency of the target behavior during that time period. And (4) obtaining, and then recording, the target behavior rate by dividing the target behavior frequency by the elapsed time.

Figure VII

Date	Book	No. Words	Time	Reading Rate per Minute
11/1	Book A-pp. 3-5	500	5 min.	100
11/8	Book A-pp. 5-7	360	4 min.	90
11/15	Book A-pp. 7-9	800	8 min.	100

Corine's reading rate per minute would be graphed as follows:

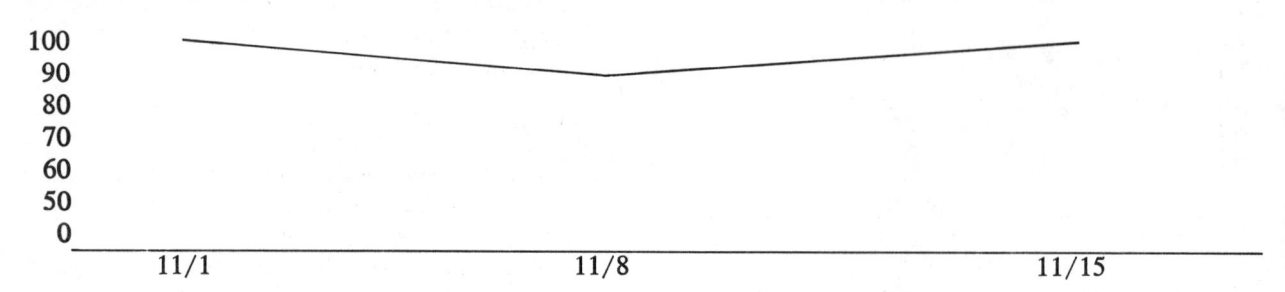

Figure VII illustrates the use of the rate baseline measurement procedure. The target behavior is oral reading; the rate procedure would operate by Corine reading from a predetermined source for a predetermined length of time, and then the practitioner dividing the number of words read by the amount of elapsed time.

Percentage

The percentage baseline measurement procedure is a versatile yet simple means of reporting the incidence of target behavior, particularly regarding academic behavior where percentage of accuracy is desired to show student progress. This procedure operates by the following steps: (1) Select a time-sampling method (usually tally sampling); (2) select an appropriate time period within which the target behavior is to be counted; (3) count and record the frequency of correct behavior, and count and record the total frequency with which the correct as well as incorrect behavior is expressed; (4) divide the correct behavior frequency by the total behavior frequency and multiply the result by 100; (5) record the resulting percentage of target behavior on the baseline measurement grid. This procedure is appropriate for obtaining the incidence of target behavior whenever it is possible to count the correct behavior frequency as well as total behavior frequency. Since time is not an ingredient, this procedure is very versatile.

The following example illustrates the use of the percentage baseline measurement procedure. The target behavior is two-digit addition problems, where Betsy correctly completed five out of ten problems on November second, and eight out of ten on November third. The percentage procedure would operate by dividing the five correct problems by the total of ten problems, and then eight by ten, multiplying by 100, and recording the results on the baseline measurement grid as shown in Figure VIII.

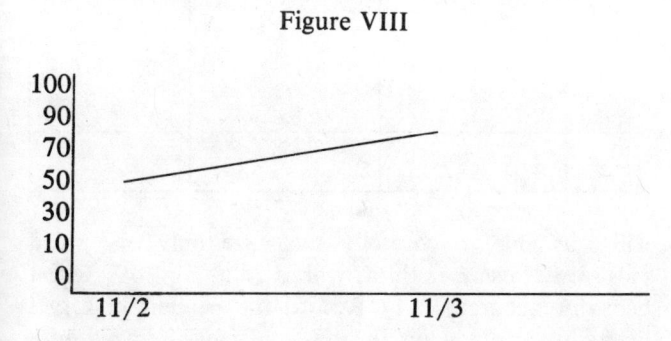

Figure VIII

```
100|
 90|
 70|          _____
 50|_____/
 30|
 10|
  0|_____
    11/2                11/3
```

The above example illustrates the use of the percentage procedure without the ingredient of time. The following example illustrates the use of the percentage procedure with time as an ingredient. The target behavior is attending, where attending is defined as having eye-contact with the assigned worksheet. The percentage-time procedure operates as follows: (1) Select an appropriate time-sampling method. (2) Select an appropriate time period, which normally should involve many short-interval time periods (e.g., 6-10 five minute time periods during a given day). (3) Observe the subject only once during each of the short interval time periods. (4) Record whether the subject is or is not attending by rendering a + for attending and a 0 for not attending. (5) Divide the frequency of correct (attending) behavior by the number of time intervals (not the length of time intervals). (6) Multiply the resulting figure by 100, which will result in the percentage of target behavior.

Figure IX

TIME	RESPONSE
9:00	+
9:05	0
9:10	+
9:15	+
9:20	+
% of time	80%

By means of Figure IX, and with respect to the percentage-time baseline measurement procedure, the reader will recognize that the subject was attending 80% of the time.

This particular time-based use of the percentage procedure represents a baseline advantage in that the practitioner is not required to be in constant observation of the subject in order to count and record the frequency of target behavior. In the above example, only one quick observation during each of the five-minute time intervals was sufficient to count and record the target behavior.

Duration

The duration baseline measurement procedure is a variation of the percentage procedure. The duration procedure is especially appropriate for counting and recording target behavior which occurs infrequently and which persists over a long period of time (such as thumb sucking). The procedure requires the use of a watch or clock with a second hand to record the amount of time a subject is engaged in the target behavior. The duration procedure operates by the following steps:

(1) the selection of a time-sampling method (fixed time or tally); (2) the selection of an appropriate time period during which target behavior is to be measured; (3) the determination of the amount of time the subject engaged in the target behavior (e.g., thumb sucking). (4) the determination of the elapsed time during which the subject was observed (the length of the time period). (5) the division of the elapsed time into the target behavior time and the conversion of that figure into a percentage by multiplying that figure by 100; and (6) the recording of the percent figure on the baseline measurement grid.

For example, Robley sucked her thumb for a period of 10 minutes out of an observed time of 15 minutes. The elapsed time (15 minutes) is divided into the target behavior time (10 minutes), and that figure multiplied by 100. The percent result of 67 is then plotted on the baseline measurement grid.

Specific Application of Baseline Measurement

Reading

Three reading skill components are: word recognition, oral reading, and comprehension. The following discussion analyzes each of those components relative to appropriate procedures for baselining reading skill behavior.

Word recognition

Word recognition involves the identification of words that are presented for recognition purposes. Counting and recording word recognition target behavior could involve the following steps: (1) List and then number the words to be taught in the order that they appear in the instructional material. The graph model which is presented in Figure X can be used for that listing and numbering purpose.

Figure X

No	Word	RESPONSE				
		11/3	11/4	11/5	11/6	11/7
1	his					
2	live					
3	was					
4	street					
5	just					
% Correct						

(2) Begin the word recognition teaching process. Use the graph model presented below for the purpose of recording, by a + or 0 relative to the particular date, whether the given word was correctly or incorrectly recognized. (3) Convert the target behavior frequency for a particular date into a percentage figure by dividing the number of words presented into the number of words correctly recognized and multiplying the result by 100. Referring to Figure XI, it can be seen that Bill was able to correctly recognize only one word (his) on November third, with a resulting 20% target behavior accuracy. (4) Record the percent of target behavior accuracy on the baseline measurement grid.

By means of Figure XI, it is possible to identify those words that have been learned by drawing a line through the dates which are subsequent to the third (or whatever is appropriate) consecutively correct answer.

Figure XI

No	Word	RESPONSE						
		11/3	11/4	11/5	11/6	11/7	11/8	11/9
1	his	+	+	+	---	---	---	---
2	live	0	+	+	+	---	---	---
3	was	0	0	0	+	+	+	---
4	street	0	0	0	+	+	+	---
5	just	0	0	0	0	+	+	+
% Correct		20	40	40	80	100	100	100

Oral reading

Baselining oral reading involves the identification of the frequency with which oral reading errors are made. Oral reading errors are defined as: word substitutions, word omissions, word mispronounciation, and pauses of more than five seconds between words. The oral reading baselining procedure involves the following steps: (1) Select an appropriate time-sampling method (usually fixed time). (2) Select an appropriate time period during which target behavior is to be counted. (3) Establish the preintervention target behavior frequency. (4) Prepare an oral reading record sheet, as illustrated by Figure XII. (5) Count, and then record on the graph, the number of words read and the number of errors made. (6) Divide the words read figure into the number of errors and multiply the result by 100 to obtain a percentage of correct figure (percentage of target behavior accuracy). (7) Divide the time figure into the words read figure to obtain a words read per minute figure. (8) Plot the frequency of target behavior accuracy (% correct) on the baseline measurement grid; if appropriate, also plot the words read per minute figure on the baseline measurement grid.

Figure XII

Date	Session	Book	Pages	Words Read	Errors	% Correct	Time	Words Read Per Minute
1-5	1	A	14-16	200	10	95	2	100

Reading comprehension

Baselining reading comprehension involves identifying the frequency with which reading comprehension errors are made. The simplest means of measuring such target behavior is by asking the subject questions about what he has read. There are four basic reading comprehension components, which are listed below, and at least one question representing each of the four components should be asked of the subject in order to determine the frequency of reading comprehension errors.

1. Recall: The ability to repeat important concepts from memory relative to the previously read information.
2. Sequence: The ability to repeat important concepts from memory in the sequenced order in which

they appeared in the previously read information.
3. Summarization: The ability to conceptually summarize the significant ideas presented in the previously read information.
4. Inference: The ability to identify cause-effect relationships that exist between previously read concepts.

Figure XIII

				Recall	Sequence	Summarization	Inference	
Date	Story	Pages	Words	1	2	3	4	% Comprehension
1/31	L	36-38	250	+	+	+	0	75

Figure XIII represents one way of recording the frequency of reading comprehension errors. It operates by the following steps: (1) Select an appropriate time-sampling method (usually fixed time). (2) Select an appropriate target behavior counting time period. (3) Present the reading material. When finished reading, ask at least one question from each of the four reading comprehension components. (4) Record a + or a 0 for correctly or incorrectly answered questions. (5) Divide the total number of questions into the number of correctly answered questions and multiply the result by 100 in order to obtain a percent of comprehension figure (frequency of target behavior accuracy). (6) Plot the percent of comprehension figure on the baseline measurement grid.

Spelling

Since baselining the frequency of spelling errors is so similar to baselining the frequency of reading errors, no special attention will be given to spelling baseline measurement procedures here.

Mathematics

The percentage baseline measurement procedure is most commonly used for counting and recording the frequency with which mathematics errors occur. There are three types of math target behaviors which are commonly counted and recorded: (1) the percentage of problems accurately completed; (2) the percentage of assigned problems accurately completed; and (3) the time required to complete the assigned task. All three target behaviors are easily computed and recorded. Regarding numbers one and two above, the number of problems completed or assigned is divided into the number of problems accurately completed and the result multiplied by 100. Regarding number three above, the elapsed time is determined by clocking the length of time involved with the task.

Figure XIV

Date	Work-Sheet	Number Assigned	Number Completed	% Completed	Number Correct	% Correct	Time Needed	Completion Rate/min.
11-14	1	20	20	100	15	75	40	.5

Figure XIV illustrates one way of recording the frequency with which math target behavior occurs. The following steps are involved: (1) Identify an appropriate time-sample method (usually fixed time). (2) Identify an appropriate target behavior counting time period. (3) Conduct the math task. Count the number of correct answers. (4) Divide the number of problems assigned, or the number of problems completed, into the number of correctly completed problems and multiply the result by 100 in order to obtain a percentage correct figure (frequency of target behavior accuracy). (5) If desired, divide the amount of time needed to complete the task into the number of problems completed in order to obtain a completion rate per minute figure. (6) Plot the percentage of correct answers, and if desired, the completion rate per minute figure, on the baseline measurement grid.

THE EVALUATION AND ACCOUNTABILITY SYSTEM OF THE MANAGEMENT MODEL

Baseline measurement provides the management model with a built-in accountability system. That system is made possible by the counting and recording of preintervention, continuing-intervention, and postintervention target behavior frequency. The system can operate in one or more of three ways: (1) The evaluation of intervention progress. If the continuing-intervention baseline measurement reveals positive target behavior change, the intervention program has made progress (successful to that point), and the various intervention strategies in use should be continued. If the continuing-intervention baseline measurement reveals no target behavior change, or change in the wrong direction, the intervention program has not made progress (not successful), and the intervention strategies in use should be changed. (2) The evaluation of behavioral-instructional objective and/or task analysis step achievement. If, at any time the continuing-intervention target behavior frequency, or the postintervention target behavior frequency, meets the success criteria established for the terminal behavior, the relevant objective has been met. (3) The evaluation of overall IEP intervention progress. Intervention progress is a function of positive target behavior change. The evaluation of IEP progress is determined by comparing current target behavior frequency, or postintervention target behavior frequency, with preintervention target behavior frequency. The resulting indication of target behavior change represents the overall IEP intervention progress.

By means of the management model accountability system the practitioner is able to declare that the intervention program: (1) made progress (but did not reach the established objective); (2) reached the established objective; or (3) did not make progress.

SUMMARY

An assortment of baseline measurement procedures has been discussed. The decision that rests with the practitioner is which of these various procedures to use. We can offer the following guidelines: (1) Use the easiest procedure. (2) The baseline measurement procedure should relate to the intervention objective and task analysis. Therefore, choose the baseline procedure which best complements the nature of the presenting problem, the objective, and the task analysis. (3) Select the baseline procedure based on the availability of the ingredients (e.g., watch with a second hand) that are essential to the effective operation of that procedure. (4) Select the baseline measurement procedure based on the degree of precision with which the practitioner wishes to count and record the frequency of target behavior. If the purpose of baselining is to account for professional behavior to a board of education, the precision with which target behavior frequency is counted and recorded will be greater than if the purpose of baselining is purely for an internal indication of intervention progress.

PART VII

THE SIXTH COMPONENT OF THE EDUCATION INTERVENTION AND MANAGEMENT MODEL:

Behavior Modification and Change Agents

Behavior modification and change agents is defined as any agent of manipulation which is designed to create systematic behavior change. Behavior modification has almost unlimited versatility, and when used wisely, is a productive agent of behavior change. We endorse the use of behavior modification in terms of the increased efficiency with which presenting problem resolution can be effected.

Section I

Behavior Modification and Change Agents: General Application

Chapter 28

Positive Reinforcement

The sixth component of the management model is behavior modification and change agents, which represents the last component to be put into use relative to a learning or behavior problem intervention.

We regard the behavior modification component of the education intervention and management model as representing the most powerful of all management model change concepts. We define behavior modification and change agents as any agent of manipulation that is designed to create systematic behavior change. Although there is a definite set of procedural laws which should be followed when earnestly applying behavior modification strategy, the applicability of the strategy is immensely variable. With the exception of medication, we regard behavior modification as the most powerful agent of short-term behavior change, and as one of the most powerful agents of long-term behavior change. Behavior modification is particularly appropriate for public educators in their attempt to successfully intervene by means of IEPs with subject and parent presenting problems. We endorse behavior modification for the purpose of markedly increasing the likelihood of intervention success relative to subjects with learning or behavior problems.

Basic law

The basic behavior modification law is that behavior is a function of its consequences. This means that what follows behavior will determine whether that behavior is strengthened or weakened. Applying this concept to human behavior, the basic law means that if a subject is reinforced for certain behavior that behavior will be strengthened and will tend to reoccur; conversely, if a subject is not reinforced for certain behavior, or if certain behavior of a subject is followed by something aversive (unpleasant), that behavior will be weakened and will tend not to reoccur.

Behavior modification and psychodeterminism

The reader may detect an apparent conceptual inconsistency. It has just been stated that behavior is a function of its consequences. Yet previously it was stated that behavior is psychosocially determined. Actually, the two concepts are mutually compatible, for despite the fact that most behavior originates with the metabolic processes of the body, the behavior that is ultimately expressed usually has been substantially changed in form from the original state of drive-tension by the mastery function of the ego. This means that the ego, in relation to the conscience values, controls the way and form in which behavior is expressed, despite the fact the behavior may have originated with the metabolic processes. Since the ego-conscience system controls the way and form in which behavior is expressed, and since the ego-conscience system is learned in relation to the helpless infant-child being dependent on powerful authority figures who dispense praise and punishment for acceptable and unacceptable behavior, behavior then is learned, and is a function of the expected or actual authority figure (later conscience and authority figure) reaction to that behavior. This means that behavior, although psychosocially determined, is a function of its consequences. Since behavior is learned, behavior can be changed by manipulating the consequences of that behavior.

Behavior modification and conscience administered esteem

The basic behavior modification law is simple to state and easy to understand but deceptively difficult to properly apply. Since the conscience represents an internalized control system (originally external in the form of parental-societal values and attitudes, then learned, then internalized as one's own), and since that internalized control system serves primarily to dispense self-praise (esteem) and self-punishment, one of the most powerful reinforcers is conscience administered esteem. This esteem process cannot be seen, except as it is manifested in pride. Thus, behavior can be maintained not only by external reinforcement that can be seen (a smile, a verbal comment, good personnel reports, salary increases, etc.), but also by the internal reinforcement of conscience administered self-esteem. Since behavior is a function of its consequences, and since internal self-esteem often is the consequence of behavior, it can be extremely difficult to modify behavior that is maintained by subject self-esteem.

About the best way to modify undesirable behavior which is maintained by self-esteem (or guilt) is the application of behavior management and/or counseling techniques to the modification of the subject's conscience system, thereby changing prevailing values, thereby changing what the subject regards as praiseworthy, and thereby changing the behavior for which the subject rewards himself by self-esteem.

The right to modify behavior

The basic behavior modification law means that it is possible to change behavior by manipulating what happens after that behavior. Such behavior shaping power gives rise to a natural philosophical-professional controversy: whether the educator, or anyone else except parents, has the right to change subject behavior without explicit parental approval. We answer the controversy by contending that unsystematic behavior modification principles are unknowingly applied to everyone by everyone daily. The smile, the head-nod, the school letter-grade or gold star, the red bird school grouping, the interest or disinterest expressed by a friend, etc., are all behavior modification strategies which serve to strengthen or weaken the behavior which precedes the particular strategy but which usually are expressed unknowingly and unsystematically. Since behavior modification is such a powerful agent of change, and since behavior modification strategies are unknowingly and unsystematically used as a normal product of human interaction, we contend that professional change agents (educators, mental-health workers, etc.) who are charged with education and socialization responsibility should be equipped with the most powerful professional change-tools possible, although in a knowing and systematic way. Since we regard behavior modification as one of the most versatile and productive agents of behavior change, and since educators need as much professional advantage as possible in order to accomplish their awesome responsibility, we endorse the use of behavior modification principles for educators, presuming the knowledgable and professional application of those principles.

Behavior modification as a bribe

It is alleged that behavior modification is tantamount to a bribe and on that basis should be regarded as unconscionable. We rebut this allegation with the contention that unknowing and unsystematic behavior modification principles have been applied by humans to human interaction since the history of time. In fact, all of us have been either recipients or proponents of behavior modification, in terms of either having had our parents respond to us with praise or punishment subsequent to certain behavior, or as parents ourselves, responding to our children with praise or punishment subsequent to certain behavior. This normal parent-child interaction is nothing more than the application of the unsystematic socialization process by the unknowing use of behavior modification principles. These principles, which distill to nothing more than the dispensing of praise or punishment for acceptable or unacceptable behavior, are the way in which the ego and conscience systems are learned and the way in which the entire world has become sufficiently civilized to permit lawful human coexistence. Behavior modification principles cannot be a bribe, for if they were, the entire development of lawful human interaction would be based on a giant bribe, in which case life itself would be ungenuine and shallow.

Behavior modification and positive reinforcement

The basic behavior modification law means that it

is possible to shape behavior by manipulating what happens to a subject after that behavior. Positive reinforcement refers to one of several formal components of behavior modification theory, and represents systematic ways in which desirable behavior may be either originated or maintained by manipulating the consequences of that desirable behavior.

One of the basic models associated with positive reinforcement is that of Skinner's operant conditioning (Hilgard, 1975, Skinner, 1965, 1975). We translate that model into the formula R-Rd, where R refers to behavior or response, and Rd refers to reinforcement. This formula simply expresses the basic behavior modification law, which is that behavior is a function of what follows that behavior. The formula also expresses a basic positive reinforcement principle, which is that desirable subject behavior may be either originated or maintained by reinforcing the subject for engaging in that desirable behavior after it occurs.

We contend that in most educational behavior-management situations the Skinnerian model represents a relative loss of power, in that the practitioner must wait for the desirable subject behavior (or an approximation) to occur before applying positive reinforcement. As such, we usually prefer the Thorndikian learning theory model (connectionism) (Hilgard, 1975; Thorndike, 1913, 1932). We translate that model into the formula S-R-Rd, where S represents a stimulus that is created by the practitioner for the purpose of evoking a desirable response (R), after which an appropriate reward or reinforcer (Rd) is applied. By means of the Thorndikian model (S-R-Rd) the educator has more power with which to control the learning atmosphere, in terms of actually creating the stimulus ("sit down Troy"), which is designed to evoke the desirable subject response (Troy sitting down), after which an appropriate reinforcement is offered ("Thank you Troy"). Using the Skinnerian model (R-Rd), the educator would have to wait until the desirable subject behavior (or an approximation) occurred (Troy sitting down), after which the appropriate reinforcement would be administered. By means of the Thorndikian model, the practitioner has the increased behavior modification power of providing whatever stimulus is necessary in order to evoke desirable subject behavior.

Behavior modification precepts

There are some behavior modification precepts which should be systematically followed in order for behavior modification to be effective. Those precepts are:

Behavior modification and the use of the stimulus (S)

The practitioner should present the stimulus (prompt or cue) to the subject in a clear and understandable way so as to permit the subject to discriminate exactly what is to be done. For example: "Sit down Troy" is a more precise hence better stimulus than, "You guys stop messing around," since the latter ambiguous cue would probably generate confused behavior, a situation which would lead to chaos were such behavior reinforced.

Behavior modification and the administration of the reward (Rd)

1. The reward, reinforcement, or payoff (all of which are synonymous) should be need-satisfying to the subject in order to have reinforcing power. Thus, for example, M & M's will not be reinforcing unless they are need-satisfying to the particular subject. The identification of what a subject regards as need-satisfying and therefore reinforcing is critical to the effective use of behavior modification. We have presented the Reinforcement Inventory which is designed to elicit what the subject regards as reinforcing and aversive. Such an instrument, as well as subject-parent interviewing and observation procedures, are essential to the identification of this important behavior modification ingredient.

2. The reinforcement should be administered to the subject immediately after the desirable response. Because of the relative inability to delay impulse gratification, the younger the subject, and/or the more disturbed the subject, the more the payoff must be administered immediately after the desirable response. Gradually, however, as the subject acquires the desirable behavior, the immediacy of the payoff administration can be systematically relaxed into an intermittent payoff schedule, until, often after a great length of time, the desirable behavior can be maintained by only occasional reinforcement. However, initially, the payoff should be immediate, and thus the typical

classroom practice of waiting until Friday to administer the gold star (assuming the gold star is need-satisfying) is technically wrong, due to the lapse of time between the desirable behavior and the administration of the payoff.

3. The reinforcement should be administered to the subject immediately after every desirable response until that response is learned, at which time the payoff should be administered on a deliberate but intermittent basis. Two concepts are important: one, until learned, desirable behavior should be reinforced each time it occurs. By skipping a time or two, the effectiveness of the behavior modification will be weakened. And two, paradoxically, after desirable behavior has been learned, administering a payoff each time the behavior occurs will result in that behavior weakening (extinguishing). Thus, to maintain behavior that has been learned, an intermittent payoff schedule should be used, which involves gradually reducing the frequency with which the payoff is administered. An intermittent payoff schedule normally involves one of two payoff practices: one, a ratio payoff schedule, or two, an interval payoff schedule. These two intermittent payoff practices can be further classified into a fixed or variable ratio schedule and a fixed or variable interval schedule. A fixed ratio payoff schedule involves reinforcing desirable behavior on a fixed ratio basis; i.e., after every second, third, or fourth, etc., time the behavior occurs. A variable ratio payoff schedule involves reinforcing behavior on a random basis; i.e., after a desirable response, but on an increasingly occasional and non-scheduled behavior basis. A fixed interval payoff schedule involves reinforcing desirable behavior after every 5, 10, or 15 minutes, etc., have elapsed, on a scheduled time-interval basis. And, a variable interval payoff schedule involves reinforcing behavior on a random time basis; i.e., after desirable behavior, but on an increasingly occasional and non-scheduled time basis.

Whether to use a ratio or interval intermittent payoff schedule should be decided on the basis of the kind of behavior that is being reinforced, as some behavior does not express itself compatibly with a ratio schedule, just as some behavior does not express itself compatibly with an interval schedule. We prefer the fixed (ratio or interval) intermittent payoff schedule for a short period of time after desirable behavior has been learned (i.e., reinforcing after every second, then third, then fourth response, or after every five minute period, ten minute period, etc.). However, after a brief fixed intermittent payoff schedule, we prefer to shift to a variable (ratio or interval) schedule, in that the variable (random) payoff schedule is probably the most powerful way of maintaining subject behavior after it has been learned. As the behavior becomes part of the subject's habit structure, the frequency with which the payoff is administered to the subject should gradually be reduced until the desirable behavior is maintained by only an occasional (but random) reinforcement.

4. The reinforcement schedule should be consistently applied, day in and day out. This means that even a well thought-out reinforcement schedule will not work effectively if, for example, it is applied conscientiously on Monday, loosely on Tuesday, nothing on Wednesday, vigorously on Thursday, etc.

The consistency concept also means that behavior modification should be systematically applied during as much of the subject's twenty-four hour day as possible. This means that parents, as well as other significant adults, should be involved in the remediation process, and among other things, trained to continue the school oriented behavior modification program at home. With respect to this issue, it is our contention that a school based remediation program which has the cooperation of the parents has a greater chance of success than a program which operates without the cooperation of the parents.

By now, it should be clear that the effective application of behavior modification strategy involves no magic and is not a panacea. Rather, it is hard and premeditated work, which, however, usually has need-satisfying payoff.

5. The subject of behavior modification should receive progress feedback. This feedback is a kind of baseline measurement for the subject and serves to provide a continuing record of behavior change. The feedback may be in any form, although we use feedback charts, which in the classroom

manifest themselves in a foot-high and blackboard-long strip of plain paper, placed above the blackboard, and divided into as many equal spaces as there are students in the class. These feedback charts are labeled with the student names, calibrated in terms of days of the week or weeks of the month, and then used to record a student's daily or weekly progress. The point is that a subject is usually more motivated to make change if the progress of that change can be measured and then visually displayed.

6. Lastly, the subject should be aware of the reinforcement and should know why he is being reinforced. If a subject were not aware of reinforcement, there could be no systematic behavior modification. Similarly, if a subject did not realize that a particular payoff was in response to certain behavior, the result might be the reinforcement of nontarget behavior (either the behavior that occurred immediately before receiving the payoff or the behavior for which the subject thought he was being reinforced). This situation would be an example of the undesirable application of behavior modification. To avoid this situation, the practitioner may simply inform the subject as to why the payoff was administered (e.g., "Barbara, I'm going to give you five checkmarks for waiting your turn.").

Behavior Modification in relation to the kinds and potency of reinforcers

Appropriate reinforcement is critical to effective behavior modification. As such, it is important to be aware of the various kinds of reinforcers and their relative payoff strength. The following discussion relates to a hierarchy of payoff potency, which represents a classification of the important kinds of reinforcers and their relative reinforcement potency. The hierarchy is based on the principle that the most potent reinforcer is that which is most need-satisfying to an individual. Typically, the most powerful human needs that require satisfaction, in descending rank order, and beginning with the most fundamental need of man, are: biological-physiological, love, safety-protection, esteem, production, creativity, and self-actualization (Maslow, 1970). The following hierarchy of payoff potency is based on a descending rank order of reinforcement potency, beginning with the most potent reinforcer, as that relates to the most fundamental need of man:

1. Edibles, or that which can be eaten (M & M's, peanuts, raisins, juice, milk, cereal bits, peanut butter, carrot sticks, marshmallows, etc.).
2. Physical contact as an expression of care (pat on shoulder, rocking a subject, holding hands, simple touching, etc.).
3. Verbal priase ("Good job John"; "You look pretty today Jonna").
4. Social praise (recognition by peers). Social praise is one of the most powerful adolescent reinforcers, but often operates to the disadvantage of the educator. If undesirable student behavior is being maintained by social praise, the educator will need to search long and hard for a payoff that is more powerful than the social praise. It may become necessary to separate the subject whose undesirable behavior is being maintained by the social praise from the individuals offering that social praise, or actually take into your confidence those individuals who are dispensing the social praise, ask them to help with the reinforcement strategy, reward them for desirable behavior, and then reward the subject for modeling his peers.
5. The use of: checkmarks, tallies, and tokens.
6. Structured free time activity. Free time activity has good payoff value if the activity is of high-interest to the subject. Free time activity can vary greatly, in terms of structured free time in a free time area, a free time period of a preestablished duration with the teacher or parents, reduced (or lengthened) time at school, etc.

Behavior modification and primary, secondary, and tertiary reinforcers

Reinforcers can be classified into primary, secondary, and tertiary reinforcers. Primary reinforcers are those which sustain life (e.g., edibles), which therefore are physiological and nonsocial in nature, and which represent the lowest-order, but for some subjects the most powerful, of all reinforcers. Secondary reinforcers are social in nature (e.g., a smile, verbal praise, etc.), are external to the subject, and represent a higher-order, but for some subjects the most powerful, kind of reinforcer. Tertiary reinforcers are internal, in the form of conscience-dispensed feelings of pride and esteem, and as such represent the highest order, and the most difficult level to attain, of all reinforcers.

Since behavior is a function of its consequences, then all behavior, except the pure physiological startle-like response, is maintained by some kind of external and/or internal reinforcement. Generally, the level of reinforcement power at which a subject operates to maintain behavior is a function of ego strength. For secure subjects, the tertiary and secondary levels of reinforcement, in that order, are sufficient to maintain behavior. However, as ego strength declines, the level of reinforcement power necessary to maintain behavior also declines, from tertiary, to tertiary-secondary, to secondary, to secondary-primary, to primary reinforcement, etc. As a rule, the younger and/or more emotionally disturbed a subject, the more a combination of need-satisfying primary and secondary reinforcers (e.g., M & M's and verbal praise) represents the level of reinforcement power necessary to sustain subject behavior.

Behavior modification and reward pairing

The ultimate goal of a behavior modification program is to effect self-maintaining desirable behavior. This goal almost always involves a change in the ego-conscience system of the subject, in terms of altering existing values and/or originating new values with respect to given behavior. The ultimate behavior modification goal is impossible to achieve by the exclusive use of primary reinforcers, as primary reinforcers in and by themselves are not at a sufficiently high reinforcement level to effect internal and conscience based change. Thus, effective behavior modification becomes a process of parsimony: this means wisely selecting, and then using, only those reinforcers which are minimally necessary to get the job done, and moving from primary to secondary to tertiary reinforcers as quickly as the subject's ego strength will permit. Thus, it is almost never acceptable to use a more powerful reinforcer when a less powerful reinforcer is adequate. Also, it is almost never acceptable to continue a subject on a particular reinforcement schedule beyond the time when that full schedule ceases to be necessary. However, the younger the subject, and/or the more disturbed the subject, and/or the more impact the practitioner wishes to have by means of the behavior modification program, the more powerful the payoff must be. Thus, simple verbal praise may be sufficient to maintain the desirable behavior of a well functioning adolescent. On the other hand, edibles and physical contact might be necessary to begin the shaping process of a young emotionally disturbed subject.

The ultimate goal of any behavior modification program is self-maintaining desirable behavior. That goal is usually achieved only by changing the values of the subject's ego-conscience system. It is precisely that change in the ego-conscience system that represents the tertiary, and highest level, of behavior modification reinforcement. Such reinforcement is the payoff that is derived from knowledge that something was done well because you feel good about it. Thus, the ultimate goal of any behavior modification program is desirable behavior which is maintained by tertiary level reinforcement.

In order to accomplish tertiary level reinforcement of desirable behavior it is essential to use only those reinforcers which are compatible with the most minimal level of reinforcement power necessary to maintain the behavior. Thus, it is important not to over-kill by means of reinforcers. In addition, the practitioner should always pair (associate) the lower-order reinforcer used with a slightly higher-order reinforcer so that the higher-order reinforcer will gradually assume the same payoff power as the lower-order reinforcer and therefore maintain the target behavior without the necessity of using the lower-order reinforcer. So, if a primary reinforcer is needed, pair a social reinforcer with that primary reinforcer. Similarly, as soon as a subject's ego strength permits, the transition from secondary to tertiary reinforcement should begin, by pairing a secondary reinforcer (smile) with a tertiary reinforcement cue (for example, "It feels good to get the answers right, doesn't it?"). Through pairing, higher-order reinforcers can come to assume the same payoff power as lower-order reinforcers, the process of which is the behavior modification bridge to self-maintaining desirable subject behavior.

Behavior modification and fading

The various categories of reinforcers have been presented by means of the hierarchy of payoff potency (edibles, social praise, checkmarks, etc.). Of those categories, all but checkmarks represent reinforcement which may be administered on a random basis. This means that such payoffs as edibles, verbal praise, physical contact, etc., may be administered after any desirable behavior, as opposed to every 20 minutes, every fifth correct answer, etc. However, the inappropriate continuation of reinforcers can lead to adverse results. As such, the concept of fading is important relative to making the necessary transition from primary to secondary, or secondary to tertiary, levels of reinforcement.

The application of the fading technique involves two components: First, the gradual reduction (fading) of the stimulus (which is presented by the practitioner in order to evoke desirable subject response), so that the desirable behavior ultimately tends to be maintained more by the internal cues of the subject than by the practitioner's external stimulus. But, too rapid a stimulus fading will result in the extinction of the desirable behavior; so the practitioner will need to sense the appropriate time and amount by which the stimulus may be reduced. The subsequent degree to which there is a sudden negative change in the baselined target behavior will indicate that the stimulus fading was either too sudden and/or too much. Second, the fading technique also involves the gradual reduction (fading) of the reinforcers used to maintain the target behavior so that the target behavior eventually comes to be maintained by subject internal (tertiary level) motivation. Again, too sudden a fading of reinforcers will extinguish the target behavior, so the practitioner must sense the time and amount by which the reinforcers may gradually be reduced. As with stimulus fading, the baseline indication of negative target behavior change immediately subsequent to reinforcement fading will indicate if the fading was too sudden and/or too much.

The fading technique is insufficient in and by itself to effect tertiary level behavior. Thus, the combination of fading and pairing higher-order reinforcers with lower-order reinforcers (smile with M & M's) is more likely to result in self-maintaining desirable subject behavior than is the use of fading by itself.

Behavior modification and the checkmark system

One of the reinforcers identified in the previously discussed hierarchy of payoff potency is that of checkmarks. The checkmark system of reinforcement operates by administering checkmarks to subjects on a regular time-interval basis for the demonstration of prearranged desirable subject behavior. The checkmark system operates on a scheduled (nonrandom) basis of reward administration, the rationale of which is the predictable opportunity of a subject to earn reinforcement for having engaged in desirable behavior. We regard the checkmark system as not only excellent, but one without which a structured behavior modification program should not operate.

We suggest that a fresh checkmark card be given to each student each school morning (or once a week if the card can accommodate that much calendar). The card should be taped to the student's desk, and at every time interval, the teacher or aide should make one checkmark in the appropriate box for acceptable behavior and no checkmark (checkmark withdrawal) for unacceptable behavior. Consistent with the concept of pairing, the person administering the checkmarks should provide a secondary reinforcer (e.g., smile, verbal praise, etc.) at the time the checkmark is administered, and in the case of a checkmark withdrawal, the student should be briefly apprised as to why a checkmark was not given. We recommend that no more than two checkmark columns plus one bonus column be used, that no more than one checkmark per concept-box be administered per time interval, and that no more than two bonus checkmarks be awarded per time interval. Such a sparing policy of checkmark administration seeks to avoid the possibility of a subject becoming satiated regarding checkmarks, a situation which could result in checkmarks losing their reinforcing property.

The receipt of a checkmark from a significant adult is usually reinforcing in and by itself. In addition, the association of the checkmark with a secondary reinforcer makes the checkmark even more rewarding. However, for many subjects, the real payoff of the checkmark system is that subjects may cash-in the total number of checkmarks accumulated during a specified time for displayed objects of interest. At the end of the day for young or disturbed subjects who cannot delay their gratification, or at longer intervals (one week usually) for other subjects, the subjects may surrender the total number of checkmarks accumulated during that length of time for objects which are displayed on the classroom bulletin board and which are affiliated with known surrender values. Thus, a subject at the end of a week could surrender his checkmark total of, for example, 132 points for a model horse, the displayed value of which is between 100 and 150 points.

We recommend that the checkmark system be included in all structured behavior modification programs. Not only does the checkmark system provide a predictable opportunity to earn rewards, but also the opportunity to use withdrawal of rewards as an extinction technique.

Table XXXI presents a sample checkmark card. The column headings can be whatever is descriptive of the behavior to be modified, although we recommend no more than two behavior columns and one bonus column. The time intervals should be appropriate to the subject and target-behavior, and be the same as the instructional time intervals on the subject's learning contract. As a rule, young and/or disturbed subjects warrant shorter time intervals, although probably not shorter than 15 minutes.

Behavior modification and the tally system

The tally system is another positive reinforcement strategy which is identified in the previously discussed hierarchy of payoff potency. The tally system operates in a way similar to the checkmark system in that the teacher makes a tally on a large and visible masterchart, which is attached to the front of the room, each time a subject performs in a desirable way. At the end of a specified time (one week usually), the subject has the opportunity to cash-in his tally total for an item of value which is displayed on the bulletin board. The tally system works better if the subject is aware of the exact behavior which can earn a tally, so it is helpful if the teacher and involved subjects preestablish the nature of desirable and undesirable bheavior. Although it is possible (but not recommended) to use the tally system concurrently with the checkmark system, the practitioner should guard against the overuse of reinforcers.

Behavior modification and the token system

The token system is another positive reinforcement strategy which is identified in the hierarchy of payoff potency. The token system involves the use of tokens (poker chips, wooden chips, etc.) as positive reinforcers. The tokens should be associated with different point values, based on either the color or size of the tokens. Token-values may be randomly administrered relative to desirable subject behavior, or certain subject behavior can be preestablished as having particular token-value, in which case tokens of that value may be awarded the subject subsequent to the valued behavior.

In either case, the subject may surrender the amount of token value, either by itself or in conjunction with checkmarks or tally values, for items displayed on the bulletin board. It is possible (but not recommended) to use the token system in conjunction with checkmarks or tallies, but the reason for so doing would need to be compelling, and caution should be used not to over-kill.

Behavior modification and negative reinforcement

Negative reinforcement is a positive reinforcement technique. Despite the connotation, negative reinforcement is not a form of punishment, nor is it an extinction technique. The basic negative reinforcement principle is: behavior which stops or avoids a painful event will be strengthened and will tend to reoccur. This means that behavior which results in the removal of an aversive (unpleasant) stimulus will be strengthened, because the removal of an aversive stimulus has the effect of strengthening behavior.

Another way of expressing the mechanics of negative reinforcement is: whereas behavior is positively reinforced by being rewarded, behavior is negatively reinforced by that behavior removing an aversive stimulus. This is because the removal of an aversive stimulus has positive reinforcing properties.

An illustration of negative reinforcement involves the modern car and driver: when the engine is turned on, but the seat belts are not buckled, an aversive buzzer and flashing red light emit from within the car. The resulting driver-behavior is to buckle the seat belt. This seat belt-buckling behavior removes the aversive stimuli of the buzzer and flashing light, and as such, the buckling behavior is reinforced and strengthened. In the future, the driver will likely buckle the seat belt prior to turning on the engine. The seat-buckling has been negatively reinforced.

Negative reinforcement is a good positive reinforcement technique. To negatively reinforce desirable behavior the practitioner should arrange for the subject to terminate a mildly aversive situation by performing that desirable behavior. By performing the desirable behavior, the subject removes the aversive situation, which reinforces and strengthens the desirable behavior. For example: if Harlan is too noisy, send him to his room (aversive situation), and indicate that he may come out whenever he can be quiet (desirable behavior). In order to remove himself from the aversive situation (room), Harlan must be quiet (desirable behavior). By being quiet, Harlan avoids the aversive situation, which strengthens the desirable (quiet) behavior.

Several features of negative reinforcement mechanics justify closer attention. (1) The aversive situation which is avoided by the desirable subject behavior should truly be aversive to the subject. (2) The aversive situation which is presented in order to be removed by the desirable behavior should be only mildly aversive, and not unduly painful. (3) The aversive situation which is presented in order to be removed by the desirable behavior should be capable of relatively easy removal by the subject. Thus, the subject should always be able to remove the aversive situation, for it is by means of that removal that the desirable behavior is strengthened. (4) The behavior that removes the aversive situation must be desirable behavior, because whatever behavior (desirable or undesirable) removes the aversive situation will be strengthened. It would be foolish to strengthen undesirable behavior by, for example, permitting Harlan to come out of his room screaming.

The reader should now understand that the aversive situation ends when the deirable behavior occurs; it is that desirable behavior which is strengthened.

Table XXXI

Checkmark Reinforcement System

	In-seat	Raises Hand	Bonus
8:30			
9:00			
9:30			
10:00			
10:30			
11:00			
11:30			
1:00			
1:30			
2:00			
2:30			
TOTALS			

3 x 5 Card

Double reinforcement

Double reinforcement is not a behavior modification technique but rather the result of behavior modification. Double reinforcement occurs when a practitioner's reinforcing behavior of a subject is reinforced by that subject's behavior modification induced progress. This is to say that a practitioner's behavior modification success is usually reinforcing to that practitioner. If the practitioner is not careful, his reinforcing behavior of a subject can be reinforced by that subject's behavior-change progress. In effect, a shrewd subject could shape the practitioner into providing that subject with desirable reinforcement.

SELECTED REFERENCES

Hilgard, E. *Theories of Learning* (4th ed.). New York: Appleton-Century-Crofts, 1975.

Krumboltz, J.D., and Krumboltz, H.D. *Changing Children's Behavior.* New Jersey: Prentice-Hall, 1972.

Maslow, A. *Motivation and Personality,* (2nd ed.). New York: Harper and Row, 1970.

Patterson, G., and Guillion, M.E. *Living with Children.* Illinois: Research Press Company, 1976.

Skinner, B.F. *The Behavior of Organisms: An Experimental Analysis.* New York: Appleton-Century-Crofts, 1975.

Skinner, B.F. *Science and Human Behavior.* New York: Macmillan, 1965.

Sulzer, B., and Mayer, G.R. *Behavior Modification Procedures for School Personnel.* Hinsdale, Illinois: Dryden Press, 1972.

Thorndike, E.L. *The Fundamentals of Learning.* New York: Teachers College Press, 1932.

Thorndike, E.L. *The Psychology of Learning.* New York: Teachers College Press, 1913.

Chapter 29

Extinction Techniques

The basic behavior modification law means that behavior that is reinforced will be strengthened and behavior that is not reinforced will be weakened. Extinction techniques are designed to weaken or extinguish undesirable behavior. By making extinction techniques a consequence of undesirable subject behavior it is possible to extinguish that undesirable behavior. Extinction techniques, like positive reinforcement, represent a formal component of behavior modification theory. The following discussion identifies and analyzes various extinction techniques.

Consistent ignoral

Consistently ignoring undesirable behavior is a good extinction technique. Most behavior, with the exception of pure physiological reactions (e.g., the startle response), is maintained by some external or internal reinforcement. By ignoring undesirable behavior, the likelihood of that behavior being fortuitously reinforced is reduced. For example, if the teacher ignores Gary's constant hand-waving behavior the teacher would be eliminating any teacher reinforcement that might serve to maintain that hand-waving behavior.

Several ignoral concepts need clarification. In order for ignoral to be an effective extinction technique the ignoral should be total and consistent. This is to say that ignoral, then attention, then ignoral, etc., will not only be ineffective in extinguishing undesirable behavior, but such irregular ignoral-attention could have the effect of intermittent positive reinforcement and could actually result in strengthening the undesirable behavior. In order for ignoral to be effective as an extinction technique attention to the undesirable behavior should be totally and consistently withheld.

The rationale of the success of the ignoral extinction technique is based on the assumption that there is little human behavior that is maintained without some external or internal reinforcement. Thus, by ignoring Gary's undesirable classroom behavior, the teacher is doing what can be done in that classroom, by the teacher, to extinguish that behavior, by that behavior modification strategy. When using ignoral as an extinction technique, it is important to control the subject's total environment as much as possible so that whatever extinction progress has been made will not be spoiled by other individuals unknowingly reinforcing the undesirable behavior. For this reason, it is important to continue the school-based behavior modification program at home, which means gaining parental cooperation, training the parents, actually shaping their behavior, etc.

The extinction technique of ignoral is often misunderstood. For example, because of unacceptable behavior, the teacher sends Jack out of the room to sit in the hall, presuming that Jack will thereby be ignored and thus punished. However, while in the hall, Jack receives attention from his friends, thus reinforcing the undesirable behavior which resulted in Jack being sent from the room. Under these circumstances, Jack's undesirable behavior probably would be strengthened.

Desensitization

Desensitization can be effective relative to the elimination of undesirable subject-fear behavior. Desensitization operates on the basis of gradually exposing a subject to the feared stimulus, and reinforcing the subject each positive step of the way. The rationale is that by gradual exposure the ego will be able to master the resulting fear (or anxiety) in manageable amounts, thus ultimately permitting the subject to effectively cope with the once-feared stimulus. The mechanics of gradually exposing a subject to the feared stimulus involve a process similar to the concept of task analysis. The feared stimulus is broken down into its component parts and each part in sequence is gradually exposed to the subject. For example, a subject who fears going to school could be reinforced for getting out of bed; reinforced for going to the front door; reinforced for stepping outside; reinforced for walking one block to school; reinforced for walking two blocks to school; . . .

reinforced for walking to the school steps; ... walking to the class door; stepping inside; etc.

Counter conditioning (reciprocal inhibition [Wolpe, 1964])

Counter conditioning is a powerful extinction technique. It involves extinguishing undesirable behavior by reinforcing desirable behavior which is antagonistic to the undesirable behavior. Since two antagonistic behaviors cannot occur simultaneously, the undesirable behavior will extinguish due to the reinforcement of the competing desirable behavior. For example, it would be impossible for Gary to frantically hand-wave while at the same time using that hand to constructively write. Therefore, if the teacher wished to extinguish Gary's hand-waving by counter conditioning, the teacher would need to think of creative ways in which to encourage Gary to write with that hand-waving hand and then reinforce the writing behavior. Since writing and the undesirable hand-waving cannot simultaneously occure, the latter would gradually extinguish due to the reinforcement of the competing desirable behavior. The key to this extinction technique is the creative identification of desirable behavior that is antagonistic to the undesirable behavior (e.g., an angry person cannot at the same time be relaxed; a high-frequency chatterer cannot at the same time chew many sticks of gum; the graffiti artist would find it difficult to, at the same time, be in charge of the school's anti-graffiti campaign; etc.).

Aversive stimuli (punishment)

Aversive stimuli means unpleasant experiences. Aversive stimuli is a controversial but sometimes necessary extinction technique. Undesirable behavior may be extinguished by administering aversive stimuli to th subject after the expression of the undesirable behavior. However, as with positive reinforcement, certain laws prevail: (1) The aversive stimulus should be meaningfully unpleasant to the subject. If it were unpleasant only to the practitioner, but actually pleasant to the subject, the effect would be to reinforce the undesirable behavior. The Reinforcement Inventory is designed to identify what a subject regards as reinforcing and aversive, and it is for the reason expressed above that this kind of information is valuable. (2) The practitioner should present the subject with a cue which is designed to signal the subject to stop the undesirable behavior. (3) The aversive stimulus should be applied to the subject immediately after every undesirable target-behavior. However, the cue as well as the frequency with which the aversive stimulus is applied should gradually be faded until the subject operates on a self-maintaining behavior basis. (4) The application of the cue and aversive stimulus should be consistent, at least until the fading process reaches the intermittent extinction stage.

The rationale of the success of this extinction technique is that the subject learns to expect the aversive stimulus at the thought or execution of the undesirable behavior, dislikes the aversive stimulus, and therefore eliminates the undesirable behavior rather than experience the aversive stimulus. This rationale suggests that pain can be more persuasive than pleasure.

The application of aversive stimuli serves only to stop the expression of undesirable behavior. In order to convert the aversive stimuli extinction technique into a positive reinforcement strategy, we recommend: (1) applying the aversive stimuli to the subject, (2) describing to the subject what the subject could have done that would have been more acceptable than the undesirable behavior, (3) have the subject actually perform that acceptable behavior, and (4) reinforce the subject for performing that acceptable behavior.

There are potential dangers involved with the use of aversive stimuli. (1) The aversive stimulus may not be aversive to the subject, and instead may serve as positive reinforcement for the undesirable subject behavior. This danger is particularly applicable to subjects who are starved for attention and for whom almost any kind of pleasant or unpleasant adult contact is reinforcing. (2) The administration of aversive stimuli may create anxiety or fear on behalf of the subject. Such a situation should be avoided. (3) In response to the administration of aversive stimuli a subject might fight back or withdraw. Again, such a situation should be avoided. (4) In response to the administration of aversive stimuli the subject may learn, by negative reinforcement, to avoid the practitioner who is associated with the aversive stimulus. But if the subject avoids the practitioner, the practitioner will not be able to carry out the behavior modification program! Another ramification of this same danger concept is that the subject might feel guilty about avoiding the practitioner, which would only compound an already unfavorable situation. (5) Aversive stimuli should be carefully administered so as to extinguish only undesirable behavior and not desirable behavior that might accompany the undesirable behavior. For example, you have been trying to teach Ann to tell the truth. Ann admits a theft. You then administer aversive stimuli in order to extinguish the theft behavior. But, that aversive stimuli probably will also extinguish Ann's truth telling behavior. In such a situation, it would be necessary to separate the two kinds of behavior for Ann, reinforce the truth telling behavior, and extinguish the theft behavior.

With the various dangers involved, the aversive stimuli extinction technique assumes a dimension of risk. However, there are instances where the behavior stopping property of aversive stimuli is necessary, in which case the technique is defensible as long as the practitioner offers the subject a cue which indicates what the subject could have done that would have been acceptable.

Satiation

The satiation extinction technique is controversial and risky. Satiation operates by obliging the subject to continuously repeat the identical undesirable behavior that is sought to be extinguished. Through boredom and/or fatigue the continuously repeated undesirable behavior will often extinguish. However, there are two conditions under which satiation should not be used: (1) when the undesirable subject behavior is dangerous, harmful, or illegal (for example, smoking), and (2) when the repetition of the undesirable behavior turns into positive reinforcement (e.g., in class, Curt is obliged to endlessly repeat an offensive word, but by so doing he gains hero stature; the resulting social praise could turn the satiation attempt into positive reinforcement of the word-saying behavior).

We recommend satiation only under prudent circumstances (for example, extinguishing the habit of typing a wrong letter by the subject continuously repeating the typing error until fatigue or boredom creates satiation).

The reader will recognize that the satiation technique is the conceptual opposite of the ignoral technique.

Withdrawal of rewards

Withdrawal of rewards is an effective extinction technique, but only if the rewards that are withdrawn are available on a systematic (nonrandom) basis. The administration of rewards on a scheduled time interval basis creates motivation for desirable behavior in terms of the subject anticipating the receipt of the rewards. As such, the withdrawal of randomly administered rewards is not an effective extinction technique because the recipient is not able to anticipate the receipt of a random reward, and as such, would not miss it were it not administered. In order to effectively use withdrawal of rewards as an extinction technique the rewards should be offered on a scheduled basis, which is the justification for using the above-described checkmark system. The checkmark system serves not only as a technique of positive reinforcement, but also as an extinction technique.

It is important to distinguish between withholding a reward not yet given and taking from a subject a reward that has already been administered. The former is compatible with the withdrawal of rewards extinction technique; the latter is punishment and should be avoided. Do not take back a reward that has already been given; such a practice has no theoretical justification.

Positive reinforcement as an extinction technique

A good extinction technique is that of positively reinforcing a subject for not engaging in undesirable behavior. This is an operant conditioning technique, and simply involves reinforcing a subject when not engaged in the undesirable behavior. For example, when Gary is not frantically hand-waving he occasionally should receive appropriate positive reinforcement, with an indication as to why the reinforcement is being administered (for example, "Thank you Gary for not waving your hand.").

The most powerful application of extinction techniques

The most powerful application of extinction techniques involves the appropriate combination of two or more of the previously discussed extinction techniques. Thus, to extinguish a particularly stubborn undesirable behavior, a combination of withdrawal of rewards and counter conditioning might be considered. However, the practitioner should guard against the use of unnecessary behavior modification power, for behavior modification over-kill can result in difficulty reaching the tertiary level of self-maintaining behavior.

The most powerful use of behavior modification techniques

The most powerful use of the behavior modification techniques so far discussed involves the appropriate combination of positive reinforcement and extinction techniques. Relative to that particularly stubborn undesirable subject behavior, a potent behavior management program might involve weakening the undesirable behavior by ignoral, while at the same time strengthening competing desirable behavior by appropriate reinforcers. However, it is important to practice behavior modification parsimony, and use only those techniques which are minimally necessary to accomplish the objective.

SELECTED REFERENCES

Wolpe, J. "The Comparative Clinical Status of Conditioning Therapies and Psychoanalysis." In J. Wolpe, A. Salter, and L. J. Regna (Eds.), *The Conditioning Therapies*. New York: Holt, Rinehart and Winston, 1964.

Section II

Behavior Modification and Change Agents: Specific Application

Chapter 30

Change Agents

Change agents are behavior modification strategies that are appropriate for use in public education. The following discussion presents different kinds of change agents, all of which can be applied to the operation of the management model for the purpose of increasing the likelihood of presenting problem resolution.

Contingency management

Contingency management is often used as an umbrella term to express the general concept of behavior modification. However, we regard contingency management in a more restricted fashion, and limit the application to: (1) contingency contracts; (2) the use of free time; (3) the daily class schedule; and (4) the use of high-interest materials. The common denominator of our use of contingency management is the Premack principle (Premack, 1965), which we consider to mean that a high-probability (high interest) task which is available immediately following a low-probability (low interest) task will increase subject motivation to complete the low-prob task in order to gain the high-prob task. The following discussion applies the Premack principle to contingency management concepts.

Contingency contracts

Contingency contracting involves the drawing-up of a written or oral behavior contract, by the teacher and student, in which the student contracts to engage in a particular low-prob task, at the successful completion of which the teacher contracts to provide the student with a high-prob task. For example, the teacher could contract with Jeff to correctly solve fifteen arithmetic tasks on five successive days, at the successful completion of which the teacher would treat Jeff to a movie. Although the contracting can be oral in nature, we prefer a simple written contract. As the reader may recall, contingency contracts are important to the operation of the learning menu classroom.

Examples of high-appeal contingency contracts appear in Chapter 22.

Structured free time

The free time concept operates by permitting a subject to engage in structured free time activity as a high-prob task after having successfully engaged in a low-prob task. Free time can be used in conjunction with contingency contracts and/or a free time classroom area, or can exist by itself as a form of positive reinforcement. The use of free time is an effective secondary student payoff, particularly in terms of accumulating sufficient free time to earn a school sponsored dance, auto show, movie, etc. The interest center, learning center, and learning menu classrooms use free time as a major source of reinforcement. However, in order to be reinforcing, the use of free time should be need-satisfying to the subject.

The daily class schedule

We recommend the use of contingency management with respect to the daily class schedule. This can be arranged by following each low-prob task with a high-prob task. With respect to the daily class schedule component of the learning contracts presented in Chapter 22, the reader will note that a high prob task begins and ends the day, and follows each low-prob task. This represents an attempt to increase subject motivation to attend school, as well as to complete the various low-prob tasks because of the contingent high-prob tasks. By interspersing high-prob with low-prob tasks, the student has something positive to anticipate throughout the school day.

High-interest materials

The last contingency management concept involves increasing the stimulus value of a learning experience by using high interest (and in some cases low vocabulary) educational materials. The use of high interest materials is designed to increase student motivation relative to performing what normally is a low-prob tool-subject task for that student but what is up-graded to a high-prob task by the use of high interest materials. The ERC represents a source a high interest materials, as does Appendix I.

Token economy

Token economy is a self-contained behavior modification strategy which has the versatility to be effective by itself. Token economy operates by the use of poker chip size tokens which simulate currency by having one-cent, five-cent, ten-cent, twenty-five cent, or fifty-cent values stamped on them. All the previously discussed behavior modification precepts pertain to the administration of the tokens. However, there are some procedures that are unique to the token economy system which should be discussed: the system can function on a classroom-wide basis, or on an individual student basis. Relative to the former situation, four or five classroom-wide desirable target behaviors should be clearly identified on large posters. Each behavior should be associated with a certain token value. The posters should be prominently displayed in the classroom. Whenever a student engages in desirable target behavior the appropriately priced token should be awarded that individual. At regularly scheduled times (e.g., once a day for young and/or disturbing students, much longer intervals for older and/or more adaptive students), a classroom-based store with a student storekeeper should open for business, at which time students may surrender the total value of their tokens for appropriately priced high-probability objects.

If the system operates on an individual student basis, then each involved student should have a small card taped to his desk on which is identified three or four desirable target behaviors, each of which should be associated with a certain token value. Whenever the student engages in that desirable target behavior the appropriately priced token should be awarded. At regularly scheduled times, involved students should be permitted to purchase high-value objects at the classroom store.

As with any positive reinforcement technique, the appropriate token should be administered to the subject immediately after the earning behavior. Also, the administration of the token should be paired with a social reinforcer (verbal praise in particular). In addition to the tokens having store purchase value, the tokens could be used to buy free time, food, trips, movies, etc. It is in this total purchase capacity that the token economy system can operate as a self-contained behavior modification procedure.

We have found the token economy system to be effective. We have also found that the effectiveness of the system is increased: if a real store-front, built by the students, is used; if the student store keeper dispenses the purchased objects in conjunction with the teacher; if actual token change is made; and if the teacher wears a multipocket apron, one pocket for each token denomination.

Although the token economy system could be used in conjunction with the checkmark system, the rationale for so doing would have to be persuasive, in terms of avoiding reinforcer over-kill.

Body image

Body image is defined as the adequacy with which one regards one's physical appearance, physical structure, and physical ability. In essence, body image is the motor component of the self concept. We contend that because of perceptual problems, actual physical disability, poor reality testing, etc., most special education students have body-image problems. For this reason, we endorse a physical classroom design which makes use of the body-image center concept. Body-image activities should be scheduled for 10-15 minutes each, one or two times a day. The body-image activities should be regarded as a high-prob task, and should thus follow low-prob tasks.

The body-image center concept should be seriously regarded as one means of resolving body-image problems. As such, the body-image activities should not be an unorganized expression of physical education exercises, but rather a coordinated effort to build body-image adequacy by having body-image goals for each subject and by relating the body-image activities to each other.

The body-image center is important to the operation of the interest center, learning center, and learning menu classrooms. Irrespective of the kind of classroom, a body-image area should include the objects necessary for subjects to: cut, paste, throw, catch, kick, run, skip, hop, march, do calisthenics, do left-right and up-down orientation exercises, match and sort objects, discriminate objects, color, trace, and draw, and engage in such activities as swimming, weight-lifting, Simon says games, memory activities, naming body part games, balance beam exercises, trampoline exercises, silhouette-part games, grooming, posture, and, cosmetic and domestic activities. Reference to specific body image materials and activities appears in Chapter 22.

Tally system

The tally (point) system can operate in three different ways, all of which employ a small spiral-bound notebook and the recording of tallies on both the left and right pages.

1. The first tally system use is for the purpose of identifying the frequency with which desirable and undesirable behavior occurs. One tally (pencil mark) is made on the left page of the notebook each time a desirable behavior occurs, and one tally made on the right page each time an undesirable behavior occurs. This tally use is effective for parents and teachers relative to objectively demonstrating the frequency with which desirable or undesirable behavior occurs. It is often reality-awakening to parents who protest that their child never does anything wrong to realize the tally build-up on the undesirable page.

2. The second tally system use is for the purpose of identifying the frequency with which a reinforcer or an aversive stimulus is administered. Again, one tally on the appropriate notebook page for each kind of behavior. This tally system use is also effective for parents and teachers in terms of objectively demonstrating the frequency with which they administer praise and punishment. Relative to (1) and (2) above, it is important, especially for parents, that the tally system be objectified in the following fashion: specific desirable and undesirable subject behavior should be identified, in list form, in order to standardize the tally administration procedure. Similarly, the specific kinds of subject behavior that may be reinforced or receive an aversive stimulus should be identified in list form.

3. The third tally system use is for the purpose of serving as a positive reinforcer or aversive stimulus, where each tally is regarded as a reinforcer or aversive stimulus. However, this tally use is effective as a behavior management strategy only in relation to certain administrative precepts, which follow. First, desirable and undesirable behavior should be clearly identified so that the subject can anticipate earning a tally by engaging in known desirable behavior. Second, in order to have any value, the subject must be aware that a reinforcer or aversive tally has been administered at the time of that administration. Third, the administration of the tally should be paired with a social reinforcer, usually of a verbal-praise nature. Gradually, the social reinforcer should thereby assume the same reinforcement power initially associated with the tally. Fourth, a tally which is used as a positive reinforcer should be administered to the subject immediately after the desirable response. Fifth, the subject should be permitted to surrender the tally total at the end of a given time period for objects which have pre-established surrender value. In this context, the tally system is similar to the checkmark system. Sixth, it is possible to use the tally system as an extinction technique by identifying specific undesirable subject behavior, administering a tally for each expression of the undesirable behavior, and at the end of the time period, adding the number of undesirable tally points to the point value of the surrender objects, thus making it more difficult to earn those objects by the degree to which undesirable tally points were administered. And seventh, most of the positive reinforcement principles which are discussed in the positive reinforcement chapter apply to the administration of the tally system.

Time-out

The time-out strategy is a powerful extinction technique. It operates by placing an offending subject in an area which is devoid of everything except a chair. The rationale of the time-out strategy is one of punishment and removing the subject from a reinforcing environment. Therefore, the time-out area should be used only for punishment purposes and never as a study booth.

Optimally, the time-out area should be a small room that is external to, but contiguous with, the classroom. In order to reduce the possibility of the time-out area being reinforcing, the area should be bare, except for a chair. If there is no external room, a time-out area can be made within the classroom by means of plyboard, heavy-duty screen, or even a large moving box. As with the extinction technique of ignoral, sending a subject out of the classroom to the office, or sending a subject at home to his room, is an inappropriate application of the time-out concept due to the reinforcement that is available from peers in and around the office, and from toys in the room. We would expect those subjects to engage again in the undesirable behavior in order to be sent to the office or room.

Some important time-out mechanics are:
1. In order to be effective, the time-out concept should be aversive to the subject. It probably would not be an aversive experience for a social isolate to be sent to the time-out area; as such, the desired behavior modification would likely not occur.
2. Because of the physical isolation involved, the time-out strategy should be regarded as a last resort extinction technique.
3. The offending student should be placed in the time-out area with as little communication as possible in order to avoid reinforcement by means of practitioner attention. Nonetheless, the practitioner should indicate to the subject that the subject behaved in an unacceptable way, briefly explain the specific nature of that unacceptable behavior, and then indicate that the subject must spend 10 minutes in the time-out area after which he may rejoin the group.
4. The length of each time-out placement should not exceed 10 minutes.
5. If a student is so unadaptive that the undesirable behavior is still operative after three time-out experiences in a given day, that student should be suspended from school for the rest of that day.

It is possible to use the time-out strategy as a means of negative reinforcement. Assuming that placement in the time-out area is aversive, the subject may be placed in the time-out area with instructions to come out only when he is capable of desirable behavior. When the subject removes the aversive situation by the desirable behavior, that desirable behavior will be negatively reinforced. If this application of the time-out strategy is used, the specific nature of the desirable behavior in which the subject must engage in order to leave the time-out area should be identified to the subject.

We have found the time-out strategy to be very effective. However, within public education it is an unconventional classroom management technique and the operator should be prepared to obtain permission for, and defend, its use.

Modeling

The modeling concept (Bandura, 1969) operates on the assumption that behavior is learned by imitation. As such, if Lamar's hero can be identified (through, for example, a sociometric device), and if Lamar models his hero's behavior, then Lamar's behavior can be modified by shaping the behavior of the hero through positive reinforcement and/or extinction techniques. Thus, the modeling strategy is a once removed behavior modification tactic, and should be guided by all the previously discussed behavior modification precepts.

We have found the modeling strategy to be effective, especially by using older students, the principal, the coach, the janitor, and cafeteria workers as models.

Medication

Behavior modification techniques are not as effective with behavior problems that are due to a central nervous system dysfunction. We contend that lawful medication is the best way to bring organically based subject behavior problems under initial control, after which behavior modification strategies are likely to be more effective. Educators should be knowledgable about the various kinds of medication as well as the medical practitioners in the community who are helpful with school-based learning and behavior problems. However, it is never acceptable to refer a minor school subject directly to a physician; any medical concern about a subject should be expressed through the school chain of command, to the parents, and then by them to the practitioner of choice.

The following information relates to various medicines which are often prescribed for the control of the associated symptoms:

1. Dilantin: seizure control.
2. Phenobarbital: seizure control; and, a slow acting sedative for children.
3. The combination of Dilantin and Phenobarbital is often used for seizure control.
4. Stelazine, and Thorazine: antipsychotic medicine.
5. Librium, and Valium: mild tranquilizers.
6. Dexedrine, and Benzedrine: antidepressant medication (stimulants).
7. Nembutal, and Seconal: rapid acting sedatives.

Crisis Intervention

Crisis intervention is a short-term change agent which is applicable to a large size school. Crisis intervention operates by: (1) Assigning a crisis teacher to a classroom which is engineered in terms of interest centers. (2) Having regular teachers contact the crisis teacher relative to acute student behavior crises. (3) Having the crisis teacher take the offending student to the crisis classroom, and by isolation, structured environment, behavior modification techniques, and order-tasks which are designed to promote success, assist the offending student to regain control. (4) As soon as possible, return the student to the regular class. The crisis intervention concept works best: on a period-to-period or day-to-day basis; if no more than 10 students are in the classroom at one time; if the orientation of the classroom is nonpunitive, and designed to help the student regain control of his emotions; and if the crisis teacher has no educational responsibility except to return the student to the regular class as soon as possible.

Limited day

Every state has a compulsory school attendance law. This means that students between certain ages are compelled to attend school. However, we argue that a teacher has the right not to have a disturbing student in class after all remedial strategies have been exhausted and after all have been found ineffective. After all conventional strategies have been exhausted, one last resort strategy that can be employed is the limited day. This strategy operates by exposing a student to only that part of the school day to which a successful adjustment can be made. Gradually the length of successful adjustment time may be increased according to the coping limits of the student. For example, a student may come to school for only 15 minutes per day for the first three weeks; then 30 minutes; 60 minutes; 90 minutes; etc.

Although behavior management is a desirable goal, it is important for educators not to feel guilty about an inability to effectively manage the behavior of all subjects. For whatever management strategies are employed, there will always be a few individuals whose behavior is not amendable to acceptable classroom control techniques. The problems of these subjects often precede school attendance, and although teacher concern is commendable, painful guilt feelings relative to the inability to cope with this kind of subject represent incorrect blame. The practical solution for these individuals is the application of the least restrictive educational environment concept.

Student group dynamics

The concept of student group dynamics operates in three different ways, all for the purpose of helping subjects understand themselves in relation to others. The three ways are role playing, psychodrama, and counseling.

Role playing

Role playing typically involves two subjects acting-out opposing social-personal roles for the purpose of gaining greater understanding regarding the feelings associated with those roles. Role playing is a tool of understanding, and is most effective with respect to issues, as opposed to problems, that deal with interpersonal relations. Role playing is a flexible tool, and can be used spontaneously to examine interpersonal issues of recent onset. Usually, the teacher assigns students to act-out roles on the basis of the needs of the students in relation to the nature of the interpersonal issue. The role playing actors should be spontaneous in their expression of the roles, and usually two opposing roles encourage such spontaneity.

The self-understanding objective of role playing can be facilitated by conducting a group discussion subsequent to the role playing, which focuses on the nature of the feelings expressed, the way the role played issue was resolved, etc. Unlike counseling, role playing is not a tool of choice for chronic problem understanding, but rather, effective for the shallow working through of interpersonal issues that need to be experienced in order to be understood. For example, role playing is helpful to mental retardates in terms of developing appropriate behavior in response to name-calling (e.g., weirdo, retardo, etc.).

Psychodrama

Psychodrama involves subjects acting-out assigned social-personal roles, based on teacher written scripts, for the purpose of achieving understanding of the feelings involved with those roles. The scope of psychodrama as a tool of understanding should be limited in the classroom to acute social-personal problems. Nonetheless, the effectiveness of the psychodrama tool is enhanced if the actors and student audience have the opportunity to discuss the feelings expressed and the problem resolution subsequent to the skit. Teacher written scripts can be very effective where the script deals with particular student problems and where students are assigned roles that are based on their relationship to those problems. The psychodrama skit can be either closed ended or open ended. The former means that the script directs the ending. The latter, which is a more powerful understanding tool, involves the script ending at a crucial midpoint, with the actors projecting themselves into the way in which the problem is resolved.

Counseling

Counseling is designed to help individuals understand themselves in relation to others. The counseling process operates by providing an accepting atmosphere of empathy and genuineness for the purpose of facilitating that understanding. The counseling process can be of an individual or group nature, and can involve at least three different counselor techniques: reflection of feeling; clarification, support, and advice; and interpretation of symbolism.

Reflection of feeling. (Regers, 1973). This counseling technique involves the sensitive understanding of a subject's internal frame of reference, and the consequent reflection by the counselor to the subject of how the subject really feels or what the subject really meant to say. In a nonthreatening atmosphere, reflection of feeling permits the subject to experience himself in an accepted way, which gradually permits the ego to master those feelings that have previously been disguised due to their inherent threat. It is essential to the welfare of the counseling client, as well as to the effectiveness of the counseling process, that the content of the reflected feeling never be more than that which the subject can understand and for which the subject is emotionally ready. It is professionally wrong to blast a subject with a full emotional exposure to himself when that subject is not able to cope with the nature of the information. Reflection of feeling is not as easy as it may seem, as a great deal of perceptiveness, empathy, and the personal security necessary to understand and give to others is involved.

Clarification, support, and advice. This counseling technique involves engaging in problem solving with the subject on a clarification and advice basis, and providing the support necessary to build the ego strength of emotionally fragile individuals. This is more directive than the reflection of feeling technique, as the latter involves the delicate attempt to focus on, and then reflect, the inner dynamics of the subject.

Interpretation of symbolism. This counseling technique is very sophisticated and should not be conducted by counselors not trained in the psychology of symbols. Basically, the counselor attempts to help the subject understand himself by interpreting to the subject the meaning of the verbal, motor, written, fantasy, dream, etc., symbols used by the subject. This is not a technique that the casually trained counselor should employ.

Counseling mechanics.

We recommend that teachers of self-contained special education classes conduct, or arrange to have conducted, student group counseling for the purpose of increasing self-understanding, understanding of others, and general coping skills. The mechanics of the counseling process should operate in the following fashion:

1. We recommend a group cocounselor whenever possible. This could involve the school counselor, a teacher who has the necessary training, etc.
2. Optimally, no more than eight subjects should be included in a counseling group.
3. The physical group counseling arrangement should involve chairs in a circle.
4. Once the counseling group begins, it should be closed to additional subjects, regarded as confidential, and operate without visitors.
5. The group counseling session should be conducted once a week, for 30 to 45 minutes in length, depending on the age of the subjects. Normally, the younger the subjects, the shorter the session length. Also, for subjects younger than seven or eight years, play activities are a better way of conducting counseling than verbal discussion.
6. We recommend that the counseling session be conducted during the next to last period of the school day, and that the subjects be provided with a controlled activity period subsequent to the counseling session for the purpose of draining residual feelings prior to leaving school.
7. The counseling sessions should be offered on a scheduled basis, and that schedule should be conscientiously maintained.
8. In order to foster a nonthreatening group counseling atmosphere, behavior controls should be minimal. However, some guidelines should be established; viz., no personal or property damage, no obscene language, no out-of-seat physical activity, etc.

9. No one should operate as a counselor without the necessary training and without a philosophical understanding of man.

Parent group-dynamics

We recommend that special education teachers conduct, or arrange to have conducted, class related parent group counseling. This change agent technique operates in a way similar to that of student group counseling. We recommend: a trained coleader (counselor, nurse, etc.); no more than 15 people in the group, which optimally should involve both parents; and that the group meet once a month, at the home of the various parents, on a rotating parent responsibility basis.

Parent groups can be conducted by at least three different counselor techniques: (1) reflection of feeling; (2) clarification, support, and advice; and (3) instruction in behavior modification techniques. Numbers one and two above represent the same concepts as discussed in the preceding counseling section. Number three, instruction in behavior modification techniques, involves training parents in formal behavior modification strategy so that the parents may continue the school-based behavior management program at home. We recommend loaning the parents a good but simple book on behavior modification, asking the parents to read the book, and then teaching behavior modification concepts from the book. In conjunction with behavior modification techniques, the parents might also be taught the concepts of behavior-instructional objectives, task analysis, and baseline measurement.

It is important to conduct parent groups for at least three reasons:
1. To offer advice to parents relative to effective ways of coping with their special education child, and to offer advice relative to effective ways of helping the child cope with the reality demands of the environment.
2. We contend that parents of exceptional children are no different than parents of regular children except that the former must cope with the additional stress incurred by the exceptionality of their child, as well as the stress incurred by the guilt based assumption of the responsibility for their child's exceptionality. Parent group counseling presents an opportunity to help parents work through those guilt feelings for the purpose of making the relationship with their exceptional child more emotionally honest.
3. Many parents of exceptional children cope with the stress of their child's exceptionality by emotional suppression, a situation which eventually could manifest itself in parental irritability, body complaints, decreased efficiency, etc. Parent groups are a good way to provide a safe opportunity for the expression of bottled-up feelings of frustration and helplessness.

For the reasons stated above, we recommend the routine classroom conduction of student and parent group counseling. However, the practitioner should never operate groups at a level above that person's professional competence, the groups should be conducted on a scheduled basis and should not be sacrificed for activities of lesser importance, and it is important for the reader to understand that behavior change due to individual or group counseling is a function of not only the people and techniques involved, but also time. The expectation of immediate behavior change due to counseling is totally unrealistic, and if progress can be identified within four or five months, the practitioner should feel successful.

Teacher aides

The operation of a prescriptive teaching classroom is facilitated by the use of teacher aides. There are three basic kinds of aides: paid adult aides, volunteer adult aides, and student aides.

It is most desirable to have a full-time adult salaried aide. In such a case, it is important to provide inservice training for the aide with respect to educational philosophy, differentiation of teacher and aide duties, behavior management techniques, and instructional methodology.

In the event that a full-time salaried adult aide is impossible, it is desirable to use volunteer adult aides, such as parents or senior citizens. It is particularly desirable to use parents of special education students as aides. The use of such parents is desirable in terms of exposing the parents to their child's school behavior, and exposing the parents to the school-based remediation program, a situation which makes easier the parental continuation of that program at home. When using special education parents as aides, it is important to avoid having parents work with their own children. Again, the parent aides should receive in-service training.

With or without the use of paid or volunteer adult aides, the use of student aides can be effective. The concept of student aides has a variety of applications: older students with younger students (cross-age tutors); brighter students with duller students; tough older students with tough younger students (for control purposes); good readers with poor readers; shy older students with normal younger students (for the purpose of social-personal confidence); etc.

The deductive strategy

The deductive strategy is not so much a change agent technique as it is a systems approach to the logical resolution of a presenting problem. The strategy operates by the practitioner performing three procedural steps: (1) defining the presenting problem; (2) determining the environmental events which reinforce undesirable subject behavior; and (3) manipulating the environment in order to eliminate the reinforcement of that undesirable behavior. Thus, it is necessary to identify who or what reinforces target behavior; when the reinforcement occurs; and then to execute the behavior modification procedures which will extinguish the undesirable behavior and/or strengthen competing desirable behavior. The deductive strategy is an excellent behavior modification plan of action whenever it is possible to precisely determine the environmental events which reinforce the presenting problems.

Kitchen timer

The kitchen timer change agent technique is a good positive reinforcement strategy, particularly when using a variable interval reinforcement schedule. The timer technique involves the use of a one-hour kitchen timer, randomly setting it, and then rewarding those subjects who are engaged in specific desirable behavior when the timer rings. In order for this technique to be effective, the desirable behavior should be identified prior to the use of the timer.

Feedback

Feedback of subject behavior-change progress is reinforcing and necessary. We recommend one of two feedback techniques: one, taping a feedback baseline-type grid to the desk of each subject; or two, taping to the classroom wall a wide strip of paper on which is drawn one feedback grid for each subject. By using the major behavioral or instructional objectives for each subject, then averaging the baselined progress with respect to those objectives, and then converting that sum into a percent figure, it is possible to plot one figure on the feedback grid per day or per week for the purpose of serving as subject feedback information. The decision as to the frequency of plotting (daily, weekly, etc.) should be made on the basis of the maturity and delay of gratification capacity of the subjects. Although it is usually the province of the teacher to compute and plot the figures, it is acceptable to teach the subjects to so compute and plot.

Guidance room

The guidance room is a last resort change agent strategy for disturbing students and is particularly applicable to large size schools. The guidance room functions by assigning a full-time male and female teacher-counselor to a classroom which operates on the basis of a therapeutic milieu. The male and female teacher-counselors are symbolic of an intact family, with the male serving as the major disciplinarian and the female serving as the receptive mother-figure. The purpose of the guidance room is to assist high-risk students to learn coping skills in a self-contained therapeutic atmosphere. As such, the guidance room teachers have exclusive and long-term (school-year or years) responsibility for the students assigned them. Academic studies are conducted within the guidance room, although the students should be merged with mainstream education whenever possible.

The guidance room should be physically arranged in terms of three rooms: a main room which serves as an interest center-based problem solving area; an activity room contiguous to the problem-solving area; and a conference-counseling room contiguous to the other side of the problem-solving area. The operating mechanics involve assigning not more than 10 disturbing students to the guidance room on a full-time basis, and through the vehicles of behavior modification, counseling, and success-oriented educational tasks, helping the students to develop appropriate social-personal coping skills.

Subject involvement

A simple but often overlooked change agent strategy is that of developing intervention objectives and task analyses in conjunction with the involved subjects.

Objectives and task analyses which are developed with a subject have a greater high-probability factor than do objectives and task analyses which are developed by the teacher only.

Ingenuity

Effective reinforcers should be need-satisfying to the subject. Behavior modification should represent for the practitioner a creative opportunity to devise ways of shaping subject behavior. Thus, ingenuity is an asset. As an example, we remember a scientifically oriented teacher and an equally scientifically oriented emotionally disturbed student who devised a clever remote-controlled behavior modification system. The system operated by the teacher pushing one button on a small control panel immediately after desirable subject behavior and pushing another button immediately after undesirable subject behavior. The first button activated a reinforcing green light and sweet tone in a receiver box carried by the subject, whereas the second button activated an aversive red light and unpleasant tone.

The structured classroom

The structured classroom is one of the best classroom-oriented change agents, particularly with respect to hyperactive and distractible students. The basic philosophy of the structured classroom involves the provision of as much meaningful classroom structure as possible so as to help students gain internal control of their feelings by means of the external control of the classroom. The structured classroom has many components, which follow.

1. The classroom should operate on the basis of a definite routine. This means a dependable daily schedule which does not arbitrarily vary; the use of carefully controlled interest centers; and the use of pass-keys, which physically represent the permission subjects must obtain in order to move within or without the class.

2. The teacher should expect student production compatible with student ability; and the teacher should be consistent, follow through, and not accept substandard work.

3. The structured classroom should operate on the basis of contingency management principles, particularly regarding high-prob tasks that follow low-prob tasks, learning contracts, and the use of high interest materials. In addition, the physical classroom arrangement should avoid excess space and should include study booths.

4. Lastly, the structured classroom should be designed to reduce extraneous environmental stimuli. Optimally, the floor should be carpeted; the overhead lights muted; the windows curtained; the classroom located away from distracting environmental sounds; the furniture fixed; the classroom color scheme bland and constant throughout; the carrels enclosed; the teacher's clothing conservative and without noisy jewelry and/or distracting colors; and, problem solving tasks should be color-coded and structured in order to focus subject attention on the task-figure as opposed to task-ground.

Clinical teaching

Clinical teaching is a form of bibliotherapy. It operates by inducing behavior change through the use of educational materials. Specifically, clinical teaching assists students with the understanding of social-personal problems by providing reading assignments the content of which meaningfully deals with the subject's problem. For example, a withdrawing student could be assigned to read a book the hero of which is similar in age to the student and who successfully overcomes shyness problems. Subsequent to having read the book, the student and target-problem should be worked into psychodrama attempts to help the student gain further understanding of the problem. Although it is difficult for a teacher to keep current with the vast amount of bibliotherapy materials, it is the province of the ERC to provide such information.

Immediate feedback interview

The immediate feedback interview permits an on-the-spot resolution attempt of minor classroom conflicts. In a fashion similar to Redl's Life-Space Interview (Redl, 1969), the teacher, without moralizing: (1) isolates the offending student; (2) determines the student's perception of the conflict situation; (3) expresses the teacher's perception of the conflict situation; (4) mutually determines what must occur in order to correct the conflict situation; and (5) contracts with the student for success by contingency management and positive reinforcement techniques. In essence, a behavior contract is drawn up which specifies what the student will do, what the teacher will do, and what specific reinforcers (free time, a certain number of tokens, etc.) will be used to assure that the contract terms will be met.

Group negative reinforcement

Group negative reinforcement is a powerful but risky behavior modification technique. The concept operates by exerting group pressure on a subject to effect subject change. For example, the teacher could refuse to permit the class to go out for recess until Judy is quiet. When the desired subject behavior occurs, the teacher would immediately excuse the class.

In order for group negative reinforcement to be effective, certain conditions should prevail: (1) The prospect of group pressure should be aversive to the subject. (2) The teacher should structure the event so that the subject behavior which removes the aversive situation is desirable behavior, for, as discussed in the negative reinforcement section, whatever kind of subject behavior (desirable or undesirable) removes an aversive situation will be reinforced. Thus, the teacher should structure the event so that the subject's group-pressure removing behavior is desirable, so that it is the desirable behavior that is reinforced. (3) Group negative reinforcement is more risky than individual negative reinforcement. Irrespective of whether the negative reinforcement is group or individual in kind the practitioner should be willing to accept the behavioral consequences of the subject not removing the aversive stimulus. Thus, if Judy's teacher elected to use group negative reinforcement, the teacher should be willing to accept the possibility of, for example, Judy choosing not to be quiet, in which case the teacher would be confronted with a class of smoldering students who are impatient to go to recess. The increased risk associated with the use of group negative reinforcement results from behavior modification strategy that backfires and the subsequent possibility of group resentment and frustration as well as difficulty in regaining teacher-class rapport.

We do not recommend this technique unless there is good reason to believe that the subject regards group pressure as sufficiently aversive to quickly yield, and unless there is good reason to believe that there will be no group reprisal for the inconvenience suffered because of the offending subject.

Chaining, and reverse chaining

The concepts of chaining and reverse chaining represent more of a logical approach to presenting problem resolution than a technique of behavior modification. The concepts are similar to the diagnostic-prescriptive teaching concept of task analysis. All behavior can be broken down into the component parts of that behavior. Chaining and task analysis simply involve the identification of the component parts of a given behavior, ranking those parts in sequential order, and then mastering the behavior by mastering the component parts of that behavior. For example, if the behavioral objective were for Chris to tie his shoelaces, the chaining concept would operate by identifying the component parts of shoelace tying, sequencing those parts (from holding a lace in each hand to pulling the bows), and then mastering shoelace tying by mastering each component part in its sequenced order. Thus, Chris would begin with holding a lace in each hand, then crossing hands, then tucking one lace under the other, etc. This sequential step process is also called successive approximation, and shaping. Thus, by means of chaining (or task analysis), Chris' behavior would gradually be shaped into shoelace tying.

Reverse chaining operates in the same fashion as chaining except the sequential order of the component parts is reversed, and the subject begins with the last sequential step and works backwards to the first sequential step. With respect to shoelace tying, Chris would begin with the last step, i.e., pulling the shoelace bow tight. After mastering that step, Chris would learn the preceding step, and then combine, and then master, both steps. And similarly with the remaining steps. The advantage of the reverse chaining concept is that it permits a subject to experience the complete behavior first, from which the subject works backward to the initial step.

We advocate the application of the chaining (task analysis) concept to all systematic intervention with learning and behavior problems. Reverse chaining does not have the variety of application that chaining does, although because of the exposure to completed tasks, it is often appropriate relative to the education of mental retardates.

Conclusions

We identify the appropriate use of behavior modification and change agents as a reinforcement schedule. A reinforcement schedule is designed to effect change. Nonetheless, the schedule should employ only those behavior modification strategies that are minimally necessary to achieve the intervention objective. If too many strategies are employed and/or if strategies are employed that are too powerful, the transition from primary to secondary to tertiary levels of reinforcement will likely be impeded.

We have found that IEP intervention failure is often due to one or both of two conditions: (1) The task analysis sequential steps are too large to permit the subject to make a succesful transition from one step to the next. (2) The reinforcement schedule is inappropriate, usually in terms of the payoffs being insufficiently need satisfying. Often, both of these failure conditions are due to insufficient information about the learner.

Even though an intervention is successful, we contend that success should never be judged in isolation, but solely in terms of the overall goal of education: viz., student acquisition of coping skills relative to economic and social survival in a vastly complex and competitive world.

SELECTED REFERENCES

Bandura, A. *Principles of Behavior Modification*. New York: Holt, Rinehart and Winston, 1969.

Premack, D. "Reinforcement Theory." In D. Levine (Ed.), *Nebraska Symposium on Motivation*. Lincoln: University of Nebraska Press, 1965.

Redl, F. "Why Life Space Interview?" In H. Dupont (Ed.), *Educating Emotionally Disturbed Children, Readings*. New York: Holt, Rinehart, and Winston, 1969.

Rogers, C. *Client-Centered Therapy*. Boston: Houghton Mifflin, 1973.

PART VIII

LEGISLATION RELATING TO SPECIAL EDUCATION

Diagnostic Prescriptive Teaching and Programming as well as the Management Model exist in order to facilitate the educational success of handicapped individuals. Recent Federal legislation serves to dramatically facilitate that educational success.

Chapter 31

Public Law 94-142

P.L. 94-142 is the Education for All Handicapped Children Act of 1975. The purpose of the Act is to ensure that all handicapped children have a free appropriate public education, which includes special education and related services, and to ensure that the rights of handicapped children and their parents are protected. Some specific components of the Act are identified below.

SPECIAL EDUCATION
1. The reference to "special education" means "specially designed instruction, at no cost to the parent, to meet the unique needs of a handicapped child, including classroom instruction, instruction in physical education, home instruction and instruction in hospitals and institutions."

RELATED SERVICES
2. The reference to "related services" means "transportation and such developmental, corrective, and other supportive services as are required to assist a handicapped child to benefit from special education, and includes speech pathology and audiology, psychological services, physical and occupational therapy, recreation, early identification and assessment of disabilities in children, counseling services, and medical services for diagnostic or evaluation purposes."

VOCATIONAL EDUCATION
3. The reference to "special education" also "includes vocational education if it consists of specially designed instruction, at no cost to the parents, to meet the unique needs of a handicapped child."

BEGINNING DATES
4. "Each State shall ensure that free and appropriate public education is available to all handicapped children aged three through eighteen within the State no later than September 1, 1978, and to all handicapped children aged three through twenty-one within the State not later than September 1, 1980."

RESIDENTIAL PLACEMENT
5. "If placement in a public or private residential program is necessary to provide special education and related services to a handicapped child, the program, including non-medical care and room and board, must be at no cost to the parents of the child."

6. "Each public agency shall take steps to provide nonacademic and extra curricular services and activities in such manner as is necessary to afford handicapped children an equal opportunity for participation in those services and activities."

"Nonacademic and extra curricular services and activities may include counseling services, athletics, transportation, health services, recreational activities, special interest groups or clubs sponsored by the public agency, referrals to agencies which provide assistance to handicapped persons, and employment of students . . . "

PHYSICAL EDUCATION
7. "If specially designed physical education is prescribed in a child's individualized education, the public agency responsible for the education of that child shall provide the services directly, or make arrangements for it to be provided through other public or private programs."

IEP
8. "On October 1, 1977, and at the beginning of each school year thereafter, each public agency shall have in effect an individualized education program for every handicapped child who is receiving special education from that agency."

9. "Each public agency is responsible for initiating and conducting meetings for the purpose of developing, reviewing, and revising a handicapped child's individualized education program."

IEP ANNUAL MEETING

10. "Each public agency shall initiate and conduct meetings to periodically review each child's individualized education program and if appropriate revise its provisions. A meeting must be held for this purpose at least once a year."

11. "The State educational agency shall ensure that an individualized education program is developed and implemented for each handicapped child who:
    (1) Is placed in or referred to a private school or facility by a public agency; or
    (2) Is enrolled in a parochial or other private school and receives special education or related services from a public agency."

COMPOSITION OF IEP MEETING

12. "The public agency shall ensure that each meeting includes the following participants:" a representative of the public agency, other than the child's teacher, who is qualified to provide, or supervise the provision of, special education; the child's teacher; one or both of the child's parents; the child, where appropriate; other individuals at the discretion of the parent or agency.

13. "For a handicapped child who has been evaluated for the first time, the public agency shall ensure:
    (1) That a member of the evaluation team participates in the meeting; or
    (2) That the representative of the public agency, the child's teacher, or some other person is present at the meeting, who is knowledgeable about the evaluation procedures used with the child and is familiar with the results of the evaluation."

PARENTS AT MEETING

14. "Each public agency shall take steps to ensure that one or both of the parents of the handicapped child are present at each meeting or are afforded the opportunity to participate, including:
    (1) Notifying parents of the meeting early enough to ensure that they will have an opportunity to attend; and
    (2) Scheduling the meeting at a mutually agreed on time and place."

"If neither parent can attend, the public agency shall use other methods to ensure parent participation, including individual or conference telephone calls."

IEP CONTENT

15. "The individualized education program for each child must include:
    (a) A statement of the child's present levels of educational performance;
    (b) A statement of annual goals, including short term instructional objectives;
    (c) A statement of the specific special education and related services to be provided to the child, and the extent to which the child will be able to participate in the regular educational programs:"
    (d) The projected dates for initiation of services and the anticipated duration of the services; and
    (e) Appropriate objective criteria and evaluation procedures and schedules for determining on at least an annual basis, whether the short term instructional objectives are being achieved."

16. "Each public agency must provide special education and related services to a handicapped child in accordance with an individualized education program."

PRIVATE SCHOOL

17. Regarding handicapped children in private schools placed or referred by public agencies: "each State educational agency shall ensure that a handicapped child who was placed in or referred to a private school or facility by a public agency:
    (a) Is provided special education and related services;
       (1) In conformance with an individualized education program . . .
       (2) At no cost to the parents; . . ."

Regarding handicapped children in private schools not placed or referred by public agencies: ". . . Each local educational agency shall provide private school handicapped children with genuine opportunities to participate in special education and related services consistent with the number of those children and their needs."

WRITTEN NOTICE (due process)

18. "Written notice . . . must be given to the parents of a handicapped child a reasonable time before the public agency:
    (1) Proposes to initiate or change the identification, evaluation, or educational placement of the child or the provision of a free appropriate public education to the child . . ."

The written notice must contain a full explanation of all the procedural safeguards available to the parent; a description of the action proposed or refused by the agency; an explanation of why the agency proposes or refuses to take action; and a description of any options the agency considered and the reasons why those options were rejcted.

The parent must be fully informed of all information relative to the activity for which consent is sought; the consent must be voluntary; the parent must agree in writing to the activities for which the consent is sught; and the consent must identify those records which will be released and to whom those records will be released.

PARENTAL CONSENT (due process) 19. "...Parental consent must be obtained before:

(i) conducting a preplacement evaluation; and

(ii) initial placement of a handicapped child in a program providing special education and related services."

The written notice must be in a "language understandable to the general public," and must be "provided in the native language of the parent or other mode of communication used by the parent..."

EDUCATIONAL EVALUATION 20. "Before any action is taken with respect to the initial placement of a handicapped child in a special education program, a full and individual evaluation of the child's educational needs must be conducted..."

The tests and other evaluation materials: must be provided and administered in the child's native language or other mode of communication, unless it is clearly not feasible to do so; have been validated for the specific purpose for which they are used; administered by trained personnel in conformance with the instructions; and the test and evaluation materials should include "those tailored to assess specific areas of educational need and not merely those which are designed to provide a single general intelligence quotient...."

MDT No single evaluation procedure may be used as the sole criterion for determining an appropriate educational program for a child.

The evaluation must be made by a multidisciplinary team or group of persons, including at least one teacher or other specialist with knowledge in the area of suspected disability.

The child must be assessed in all areas related to the suspected disability, "including, where appropriate, health, vision, hearing, social and emotional status, general intelligence, academic performance, communicative status, and motor abilities."

21. "Testing and evaluation materials and procedures used for the purposes of evaluation and placement of handicapped children must be selected and administered so as not to be racially or culturally discriminatory."

INDEPENDENT EDUCATIONAL EVALUATION 22. A parent has the right to an independent educational evaluation at public expense if the parent disagrees with the evaluation obtained by the public agency. However, the public agency may initiate a hearing to show that its evaluation is appropriate. If the final decision is that the evaluation is appropriate, the parent still has a right to an independent educational evaluation, but not at public expense.

If the parent obtains an independent educational evaluation at private expense, the results of the evaluation must be considered by the public agency in any decision made with respect to the provision of a free appropriate public education to the child, and may be presented as evidence at a hearing regarding that child.

EDUCATIONAL PLACEMENT DECISION 23. The educational placement decision regarding each child must be "made by a group of persons, including persons knowledgeable about the child, the meaning of the evaluation data, and the placement options..." The group must use information from a variety of sources, including aptitude and achievement tests, teacher recommendations, physical conditions, social or cultural background, and adaptive behavior.

The educational placement decision must be made in conformance with the least restrictive environment rules.

If a determination is made that a child is handicapped and needs special education and related services, an individualized education program must be developed for the child.

An evaluation of the child must be conducted every three years, or more frequently if conditions warrant or if the child's parent or teacher requests an evaluation.

LEAST RESTRICTIVE EDUCATIONAL ENVIRONMENT 24. "Each public agency shall ensure:

(1) That to the maximum extent appropriate, handicapped children, including children in public or private institutions or other care facilities, are educated with children who are not handicapped, and

(2) That special classes, separate schooling or other removal of handicapped children from the regular educational environment occurs only when the nature or severity of the handicapped is such that education in regular classes with the use of supplementary aids and services can not be achieved satisfactorily."

"Each public agency shall ensure that a continuum of alternative placement is available to meet the needs of handicapped children for special education and related services." The continuum of alternate placements must include instruction in regular classes, special classes, special schools, home instruction, and instruction in hospitals and institutions.

25. Unless a handicapped child's individualized education program requires some other arrangement, the child must be educated in the school where he or she would attend if not handicapped.

PARENT REVIEW OF RECORDS

26. The parents of a handicapped child shall be afforded the opportunity to inspect and review all educational records with respect to the identification, evaluation, and educational placement of the child, as well as the provision of a free appropriate public education to the child."

27. Each agency shall permit parents to inspect and review any education records relating to their children which are collected, maintained, or used by the agency, without unnecessary delay, and in no case more than forty-five days after the request has been made.

The parents have a right to a response from the participating agency relative to reasonable requests for explanations and interpretations of the records.

A parent who believes that information in education records collected, maintained, or used is inaccurate or misleading or violates the privacy of or other rights of the child may request the participating agency to amend the information. If the agency refuses to amend the information, it shall inform the parent of the refusal, and advise the parent of the right to a hearing.

HEARING

28. A parent or a public educational agency may initiate a hearing regarding the identification, evaluation, or educational placement of the child, or the provision of a free appropriate public education to the child.

The hearing is conducted by the State education agency or the public agency directly responsible for the education of the child.

The hearing may not be conducted by a person who is an employee of a public agency which is involved in the education or care of the child, or by any person having a personal or professional interest which would conflict with his or her objectivity in the hearing.

29. The regulations of the Education of the Handicapped Act are published in the *Federal Register,* Volume 42, #63, Tuesday, August 23, 1977.

Chapter 32

Procedures for Evaluating Specific Learning Disabilities:

Supplement to the Education of the Handicapped Act

DEFINITION OF LEARNING DISABILITY

1. Specific learning disability is defined as a "disorder in one or more of the basic psychological processes involved in understanding or in using language, spoken or written, which may manifest itself in an imperfect ability to listen, think, write, spell, or to do mathematical calculations. The term includes such conditions as perceptual handicaps, brain injury, minimal brain disfunction, dyslexia, and developmental apahsia. The term does not include children who have learning problems which are primarily the result of visual, hearing, or motor handicaps, of mental retardation, of emotional disturbance, or of environmental, cultural, or economic disadvantage."

EVALUATION TEAM COMPOSITION

2. In addition to the composition requirements of the multidisciplinary evaluation team as specified by P.L. 94-142, the team evaluating a child suspected of having a specific learning disability shall include: the child's regular teacher; if the child does not have a regular teacher, then a regular classroom teacher qualified to teach a child of his or her age; for a child of less than school age, an individual qualified by the State educational agency to teach a child of his or her age; and at least one person qualified to conduct individual diagnostic examinations of children, such as a school psychologist, speech-language pathologist, or remedial reading.

COMPONENTS OF LEARNING DISABILITY

3. A team may determine that a child has a specific learning disabiity if:

The child does not achieve commensurate with his or her age and ability levels in one or more of the areas listed below, when provided with learning experiences appropriate for the child's age and ability levels; and

The team finds that a child has a severe discrepancy between achievement and intellectual ability in one or more of the following areas:

oral expression;
listening comprehension;
written expression;
basic reading skills;
reading comprehension;
mathematics calculation; or
mathematics reasoning.

The team may not identify a child as having a specific learning disability if the severe discrepancy between ability and achievement is primarily the result of:

a visual, hearing, or motor handicap;
mental retardation;
emotional disturbance; or
environmental, cultural, or economic disadvantage.

4. "At least one team member other than the child's regular teacher shall observe the child's academic performance in the regular classroom setting.

343

In the case of a child less than school age or out of school, a team member shall observe the child in an environment appropriate for a child of that age.

WRITTEN REPORT

5. "The team shall prepare a written report of the results of the evaluation.

The report must include a statement of:

(1) Whether the child has a specific learning disability;
(2) The basis for making the determination;
(3) The relevant behavior noted during the observation of the child.
(4) The relationship of that behavior to the child's academic functioning;
(5) The educationally relevant medical findings, if any;
(6) Whether there is a severe discrepancy between achievement and ability which is not correctable without special education and related services; and
(7) The determination of the team concerning the effects of environmental, cultural, or economic disadvantage.

Each team member shall certify in writing whether the report reflects his or her conclusion. If it does not reflect his or her conclusion, the team member must submit a separate statement preesenting his or her conclusions."

GUIDELINE

6. An important guideline obtained in the Supplement follows:

"Those with specific learning disabilities may demonstrate their handicap through a variety of symptoms such as hyperactivity, distractability, attention problems, concept association problems, etc. The end result of the effects of the symptoms is a severe discrepancy between achievement and ability. If there is no severe discrepancy between how much should have been learned and what has been learned, there would not be a disability in learning. However, other handicapping and sociological conditions may result in a discrepancy between ability and achievement. There are those for whom these conditions are the primary factors affecting achievement. In such cases, the severe discrepancy may be primarily the result of these factors and not of a severe learning problem. For the purpose of these regulations, when a severe discrepancy between ability and achievement exists which can not be explained by the presence of other known factors that lead to such a discrepancy, the cause is believed to be a specific learning disability."

Chapter 33

Section 504 of the Rehabilitation Act of 1973

PURPOSE
1. The purpose of Section 504 of the Rehabilitation Act of 1973 is to establish that "no qualified handicapped person shall, on the basis of handicapped, be excluded from participation in, be denied the benefits of, or otherwise be subjected to discrimination under any program or activity which receives or benefits from Federal financial assistance."

2. "A recipient, if providing any aid, benefit, or service, may not, directly or through contractual licensing, or other arrangements, on the basis of handicap:

PROVISIONS

Deny a qualified handicapped person the opportunity to participate in or benefit from the aid, benefit, or service;

Afford a qualified handicapped person an opportunity to participate in or benefit from the aid, benefit, or service that is not equal to that afforded others;

Provide a qualifiied handicapped person with an aid, benefit, or service that is not as effective as that provided to others;

Provide different or separate aid, benefits, or services, to handicapped persons or to any class of handicapped persons unless such action is necessary to provide qualified handicapped persons with aid, benefits, or services that are as effective as those provided to others; . . ."

". . . aids, benefits, and services, to be equally effective are not required to produce the identical result or level of achievement for handicapped and nonhandicapped persons, but must afford handicapped persons equal opportunity to obtain the same result, to gain the same benefit, or to reach the same level of achievement in the most integrated setting appropriate to the person's needs."

SPECIAL EDUCATION
3. "A recipient that operates a public elementary or secondary education program shall provide a free appropriate public education to each qualified handicapped person who is in the recipient's jurisdiction, regardless of the nature or severity of the person's handicap."

The provision of an "appropriate education" means the provision of regular or special education and related aids and services that are designed to meet individual educational needs of handicapped persons as adequately as the needs of nonhandicapped persons are met.

IEP
"Implementation of an individualized education program developed in accordance with the Education of the Handicapped Act is one means of meeting the standards established . . ." in the previous paragraph.

A recipient may place a handicapped person in or refer such person to a program other than the one that it operates; if so, the recipient remains responsible for ensuring that the requirements of this standard are met with respect to any handicapped person so placed or referred.

TRANSPORTATION
4. "If a recipient places a handicapped person in or refers such person to a program not operated by the recipient as its means of carrying out the requirement of this subpart, the recipient shall ensure that adequate transportation to and from the program is provided at no greater cost than would be incurred by the person or his or her parents or guardian if the person were placed in the program operated by the recipient."

RESIDENTIAL PLACEMENT
5. "If placement in a public or private residential program is necessary to provide a free appropriate public education to a handicapped person because of his or her handicap, the program, including non-medical care and room and board, shall be provided at no cost to the person or his or her parents or guardian."

PRIVATE SCHOOL
If a recipient has made available a free and appropriate public education to a handicapped person and the person's parents or guardian choose to place the person in a private school, the recipient is not required to pay for the person's education in the private school.

LEAST RESTRICTIVE EDUCATIONAL ENVIRONMENT
6. A recipient shall educate, or shall provide for the education of, each qualified handicapped person in its jurisdiction with persons who are not handicapped to the maximum extent ap-

propriate to the needs of the handicapped person. "A recipient shall place a handicapped person in the regular educational environment operated by the recipient unless it is demonstrated by the recipient that the education of the person in the regular environment with the use of supplementary aids and services can not be achieved satisfactorily."

If a recipient ". . . operates a facility that is identifiable as being for handicapped persons, the recipient shall ensure that the facility or the services and activities provided therein are comparable to the other facilities, services, and activities of the recipient."

EVALUATION 7. A recipient that operates a public elementary or secondary education program shall conduct an evaluation ". . . of any person who, because of handicap, needs or is believed to need special education or related services before takikng any action with respect to the initial placement of the person in a regular or special education program and any subsequent significant change in placement."

A recipient ". . . shall establish standards and procedures for the evaluation and placement of persons who, because of handicap, need or are believed to need special education or related services which ensure that:

(1) Tests and other evaluation materials have been validated for the specific purpose for which they are used and are administered by trained personnel in conformance with the instructions provided by their producer;

(2) Tests and other evaluation materials include those tailored to assess specific areas of educational need and not merely those which are designed to provide a single general intelligence quotient; and

(3) Tests are selected and administered so as to best ensure that, when a test is administered to a student with impaired sensory, manual, or speaking skills, the test results accurately reflect the student's aptitude or achievement level or whatever other factor the test purports to measure, rather than reflecting the student's impaired sensory, manual, or speaking skills (except where those skills are the factors that the test purports to measure)."

PLACEMENT 8. "In interpreting evaluation data and making placement decisions, a recipient shall (1) draw upon information from a variety of sources, including aptitude and achievement tests, teacher recommendations, physical condition, social or cultural background, and adaptive behavior, (2) establish procedures to ensure that information is obtained from all such sources, is documented and carefully considered, (3) ensure that the placement decision is made by a group of persons, including persons knowledgeable about the child, the meaning of the evaluation data, and the placement options . . ."

REEVALUATION 9. A recipient shall establish procedures for the periodical reevaluation of students who have been provided special education and related services. "A reevaluation procedure consistent with the Education for the Handicapped Act is one means of meeting this requirement."

PROCEDURAL SAFEGUARDS 10. A recipient that operates a public elementary or secondary education program shall establish and implement, with respect to actions regarding the identification, evaluation, or educational placement of persons who, because of handicap, need or are believed to need special instruction or related services, a system of procedural safeguard that includes notice, and opportunity for the parents or guardian of the person to examine relevant records, and impartial hearing with opportunity for participation by the person's parents or guardian and representation by council, and a review procedure.

NON ACADEMIC SERVICES 11. A recipient shall provide non-academic and extracurricular services and activities in such manner as is necessary to afford handicapped students an equal opportunity for participation in such services and activities.

Non-academic and extra-curricular services and activities may include counseling services, athletics, transportation, health services, recreational activities, special interest groups or clubs sponsored by the recipient, and referrals to agencies which provide assistance to handicapped persons.

COUNSELING 12. A recipient that provides personal, academic, or vocational counseling, guidance, or placement services to his students shall provide the services without discrimination on the basis of handicap. The recipient shall ensure that qualified handicapped students are not counseled toward more restrictive career objectives than are not handicapped students with similar interests and abilities.

PHYSICAL EDUCATION 13. In providing physical education courses and athletics and similar programs and activities to any of its students, a recipient may not discriminate on the basis of handicap. A recipient that offers physical education courses or that operates or sponsors interscholastic, club, or intramural athletics shall provide to qualified handicapped students an equal opportunity for participation in these activities.

PRESCHOOL OR ADULT EDUCATION
14. A recipient that operates a preschool education or day care program or activity or an adult education program or activity may not, on the basis of handicap, exclude qualified handicapped persons from the program or activity and shall take into account the needs of such persons in determining the aid, benefits, or services to be provided under the program or activity.

PRIVATE SCHOOL
15. A recipient that operates a private elementary or secondary education program may not, on the basis of handicap, exclude a qualified handicapped person from such program if the person can, with minor adjustments, be provided an appropriate education within the recipient's program.

16. "A recipient that operates a public elementary or secondary education program shall annually:

(a) Undertake to identify and locate every qualified handicapped person residing in the recipient's jurisdiction who is not receiving a public education; and

(b) Take appropriate steps to notify handicapped persons and their parents or guardians of the recipient's duty . . ."

PART IX

DIAGNOSTIC-PRESCRIPTIVE TEACHING AND PROGRAMMING AS A CROSS-CATEGORICAL SPECIAL EDUCATION MODEL

Diagnostic-Prescriptive Teaching and Programming emphasizes the application of appropriate strategies to the resolution of presenting problems without regard to educational placement or special education category.

Chapter 34

D-PT Similarities and Differences Regarding Educationally Handicapped Individuals

We define educational handicap (EH) as mild through severe learning or behavior problems not caused by sensory impairment or cultural difference. Although we do not reject the existence of traditional special education categories (emotional disturbance, learning disabilities, mental retardation, etc.), we think there are many more teaching and programming similarities than differences relative to those categories. As such we suggest that more special education thought, practice, and legislation be directed to the common outcome of resolving presenting problems than to categorical identification, placement, remediation, and financing, and the magical presumption that once an individual is labeled the problem goes away. In essence, we think the non-categorical or cross categorical programming of educationally handicapped individuals is more practical and defensible than artificially distinct categorical special education, because of the programming similarities.

What follows is a discussion of the EH programming similarities and differences.

Similarities

A. Management Model

1. Learner

The learning characteristics of attention, physical factors, input, memory, meaning, output, achievement level, IQ, personality factor, reinforcers, and self structuring capability are applicable to anyone, without regard to special education placement or category, as are the many formal and informal psychoeducational assessment instruments by which they are measured and which are discussed in Part II of this book.

2. Behavioral-Instructional Objectives

An objective identifies measurable terminal behavior in which an individual must engage in order to demonstrate the achievement of the objective. Objectives are necessary to provide direction and accountability to IEP-IIPs, and are applicable to anyone.

3. Task Analysis

Task analysis involves breaking down an objective into its major component parts, sequencing those parts from first to last, and then teaching the content on a sequential step by step basis until the objective has been reached. Like objectives, task analysis is applicable to anyone, and as such is cross categorical.

4. Individualization and Success

a. Curriculum Match. The Curriculum Match criteria of physical factors, attention, input, memory, meaning, output, achievement level, IQ, self-structuring capability, etc., are non-categorical, and as appropriate for a gifted LD subject as for a TMR individual.

b. Curriculum Materials. With the exception of curriculum guides for the mentally retarded and materials for sensory impaired individuals, curriculum materials are cross categorical. Thus, skill continua, remedial exercises relative to the learning circuit model concepts, tool-subject materials, high-interest/low-vocabulary reading programs, body image activities, etc., are equally applicable to everyone.

c. The Learning Circuit Model. The concepts of auditory, visual, verbal, graphic, and haptic input, memory, meaning, and output are equally applicable to everyone, without regard to regular or special education.

d. The concepts of classroom engineering, student grouping, body image, career education, sex education, x-work, teaching to the student's strength, direct instruction, learning contracts, skill continua, etc., are non-categorical, and are just as appropriate for an ED student as for a non-handicapped student.

5. Baseline Measurement and Accountability

Baseline measurement and accountability procedures operate by counting and recording target behavior. The counting and recording procedures are no different for an EMR student, an LD student, or a gifted individual.

6. Behavior Management

Behavior Management seeks to create systematic behavior change by means of positive and negative reinforcement, extinction techniques, change agents, etc. All the strategies are equally appropriate for everyone, and the application would not differ or change on the basis of special education category.

B. Individualized Education Programs

The legislation mandating IEPs, and the required IEP components, and the various IEP and IIP formats are all cross-categorical.

C. Treating the cause, not the symptom.

A dominant D-PT concept is that most behavior is caused. As such, many special education presenting problems are symptoms of an underlying cause. Thus, stuttering, hyperactivity, graphic output symbol reversals, truancy, memory problems, tool-subject underachievement (as well as over-achievement), receptive language difficulty, fighting, poor handwriting, avoiding eye-contact, etc., could be symptoms of an underlying cause.

Usually, underlying causes involve either emotional stress and/or a central nervous system dysfunction. To efficiently treat a special education presenting problem, we think it is necessary to identify the cause of the problem and then remediate that cause, as opposed to wasting time attempting the remediation of a symptom.

The treatment for a stress-based problem is the identification of the cause of the stress (for a minor individual, usually the parent-child relationship), and then the provision of psychotherapy, counseling, behavior modification, and/ possibly medicine, relative to those people involved in the stress syndrome. The educational treatment for a CNS-based problem is teach to the strength, remediate the weakness, perhaps medicine, behavior modification, and special programming and materials designed to help the brain accommodate the learning weakness.

The theory and practice of treating the cause is appropriate for all individuals, irrespective of special education label or category.

D. Identification of the Presenting Problem

All special education students have one or more presenting problems or they would not be in special education. In order to effectively program for the resolution of a given presenting problem it is first necessary to precisely define that problem. The manner by which presenting problems can be defined is common to all special education individuals, irrespective of label, category, or educational placement.

Pinpointing the nature of an educational presenting problem in order to facilitate remediation has an excellent precedent relative to the medical model. This is to say that were an individual to consult a physician regarding a body pain, it would be likely that the physician would attempt to identify the cause and nature of the presenting problem in order to determine the most effective treatment. In our opinion, an educational presenting problem should be attacked in the same way; that is, identify the cuase and nature of the problem prior to treatment. For example:a reversal problem ("was" for "saw") could be caused by brain dysfunction induced learning disability or by emotional stress. The effective remediation of such a reversal problem is a function of identifying the cause of the problem. Should it be determined that the reversal problem is caused by a brain dysfunction, then certain kinds of instructional activities are appropriate. On the other hand, should it be determined that the reversal problem is caused by emotional stress, then instructional activities would not be particularly appropriate; rather counseling or behavior management would be the treatment of choice relative to reducing the stress which in turn would reduce or eliminate the reversal problem.

The means by which the cause of an educational presenting problem can be understood involve:
1. Formal psycho-educational assessment, including the appropriate Wechsler test, Bender-Gestalt, DAP, Rorschach, etc.
2. Informal psycho-educational assessment, including the SILI.
3. The Comprehensive History.
4. Conducting a certain line of inquiry relative to the person making the referral. Generally, referrals are described in vague and unspecific terms (e.g., "Harlan has a reading problem."). By repeatedly asking the following question, it is possible to refine

and pinpoint the nature of the presenting problem: "What specifically does the subject do that convinces you he has a problem?" This inquiry is designed to evoke an increasingly more differentiated behavioral description of the presenting problem. As a result, after four or five such questions, information may be obtained to the extent that Harlan does not in fact have a reading problem, rather a visual discrimination problem. In such a case, the "reading" problem would represent a symptom of the visual discrimination cause. As with the medical model, problem resolution is greatly facilitated by treating the cause rather than the symptom.

The above-identified line of inquiry is effective regarding another component of the process by which it is possible to define the nature of the presenting problem. Such line of inquiry can result in the development of hypotheses regarding the nature of the presenting problem to the extent that formal and/or informal psycho-educational tests can be selected which are designed to yield information about the nature of the presenting problem. Without such hypotheses, the selection of a test battery is random, and may not lead to relevant information about the nature of the presenting problem.

E. D-PT Programming Sequence

The sequence of D-PT activities is the same for anyone, irrespective of educational placement or special education category. That sequence involves:

1. Determine the age and school grade-level placement of the students, and the presenting problem.
2. Conduct formal and/or informal psycho-educational assessment of the students relative to learning-behavior strengths and weaknesses.
3. Identify a learning contract-schedule system, including a daily class schedule.
4. Based on the psycho-educational assessment, and in relation to the daily class schedule, determine a curriculum match for each subject.
5. For each subject, develop long and short term behavioral-instructional objectives and task analyses, including curriculum materials based on #4 above.
6. Select X-work or independent student activities.
7. Select a classroom engineering design, and student grouping procedure.
8. Select a systemtic as well as random behavior management program.
9. Identify the baseline measurement system.
10. Develop an overall behavioral and instructional accountability system.
11. Using the above and other germane information, develop and execute an IEP and IIP for each special education student.

F. Counseling

A common goal of counseling is self-understanding and self-acceptance. To this extent, the counseling process is applicable to anyone, irrespective of educational placement or special education category. However, the counseling vehicle by which such self-understanding and acceptance is facilitated is to some extent a function of the kind and degree of presenting problem, a situation which is discussed subsequently under EH differences.

Differences

A. Definitions of the special education categories which commonly comprise the EH classification:

1. Emotional Disturbance
   Emotional disturbance is defined as acting-out or acting-in behavior which is symptomatic of the individual's stress management threshold having been exceeded.
2. Learning Disabilities
   Learning disabilities is defined as problems with learning that are due to a learning circuit defect which in turn is a result of a central nervous system dysfunction. Learning disabilities must involve a severe discrepancy of minimally one to two years between current and potential tool-subject ability, and LD may not be due to emotional disturbance, mental retardation, cultural difference, sensory impairment, and/or improper instruction.
3. Mental Retardation
   Mental retardation is defined as a global and irreversible problem-solving deficiency which is generally a result of a central nervous system dysfunction and which can be assessed on a multiple criteria basis: (1) psychoeducational testing, where all IQ's are below 75 and all scaled scores are below 7 or 8; (2) the subject's developmental history, where all relevant

developmental landmarks corroborate the problem-solving deficiency associated with the mental retardation; (3) the subject's educational history, where the subject's history of low profile educational problem-solving corroborates the mental retardation condition; and (4) the subject's social history, where all social problem-solving corroborates the mental retardation condition.

B. Educational Symptoms

1. Education symptoms represent another EH programming difference. The primary educational symptoms of emotional disturbance are: acting-out; acting-in (withdrawal); attending and/or responding problems; odd ideas and/or behavior; poor reality testing; minimal respect for authority and/or the rights of others; too much emotional stress; minimal anxiety and/or guilt relative to circumstances which normally would generate anxiety and/or guilt; too much anxiety and/or guilt; fear of authority figures; marked mood swings; chronic depression or elation; inability to establish and/or maintain meaningful interpersonal relations; chronic rigidity, perfectionism, and tenseness; lack of humor; chronic emotional coldness; chronically emotionally flat; chronic aggression, belligerence, and destructiveness; chronic sensitivity, touchiness, and irritability; chronic dishonesty; defensiveness; chronic underachievement; incontinence; hyperactivity; and medically unfounded body complaints.

2. The primary educational symptom of learning disabilities is tool-subject difficulty, most typically caused by the following learning characteristic weaknesses: auditory and/or visual input, memory, and meaning; and verbal, graphic, and/or haptic output. Further educational symptoms of learning disabilities are: marked tool-subject and learning characteristic strengths and weaknesses; hyperactivity; physical coordination problems; good interpersonal relationships; respect for authority and the rights and property of others; minimal willful behavior problems; personal sincerity; eager to please; and motivation to do well, but the individual nonetheless often experiences frustration and failure.

3. The primary educational symptoms of mental retardation are: chronic, simple, global, and flat-profile problem solving; social and emotional immaturity in the context of friendly interpersonal relations; IQ's below 75 and scaled scores below 8; very limited abstract problem solving ability; difficulty generalizing learned principles to new situations; better long-term than short-term memory; a need for repetitive educational drill; and a limitation of 5th or 6th grade tool-subject attainment.

C Prevalence of emotional disturbed, learning disabled, and mentally retarded subject.

1. Emotional Disturbance: about 4% of the general population.
2. Learning Disabilities: about 4 or 5% of the general population.
3. Mental retardation: about 3% of the general population relative to the AAMD definition of mental retardation; about .02% of the general population relative to our multiple criteria definition of mental retardation.

D. Causation as an EH programming difference.

1. Emotional Disturbance

The cause of emotional disturbance is almost always emotional stress, the origin of which in a minor individual usually relates to the parent-child dynamics. It is possible that some forms of emotional disturbance could have a genetic referent, a situation about which little is understood at this time.

Generally, emotional disturbance expresses itself either in acting-in or acting-out behavior. Either way, the emotional disturbance is a function of too much conscience (acting-in), or insufficient conscience (acting-out). With the exception of the little understood genetic contribution to emotional disturbance, such conscience control problems are learned, primarily in relation to the early parent-child dynamics. Specifically, the normal individual receives an appropriate amount of parent love, dependency gratification, security need satisfaction, limit setting, discipline, reasonable task expectation, support and reinforcement, and minimal threat, harshness, and failure. On the other hand, the acting-in emotionally disturbed subject may receive minimal love and security-need satisfaction from the parents, but develop a strict and harsh conscience based primarily on the rigid and demanding attitudes and values of the parents. Therefore, the more strict, rigid, moralistic, and demanding the parents, the more likely the subject will have a harsh and punitive concience which interprets even normal behavior as unacceptable, which creates a constant state of subject threat, which in turn results in too much stress, and which is characterized by acting-in behavior.

The acting-out emotionally disturbed individual often does not receive even minimal security-need satisfaction from the parents, a situation which creates a critical defect in the trust and love system of the subject. In addition, such a subject usually has a defect in the conscience system, which usually is a function of parental conscience defect, and which expresses itself in little respect for authority, little respect for the rights and/or property of others, minimal guilt and anxiety, acting-out behavior on the basis of minimal internal controls, minimal ability to delay gratification, greedy behavior, often difficulty with the law, difficulty receiving and giving meaningful love, difficulty establishing long-term and satisfying interpersonal relations, minimal ability to profit from experience, poor work ethic, difficulty fitting into the system, and in general, defiant and rebellious behavior without much concern for other people.

2. Learning Disabilities

The cause of learning disabilities is a central nervous system dysfunction. Such a dysfunction can involve: a. frank brain damage; b. the hypothesis of brain damage, which is supported by "soft" signs of brain damage, a situation which is identified as minimal brain damage; c. and/or neurological immaturity, which need not be caused by brain damage, although would relate to immature central nervous system development. All three kinds of central nervous system dysfunction can cause the same kind and degree of presenting problem. The primary educational difference between the three kinds of dysfunctions relates to the fact that frank and minimal brain damage probably can never be reversed, but neurological immaturity may dissipate over a period of time due to nervous system maturation. This is to say that the neurologically immature subject could grow out of such immaturity, in which case the presenting problem would dissipate. However, since brain cell damage is probably irreversible, a presenting problem the cause of which is brain damage will not dissipate over time, and special instruction is necessary for those behaviors which are defective because of the central nervous system dysfunction.

3. Mental Retardation

The cause of mental retardation is the same as for learning disabilities, viz., a central nervous system dysfunction. The primary difference between brain dysfunction causing mental retardation and that causing learning disabilities relates to the amount of dysfunction or damage. Generally, the more massive or systemic the damage, the more likely the result will be mental retardation. In essence, a learning disability is caused by minimal brain damage, whereas mental retardation is caused by diffuse and often massive brain damage of dysfunction.

As brain damage is probably irreversible, a subject who is truly mentally retarded will always be mentally retarded. It is only on this irreversible basis that the use of life-experience and survival-based mental retardation curriculum guides can be justified with mental retardates. Such curriculum guides cannot be justified with pseudo mental retardates.

Although the overwhelmingly predominate cause of mental retardation is brain dysfunction, a psychogenic form of mental retardation does exist. This condition involves a severe and irreversible form of psychopathology which is part of the subject's character structure. In this sense, psychogenic mental retardaton relates to a character disorder, the cause of which is very early and grim maternal rejection and emotional harshness, which creates severe emotional stunt, and which is expressed as symptomatic mental retardation without any concomitant brain damage.

As with the condition of learning disabilities, many of the known causes of brain damage and consequent mental retardation are identified in the Comprehensive History. Exclusive of obvious post-natal trauma (such as an auto collision, falling off the house roof, etc.), the developmental time-period which is most susceptible to brain damage is the first trimester of pregnancy, during which such maternal anomalies as anoxia, infection, virus, drugs, etc., can cause brain damage and hence mental retardation. A second time-period which is very susceptible to brain damage and hence mental retardation is that of conception, during which time genetic aberrations can cause severe pathology, the most typical of which is Down's syndrome.

Frank and minimal brain damage as well as neurological immaturity can result in the same presenting problem. However, in terms of cause, the distinction is not always easy to make. Generally, frank and minimal brain damage will express themselves by means of Comprehensive History resuls which suggest the possibility of the brain dysfunction. Often, however, neurological immaturity does not have a correlate in the Comprehensive History, and other psycho-educational assessment instruments, such as theBender-Gestalt, must be used to distinguish between immaturity and brain damage. With respect to such distinction, the Bender results of the subject with brain damage in the graphic output area will often be characterized by design destruction, rotation, and/or dog ears. On the other hand, the Bender results of a subject with neurological immaturity will often be characterized by the same triad of symptoms, yet without as much crude damage to the integrity of the designs. Thus, the Bender results of the neurologically immature subject are a little more intact and "clean" than the subject with brain damage.

The importance of the distinction between brain damage and neurological immaturity relates to consequent educational programming. This is to say that the nuerological immaturity may decrease over a period of time to the extent that the subject's neurology catches up with his chronology. As such, retention in the primary grades is an appropriate prescriptive strategy if there is reason to believe that the subject will have more problem solving success in the retained grade than experienced initially. This is not the case with the brain damaged individual, whose problems probably will not dissipate simply with the passage of time, and for whom grade retention on the time-dissipation assumption is not an appropriate prescriptive strategy.

E. Counseling

Counseling represents another EH programming difference. Although the common counseling goal is self-understanding and self-acceptance, and therefore applicable to almost anyone, the counseling process is contraindicated relative to the primary resolution of some presenting problems.

1. Emotional disturbance

Emotional disturbance regarding a minor individual is primarily a function of stress which relates to the parent-child relationships. As such, one of the premier ways by which to resolve emotional disturbance is through the counseling or psychotherapy of those people involved with the stress syndrome.

2. Learning disabilities

Learning disabilities are caused by a central nervous system dysfunction. Since the counseling or psychotherapy process is not able to affect brain chemistry, neither counseling nor psychotherapy is an appropriate primary change agent relative to presenting problems the cause of which is brain dysfunction. Nonetheless, the self-understanding and acceptance goals of the counseling process might be helpful to a learning disabled subject with an emotional overlay, which could be expressed as anxiety, guilt, low esteem, etc. Even so, such a counseling function would be secondary in nature, and would not effect the basic problem of brain damage.

3. Mental Retardation

The relationship between the counseling or psychotherapy process and mental retardation is the same as discussed under Learning disabilities above.

Chapter 35

IEP Forms

To facilitate IEP-IIP development and delivery, and in conjunction with learning contracts, we suggest the use of a form such as that which appears in Table XXXII. This form is applicable to all handicapped individuals, without regard to educational labels or category.

Table XXXII

IEP Form 1

Subject's Name_____ Age_____ Grade_____ Teacher _____

School_____

Precise Presenting Problem:

Comprehensive History:
    Family:

    Developmental:

    Emotional:

    Educational:

Test Data:

WISC (WAIS)
VIQ _____ PIQ _____ FIQ _____

		Achievement	_____	ITPA			
		Reading	_____	AR _____		VE _____	
		Spelling	_____	VR _____		GC _____	
I _____	PC _____	Arithmetic	_____	VSM _____		ME _____	
C _____	PA _____	_____	_____	AA _____		AC _____	
A _____	BD _____	_____	_____	ASM _____		SB _____	
S _____	OA _____	_____	_____	VA _____		MSS _____	
V _____	C	_____	_____	VC _____		CPLA _____	
DS _____							

SILI Strengths and Weaknesses:

Other Test Data:

Reinforcers:

Curriculum Match Statement:

Least Restrictive Educational Environment:

Environmental Considerations:

Beginning and Ending Dates:

Criteria for Annual Evaluation:

Committee members:

Individual Program
IEP Form 2

Subject's Name_____ Age_____ Grade_____ Teacher_____

School _____ Problem _____

Annual Behavioral/Instructional Objectives:_____
_____
_____
_____
_____
_____
_____

Short Term Objectives:_____
_____
_____
_____
_____
_____
_____
_____
_____
_____
_____
_____
_____
_____
_____
_____
_____
_____

Behavior Management Program: _____
_____
_____
_____
_____
_____
_____
_____
_____

Name_____   Date_____

IEP Form 3

Learning Contract/Schedule

TIME	CENTER	SUBJECT	ASSIGNMENT	COMPLETED

IEP Form 4

Baseline Measurement and Accountability:

Record: Date, %, Rate, Frequency, etc.

Session	1	2	3	4	5	6	7	8	9	10	11	12	13	14	15
Date															
%															
Rate															
Frequency															

	16	17	18	19	20	21	22	23	24	25	26	27	28	29	30
Date															
%															
Rate															
Frequency															

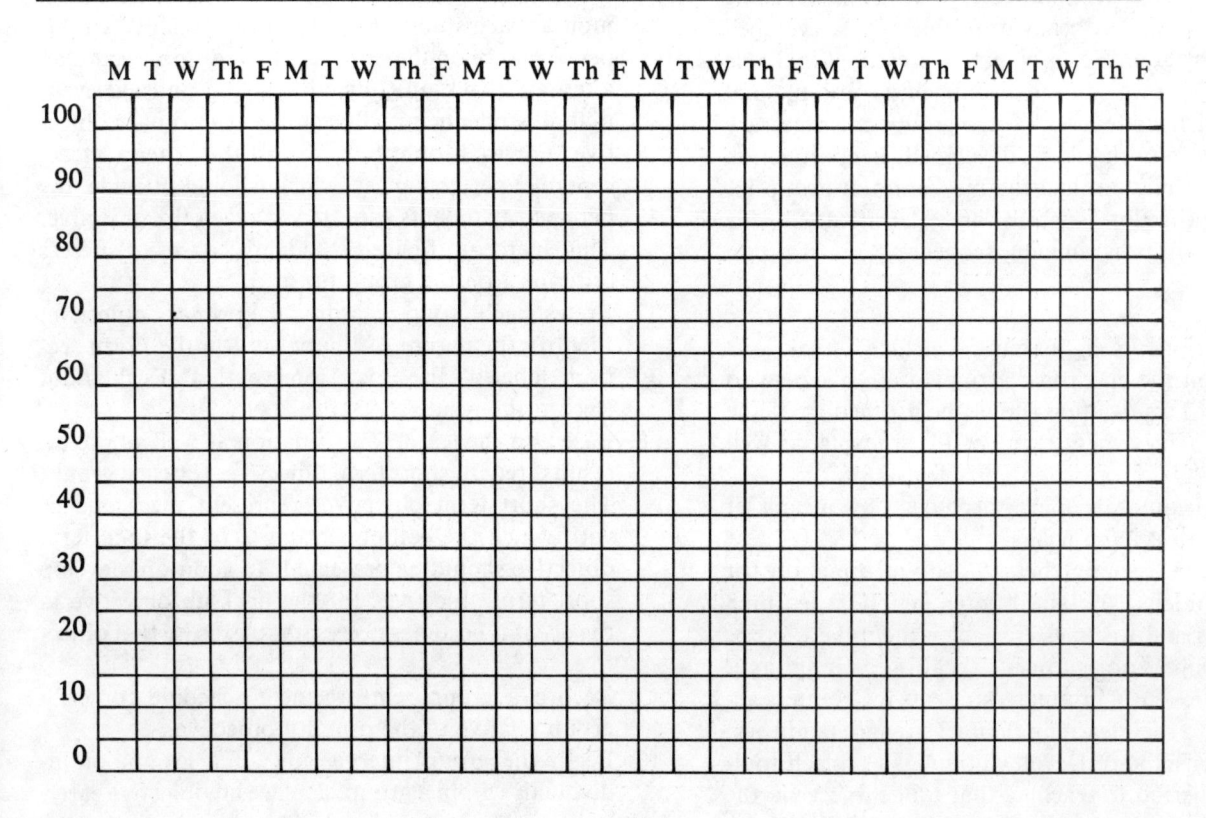

Comments:

Chapter 36

Group Program Form

Group programming is more difficult than individual programming if for no other reason than the additional number of students involved with group intervention. In order to provide a systematic referent for intervening with group learning or behavior problems we developed the Group Program Form, which is presented in Table XXXIII. For each major group intervention, and relative to each student within the group, the necessary Form information should be developed, in conjunction with IEP information, and the mechanics of group intervention procedures which are identified by the following group programming sequence.

Group prescriptive programming sequence
1. Decide on the classroom grouping arrangement to be used. This decision should be a function of the age and achievement range of the students, as well as the kinds of presenting problems.
2. Insure flexible grouping mechanics by means of movable desks and chairs.
3. Obtain the learning characteristic information for each student (obtained-potential IQ, learning strengths and weaknesses, achievement data, etc.).
4. For each tool-subject (reading, language, arithmetic, etc.), group the students into centers according to their learning channel strength (auditory, visual, or haptic). Devote about 75% of each tool-subject period to teaching that tool-subject via the student's learning channel strength. For those students who have no learning channel strength use the VAKT procedure within the haptic or VAKT center.
5. With a diversity of student ability and/or kind of presenting problem, it may be instructionally helpful to divide the learning-strength groups into grade level based subgroups for each tool-subject.
6. For each group, record on the Form a long term instructional or behavioral objective (e.g., within six months each student will improve by 25 percent his performance on the pre-test). In addition, record an alternate (back-up) objective in the unusual event that all students initially achieve the primary objective. For each objective, record the criteria of acceptable performance, which should include the percent of students expected to reach the objective. This percent figure is identified as "success criterion" on the group Form.
7. Pretest each group regarding the primary objective. Identify the nature of the pre-test in the Form section labeled Pre-Post Intervention Evaluation. Record the results.
8. Based on the learner information as well as pretest results, record short term objectives for each group. The short term objectives represent the sequence with which the component parts of the long term objective should be presented. In addition, develop short term objectives for the back-up objective in the event it becomes necessary to execute that objective.
9. Record a group reinforcement schedule for each group relative to the primary objective.
10. Begin the group intervention. If a group, or individuals within a group, achieve an objective early, use them as instructional aides relative to the unfinished groups. If a group, or individuals within a group, chronically finish early, provide more challenging objectives for those individuals, or X-work.
11. When the objective has been met, or when the in-

structional time has elapsed, give the students the pre-test in the form of a post-test. Record the pre-post intervention test results for each student in the Evaluation Results section of the Form.

12. Indicate on the Form if the objective was met, and express any observations or recommendations for change.

The following group programming sequence is applicable to those students whose tool-subject remediation is conducted by means of the learning channel weakness.

13. Each tool-subject is taught via student learning channel strength for about 75% of each tool-subject period. During the remaining 25% of each tool-subject period, regroup the students into centers according to their learning channel weakness (primarily auditory or visual), and attempt to remediate the tool-subject problem by remediating the learning channel weakness. For those students with multichannel and therefore general learning weakness, use the VAKT procedure within a VAKT or haptic center. The disproportionate emphasis placed on teaching tool-subjects to the learning channel strength is a result of only minimal evidence indicating that tool-subject remediation can occur by means of an exclusive remedial emphasis on the learning channel and/or tool-subject weakness.

14. If there is a diversity of student ability and/or kind of presenting problem, it may be helpful to divide the learning-weakness groups into grade level subgroups for each tool-subject.

15. Record on a separate Form a long-term instructional or behavioral objective for each group relative to the remediation of the learning channel weakness. In addition, record an alternate objective in the event that all students initially meet the primary objective.

16. Pretest each group with respect to the primary objective. Record the pretest nature and results.

17. Based on the learner information as well as pre-test results, record short term objectives for each group. The short term objectives represent the sequence with which the component parts of the long term objective should be presented. In addition, develop short term objectives for the back-up objective.

18. Record a reinforcement system for each group.

19. Begin the group intervention. Use early finishers as instructional aides. Provide more challenging objectives for chronic early finishers, or X-work.

20. Give each student the pre-test as a post-test. Record the pre-post intervention test results on the Form.

21. Indicate on the Form if the objective was met, and express any observations or recommendations for change.

Table XXXIII

Group Program Form

Date_____ Session_____ Name(s)_____

Subject or Activity:_____

Behavioral/Instructional Objective (include success criterion): _____
_____
_____
_____
_____
_____
_____
_____

Alternate Objective: _____
_____
_____
_____

Short Term Objectives: _____
_____
_____
_____
_____
_____
_____
_____
_____
_____
_____
_____
_____
_____
_____
_____
_____

Reinforcement Schedule: _____
_____
_____
_____

Pre-Post Intervention Evaluation: _____
_____
_____
_____
_____

Evaluation Results: _____
_____
_____
_____
_____
_____
_____

Objective: _____ Met _____ Failed

Observations:

Recommendations for Change:

Chapter 37

Part X

SAMPLE IEPs

In order to illustrate the result of diagnostic-prescriptive teaching and programming, the following chapter presents several IEPs. These IEPs are not offered as samples of perfect intervention strategy, but rather as real-life examples of the management model process.

IEP Number 1

CA 16.9, Grade 11.5

Presenting Problem: Trudy was referred for evaluation by her mother, who did not concur with the school district's label of Mental Retardation and wanted to know the nature of Trudy's learning problems. Trudy was labeled "MR at the age of ten" and "reads on the fourth grade level."

Physical Characteristics	Attentional Factors	Ob./Pot. IQ	Achievement Data	Input
mild gross motor problems	Aud—60 minutes Vis—60 minutes	V-82/95 P—82/90	PIAT M—4.4 RR-4.8 RC-3.9	Auditory & Visual

Meaning	Output	Self-Structuring	Emotional Factors:	Reinforcers
Auditory & Visual	Graphic & Verbal	Moderately	mod. self-concept probs. not spontaneous mild depression mild body image probs. in relation to female role stubborn streak insecure about relationship with natural parents.	praise, success, smiles, hugs, time to talk on phone, watch TV, art projects, new clothes, activities along with Mom or Dad

Curriculum Match: Trudy needs materials geared to a moderately self-structuring 17-year-old with an obtained IQ of 81 (Mental Age—13.8); a mid-third to fourth grade reading level; a mid-fourth grade math level; with equal emphasis on auditory and visual input, and graphic and verbal output; which are high interest-low vocabulary; and which emphasize survival and career education skills.

Long/Short Term Instructional/Behavioral Objectives: The following objectives will be achieved by January 31.

Reading: After pretesting into System Fore, Trudy will achieve objective 7.23.1 (recognizes assumptions) with 4 out of 6 correct responses.

Language: Given a choice of: 1. applying for a job, 2. requesting information, or 3. complaining about a product, Trudy will write a business letter to include heading, inside address, salutation, body, closing, signature, and enclosures, within 45 minutes with 5 out of 7 parts correctly incorporated. (3.29.3)

Math: Given x amount of money and a list of expenditures (rent, utilities, food, clothing, medical care, transportation, savings, and spending money), Trudy will write, in chart form, a balanced monthly budget, within 45 minutes and including all eight items.

Art: Trudy will complete at least one art project a month, each with a minimum passing grade of C.

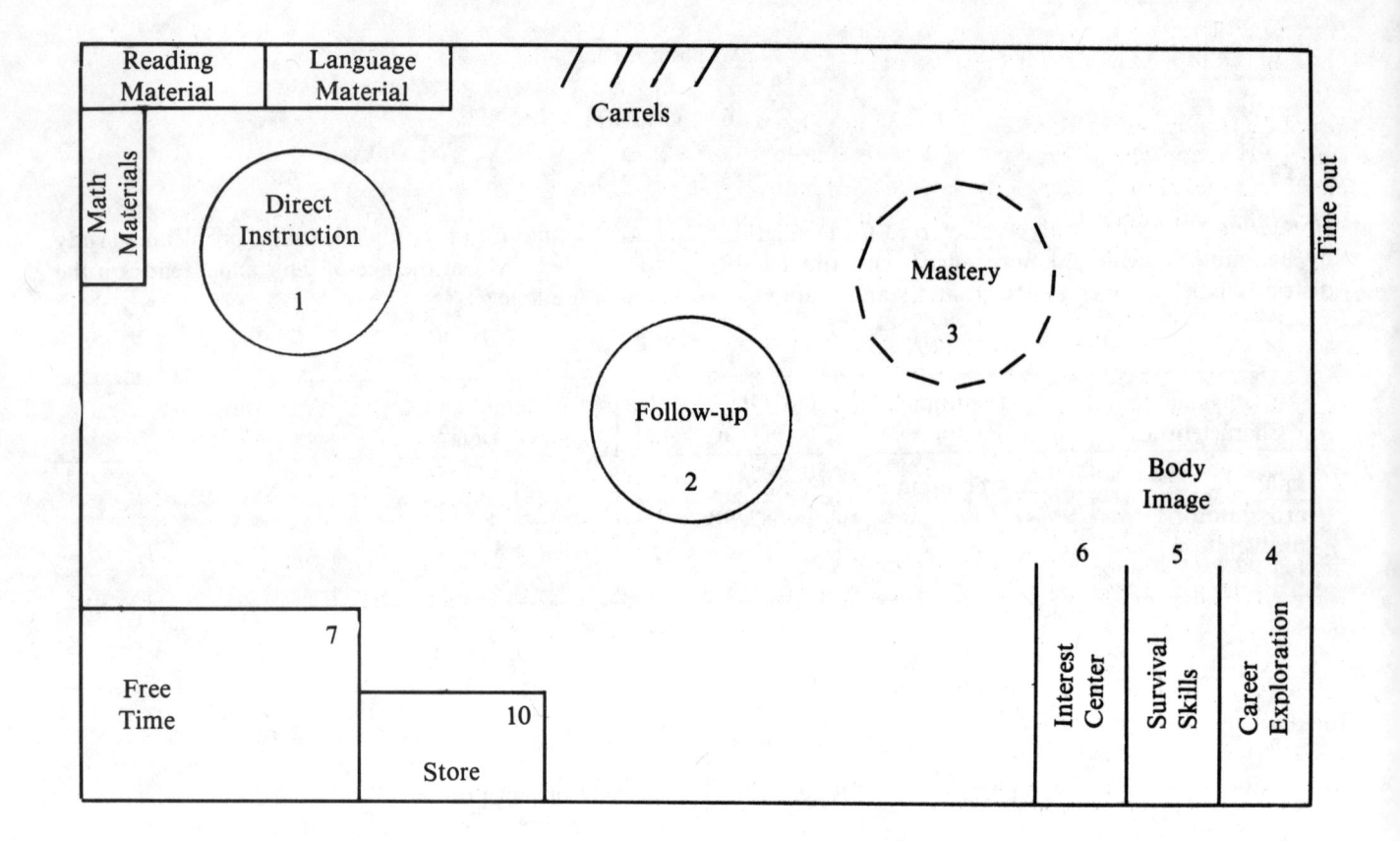

Behavior Grid:

Time	Initiate Conversation	Refrain from Self-Derogatory Remarks	Bonus
8:15			
8:30			
9:15			
10:15			
11:00			
Etc.			

Home Ec: Trudy will plan a menu for one full week, utilizing the four basic food groups, within 45 minutes.

Sex Ed.: Trudy will graphically or verbally list the cause, two symptoms, two eventual effects, one treatment, and one place or person to contact for treatment of syphillis and gonorrhea, within 10 minutes with 10 out of 14 correct responses.

Body Image: Upon request, Trudy will demonstrate one exercise to improve the following body parts: upper arm, thigh, calf, ankle, abdomen, buttocks, chest, knee, lower back, and shoulder, each within three minutes.

Career Education: Given a list of 116 jobs arranged in career clusters, Trudy will select and explore (as defined by a written contingency contract between Trudy and the teacher) a minimum of 20 jobs, answering 20 comprehension questions about each job with 80% accuracy in a 45 minute period.

Vocational Education: Trudy will contract for and fulfill job training requirements for three OJT stations, each lasting approximately three months for a minimum of two hours a day, Monday through Friday.

Behavioral: 1. Trudy will initiate conversation (ask a question, answer a question without being asked, state her opinion) three times during any given small group (no more than five students) discussion of 20 minutes in length. 2. Trudy will refrain from making self-derogatory remarks during a randomly selected 45-minute period, five days in a row.

Short Term Objectives, Reading. By April 1: After pretesting into System Fore, Trudy will achieve those objectives not mastered that precede her mastery level, with success criteria as specified in the continuum. 2. By May 20: Trudy will achieve objective 8.16.4 (organizes related ideas under given topic heading) with 3 out of 5 correct responses, within 10 minutes. 3. By October 1: Trudy will achieve 8 out of 9 objectives in Level 18 (Strands 5-8) with success criteria as outlined in System Fore. 4. By November 1: Given a list of 5 words and their antonyms in columns, Trudy will match (draw a line between) each word and its antonym, all in 5 minutes at 80% accuracy. (7.20.2) 5. By December 1: Trudy will achieve objective 7.22.1 (making inferences about reading material) with success criteria as outlined in System Fore.

Grouping and Classroom Engineering: Grouping is accomplished by means of a "Center" column on the Learning Contract, which routes Trudy and her classmates to various centers.

Behavior Management: Strategies: Checkmark system in which Trudy deposits checkmarks and writes checks for desired back-up reinforcers; written contingency contracts; classroom rules and daily goal setting sessions; Premacking; modeling; response cost. Time out is not appropriate for Trudy.

Reinforcers: home-school program to earn clothes, TV time, shopping trips or lunch out with Mom; school reinforcers such as extra art time, pop, free time to read high interest materials (mysteries, etc.), prearranged cooking, sewing, dance lessons.

Punishers: response cost of checkmarks; loss of privileges (TV, phone). Avoid derogatory, negative comments.

Schedule: Checkmarks: fixed interval at the end of each subject; trade in checkmarks weekly. Praise, smiles: variable ratio 1 to 3.

LREE: Trudy can be identified as a learning disabled (LD) individual. She should receive tool subject (reading, language, math, body image, career education) in a Special Education Resource Room, with an emphasis on self concept development and career education. She should participate in regular education classes such as art and home ec. In addition, Trudy should spend a minimum of two hours a day at job sites matched to her interests.

Beginning Date: February 1. *Ending Date:* Trudy's graduation.

Related Services: Professional psychotreatment; liaison person to coordinate school, home, and community programs.

Environmental Considerations: 1. Trudy needs a crash program of self concept development through counseling, success at school, and increased security at home. 2. Mrs. Nelson and Trudy should have time together daily to cook, shop, go out to lunch, etc. 3. Trudy should be reinforced for spontaneity, i.e. volunteering information. 4. Should Trudy continue to have balance problems, she should have an inner ear examination by a qualified MD. 5. Trudy should continue to take her birth control pills. 6. Don't let Trudy drop out of school. 7. Structure Trudy's day so that she has a minimum of free time. Too much freedom is not beneficial to Trudy at this time. 8. Encourage Trudy to do things with female friends, such as social activities, clubs, dancing classes, etc. 9. A complete assessmnt of Trudy's voational skills should be given immediately. (The VESEP enabling skills inventory may be helpful.) 10. Continued use of medication should be monitored by Mrs. Nelson. 11. Be aware that an increase in sleeping problems may be an indication of increased stress.

Reevaluation: 1. Trudy's progress toward academic and behavioral goals should be evaluated monthly by means of a conference set up by the liaison person. 2. Trudy should be reevaluated in January, with a complete psychoeducational battery, including intelligence, achievement, projective, and career/vocational assessment.

LEARNING CONTRACT/SCHEDULE

Time	Task No.	Subject	Center	Assignment	Completed
8:15	1	Goal	3	Establish daily goal.	
8:30	2	Reading	1	Changing Times Reading Skills—Real People at Work—new vocabulary, define 7 of 10 words correctly.	
	3	Reading	2	Changing Times—read story, p. 1-5 using Neurological Impress Method. Accuracy is completion of assign.	
	4	Reading	3	Changing Time—Skills sheet 1-10 comprehension questions, 80% correct. (6.14.5)	
9:15	5	Body Image	9	Chicken fat record. Accuracy is completion.	
9:30	6	Language	1	Corrective Reading—comprehensive B lesson 10—no more than 2 errors.	
10:15	7	Home Ec (MWF)			
		Art (T, Th)		Art (2/21)—Design "feelings" mobile—draw or find picture to depict happy, angry—accuracy is completion.	
11:00	8	Math	1	Teacher made exercise—making change to $25.000—80% on checkout (11.23.4)	
	9	Math	2	Pacemaker Practical Arithmetic Series—p. 27-28, 9/12 correct. (11.23.4)	
	10	Math	3	Arithmetic Skill Series—Building Arithmetic Skills—p. 89-90, 75% Accuracy. (10.23.4)	
11:45	11	BI/Sex. Ed.	3	Group discussion using p. 139-140, Social & Sexual Development, Answer 10 written comps., 80% correct.	
12:45	12	Career Ed.	4	Select and listen to Eye Gate tape. Answer comp. questions—80% correct.	
1:5	13	Goal	3	Evaluate daily goal.	
2:00	14	Vocational Education	OJT	Meet job training requirements as specified in contract.	

X-Work: SLI #11.23.4

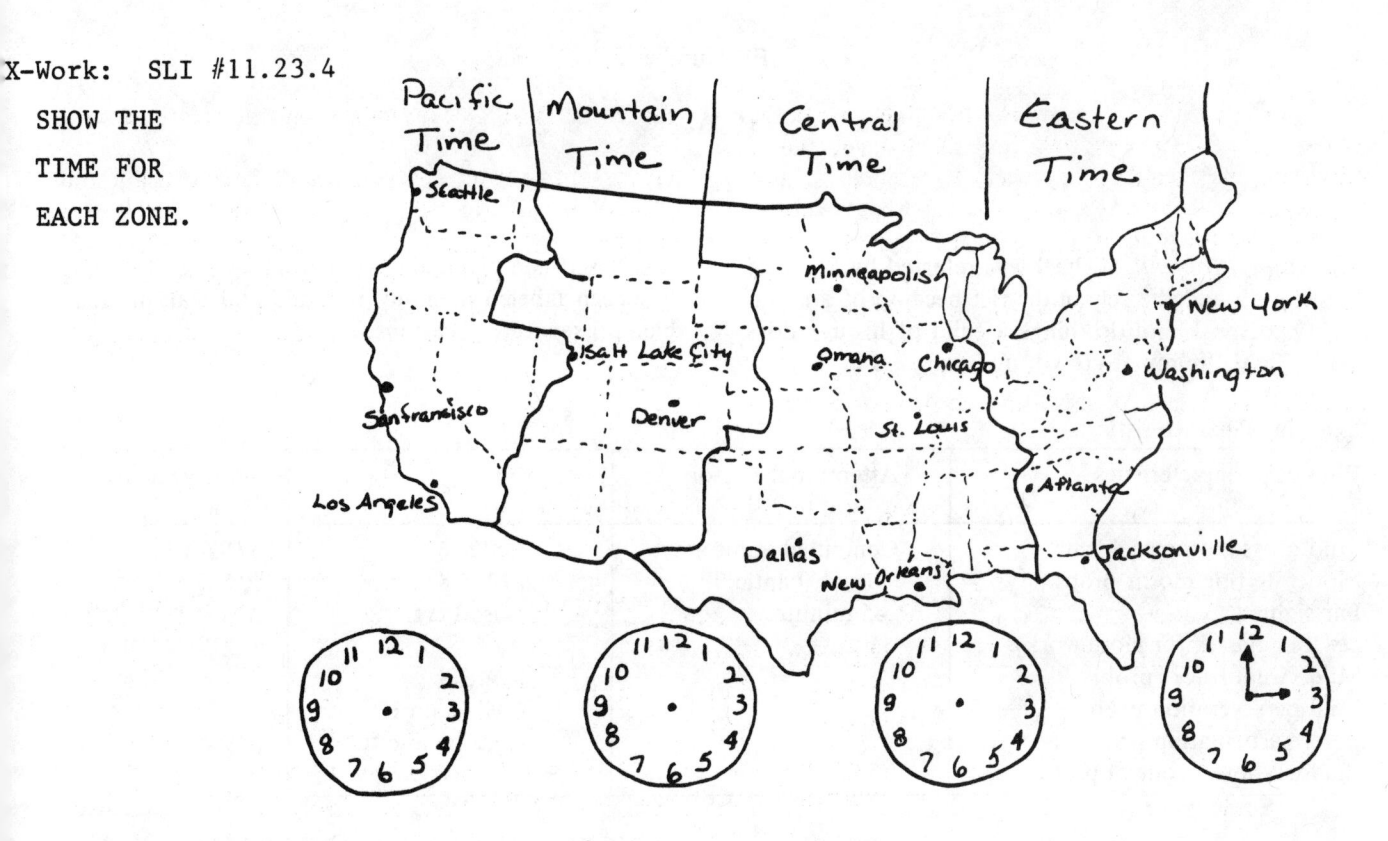

SHOW THE
TIME FOR
EACH ZONE.

Pacific Time | Mountain Time | Central Time | Eastern Time

Seattle, San Francisco, Los Angeles, Salt Lake City, Denver, Minneapolis, Omaha, Chicago, St. Louis, Dallas, New Orleans, New York, Washington, Atlanta, Jacksonville

You buy:	It costs:	You give the clerk:	Count your change:
1 can fruit drink	$0.46	$1.00	
1 jar dill pickles	$0.59	$0.75	
1 box cereal	$0.78	$1.00	
½ lb. ham	$1.05	$1.50	
2 rolls paper towels	$1.00	$5.00	
2 cans corn	$0.49	$1.00	

Total cost:

Write a check to Friendly Grocery for the total cost of the groceries.

1. 73   2. 94   3. 67   4. 75   5. 48   6. 37
   X 48   X 82   X 23   X 34   X 92   X 14

Copyright © 1976 by McGraw-Hill, Inc. All Rights Reserved.

IEP Number 2

C.A. 7.6

Presenting Problem: Michael was referred by Mr. and Mrs. Smith and the school district because of an "inability to speak and do things a child of his age does easily" and "minimal growth and progress in a structured, self-contained, individualized setting." Michael has been labeled mentally retarded and learning disabled on separate occasions.

Learning Characteristics:

Physical Characteristics	Attentional Factors	IQ	Achievement Data
Mild gross motor problems. Moderate fine motor probs. Far sighted (wears glasses for close work). Mild visual track. prob. Mild perseveration prob. Severe articulation prob. Bladder/bowel control prob.	Combined auditory, visual, haptic, 45 minutes	Leiter 62 MA 4.8 Wisc Perf. IQ 51 MA 3.8 CMMS no IQ score; was unable to do task.	WRAT R K.2 M Pk.1

Input	Memory	Meaning	Output	Self Structured	Emotional Factors
aud: + vis: - hap: ok	auditory sequential: -- aud recall: + Aud storage: - Vis. Seq: -- vis recall: -- visk storage: --	Aud: ok Vis: ok	ver: --- graph: -- hap: +	No: needs teacher direction	emotionally warm relates better to females. fearful of new situations. impulsive. temper tantrums. mod. self-concept problems.

Reinforcers:

verbal praise
physical touch
coloring
playing with cars and trucks
watching Sesame Street and Mr. Rogers on TV
helping Mom cook
roughhousing with Dad
playing games
family activities

Curriculum Match: Michael needs materials geared to a non-self structuring 7.6-year-old with an obtained Leiter IQ of 62 (mental age of 4.8); a beginning kindergarten reading level; a pre-Kindergarten math level; which utilize the VAKT method and de-emphasize verbal output; which emphasize life-survival skills and career education; which are teacher-directed, and inherently reinforcing; and which stress repetition of concepts.

Long and Short Term Objectives:

Instructional: (long term) By April 3: Given a list of the first 25 survival words in the Edmark Reading Program, Michael will correctly orally read 20 out of 25 words, each word within 15 seconds.

Behavioral: (long term) By April 3: After receiving verbal directions, Michael will complete a randomly selected 10-minute independent task to the accuracy level specified on his learning contract, three out of five consecutive days.

Remediation: (long term for visual sequential memory) By April 3: After being visually presented with a sequence of four flashcards (each containing an upper case letter) and allowed to view it for five seconds, Michael will reproduce, by manipulating the cards, the correct sequential order from memory for three out of four trials, each trial within 30 seconds. (SLI 5.7.7)

Remediation: (short term for visual sequential memory) 1. By May 15: Given a worksheet of four rows of four randomly sequenced shapes (○, △, ▭, ▢) and a different stimulus shape (○, △, ▭, ▢) for each row, Michael will correctly match by pointing each stimulus shape with its corresponding shape with 75% accuracy within two minutes. (SLI 5.4.1) 2. By October 1: When presented with a sequence of four flashcards (each with a different shape), Michael will correctly copy (by manipulating a separate set of cards containing the same shapes) the sequence for two out of three trials, each trial within 45 seconds. 3. By November 15: Michael will accomplish objective 5.6.1 (matches capital letters) by correctly matching (pointing to) three out of four of the letters within two minutes. 4. By January 1: After being visually presented with a sequence of two flashcards (each containing an upper case letter) and allowed to view it for five seconds, Michael will reproduce, by manipulating the cards, the correct sequential order from memory for three out of four trials, each trial within 30 seconds. (SLI 5.7.1) 5. By February 15: After being visually presented with a sequence of three flashcards (each containing an upper case letter) and allowed to view it for five seconds, Michael will reproduce, by manipulating the cards, the correct sequential order from memory for three out of four trials, each trial within 30 seconds. (SLI 5.7.2)

Grouping and Classroom Engineering: Grouping is accomplished by means of a "Center" column on the learning contract, which routes Michael and his classmates to various centers.

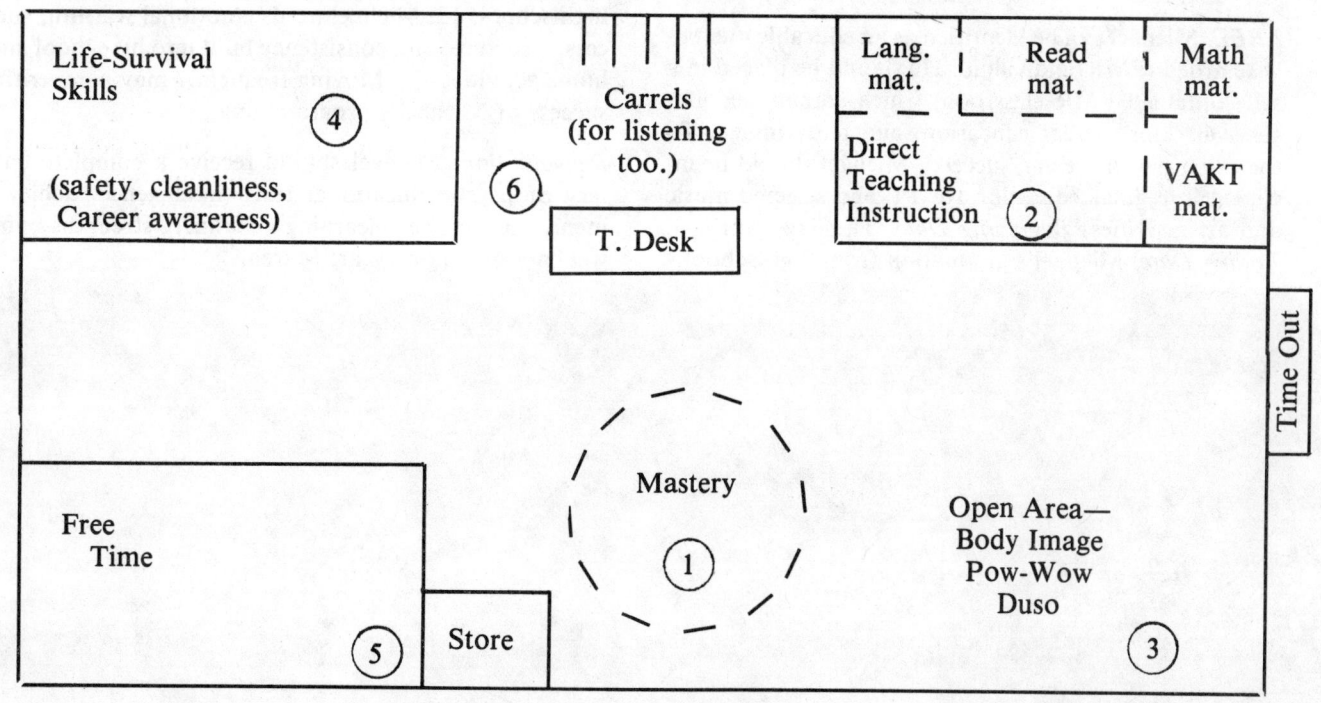

Behavior Grid:

Time	Wears Glasses	Completes Task	Bonus
8:30			
8:45			
9:00			
Etc.			

Behavior Management: Strategies: Checkmark system; contingency contracting; Premack; modeling; classroom rules and daily goal setting sessions; time out; response cost; interruption of undesired behavior.

Reinforcers: See learning characteristics grid, p. 1.

Punishers: Response cost of checkmarks; time out for aggressive behavior such as hitting. Avoid belittling, derogatory remarks.

Schedules: Checkmarks: fixed interval, at the end of each tool subject, and initially trade in at the end of the morning and afternoon; Praise: variable ratio 1 to 3; Physical touch: variable ratio 1 to 10.

LREE: Michael can be identified as an educable mentally retarded (EMR) individual. He should be placed in a self-contained EMR classroom which emphasizes life-survival skills, career education, and body image. To the extent which he can succeed, Michael should be included in regular education for PE and selected music and art activities. *Beginning Date:* Tuesday, April. 3. *Ending Date:* Michael's graduation from high school.

Related Services: 1. Speech and language therapy; 2. Liaison person to coordinate Michael's total (school, home, community) program; 3. Parent programming (weekly) relative to behavior management skills, communication skills, and their rights under PL 94-142.

Environmental Considerations: 1. Michael should receive a medical examination to determine if his bladder control problems are due to poor sphincter control. 2. Occurrences of bladder or bowel control problems should be labeled but not punished. The school's toilet schedule should be continued; a similar one should be initiated at home. 3. Michael's brothers should not be allowed to do things for Michael that he can do himself. 4. Mrs. Smith should continue with her roller skating and ceramics activities. 5. If possible, Mrs. Smith should arrange her work hours so that she is home when the children are dismissed from school. 6. The boys should sleep in separate beds. 7. Michael should wear his glasses when doing school work. 8. Michael should become involved in activities which expose him to age-appropriate peers, such as Cub Scouts, etc. 9. Michael needs time alone with each parent every day doing activities of interest to them. 10. The whole family should engage in weekend activities such as trips, hikes, camping, etc. 11. Beginning now, Michael's educational programming should include those skills that will enable him to become a working member of society. The logical extension of his program is on-the-job training in high school. 12. Michael needs emotional warmth, success, structure, and consistency built into his school and home activities. 13. Moving frequently may hamper the success of Michael's programming.

Reevaluation: Michael should receive a complete battery of psychoeducational tests (intelligence, achievement, projective, learning channel strengths and weaknesses) in one year; March.

LEARNING CONTRACT/SCHEDULE

Time	Task No.	Subject	Center	Assignment
8:30	1	Order	1	Workjobs p. 35—Hook Board—Accuracy is one washer to a hook, 25/30 correct.
8:45	2	Pow-wow	3	Set daily goal.
9:00	3	Language	2	Boehm Resource Guide—T.G. p. 1-3. Accuracy is correctly answering top or bottom 4 out of 6 times on concept card 1
	4			VAKT the circle shape—accuracy is a closed form (1.3.7)
9:30	5	Body Image	3	I CAN—Body Awareness Assessment. Accuracy is completion.
9:50	6	Reading	2	Edmark: pre-reading 2-17—2-24. Match 12 of 16 items correctly (5.5.6)
	7			VAKT is letter of name R—accuracy is correct formation in sandbox coupled with saying name of letter.
10:20		Recess/Milk Break		
10:40	8	Math	2	I CAN: Skill 2—accuracy is correctly counting 5 of 8 sets of dots (10.4.1)
	9			VAKT number "1"—accuracy is correct formation of number coupled with saying letter's name.
11:10	10	Music/Art/PE	3	Laterality and Directionality Act 9-Clap, clap, clap! Accuracy: point to 4 of 7 body parts.
11:30	11	Writing	1	Dubnoff—Level 1 P.A.-1 & 2. Accuracy is off the lines no more than 5 times. (1.3.6)
11:40	12	DUSO/Careed Ed.	3	DUSO—Introduction Story—Accuracy is pantomime one rule correctly.
12:00		Lunch		
1:00	13	Order	1	Teaching Resources Lacing Cards 1, 2—Accuracy is one shape laced correctly (10.3.2)
1:10	14	Visual/Auditory Remediation	2	Wrokjobs p. 83—same or different—Accuracy is 7 out of 10 pictures correctly matched (5.3.4)
1:30	15	Body Image	3	Body Management Activities—walk, skip, jump, hop on 6' line. Accuracy is going off line no more than 3 times per activity.
1:45	16	Spelling Language Therapy	Out	Non-Slip-SMP 2—accuracy is correctly matching 10 of 15 symbols.
2:15	17	Life-Survival	4	Cincinnati Guide PLP #1—washing face and hands—accuracy is completion of 6 out of 10 steps of teacher-made task analysis.
2:45	18	Pow-wow	3	Chart checkmarks
3:00		Dismissal		

IEP Number 3

CA 6.10, Grade 1

Presenting Problem: Cindy was referred for being "a behavior problem at school and in the home.

Comprehensive History: Family: Cindy is the younger of two children. The family is characterized by instability: 1) The family moved to "make a new go of it"; 2) There has been a history of separation; 3) The parents argue frequently in front of the children. Mrs. Black apparently is the major disciplinarian; Mr. Black apparently is lenient.

Developmental: Cindy was conceived in an attempt to save the marriage. Mrs. Black related being "really nervous" during the last two months of pregnancy; otherwise, the pregnancy was unremarkable. Mrs. Black reports that she did not enjoy Cindy at first, but that their relationship has improved since moving. Cindy's developmental history was normal except for a slight delay in speech which Mrs. Black attributed to Mike talking for Cindy.

Emotional: Cindy complains of nightmares. She wets her bed, a problem which goes in cycles. Cindy appears to have difficulty expressing her feelings, such as anger, but she can readily give and receive affection.

School: Cindy has a history of behavior problems at school. Her behavior in first grade is improved over that of kindergarten, possibly due in part to a better relationship with her teacher.

Clinical: Cindy was cute; cooperative; sustained a long attention span when interested in the task; was active but not hyperactive; was right-sided (eye, hand, and foot); and had good gross and fine motor coordination.

Learning Characteristics:

CA	IQ Ob/Pot	WRAT	Physical Characteristics	Attentional Factors	Input
6.10	V = 116/120 P = 124/140 FS = 122 (ob)	R = 1.3 S = 1.4 M = 1.8	Possible tongue thrust	Auditory: 20-30 minutes Visual: 15-20 minutes	Aud. ok Vis. ok

Memory	Meaning	Output	Self-Structuring
Auditory + Visual Sequential -	Visual and auditory: Ok	Verbal: Ok	No

Curriculum Match: Materials should: 1) emphasize auditory input; 2) utilize either verbal or graphic output; 3) require little self-structuring; 4) provide Cindy with positive reinforcement; and 5) start at beginning first grade for language arts and middle first grade for math.

Long-Range Objectives: Cindy's instructional program will utilize the System Fore continua for reading, math, and language.

Reading: Cindy will achieve objective 6.7.1 within one month at 80% accuracy.

Math: Cindy will achieve objective 11.9.2 within one month at 80% accuracy.

Language: After one month's instruction, Cindy will write from dictation, 20 CVC words containing any of the following vowels and consonants: a, i, o, r, f, m, n, t, within 15 minutes at 90% accuracy.

Classroom Engineering and Grouping: 1) Direct Instruction is given at the Direct Teaching Center. 2) Workbook assignments, X-factor work, and Order Tasks are completed at the Mastery Center. 3) The open area is used for Body Image activities DUSO, and Pow-wow. 4) Upon completion of assignments, students will be assigned X-work, structured free time, or be routed to the Interest Centers.

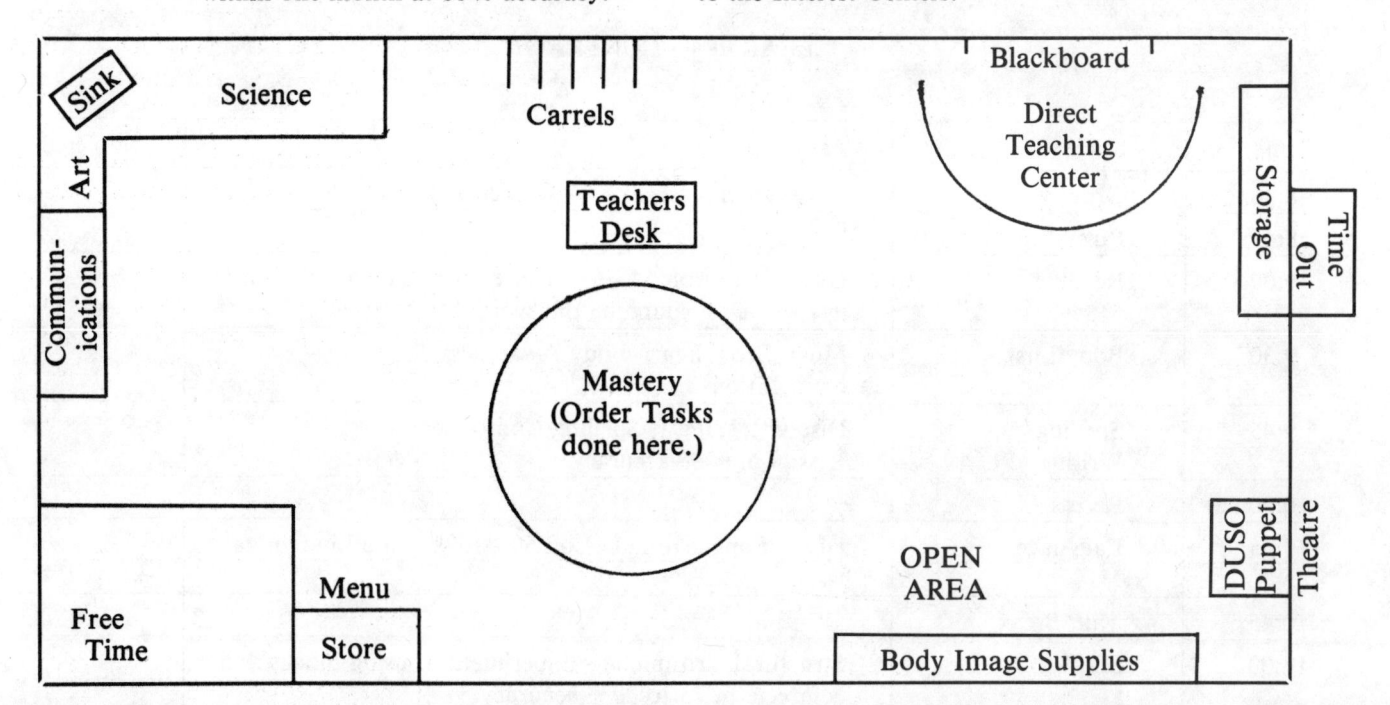

Time	Raises Hand	Keeps hands to Self	Bonus
8:30			
8:45			
9:00			
Etc.			

Behavior Management: Daily behavioral goals will set in Pow-wow. A behavioral grid will be used so that Cindy can be "paid" with checkmarks for engaging in target behavior. Possible back-up reinforcers for Cindy would include such things as being read to, free time to play a game with a friend, time after school to help the teacher, allowing her to take books home overnight, etc.

Least Restrictive Environment: The LRE for Cindy ideally is the regular classroom, employing the use of behavior management, a structured classroom (including learning contracts, daily class schedule, and engineering), and curriculum match. The teacher could be male or female, as long as the person is consistent, warm, secure, and understands the nature of Cindy's presenting problem.

Environmental Considerations:

1. Again, Cindy needs a strong, consistent behavior management program both at school and at home. A liaison person should coordinate her total program, perhaps to include family counseling.

2. Cindy should not be kept after school, except as a reward, to help the teacher. Likewise, Cindy should not be tutored at home.

3. A complete physical exam, to include hearing and vision, should be given to Cindy.

4. Cindy should be evaluated for a possible tongue thrust.

5. Cindy needs a crash program of success, self-concept development, and body image activities.

6. Her instructional program should challenge her work toward her potential, being careful to ensure success.

7. Cindy needs to be provided with a wide variety of experiences (field trips, informative movies, stories, etc.) which will broaden her experiential background and encourage her creativity.

LEARNING CONTRACT

Time	Subject	Assignment	Completed
8:30	Order	Love Order Task #1—80% Accuracy.	
8:45	Pow-wow		
9:00	Reading	Distar I, Lesson 57—6 out of 8 correct on Sounds firm-up, 100% on sounding out words.	
9:30	Body Image	Move-Grow-Learn Body Awareness Task #39—No collisions!	
9:45	Spelling/Writing	Distar Reading I, Spelling Component—Lesson 6, 90% accuracy.	
10:00	Recess		
10:45	Language	Distar Language I, Lesson 50—100% on all individual tests.	
10:45	Milk Break		
11:00	Math	Structural Arithmetic—Experiment 3, using blocks and complete p. 75 to 90% accuracy.	
11:30	Music/Art/PE	PE—"Chicken Fat" record in gym. Completion checkmark contingent on engaging in target behavior.	
11:50	Preparation for lunch		
12:00	Lunch		
1:00	Order	Distar Reading I, Lesson 57 Take-Home, 90% accuracy.	
1:10	Reading	Distar I Storybook 1, p. 1. using Neurological Impress Method—no more than three mistakes.	
1:30	DUSO	Listen to story: "The Red and White Bluebird." Follow DUSO Rules with no violations.	

Time	Subject	Assignment	Completed
1:45	Language	Distar Language I, Lesson 50 Take-Home, 100% accuracy.	
2:10	Body Image	Move-Grow-Learn Body Awareness task #40—No collisions!	
2:25	Science/Social Studies	Film on brushing teeth—accuracy is following class rules during discussion with no more than 2 violations.	
2:45	Pow-wow and charting		
3:00	Dismissal		

X-Work

6.9.1

Choose letters to make new words.

Examples: <u>c</u>ap <u>m</u>ake <u>p</u>ine

m
p
t
f
d
b
n

-ap -ake -ine
-ap -ake -ine

IEP Number 4

CA 6.10; Grade—Kindergarten

Presenting Problem: Kathy was referred in order to determine the nature of her difficulty in expressive language skills, articulation, and gross motor development.

Physical Character	Attentional Factors	Ob/Pot IQ	Achieve Data	Input	Memory
mod. gross/ fine motor problems. "lazy eye". articulation problems. laterality confusion.	combined aud. & vis. 45 minutes	83/ave.	WRAT S, Pk.7 M, Pk.8 R, K.2	Aud.-ok aud. recall ok Vis. mild weak. Haptic ok	aud. stor. - aud. recall ok aud. sequen. - vis. stor. - vis. recall ok vis. sequen. --

Meaning	Output	Self-Structuring	Reinforcers
aud. -- vis. ok	verbal -- graphic -- haptic ok	No.	verbal praise, physical touch, snacks, play games, use of puppets, positive stamps, stickers, notes, have work posted.

Emotional Factors

Mod. self concept problems
Insecure about relationship with parents.
Easily frustrated with difficult tasks.
Regresses to lower developmental level when frustrated.
Avoids unfamiliar tasks and situations.
Affectionate when comfortable.

Curriculum Match: Kathy needs materials geared to a non-self structuring 6.10-year-old with an obtained IQ of 83 (mental age of 5.8); a beginning kindergarten reading level; a pre-kindergarten math level; which emphasize the VAKT approach and deemphasize verbal output; which are teacher-directed; and which are sequential in concept formation and inherently reinforcing.

Long and Short Term Objectives:

Instructional: (long term) By February 12, given a worksheet of five addition problems (facts to 5), Kathy will write the correct answers within 5 minutes, at 80% accuracy, (SLI 11.8.2).

Instructional: (short term)

1. By April 1,: Given a list of 7 letters and 5 numerals in random order, Kathy will identify by pointing 4 out of 5 numerals within 3 minutes. (SLI 10.3.2)

2. By June 1: Kathy will achieve objective 10.5.5 (identifies larger and smaller sets) with criteria as specified in the System Fore continuum.

3. By October 1: Kathy will achieve objective 10.6.3 (indicates the set with a given number of members from among sets of various sizes) with criteria as specified in the System Fore continuum.

4. By November 15: Upon request from the teacher, Kathy will write the number 1-9, in order, correctly including 7 of the 9 numbers, within 5 minutes. (SLI 10.6.3)

5. By January 15: Kathy will achieve objective 11.8.1 (joins sets of 1-5 objects and records results using + and = signs) with criteria as specified in the System Fore Continuum.

Behavioral (long term): By February 12: After setting "completing assignments" as her daily goal, Kathy will complete at least 80% of her daily tasks within the allotted time, five days in a row. (Accuracy can be calculated by dividing the number of assigned tasks into the number of completed tasks.)

Remediation: (long term): By February 12: When verbally presented with a four step command, Kathy will perform all four steps in the correct sequence for two out of three trials, each trial within three minutes.

Behavior Management, Strategies: Checkmark system; contingency contracting; modeling; classroom rules and daily goal setting sessions; Premack; response cost; time out. *Reinforcers:* see grid, p. 1. *Punishers:* response cost of checkmarks; time out for aggressive behavior such as biting. Avoid derogatory, negative comments. *Schedule:* Checkmarks: fixed interval, at the end of each subject, and trade in at the end of the morning and afternoon, initially; Praise: variable ratio 1 to 3; Physical touch variable ratio 1 to 10.

Time	Does not bite	Starts Assign.	BONUS
8:30			
8:45			
9:00			
9:30			
9:45			
Etc.			

LREE: Kathy can be identified as a learning disabled (LD) individual. She should receive tool subject (reading, language, math, body image, writing, career education) and training to remediate her weaknesses in a Special Education Resource Room. She should participate in regular classes (music, art, etc.) to the extent that she can be successful. There should be a strong emphasis in both environments on self concept development.

Beginning Date: Monday, February 12. *Ending Date:* Kathy's graduation.

Related Services: 1. Speech and language therapy. 2. Liaison person to coordinate Kathy's total (school, home, community) program. 3. Parent programming (weekly) relative to behavior management skills, communication skills, and their rights under PL 94-142.

Environmental Considerations: 1. The family should engage in weekly activities together, such as swimming, hiking, skiing, etc. 2. Kathy should spend time with each parent (separately) each day doing things of interest to both. 3. Don't allow Mike to talk for Kathy. 4. Kathy needs good modeling. She should not be mixed in an educational environment with severely mental retarded or emotionally disturbed students. 5. Kathy needs many success experiences at home and school. 6. The use of medication may be explored if Kathy's attention or fatigue level decreases. 7. Both the school and home should provide consistency, structure, continuity, and expectations appropriate for Kathy's developmental level. 8. Kathy needs security through warm, affectional relationships. 9. Mrs. Williams should continue to have her private time. 10. Written parental permission should be obtained for further testing, and testing should be non-verbal, but not of a group nature.

Reevaluation: Kathy should receive a complete battery of psychoeducational tests (intelligence, achievement, projective, learning channel strengths and weaknesses) in one year.

LEARNING CONTRACT/SCHEDULE

Time	Task No.	Subject	Center	Assignment	Completed
8:30	1	Order	4	Work jobs—pegboard pattern—Accuracy is shape correct (5.4.19)	
8:45	2	Pow-wow	5	Set daily goal.	
9:00	3	Language	1	Syntax 1—Goal 1-TG p. 4, 5 Steps A, B, C (2-3.2.5) Accuracy: "the" plus picture word, 6/8 correct.	
	4	Aud. Seq. Memory	2	Goal ASM 1, Tasks 1-3, 4 out of 6 word pairs said in order	
9:30	5	Body Image	5	Move-Grow-Learn coordination—13 acc. is lopping or 2 feet w/beanbag between knees—3 hops	
9:45	6	Reading	1	Edmark-pre-reading 2-17—2-24 match 14 of 16 items correctly (5.5.6)	
	7		1	VAKT 1st letter of name K- acc. is correct formation in sandbox coupled w/saying name.	
	8	Visual Tracking	3	Marble Track-Body Man. Act. P. 127 acc: stop marble w/finger 2 out of 3 trials (5.1.2)	

Time	Task No.	Subject	Center	Assignment	Completed
10:15		Recess Milk Break			
10:30	9	Math	1	I CAN—SKILL 3—TG p. 12 Acc: make set of 6,4,3 (10.5.5)	
	10	Visual Discrim.	3	Workjobs p. 57—matching shapes 16 cards-13/16 correctly matched	
11:00	11	Music M&F Art TTh	Out	Laterality & Directionality Act. 9 Clap, clap, clap! acc: point to 5 of 7 body parts	
11:20	12	Writing	4	Dubnoff 1—Level 1 p. A-1 & 2 acc: off lines no more than 4 times (1.3.6)	
11:30	13	DUSO/Sex Ed/Career Education	5	Duso—Listen to story/The Underwater Problem Solvers—Be able to pantomime the rule correctly.	
11:50		Lunch prep.			
12:00		Lunch			

Color the circles

X-Work

APPENDIX I

Selected Curriculum Materials
Which Represent A Good D-PT Match

Reading

1. *Auditory Discrimination in Depth.* Teaching Resources, 100 Boylston Street, Boston, Mass. 02116.

   ADD is a multisensory program that develops the auditory-perceptual skills basic to reading, spelling, and language.

2. *Corrective Reading.* Science Research Associates, 759 East Erie St., Chicago, Illinois 60622.

   This is a complete remedial decoding and comprehension program using direct instruction, oral reading, and learning contracts.

3. *Criterion Reading.* Random House, Westminister, Maryland 21557.

   This is an excellent K-8 developmental, sequenced, criterion referenced, individualized, diagnostic and placement support system in reading, with built-in performance objectives, and with cross reference to specific teaching materials relative to basic reading programs.

4. *Distar Reading.* Science Research Associates, 759 East Erie Street, Chicago, Illinois 60662.

   This is a developmental, sequenced, criterion-based reading program that involves structured teaching methods.

5. *E.B. Press Tutorial Program.* E-B Press, P.O. Box 10459, Eugene, Oregon 97401.

   a. Word Endings. This direct instruction supplementary program is designed to increase student rate in oral discrimination of word endings.

   b. Functional Decoding and Vocabulary Building. This direct instruction supplementary program is designed to increase student rate and accuracy in oral reading as well as formulating definitions of words read.

6. *Edmark Reading Program.* Edmark, 13241 Northup Way, Bellevue, Washington 98005.

   This beginning reading and language program is designed for school-aged non-readers. Using a direct instruction and multi-sensory approach, 150 survival words are taught. Total communication is facilitated through a signing component.

7. *Fountain Valley Teacher Support System in Reading and Math.* Richard L. Zweig, Associates, Inc., 1711 McGraw Ave., Irvine, California 92714.

   This is an excellent K-6, developmental, sequenced, criterion based, individualized, diagnostic and placement support system in reading, with cross reference to specific teaching materials relative to basic reading programs.

8. *Goldman-Lynch Sounds and Symbols.* American Guidance Services, Inc., Publishers Building, Circle Pines, Minnesota 53014.

   This teacher directed program is designed to help the pre-reading child associate sounds with written symbols. The kit provides multi-sensory teaching aids and emphasizes active student involvement.

9. *The Herman Method of Reversing Reading Failure.* Romar Publications, Inc., 6380 Wilshire Blvd., Los Angeles, California 90048.

   This is a multisensory, developmentally sequenced, K-6, reading, writing, and spelling program that involves teacher-directed lessons. The program is designed to teach beginning level decoding skills by means of any or all of the four stages of the VAKT technique.

10. *Houghton-Mifflin Reading Program.* 1900 South Batavic Avenue, Geneva, Illinois 60134. Reading grade level: K-12.

    This is a sequential, visually-based reading program with scope and sequence objectives related to the development of K-12 reading and language arts skills.

11. *Houghton-Mifflin Tutorial.* Same address as above.

    Provides programmed lessons, coordinated with the Houghton-Mifflin Reading Series, to re-teach reading skills not mastered through regular class work. Designed for use by paraprofessionals and older students with individual students.

12. *Individualized Directions in Reading.* Stack-Vaughn, P.O. Box 202P, Austin, Texas 78767.

    This is a student-directed system for improving reading skills. Components include learning centers for assessment, phonics, structural analysis, and comprehension.

13. The Language Experience Reading Technique (see Figure XV).

14. The Neurological Impress Reading Technique (see Figure XVI).

15. *The New Streamlined English Series.* New Readers Press Division of Laubach Literacy, Box 131, Syracuse, New York 13210.

    This is a basic and developmentally sequenced reading and writing program, which develops decoding and comprehension skills needed to function as an adult. The series has Correlated Readers, the content of which relates to independent living.

16. *Open Court Foundation Program.* Box 599, LaSalle, Illinois 61301.

    A correlated language, spelling, reading, and writing program, sequential in design, with built-in performance objectives relative to the development of K-6 language arts skills.

17. *Peabody Rebus Reading Program.* American Guidance Service, Publisher's Building, Circle Pines, Minnesota 55014.

    These programmed materials introduce reading through rebuses (picture words), and then a combination of rebuses and traditional orthography (spelled words). The readiness level de-emphasizes verbal output through a complete introductory program which equips the learner with the skills and vocabulary necessary for transferring to the primary level of traditional programs.

18. *Reading for Survival in Today's Society, Vol. I and II.* Goodyear Publishing, 1640 5th St., Santa Monica, California 904012.

    This kit provides instruction in reading and consequent behavior relative to functional/survival skills necessary to read and interpret printed matter encountered in everyday living. Specific areas include labels, weather reports, travel information, job application forms, etc.

19. *Reading Skills Program.* Changing Times Education Service, 1729 H Street, N.W., Washington, D.C. 20006.

    This is a multisensory and developmentally sequenced reading program that uses teacher and student-directed lessons. Basic decoding and comprehension skills are taught through career education related stories.

20. *Reading Technology.* Mind, 1 Kings Highway North, Westport, Connecticut 06880.

    This audio-visual program diagnoses and teaches decoding and comprehension skills. It is a fully automated self-contained learning system that presents instruction through learning modules.

21. *Sound-Order-Sense Program.* Follett Publishing Co., 1010 West Washington Boulevard, Chicago, Illinois 60607.

    This is a series of multi-level auditory exercises designed to build auditory perception skills from the simplest spoken sentences.

22. *Sounder, A Complete Reading Tutorial System.* Edmark Associates, 13249 Northup Way, Bellevue, Washington 908805.

Sounder is a complete remedial reading/tutoring system that can be employed by using older students or adult aides as tutors. Sounder teaches phonetics and 200 sight words.

23. *System 80.* Borg-Warner, 600 West University Drive, Arlington Heights, Illinois 60004.

This reading support program is a hardware-based visual-auditory-tactual method of providing supplemental individualized instruction in basic reading skills.

24. *System FORE.* FOREWORKS, P.O. Box 9747, North Hollywood, California 91609.

The System FORE includes skill continua in Language, Reading, and Math for ages 2-12, and also Additions, plus Secondary Extension. A materials list that is cross-referenced to the skill continua is available.

This is a developmental, sequenced, criterion based, individualized, diagnostic and placement support system in reading, math, and language, with cross references to specific teaching materials relative to basic skill tasks in these disciplines.

25. VAKT. (See Figure XVII).

FIGURE XV
Use of Language Experience Approach as a Technique of Remediation

The Language-Reading Experience Approach can often be used as a successful remedial approach for many students, and as a supplemental approach when a basal book is used as the primary instructional method. This is particularly true for intermediate grade students with a primary grade instructional level, and for some students who are shy, withdrawn, and/or have a poor self-concept.

One approach to the Language-Reading Experience Approach includes the following steps:

1. Motivate the student to dictate a story by showing him pictures, having him relate his own experiences (real and/or imagined), by reading a story to him and having the student continue the story beyond the author's ending, unfinished stories, through the use of movies, etc.

2. Dictating may be done directly to the teacher or tape recorder. In either case, the teacher writes the story exactly as dictated. It is recommended that regarding dialect errors the teacher simply reread to the student what he has said, asking if that is the way he wants it written.

3. The teacher uses the story as a basis for instruction, much the same way as a regular basal reader would be used. It is not unusual for students to use words verbally that are well beyond their ability to recognize in print.

4. The student continues to dictate stories over a period of time. These stories may be bound together and used as the student's instructional "book."

5. The student may want to illustrate his stories. If so, it is recommended that he be allowed to do so.

6. A photograph of the student could be placed on the cover, or on the title page by the student-author's name. This is often helpful for children with poor self concept.

7. It is recommended that the teacher consult a basal reader manual at the instructional level of the student to insure scope and sequence of skills development. Frequently it will be necessary to consult basal manuals at reading levels below that of the student's instructional level to insure sequential skill development and/or to remediate certain weaknesses.

8. For some students with graphic problems, the use of a typewriter would be an asset relative to the student typing the dictated story.

Figure XVI
The Neurological Impress Remedial Reading Technique

The Neurological Impress Remedial Reading Technique is an economical and time-saving method of improving reading ability relative to individuals who need remedial reading. It is most effective when employed in a one to one relationship, although it can be used in a group setting if earphones are used by the students and the teacher reads into a mike while the reading material is projected onto a screen. The N.I. techique is most effective with upper elementary students through adults, when presented in consecutive daily sessions of approximately 15 minutes each over an eight to ten week period, and when high-interest reading materials are used.

The mechanics of the Neurological Impress technique are:

1. Select high-interest reading material which is at a slightly lower than usual reading level for the student.

2. The instructor and student should be seated side by side at a table with the student slightly forward so the instructor's voice is close to the student's ear.

3. The student is given minimal instruction, other than being directed to read aloud and also simultaneously with the instructor.

4. When the instructor and student read aloud together, the instructor uses his finger to underline the written word at the exact moment the word is read aloud. If desired, the student may later perform this function, or alternate between the student and the teacher.

5. Initially, the instructor should read slightly louder and faster than the student. Later, the emphasis should be on simultaneous reading.

6. No correction is done with the student, although some re-reading may be necessary in the initial stages of the program. The instructor must be sensitive to the student's level of anxiety and tolerance, and adjust his reading rate and/or materials accordingly.

7. During the eight to ten week instructional period, the instructor gradually increases the reading pace and the level of reading difficulty, thus "dragging" the student to higher levels.

8. Although the reading pace is gradually increased during the overall instructional process, the instructor should also provide short bursts of speeded oral reading in every instructional session.

After two weeks of instruction, the reading burst-pace may be increased to as fast as the instructor can real aloud without discomfort.

In summary, the Neurological Impress technique is a remedial reading technique which requires little investment in time or money. Research studies indicate significant gains are frequently attained and that these gains are maintained. Net reading gains of two years or more are not uncommon among students who have received Neurological Impress reading instruction. If a student does not respond favorably to this technique after three or four weeks of instruction, it is likely that the technique is not the remedial method of choice, and other strategies should be tried.

FIGURE XVII

The VAKT Technique

The VAKT technique is one of the most powerful but also most laborious of all remedial strategies. The technique is designed to be used with individuals who have major defects in the auditory as well as visual processing systems, and as such have experienced chronic tool-subject failure.

VAKT stands for Visual-Auditory-Kinesthetic-Tactual. The intent of the VAKT technique is to utilize any and all (multi-sensory) input systems available to the individual in order to increase the likelihood of tool-subject or instructional success. Thus, it is assumed that an individual with severe auditory and visual processing defects will learn better by means of a multi-sensory instructional technique than by a single (for example auditory or visual) instructional technique.

The VAKT technique is very time-consuming and laborious, and almost always involves a one-to-one teacher-student relationship. Nonetheless, the VAKT technique is powerful, usually results in immediate payoff for the individual, and has a high long-term yield relative to at least minimal tool-subject success, whereas previous instructional techniques resulted in chronic failure.

The VAKT technique can be used for the purpose of teaching reading, written spelling, handwriting, and written arithmetic computation. In addition, the VAKT technique can be used for the purpose of partial remediation of auditory and visual discrimination; auditory and visual storage, sequential, and recall memory; auditory, visual, and tactual meaning; and graphic output. Lastly, the VAKT technique facilitates such splinter instructional skills as phonic ability, syllabication, and left to right sequencing.

The VAKT involves four stages, and several steps within each stage.

Stage I: Tracing

1. The subject selects a word that he wants to learn to read or spell, regardless of the length of the word.
2. The word is written for the subject by the teacher by means of crayon or other substance which leaves a raised surface, in blackboard-size print.
3. The subject traces the word with his first and second fingers, and says each part of the word as he traces it.
4. This tracing-saying procedure is repeated until the subject can write the word without looking at the model.
5. The subject is allowed as much time as is necessary to master the number four procedure.
6. After the subject can write the target word from memory, the subject dictates to the teacher a brief story which includes the target-word.
7. That story is typed by the teacher, and the subject reads the story to the teacher.
8. The subject places the target word that has been learned by tracing in a word-file, which then becomes the word pool which the subject has acquired.
9. Words in the word-pool are periodically reviewed relative to the subject's ability to read (or spell) the words. If a word is forgotten, those words are re-learned by means of the tracing-saying technique.

There are some important conditions relative to Stage One.

1. It is important for the subject to trace the target words with his fingers, and not a stylus or pencil. Finger tracing provides direct tactual contact with the raised surface by which the word was printed. It is that contact which provides an additional input dimension for the subject, which is the essence of the multi-sensory VAKT technique.
2. It is critical that the subject write the target word from memory, and not by means of looking back and forth between the model and the word that he is writing.

It is thought that such looking back and forth breaks up the word into fragmentary units, thus impeding the learning process.

3. The explanation of the VAKT technique involves the subject looking at the word (V), saying the word (hearing it—A), feeling the hand movement involved with the left to right tacing (K), and feeling the raised surface as the subject's fingers trace the letters (T).
4. It is important that the saying and tracing be synchronized, so that the subject is tracing that part of the word which he is saying.
5. Target words should be written and learned as whole units, rather than by sounds or syllables.
6. The purpose of allowing the subject to select the target words is to increase the subject's motivation to endure the labor involved with the VAKT technique. However, since the VAKT technique is designed primarily for subjects who have severe auditory and visual processing problems and hence chronic instructional failure, the sudden VAKT-based ability to read or spell a few words has immense payoff value.
7. If the subject makes a mistake relative to incorrect word pronunciation, saying-tracing synchronization, or writing the word from memory, the process should stop at that point and the subject should return to the beginning and start again. Thus, erasing, mistakes, or corrections are not permitted. This "no error" policy is designed to avoid the subject learning the incorreect pronunciation, written form of expression, etc. of the target word.

Stage II: Vocalizing Without Tracing

1. Tracing is no longer necessary in Stage Two.
2. The subject looks at the high-interest printed target-word, repeatedly says the word out loud, and then writes the word from memory.
3. The Stage Two words need not be printed in raised surface form.
4. The target-words should be of high-prob value to the subject.
5. A "no error" policy is in effect for Stage Two.
6. The subject uses learned target words for the purpose of writing brief sentences, then paragraphs. Gradually, writing becomes easier, the stories become longer, and the writing of the story words reinforces the ability to read the words.

The transition between Stage One and Stage Two occurs at the time the subject naturally phases out the need to trace the target word in order to write it from memory. Stage One can last from a matter of weeks to a year, depending upon the severity of the central nervous system problem which is causing the learning defects.

One of the derivatives of Stage Two is that the subject gradually establishes the association between the sound of a word and the way the word looks. Thus, when the subject hears the word, he can revisualize it; and, when he sees the word, he can auditorize it.

Stage III: Visualizing, but no Vocalizing or Tracing

1. Vocalizing is no longer necessary in Stage Three.
2. The subject looks at the target word, and writes the word from memory without vocalizing or tracing.
3. The "no error" policy is in effect for Stage Three.
4. High-interest/low-vocabulary reading materials, and/or experience-language chart material, is used in Stage Three.
5. The subject is encouraged to read from the number four type material, and the words that he is unable to read are identified for further study. These "failure words" are learned separately by means of the Stage Three procedure.

6. An inventory of the mastered target words is made, and periodically reviewed to ensure continuing mastery.

Stage IV: Generalization

1. The fourth stage begins when the subject can generalize new words from their resemblance to known words.
2. More advanced high-interest/low-vocabulary reading materials are used.
3. The words used for Stages Three and Four should include those career education words and concepts which will be necessary for the subject's post-school social and economic survival.

The subject's progress should be constantly monitored. If failure or regression occurs, the subject should be returned to the immediately preceding Stage.

Because of the amount of subject effort involved with the VAKT technique, the subject probably should not be extensively read to, in order to prevent the subject from seeking the easy way out and inviting people to read for him, as opposed to mastering reading and spelling words by means of the VAKT technique.

Reading: High Interest/Low Vocabulary

1. *Action Libraries.* Scholastic Book Services, 904 Sylvan Avenue, Englewood Cliffs, New Jersey 07632. Reading level: 2.0-4.0. Interest grade level: 7-12.

2. *All About Sounds.* Creative Teaching Associates, P.O. Box 7766, Fresno, California 93727.

   All About Sounds is a supplemental reading system, which can be used as X-work material, whic is correlated to Distar Reading, and which is designed for use in grades K-2.

3. *American Adventure Series.* Harper and Row, 2500 Crawford Avenue, Evanston, Illinois. Reading grade level: 2-6. Interest level: 4-12.

4. *Bowman Reading Incentive Programs.* Bowman Publications Corp., Glendale, California 91201. Reading grade level: 3.0. Interest level: Elementary-High School.

5. *The Checkered Flag Series (Kit A).* Addison Wesley, 2725 Sand Hill Road, Menlo Park, California 94035. Reading grade level: 2.4-4.5. Interest grade level: 6-12.

6. *The Checkered Flag Series (Kit B).* Same address as above. Reading grade level: 3.4-4.5. Interest grade level: 6-12.

7. *Cowboy Sam Series.* Benefic Press, 1900 North Narrangansett Avenue, Chicago, Illinois 10570. Reading grade level: pre-primer to 3rd.

8. *Cowboys of Many Races.* (Same address as above.) Reading grade level: pre-primer to 5th.

9. *Dan Frontier Series.* (Same address as above.) Reading grade level: pre-primer to 5th.

10. *Deep Sea Adventure Series.* Field Educational Publications, 2400 Hanover Street, Palo Alto, California 94304. Reading grade level: 1.8-5.0. Interest level: 3-17.

11. *Frontiers of American Books.* Children's Press, 1224 West VanBuren Street, Chicago, Illinois. Reading grade level: 3. Interest level: Elementary-High School.

12. *Interesting Reading Series.* Follett Publishing Company, 1010 West Washington Blvd., Chicago, Illinois 60607. Reading grade level: 2.0-3.0. Interest level: 3-High School.

13. *The Jim Forest Readers.* Addison Wesley, 2725 Sand Hill Road, Menlo Park, California 94035. Reading grade level: 1.7-3.2. Interest level: 1-7.

14. *Know Your World.* Xerox Education Publications, 1250 Fairwood Avenue, P.O. Box 444, Columbus, Ohio 43216.

    This is a weekly classroom newspaper which covers topics suitable for secondary-level students. Skill exercises on duplicating masters are included.

15. *Morgan Bay Mysteries.* Field Educational Publications, 2400 Hanover Street, Palo Alto, California 94304. Reading grade level: 2.4-4.5. Interest level: 4-11.

16. *Pacemaker.* True Adventures, Fearon Publishers, Inc., 6 Davis Drive, Belmont, California 94002. Reading grade level: 2.0-2.5.

17. *Pal Paperbacks and Filmstrips.* Xerox Education Publications, 1250 Fairwood Avenue, P.O. Box 444, Columbus, Ohio 43216. Reading grade level: 1.5-5.5. Interest level: 5-12.

    These paperback books have correlated filmstrip-cassette tape presentations.

18. *Readers Digest Skill Builders.* Readers Digest Services, Inc., Pleasantville, New York 10597. Reading grade level: K-6. Interest level: Elementary-High School.

19. *Reading Fun I Can Do Myself.* Creative Teaching Associates, P.O. Box 7766, Fresno, California 93727.

    Reading Fun I Can Do Myself involves individual learning center activities, dealing with: rhyming, opposites, word building, contractions, following directions, and comprehension. The materials are correlated to the Distar reading program.

20. *The Top Flight Readers.* Addison Wesley, 2725 Sand Hill Road, Menlo Park, California 94035. Reading grade level: 2.3-3.5. Interest grade level: 5-12.

Language

1. *Auditory Discrimination in Depth.* Teaching Resources, 100 Boylston Street, Boston, Massachusetts 02116.

   This is an excellent K-12, structured, sequential, multisensory program that develops the auditory-perceptual skills basic to reading, spelling, and language.

2. *Boehm Resource Guide for Basic Concept Teaching.* The Psychological Corporation, 575 Third Avenue, New York, N.Y. 10017.

   This resource kit is designed to be used in teaching fundamental language concepts through concrete experiences and direct instruction. The kit includes a resource manual, picture cards, games, puzzles, and matching and classifying tasks.

3. *Corrective Reading-Comprehension.* Science Research Associates, Inc., 259 Erie Street, Chicago, Illinois 60611.

   In addition to teaching reading comprehension, this direct instruction program teaches verbal and written expressive language relative to reasoning, using information, definitions, sentence structure, developing inferences, following directions, and written communication.

4. *Developmental Syntax Program.* Learning Concepts. 2501 N. Lamar, Austin, Texas 78705.

   This is a series of eight programs designed to correct oral syntax problems within the classroom. The procedures used include ear training, production and carry-over, and generalization to a different context.

5. *Distar Games and Strategy.* Science Research Associates, 579 East Erie Street, Chicago, Illinois 60611.

   This is an educational game supplement to the Distar Language Program, and requires conversational interaction.

6. *Distar Language.* Science Research Associates, 579 East Erie Street, Chicago, Illinois 60611.

   This is a developmental, sequenced, criterion based language program which teaches language concepts essential for effective communication.

7. *Goal: Language Development.* Milton Bradley Company, Springfield, Mass. 01001.

   Goal is comprehensive multiple stimuli program designed to help children acquire the language skills basic to learning to read.

8. *Initial Expressive Language Program.* Edmark Associates, 13241 Northup Way, Bellevue, Washington 98005.

   This direct-instruction program teaches oral language skills to children who speak in phrases of less than five words. It contains placement tests, a behavioral recording system, a programmed text format in the teacher's manual, and picture cards.

9. *Peabody Language Development Program.* American Guidance Services, Publishers' Building, Circle Pines, Minnesota 53104.

   This program is designed primarily to stimulate receptive, associative, and expressive language development.

10. *Syntax-1.* Communication Skill Builders, 815 E. Broadway, P.O. Box 608, Tucson, Arizona 85733.

    This direct instruction language tutorial program is a sequenced set of lessons that teaches oral syntax skills to individuals who demonstrate a developmental lag in expressive language.

11. *System FORE.* FOREWORKS, P.O. Box 9747, North Hollywood, California 91609. The System Fore includes skill continua in language, reading, and math for ages 2-18.

    This is a developmental, sequenced, criterion based, individualized, diagnostic, and support system in reading, math, and language, with cross references to specific teaching materials relative to basic skill tasks in these disciplines. The language sequence includes components in phonology, morphology, syntax, and semantics.

Math

1. *Computapes.* Science Research Associates, 579 East Erie Street, Chicago, Illinois 60622.

   This is a self-structured supplementary math operation program that uses cassette tapes and limited graphic output. The tapes provide instruction directions, and immediate feedback.

2. *Digitor.* Centurion Industries Incorporated, Redwood City, California 94063.

   This is a high-interest calculator-like instructional tool for developing increased rate and accuracy with basic facts in addition, subtraction, multiplication, and division.

3. *Distar Math.* Science Research Associates, 759 East Erie Street, Chicago, Illinois 60622.

   This is a developmental, sequenced, and criterion based math program which involves structured and direct teaching methods.

4. *Dot Overlay Technique.* Bernie Straub Publishing Co., Inc. and Special Child Publications, 4535 Union Bay Place, N.E., Seattle, Washington 78105.

   This beginning math program uses a teacher directed and student practice format with visual and haptic input to teach basic number concepts and additional skills.

5. *The E-B Press Tutorial Series.* E-B Press, P.O. Box 10459, Eugene, Oregon 97401.

   The E-B Tutorial Programs are sets of developmental, sequenced, criterion based, and structured materials designed to provide step-by-step instruction in time telling, number skills, math combinations, and carrying and borrowing.

6. *Foundations for Mathematics.* Teaching Resources, 100 Boylston Street, Boston, Masachusetts 02116.

   This program develops basic concepts of color, shape, size, number, and order, and is designed for use with children at preschool to first grade functional levels.

7. *Fountain Valley Teacher Support System in Math.* Richard L. Zweig, Associates, Inc., 20800 1711 McGraw Ave., Irvine, California 92714.

   This is a K-6, criterion based, individualized, sequenced, diagnostic, and support system in math, with cross references to specific instructional materials for each skill in the developmental sequence.

8. *Fundamentals Underlying Numbers.* Teaching Resources Corp., 100 Boylston Street, Boston, Massachusetts 02116.

   These 96 math games are easy-to-play, non-competitive, and self-correcting. Designed to provide a basic first-year program for children of functional ages 4½ to 6, FUN develops basic math concepts relating to numbers one to nine.

9. *Goal.* Milton Bradley Company, Springfield, Mass. 01001.

   Goal is a comprehensive, multiple stimuli program designed to help children acquire beginning math concepts and skills.

10. *I Can Arithmetic Program.* Special Child Publications, 4535 Union Bay Place, N.E., Seattle, WA 98105.

    A complete beginning arithmetic program developed for slow-learning children designed to teach number/numeral concepts, addition, and subtraction. Haptic input and graphic output are emphasized.

11. *Independent Drill for Mastery.* Developmental Learing Materials, 7440 Natchez Avenue, Niles, Illinois 60641.

    This program features tests to determine student's entry levels and progress in the program. Answer keys and a class profile assist the teacher in scoring and recording test results and prescription. Self-study lessons on tape are assigned, and students listen, write and correct their practice papers with the answer/study sheets.

12. *Individual Instruction in Mathematics.* Houghton-Mifflin, 1900 South Batovia Avenue, Geneva, Illinois 60134.

This is a visually oriented, performance objective based, remedial but supplemental, computational without a quantitative reasoning emphasis, low-level high school math program with pre-post tests. K-6 equivalent program is *Math For Individual Achievement,* same publisher.

13. *Individualized Computational Skills Program, Set B.* Houghton-Mifflin Co., 1900 South Batavia Avenue, Geneva, Illinois 60134.

    This program helps identify computational skill weaknesses and provides materials to remediate these weaknesses.

14. Key Math instructional objectives as they relate to math weaknesses identified on the Diagnostic Profile. The instructional objectives can be found in the Key Math Manual, available from American Guidance Service, Inc., Publisher's Building, Circle Pines, Minnesota 55014.

15. *Learning Skill Series: Arithmetic.* McGraw-Hill, 1221 Avenue of the Americas, New York, New York 10020.

    This supplemental math workbook series provides practice in pre-vocational arithmetic skills, including money management, telling time, measurement, auto and home care, and preparing meals.

16. *Math Technology.* Mind, 1 Kings Highway North, Westport, Connecticut 06880.

    This is an individualized and student operated audio-visual math program emphasizing practice in skills relevant to occupational settings and job success. There is a behaviorally based diagnostic component used to place the student in the program.

17. *Money Makes Sense.* Fearon Publishers, Belmont, California.

    This program is designed to teach the names of coins; the value of coins; counting money; reading money values; and applying these skills in practical situations.

18. *Pacemaker Practical Arithmetic Series.* Fearon-Pitman Publishers, Inc., 6 Davis Drive, Belmont, California 94002.

    This series of three workbooks provides practice in basic arithmetic skills relative to money, checking and savings accounts, paychecks and payroll deductions, and other vocationally related math survival skills.

19. *Programmed Math: Sullivan.* McGraw-Hill Book Company, 1221 Avenue of the Americas, New York, NY 10020. Math grade level: second grade through junior high.

    This remedial and developmental math program covers math principles and skills ranging from beginning number concepts through consumer and personal math problems. The teaching and practice books use a self-instructional and self-correcting format.

20. *Structural Arithmetic.* Houghton-Mifflin Co., 1900 South Batavia Avenue, Geneva, Illinois 60234.

    This is a concrete and sequenced K-3 math program, which emphasizes visual/tactile input, and has many manipulative objects and tasks.

21. *System 80.* Borg-Warner, 600 West University Drive, Arlington Heights, Illinois 60004.

    This math support program is a hardware-based VAT (visual-auditory-tactual) method of providing supplemental individualized instruction in basic math skills.

22. *System FORE.* FOREWORKS, P.O. Box 9747, North Hollywood, California 91609. The System Fore includes skill continua in language, reading, and math for ages 2-18.

    This is a developmental, sequenced, criterion based, individualized, diagnostic, and support system in reading, math, and language, with cross references to specific teaching materials relative to basic skill tasks in these disciplines.

Spelling

1. *Continuous Progress in Spelling, Kit 2.* The Economy Co., 1901 North Walnut, Oklahoma City, Oklahoma 73125.

    Progress is individually placed in a test-study-test approach.

2. *The Herman Method of Reversing Reading Failure/Spelling Section.* Romar Publications, Inc., 6380 Wilshire Blvd., Los Angeles, California 90048.

    This is a multisensory, developmentally sequenced, K-6, reading, writing, and spelling program that involves teacher-directed lessons. The program is designed to teach beginning level decoding skills by means of any or all of the four stages of the VAKT technique.

3. *Independent Drill for Mastery: Fundamentals of Spelling.* Developmental Learning Materials, 7440 Natchez Avenue, Niles, IL 60641.

    This program features tests to determine student entry level and progress in the program. Answer keys and a class profile assist the teacher in scoring and recording test results. Self-study lessons on tape are assigned, and students listen, write and correct their practice papers with the answer/study sheets.

4. *Morphographic Spelling.* E-B Press, P.O. Box 10459, Eugene, Oregon 97401.

    This is a sequential spelling program designed to break words down into units of meaning (morphographs), and apply spelling rules to basic root words.

5. *System 80.* Borg, Warner, 600 West University Drive, Arlington Heights, Illinois 60004.

    Using an audio-visual hardware unit, these materials are designed to teach a fundamental spelling vocabulary useful in the primary grades and later writing activities.

3. Three rules of remedial spelling are: a. input must precede output. b. since spelling is an output process, and reading is an input process, the student should be asked to spell only those words that he can read. c. written spelling should be emphasized rather than oral spelling. Thus, spelling instruction should correspond closely with reading instruction, and the student should be asked to spell in writing only those words he is able to read.

Auditory Discrimination

Auditory discrimination may be defined as the ability to discriminate similarities and differences between stimuli presented auditorally.

1. *Auditory Discrimination in Depth (ADD).* Teaching Resources Inc., 100 Boylston Street, Boston, Massachusetts 02116.

    This is an excellent K-12, structured, sequential, multisensory program that develops the auditory-perceptual skills basic to reading, spelling, and language.

2. *Auditory Perception Training Program.* Developmental Learning Materials, 7440 Natchez Avenue, Niles, Illinois 60648.

    This program is designed to teach students the skill of associating a single sound with a pictorial presentation of that sound.

3. *Sound-Order-Sense Auditory Perception Program.* Follett Publishing Company, 1010 West Washington Blvd., Chicago, Illinois 60607.

    These are multi-level auditory exercises designed to build auditory perception skills from the simplest spoken sentences.

4. Teacher Directed Activities:

    a) When verbally given a target word (such as hit), have the student select the word/words that rhyme with the target word from a list of words also presented verbally. For example: Teacher says to the student: "Which of the following words rhymes with *hit?* Teacher then pronounces the words: "boy", "man", "fit." The student should select the word "fit." (If the student forgets the target word before the teacher reads the list, be sure to repeat it.)

b) With the student's back to the teacher, the teacher pronounces various word pairs; the student is asked to indicate whether the words of each pair are the same or different. Examples of word pairs to use are: tin-thin; mop-mob; robe-rode; etc. The word pairs should require the student to discriminate between sounds in the initial, medial, and/or final letter positions, from fine to gross discrimination.

c) With the student's back to the teacher (or blindfolded), the teacher produces sounds from two similar musical instruments (i.e., triangle and bell); the student is asked to indicate whether the sounds are the same or different.

d) Ask the student to say a consonant sound which can be sustained (i.e., m, s, f, etc.). Tell him to continue emitting one of those sounds while the teacher says other consonant sounds (i.e., r, l, v, etc.). Ask the student to stop as soon as he hears the teacher say the sound that he (student) is producing.

Auditory Storage Memory

Auditory storage memory may be defined as the ability to remember single concepts, facts, or data when presented verbally over a short period of time.

1. *Aides to Psycholinguistic Teaching* (2nd Ed.), Bush, Wilma Jo, and Giles, Marian T. Ohio: Charles E. Merrill Publishing Co., 1977, Chapter 5.

2. *Auditory Perception Training Program*. Developmental Learning Materials, 7440 Natchez Avenue, Niles, Illinois 60648.

   This program is designed to strengthen listening and recall skills in five areas: motor, memory, figure-ground, discrimination, and imagery.

3. *Perceive and Respond Auditory Program*. Modern Education Corporation, Box 721, Tulsa, Oklahoma 74101.

   These materials provide opportunities for practice in auditory memory. Volume I uses audio cassettes, self correcting spirit masters, and activator pens to provide experiences with environmental sounds.

4. *Sound-Order-Sense Auditory Perception Program*. Follett Publishing Co., 1010 West Washington Blvd., Chicago, Illinois 60607.

   These are multi-level auditory exercises designed to build auditory perception skills from the simplest spoken sentences.

5. Teacher Directed Activities:

   a. Direct subject to listen for the sound of one letter, e.g., b; have subject stand up when he hears the sound in a series of words pronounced by the teacher. Gradually increase the numbr of sounds which he must remember.

   b. Tell subject a key word (e.g., "store"); tell him that you will ask him to repeat the word later. Gradually increase the number of words to be remembereed as well as the time gap.

   c. Tell subject a target word (e.g., "red"). Allow 60 seconds to pass; then give him a series of five similar words, among which is the target word; ask him to raise his hand when he hears the target word. Gradually increase the number of target words.

Auditory Sequential Memory

Auditory sequential memory may be defined as the ability to remember, in the order given, a series of stimuli acquired auditorially.

1. *Aids to Psycholinguistic Teaching* (2nd ed). Columbus, Ohio: Charles E. Merrill Publishing Company, 1969. Chapter 5.

2. *Simon,* Milton Bradley Company, Springfield, Massachusetts 01115.

   An unusually high-interest "computer" type of game-format training device.

3. *Auditory Perception Training Program*.

Developmental Learning Materials, 7440 Natchez Avenue, Niles, Illinois 60628.

This program is designed to strengthen listening and recall skills in five areas: motor, memory, figure-ground, discrimination, and imagery.

4. *Auditory Sequential Memory Exercises*. Developmental Learning Materials, 7440 Natchez Avenue, Niles, Illinois 60648.

5. *Buzzer Board and Buzzer Board Pattern Cards*. Developmental Learning Materials, 7440 Natchez Avenue, Niles, Illinois 60648.

The buzzer board program is designed to increase auditory perceptual abilities, including auditory attention, discrimination, and sequential memory. The buzzer emits a series of auditory patterns which the student duplicates.

6. *The Fourth "R", Remembering*. Harp, Billie M. and Pereira, Esther R. Instructional Materials and Equipment Distributors, 1520 Cotner Avenue, Los Angeles, California 90025, 1974.

7. *Learning Disabilities*. Johnson, D. and Myklebust, H. Pp. 182-183, New York: Grune and Stratton, 1967.

8. *Perceive and Respond*. Modern Education Corporation, Box 721, Tulsa, OK 74101.

These materials provide opportunities for practice in auditory sequential memory. Volume III uses cassettes, self correcting spirit masters, and activator pens to provide experiences with directions, digits, words, and morse code.

9. *Sound-Order-Sense Program, Level II*. Follett Publishing Co., 1010 West Washington Blvd., Chicago, Illinois 60607.

10. Teacher Directed Activities:

 a) Present the subject with a sequenced series of sounds (e.g., individual letter sounds, s-t-m or k-g-g). Have the subject verbally repeat in sequence the presented sounds. Begin by presenting a series of three sounds, then extend the number of sounds in each sequence to the subject's limit.

 b) Demonstrate a hand-clap rhythm (e.g.: clap-pause - clap - clap; or clap - clap - pause -clap). Have the subject imitate the rhythm by clapping. Increase the number of components to the subject's limit.

 c) Have the subject follow a series of specific verbal directions. (For example, "Go to the bookcase," "Bring me a book," "Put it on the table," and "Open the door.") Gradually increase the number of directions given in sequence.

 d) Read a story to the subject and have him repeat the sequence of events. Begin with stories with a maximum of three major events; continue by using stories with an increasing number of events.

Auditory Recall Memory (Reauditorization)

Auditory recall Memory may be defined as the ability to spontaneously recall the names of objects that are presented non-verbally, as evidenced by the subject correctly naming the objects.

1. *Auditory Perception Training Program*. DLM, 7440 Natchez Avenue, Niles, Illinois 60648.

This program is designed to strengthen the student's listening and recall skills in five areas: motor, memory, figure-ground, discrimination, and imagery.

2. *Learning Disabilities*. Myklebust, H. and Johnson, D. New York: Grune & Stratton, 1967, pp. 114-122.

3. *Sound-Order-Sense Auditory Perception Program, Level II*. Follett Publishig Co., 1010 West Washington Blvd., Chicago, Illinois 60607.

These are multi-level auditory exercises designed to build auditory perception skills from the simplest spoken sentences.

4. Teacher Directed Activities:

 a. Teach high-use target words: With or without a visual cue (e.g., a picture of the object for which the word stands), teacher orally or in writing presents a partial sentence; have the subject complete the sentence using the target word (e.g., "I eat with a . . . *spoon*."), initially with, then later without, the visual cue.

b. Encourage the retrieval of high-use words by having the subject use those word in context.

c. Pair target words with a visual cue; have the subject say a sentence using the target word when presented with the visual cue. For example, show a picture of a school bus with children in it and have the subject say a sentence using "school bus" as a target word.

d. Timed rapid-naming drills. Have the subject say the names of as many objects in a pool of pictures as possible within 30 seconds; record the time after each drill so that progress may be monitored.

e. Oral reading drills on a one-to-one basis. After each paragraph, then page, the subject should be asked to recall what he read on that page. The number of pages recalled should gradually increase until the subject is able to recall an entire story.

f. Associate target words with other words of common usage (e.g., 'Salt and *pepper*.") Have the subject recall one of the paired target words from the visual cue of the other.

g. Associate target words with a picture of each word; write the target word name under each picture. After the subject correctly reads the word with the picture cue, remove the written word and have him identify the word by means of the picture cue; then converse.

Sound Location

Sound location may be defined as the ability to identify the direction from which sounds originate.

1. *Children With Learning Disabilities* (2nd ed). Lerner, Janet W. Boston: Houghton Mifflin, 1976, pp 194-194.

2. Teacher Directed Activities:

   a) When remediating sound location, have the subject do the exercises with an auditory trainer (phonic ear), and then without it.

   b) Start a metronome and hide it in the classroom. Have the subject find the metronome by means of sound location.

   c) Blindfold the subject. Beginning with gross sounds (e.g., ringing a bell or beating a drum), have the subject turn his face in the direction of the sound. Introduce finer sounds, such as clapping or snapping fingers.

Auditory Meaning

Auditory meaning may be defined as the ability to gain meaning from stimuli acquired auditorally.

1. *Aides to Psycholinguistic Teaching* (2nd ed). Bush, W.J. and Giles, M. Ohio: Charles E. Merrill, 1977, Chapter 3.

2. *GOAL: Language Development:* Milton Bradley Company, Springfield, Mass. 01001.

3. *Peabody Language Development Kits.* American Guidance Services, Publishers' Building, Circle Pines, Minnesota 53104.

   This program is designed primarily to stimulate receptive, associative, and expressive language development.

4. *Sound-Order-Sense Program.* Follett Publishing Co, 1010 West Washington Blvd., Chicago, Illinois 60607.

   These are multi-level auditory exercises designed to build auditory perception skills from the simplest spoken sentences.

5. Teacher Directed Activities:

   a. The following guidelines should be used with the subject when remediating auditory meaning:
      1. Ask one-concept questions.
      2. Accept concrete answers.
      3. Provide visual cues when appropriate.

   b. Have the subject listen while the teacher verbally presents analogies in which the last word is missing. Have him complete the analogies by orally supplying the missing word. (Sample analogies are: Ear is to listen as nose is to_____; Sun is to day as moon is to_____; Laughing is to happy as crying is to_____.)

c. Read the subject a riddle, such as : "I am big. You go inside me. I have rooms. You live in me. I am a_____." Have the subject complete the riddle by saying the correct word.

d. While the subject listens, say 3-5 words belonging to one category of objects, such as nickel, dime, quarter, penny. Ask the subject to tell you the category to which the named objects belong.

e. Pronounce words that are in the subject's spoken vocabulary. Ask him to give a synonym and then an antonym for the word pronounced. (For the word "lady," the synonym would be "woman," and the antonym would be "man.")

Sound Blending

Sound blending may be defined as the ability to blend isolated sounds to make a word.

1. *Auditory Discrimination in Depth.* Teaching Resources, 100 Boylston Street, Boston, Massachusetts 02116.

    This is an excellent K-12, structured, sequenced, multisensory program that develops the auditory-perceptual skills basic to reading, spelling, and language.

2. *Corrective Reading Program—Decoding A.* Science Research Associates, 759 East Erie Street, Chicago, Illinois 60622.

    This is a complete decoding program which uses sound blending as a basic word attack strategy.

3. *Goldman-Lynch Sounds and Symbols.* American Guidance Services, Inc., Publishers Building, Circle Pines, Minnesota 53014.

    This program teaches sound blending skills necessary for reading success.

4. *Perceive and Respond Auditory Program: Volume II.* Modern Education Corporation, Box 721, Tulsa, Oklahoma 74101.

    These materials provide opportunities for practice in sound discrimination and blending. Volume II uses cassettes, self correcting spirit masters, and activator pens to provide these experiences.

5. Teacher Directed Activities:

    a. Have the subject say a sustained sound (e.g., m, s, sh, v). Have him continue saying the sound while the teacher says other sustained sounds (e.g., r, m, l). Have the subject stop when he hears the same sound he is saying.

    b. Verbally present the subject with words separated into syllables, e.g, ta-ble, bas-ket-ball, etc. Have the subject verbally respond by saying the word fast. Increase the length of the pause between syllables as the subject's mastery increases.

    c. Present the subject with three flash cards, each containing one word from his reading material. Pronounce one of the words by isolating each sound at the rate of one per second (e.g., p-e-n). Have the subject pick out the correct card and say the complete word.

    d. Verbally present the subject with words, voicing each sound separately (e.g., p-e-n, h-i-ll, b-e-l-t). Have the subject say the complete word fast.

Auditory Closure

Auditory closure is defined as the ability to verbally identify the whole or complete word from a verbal presentation of that word with one or more phonemes omitted.

1. *Auditory Closure Cards.* Colbourn School Supply Co., 999 S. Jason, Denver, CO 80223.

    This progrm uses a script which directs the teacher to say an incomplete word. The learner identifies the total word by selecting the correct picture card. Cards are from the categories of animals, clothing, toys, and food.

2. *Damron Reading/Language Kit.* McGraw-Hill, Special Edition, Catalog, 1978. 1221 Avenue of the Americas, New York, NY 10020.

This kit contains activities grouped relative to the twelve areas of the Illinois Test of Psycholinguistic Ability. Each activity provides suggestions for a prescriptive approach to instruction.

3. *GOAL*. Milton Bradley Company, Springfield, Massachusetts 01101.

   GOAL is a comprehensive multiple stimuli program designed to help children acquire the language skills basic to learning to read.

4. Teacher Directed Activities:

   a) With three objects or pictures on the table, play a guessing game in which the subject guesses which picture you are thinking of from the *first* sound of the word. Later emit middle or final sounds instead of the initial sound.

   b) Help the subject learn to discriminate word and word sounds from background noise by giving him simple commands at the same time other distracting noise is being heard (taped music or motor noise such as that of a vacuum cleaner). Start with a low level of noise interference, increasing it as the subject can cope. Turn up the noise volume slowly, guaranteeing successful performance on at least fifty percent of the commands.

   c) Read familiar nursery rhymes to the subject while leaving a key rhyme-word out of the oral presentation. Have the subject stop the reader then supply the missing word that rhymes. The reader should reinforce correct response by re-reading the sentence with the key word supplied.

   d) Play telephone; omit sounds of words, or words, from the conversation. Have the subject identify the missing sounds or words.

   e) Have the subject fill in the missing sounds of words or sentences presented verbally to him. For example: "On my head I wear a ha__."

Visual Discrimination

Visual discrimination may be defined as the ability to discriminate similarities and differences between stimuli presented visually.

1. *Aids to Psycholinguistic Teaching* (2nd ed.) Bush, W. and Giles, M. Columbus, Ohio: Charles E. Merrill Co., 1977, Chapter 6.

2. *Conceptual Learning*. Siegfried Englemann, Dimensions Publishing Co., San Rafael, California 94903. Chapters I and II.

3. *Visual Matching, Memory, and Sequencing Exercises Books, Levels 1-6*. DLM, 7440 Natchez Avenue, Niles, Illinois 60648.

   This series provides developmental exercises that train students to visually match colors, figures, shapes, designs and letters.

4. *Wipe-Off Cards; Same or Different, External Differences;* and *Finding Pairs*. School Specialty Supply, Inc., Salina, Kansas 67401.

   These cards use a matching activity to train visual discrimination.

5. Teacher Directed Activities:

   a) Place duplicate objects on a table (e.g., rectangles, letters, numbers, pencils, squares, circles, forks, knives, spoons, etc.) The teacher names an object, and the subject is asked to find its mate. Work from gross to fine, large to small. Increase the number of objects in the pool, and the number of objects to be matched.

   b) Present the subject with a variety of objects, which are varied by size, color, use, shape, etc. Have him group the objects by size, color, use, shape, etc. Have him pick out individual objects when given directions, such as: "Pick up the large red circle;" "Pick up the small number 6;" etc.

   c) Place geometric shapes throughout the classroom, varying the size and color. Tell the subject that we will play a treasure hunt game. Have him find only the blue triangles in the room. Reinforce correct responses, and repeat the game varying the shape and color to be found.

d) Present the subject with five or six printed letters or numbers. Write a duplicate letter or number on the board and have the subject find the matching letter or number.

Visual Storage Memory

Visual storage memory may be defined as the ability to remember single concepts, facts, or data when presented visually over a short period of time.

1. *Aids to Psycholinguistic Teaching* (2nd ed). Bush, W.J. and Giles, M. Ohio: Charles E. Merrill, 1977, Chapter 9.

2. *Touch Type Program.* Common Signs, Modern Education Corporation, Box 721, Tulsa, Oklahoma 74101.

   This program is designed to increase visual memory skills using a visual-tactile-kinesthetic approach with common safety, road, and information signs.

3. *Visual Memory Cards.* Developmental Learning Materials, 7440 Natchez Avenue, Niles, Illinois 60648.

4. Teacher Directed Avtivities:

   a) Immediately before a recess, show subject a picture with high interest objects; name each item. When he returns from recess, have him name the object(s). Repeat this on a regular basis, varying the time of day for the activity, and the number of items to be remembered.

   b) Show subject a tray of three objects at the beginning of the school day; name each object for him. At the end of the first class period, have him identify the items from memory. Increase the number of items.

   c) Show subject an object. Allow some time lapse; then place the object in a pool of different objects. Have subject pick out the object. Increase the similarity of the objects in the group, lengthen the time lapse, and increase the number of objects shown as well as in the pool.

d) Show subject a letter cutout or a playing card. After one minute, place the card or letter cutout among a pool of letter cutouts or cards and have him pick out the original letter or card. Vary the number of letters or cards and the time lapse.

Visual Sequential Memory

Visual sequential memory may be defined as the ability to remember, in the order given, a series of stimuli acquired visually.

1. *Aids to Psycholinguistic Teaching* (2nd ed.). Bush, W. and Giles, M. Ohio: Charles E. Merrill, Co., 1977, Chapter 9.

2. *The Fourth "R", Remembering.* Harp, Billie M. and Pereira, Esther R. Instructional Materials and Equipment Distributors, 1520 Cotner Ave., Los Angeles, California 90025, 1974.

3. *Learning Disabilities.* Johnson, D. and Myklebust, H. New York: Grune & Stratton, 1967, Pp. 168-169.

4. *Visual Matching, Memory, and Sequencing Exercises Books, Levels 1-6.* Developmental Learning Materials, 7440 Natchez Avenue, Niles, Illinois 60648.

   This series provides developmental exercises that train students to visually match colors, figures, shapes, designs and letters.

5. *Visual Memory Cards.* Developmental Learning Materials, same address as above.

   These flash cards are designed to provide training in visual discrimination, sequencing, and memory.

6. Teacher Directed Activities:

   a) Give subject 3 different playing cards. Have subject look at the cards for 5 seconds. Scramble the cards. Have him return the cards to the original sequence. Vary the task by increasing the number of cards.

   b) Prepare a series of objects such as toy car, toy boat, key, etc. Prepare 3" x 5" cards with pictures of the same objects, one picture to a card. Show subject the objects arranged in a certain sequence on the table. Cover the objects and ask subject to arrange the cards in the same order. Gradually increase the complexity by increasing the number of objects.

c) Arrange 3 or 4 objects in order. Have subject look at them, then close his eyes while the objects are mixed up. Have him put them back in the correct order. Repeat the task by varying the order and the number of objects.

d) Write a combination of two letters or numbers on the chalkboard and erase them quickly. Have subject verbally repeat the combination, write the combination on the chalkboard, or point to the correct combination among several combinations presented visually on paper or the blackboard. Repeat the procedure by increasing the number of items in the combination of letters and/or numbers. Gradually decrease the amount of time before erasing the combination.

Visual Recall Memory (Revisualization)

Visual recall memory may be defined as the ability to spontaneously recall how the names of words and/or objects presented verbally look in print, as evidenced by the subject graphically reproducing the target words or objects.

1. *Aids to Psycholinguistic Teaching* (2nd ed.) Bush, W. and Giles, M. Columbus, Ohio: Charles E. Merrill Co., 1977, Chapter 6.

2. *Goldman-Lynch Sounds and Symbols*. American Guidance Services, Inc., Publisher's Building, Circle Pines, Minnestoa 53014.

3. *Independent Drill for Mastery: Fundamentals of Spelling*. Developmental Learning Materials, 7440 Natchez Avenue, Niles, Illinois 60648.

This self-structured program uses self-study lessons on tape casettes to provide verbal descriptions of words. The student listens, writes, then corrects each practice paper with the answer/study sheets.

4. *Learning Disabilities*. Johnson, D., and Myklebust, H. New York: Grune & Stratton, 1967, pages 218-227.

5. *Morphographic Spelling*. EB Press, Box 10459, Eugene, Oregon 72401.

This is a direct instructional program designed for students who demonstrate mastery of basic sound-symbol relationships, but who cannot revisualize in order to spell them.

6. VAKT Technique.

7. *Visual Matching, Memory, and Sequencing Exercise Books, Levels 1-6*. Developmental Learning Materials, 7440 Natchez Avenue, Niles, Illinois 60648.

This series provides developmental exercises that train students to visually match colors, figures, shapes, designs and letters.

8. *Wipe-Off Cards; Same or Different, External Differences;* and *Finding Pairs*. School Specialty Supply, Inc., Salina, Kansas 67401.

9. Teacher Directed Activities:

a) Prepare a set of picture completion exercises where the first picture is complete and each successive picture has an increased number of parts omitted. Have subject look at the first figure then complete each of the others without looking at the model.

b) Show subject a geometric object (e.g., a circle). Have him graphically make it, or verbally describe it, into as many different objects as he can (e.g., face, clock, ball, apple).

c) Use word completion exercises. Prepare a sheet with a word written completely, then examples with letters omitted from various positions. Have subject look at the complete word, then write in the missing letters in the examples that follow. The last example for each word should present only the blank spaces. For example: cat: __ __t; __at, c__ __; c__t, __a__; ca__ __ __.

Visual Meaning

Visual meaning may be defined as the ability to gain meaning from stimuli acquired visually.

1. *Aids to Psycholinguistic Teaching.* (2nd ed.) Bush, Wilma Jo and Giles, Marian T., Ohio: Charles E. Merrill Publishing Co., 1977, Chapter 7.

2. *Association Picture Cards.* Developmental Learning Materials, 7440 Natchez Avenue, Niles, Illinois 60648.

    This program is designed to improve visual meaning by presenting cards, each with a series of visual stimuli, regarding which the subject discriminates on the basis of categories.

3. Teacher Directed Activities:

    a) Cut pictures of foods from magazines and mount each picture on a separate piece of tagboard. Have subject sort the pictures according to fruit, vegetable, meat, dairy product, etc.

    b) Present subject with pictures of similar objects, such as a car, truck, bicycle, horse, etc., and have him verbally compare how the obects are alike and different relative to function, size, etc.

    c) Match sports figures with appropriate equipment.

Visual Tracking

Visual tracking may be defined as the ability to use both eyes in a coordinated and smooth manner when following a moving object.

1. *Ann Arbor Tracking Program.* Ann Arbor Publishers, P.O. Box 388, Worthington, Ohio 43085.

    This program is a set of self-instruction workbooks, and includes: symbol tracking; word tracking; cues and signals; number tracking; multiple tracking; letter tracking; and cursive tracking.

2. *The Fitzhugh PLUS Program.* Allied Education Council, Galien, Michigan 49113.

    The Fitzhugh PLUS Program is a remedial workbook program incorporating a self-teaching and immediate-feedback process using a magic marking pen. The spatial organization series uses shape matching and completion problems. The program is designed to allow students to work at their own pace.

3. *Motoric Aids to Perceptual Training.* Chaney, C. and Kephart, N. Ohio: Charles E. Merrill Publishing Co., 1968, Chapter 7.

4. *Visual Tracking Cards.* Colbourn School Supply Co., 999 S. Jason, Denver, CO 80223.

    These reusable cards include progressive left-to-right tracking activities. The learner is moved from simple eye movement tasks to total word recognition in left-to-right progression.

5. Teacher Directed Activities:

    a) Horizontal: Sit in front of subject with thumbtack in pencil eraser about 18 inches from the midline of his nose. Slowly move the pencil to the far-left while subject counts to 10, then to the far-right. Have subject follow the moving thumbtack with his eyes, keeping his head stationary and straight ahead.

    b) Vertical: Follow same procedure as in #a above. Start at midline of the nose. Slowly move the pencil up and down about 10 inches in each direction, staying about 18 inches from subject's body.

    c) Diagonal: Begin at subject's midline of the nose and move pencil in all directions. Change angles and starting points.

    d) Rotary: Begin at midline of the nose and have subject track the thumbtack in small circular movements. Extend size and position of circles.

    e) Take old phonograph records and make cardboard extensions with luminescent dots. Use in a darkroom at different speeds (slow, 33 1/3 to fast, 78) with subject counting the number of revolutions.

f) Have subject visually track a small penlight on a dark piece of construction paper.

g) Sit in front of subject and slowly draw lines or line patterns on paper from left to right. Have subject visually track and follow with his finger.

h) Slowly draw a line on the chalkboard; have subject follow with his eyes and finger (together) as line is drawn from left to right. Vary the pattern drawn, from simple to complex.

i) Newspaper tracking activities: Have subject circle, in sequence, the letters of the alphabet as he finds them in each newspaper column. This activity can be expanded to having him locate whole words that he is learning.

Visual-Spatial Relationship

Visual-spatial relationship may be defined as the ability to visualize positions of objects in space, as evidenced by correctly matching and/or reproducing three dimensional designs.

1. *Colored Cubes and Pattern Cards*. Teaching Resources, 100 Boylston Street, Boston, Massachusetts 02116.

   These 70 sequenced pattern cards represent a series of dimensional designs to be built with colored one-inch cubes. The student is presented with a design card which he copies with the blocks. The cards are sequenced in order of difficulty. The program may be used as direct instruction or self-structured student practice.

2. *Dubnoff School Program, I*. Same address as above.

   This is a developmental program designed to improve motor-perceptual skills, with exercises in perception, directional and spatial orientation, coordination, and fine motor control.

3. *Fairbanks-Robinson*. Teaching Resources, same address as above.

   This is a training program in the development of basic motor skills, providing a transition from gross to fine motor skills.

4. *Frostig Program for the Development of Visual Perception*. Follett Publishing Co., 1000 Washington Blvd., Chicago, IL 60607.

5. *Small Parquetry With Pattern Cards*. Teaching Resources, same address as above.

   This set of 70 sequenced cards represents patterns that can be duplicated with parquetry pieces. The student is presented with a pattern, and reproduces the pattern using the exact shape, size, and color of the parquetry pieces. This program may be used as direct instruction for self-structured student practice.

6. Teacher Directed Activities:

   a) Present subject with goemetric forms, such as cones, spheres, cubes, cylinders, triangular prisms, pyramids, etc. Have subject play, feel, and build spontaneous structures, as well as patterns from models.

   b) Construct simple designs with blocks and have subject imitate the patterns.

   c) Have subject construct mosaic tile pictures, either from a model, or spontaneously.

   d) Construct pegboard and marble board designs; have subject reproduce the designs.

   e) Have subject develop progressive tinker-toy construction projects.

   f) Using modeling clay, have subject create basic forms and construct objects.

   g) Using Parquetry Designs, have subject model the designs.

   h) With a geo-board, make a design and have subject imitate it.

Visual Closure

Visual closure may be defined as the ability to verbally identify (name) or graphically complete a visual stimulus (e.g., a picture or word), from a visual presentation of that stimulus, with one or more parts of the stimulus omitted.

1. *Aids to Psycholinguistic Teaching* (2nd ed). Bush and Giles, Ohio: Charles E. Merrill Publishing Co., 1977, Chapter 8.

2. *Erie Program, Parts 3 & 4.* Teaching Resources, 100 Boylston St., Boston, Massachusetts 02116.

   These activities and games are designed to develop basic perceptual skills such as eye-hand coordination, visual closure, and visual memory.

3. *The Fitzhugh PLUS Program.* Allied Education Council, Galien, Michigan 49113.

   The Fitzhugh PLUS Program is a remedial workbook program incorporating a self-teaching and immediate-feedback process using a magic marking pen. The spatial organization series uses shape matching and completion programs. The program is designed to allow students to work at their own pace.

4. *Visual Closure Cards.* Colbourn School Supply Co., Box 301, Casper, WY 82601.

   This self-checking material is designed to introduce or reinforce concepts of visual closure.

5. Teacher Directed Activities:

   a) Visually present subject with one partially completed number, e.g., 1, 2, 3 . Have subject look at the partially completed number, and verbally identify it, and/or graphically complete it.

   b) Visually present subject with one partially completed word, e.g., CAT, etc. Have subject look at the partially completed word and verbally identify it, and/or graphically complete it.

   c) Visually present subject with a series of partially completed numbers, e.g., his address, telephone number, etc. Have subject look at the partially completed series of numbers and verbally identify the number series, and/or graphically complete it.

   d) Visually present subject with a series of partially completed go-together words, e.g., salt-pepper; bread-butter; etc. Have subject look at the partially completed word series and verbally identify the words, and/or graphically complete the word series.

   e) Visually present subject with a sentence in which the words have some partially completed letters (e.g., ''I went to the MOVIE Startrek.'') Have subject verbally identify the partially completed word and/or graphically complete it. Then have him read the complete sentence.

Graphic Output

Graphic output may be defined as the encoding, responding, or output of stimuli by means of paper-pencil activity (such as handwriting).

1. *Dubnoff Program I (Complete Prewriting Program).* Teaching Resources Corp., 100 Boylston Street, Boston, Massachusetts 02116.

   This program provides the base for a developmental handwriting program. Its particular application is for the remediation of handwriting problems at any age or grade level.

2. *Fairbanks-Robinson.* Teaching Resources, same address as above.

   This is a training program for the development of basic motor skills, providing a transition from gross motor to fine motor skills.

3. *Learning Disabilities.* Myklebust, H. and Johnson, D. New York: Grune & Stratton, 1967, pp. 193-218.

4. *Peterson Handwriting, Let's Learn to Write.* Peterson Handwriting, 2215 Commerce St., Dallas, Texas 75201.

   This is a complete handwriting program for all levels. It uses a color-graph system to teach correct letter formation.

5. Teacher Directed Activities:

   a) Teach subject to make 5 inch size circles and lines, then numbers and letters, on the chalkboard. Provide him with dotted lines or large templates as a guide while he learns. Use the VAKT technique if necessary. Gradually reduce the size of the objects drawn.

   b) Using the chalkboard, provide subject with two dots. Have him connect the dots. Repeat this procedure by increasing the number of dots and varying their distance and/or placement on the chalkboard.

c) Have subject color objects within the lines; or draw a pencil line through increasingly complex mazes.

d) Have subject trace paper-folds.

e) Have subject trace geometric forms, then letters, numbers, and words on acetate overlays or onion skin paper.

f) Have subject draw geometric forms, then letters and numbers, from cutouts or stencils. Have him trace the result with his finger, until he can copy the model from memory.

g) Develop subject's fine motor coordination by means of Tinker toy play, jacks, stringing beads, etc.

h) Use the VAKT technique.

Haptic Discrimination

Haptic discrimination may be defined as the ability to discriminate similarities and differences between stimuli presented haptically.

1. *Detect Tactile.* Science Research Associates. 155 North Wacker Drive, Chicago, Illinois 60606.

   This tactile manipulative skills program uses textured objects, including geometric forms, numerals, and letters, to teach discrimination tasks.

2. *Haptic Perceptual Development Program.* Edmark 13241 Northup Way, Bellevue, Washington 98005.

   This program is designed to develop kinesthetic and tactile abilities. Haptic discrimination activities are included in each of five learning stations.

3. *Touch-and-Match Shapes.* Teaching Resources, same address as above.

   The program provides practice in tactile discrimination of geometric shapes.

4. *Touch-and-Match Textures.* Teaching Resources. Same address as above.

   The program provides practice in distinguishing textures.

5. Teacher Directed Activities:

   a) Blindfold subject. Have him feel a raised surface object (letter, number, etc.). While retaining that object, have him haptically find a duplicate object from a pool of raised surface dissimilar objects. Vary the difficulty level by increasing the number of pool objects, and making the target and pool objects more similar.

Affective Development

1. *Developing an Understanding of Self and Others (DUSO).* American Guidance Service, Publishers' Building, Circle Pines, Minnesota 55014.

   DUSO is designed to help develop an awareness of one's self, relationships with other people, and one's needs and goals.

2. *Toward Affective Development (TAD).* American Guidance Service. Same address as above.

   TAD is designed to develop the recognition of feelings, the acceptance of feelings, and an understanding of the relaionship between feelings and various interpersonal events. It is also designed to develop an understanding of individual differences.

3. *Transition.* American Guidance Service, same address as above.

   Transition explores the needs, goals, expectations, feelings, values, and conflicts of secondary students. It is a teacher directed program which specifically addresses the student's social and emotional needs. The program helps to develop self respect and regard for others by promoting human understanding, empathy and personal responsibility.

NAME INDEX

Bandura, A., 330
Bateman, B., 217
Bender, L., 43
Burgemeister, B., 32

Combs, A., 14
Cratty, B., 241

Dubnoff, B., 274
Dunn, L., 32, 273

Engleman, S., 273

Fairbanks, J., 274
Fernald, G., 274
Fristoe, M., 35
Frostig, M., 139, 150

Geake, R., 274
Goldman, R., 35, 274
Goodenough, F., 92

Harris, D., 92
Hartman, H., 197
Hewitt, F., 272, 281
Hilgard, E., 315
Homme, L., 274, 281
Horne, D., 274

Jacobson, L., 10
Jastak, J. & R., 34
Johnson, D., 194

Karnes, M., 273
Kirk, S., 37, 39
Koppitz, E., 67, 69

Lindamood, C. & P., 273
Lynch, M., 274

Machover, K., 89
Mager, R., 207
Markwardt, F., 35
Maslow, A., 322
Mykelbust, H., 194

Premack, D., 275

Redl, F., 335
Robinson, J., 274
Rogers, C., 332
Rosenthal, R., 10

Skinner, F., 315
Smith, D., 274
Smith, J., 273
Snygg, D., 14

Terman, L., 30

Wechsler, D., 18, 28
Wepman, J., 35
Wolpe, J., 324
Woodcock, R., 35

SUBJECT INDEX

Accountability, 3, 217, 301, 311
acting-in, 200, 201, 352
acting-out, 26, 46, 93, 182, 200, 201, 352
aggression and control, 46, 92, 180, 181
American Association on Mental Deficiency, 263
Analysis of Ingredients of a Good Objective, 209-212
anemia, fetal, 176
anoxia, 177, 178
anxiety, 26, 46, 93, 184, 202, 352
assessment, 9, 124, 9-196, 262
Association for Children with Learning Disabilities, 263
Association for Retarded Citizens, 263
auditory acuity, 135
auditory closure, 138
auditory discrimination, 136
Auditory Discrimination Test, 35
auditory figure-ground, 138
auditory learning center, 273
auditory meaning, 137
auditory processing, 136
auditory recall memory (reauditorization), 137
auditory sequential memory, 137
auditory storage memory, 136
aversive stimuli, 191, 196, 324, 325

baseline measurement, 229-231, 301, 302, 303, 305-311
baselining mathematics, 310
baselining reading comprehension, 308
baselining spelling errors, 310
behavior modification, 5, 191, 196, 201, 313-326
behavioral-instructional objectives, 4, 5, 207-214, 301
Bender Test, 43-88, 89, 91, 92
bibliotherapy, 335
bio-chemical intolerance, 176
body image, 240-241, 273, 274, 328-9
body image center, 273
brain damage, 20, 44, 49-50, 92, 178

career education, 241-243
carrel, 273, 274
chaining, 336
chaining, reverse, 224, 236
Change Agents, 327, 337
checkmark system of reinforcement, 319-320, 321
Classroom Grouping Arrangements, 280-299
"Closer Look", 251
Columbia Mental Maturity Test, 32
Comprehensive History, 173-190

conscience, 198-202
contingency contracts, 234-238
contingency management, 327
convergence, 139
cooperation, parental, 184
Council for Exceptional Children, 251, 263
counseling, 201, 332-333
counter-conditioning, 324
crisis intervention, 331
criteria of acceptable performance; accuracy, 207, 209-211
criteria of acceptable performance; difficulty level, 207, 210-211
criteria of acceptable performance; time, 207, 209-210
Criterion referenced testing, 9-10
crosscategorical special education, 3, 264, 349-354
culturally different, 26
Curriculum Match, 228-229
curriculum materials which represent a good DPT match, 383-404

D-PT Programming Sequence, 351
deductive strategy, 334
defense mechanism, 202-203
depression, 20, 26, 51, 90, 93, 176
desensitization, 323-324
difficulty level criterion, 207, 210-211
direct instruction, 266-271
Draw-A-Person Test (DAP), 89-123
drives, 197-198
duration baseline measurement procedure, 307-308

educational handicap (EH), 349
educational readiness, 46, 92
ego, 197-203
ego-conscience system, 197-203, 313-314, 317-318
emotional disturbance, 200, 318, 351-354
enabling objectives, 218-219
encephalitis, 179
engineered classroom, 272
enuresis, 179
epilepsy, 175
ethics, 262-263
ethics, testing, 16-17
evaluation of overall IEP intervention progress, 311
exploratory center, 272-3
extinction techniques, 323-326

fading, 318-319
family 173-175, 195-196
feedback, 334-336

fixed time sampling, 302-303
formal psychological tests which assess the SILI components, 168-172
fragmentation, 50
free time, 327
free time area, 273
frequency target behavior counting procedure, 305-306

group, according to student ITPA CPLA, 281
group, activity center, 281
group, chronological age, 280
group, grade in school, 280
group, grade level ability, 280
group, interest centers, 296, 297
group, learning channel weakness, 280
group, learning strengths & weaknesses, 280
group, special education category, 281
group, student learning quotients, 281
group, tool subjects according to I.Q., 280
group negative reinforcement, 336
Group IEP Programming, 360-363
guidance room, 334
guilt, 198

haptic, 27, 125, 157-158, 193, 239
Health History Form, 257-261
herpes simplex, 177
hyperactivity, 179
hypoactivity, 179

ignoral, 323
immediate feedback interview, 335-336
Individual IEP Programming, 355-359
Informal Psychoeducational Testing and Assessment, 9-10, 124-196
instructional objective (see behavioral-instructional objective)
integrating special education, 244, 341-342
intertest scatter, 27
intervention,k 3-6, 9, 14
intervention failure, 337
intratest scatter, 27
I.Q., controversy, 12-13
I.Q., Full Scale, 18-22
I.Q., Performance, 18-22
I.Q., Verbal, 18-22
itinerant teacher, 264
ITPA, 37-42

jaundice, 176, 177

Key Math Diagnostic Arithmetic Test, 35-36
Kitchen timer change agent technique, 334
Koppitz scoring system, 67-71

learner information, 9, 193
learning center, auditory, 273
learning center, visual, 274
learning centers, 273
learning channel strength and weakness, 27, 124-172, 193, 239
learning channels, 27, 124-125, 239
learning characteristics, 10, 27, 124, 193
learning circuit model, 239
learning contract-schedule, 229, 231
learning disability, 26, 273, 343-344, 351-354
Learning quotient, 194, 281, 291
least restrictive educational environment, 244
limited day, 331

mainstreaming, 244
management model, 4-6, 349-350
mastery center, 273
mechanical aspects of baseline measurement, 305-311
medication, 330
mental retardation, 21, 26, 27, 44, 91-92, 150, 152, 351-354
modeling, 330
models, importance of, 203

negative reinforcement, 320-321

objective, enabling, 218-219
obsessive-compulsive, 20, 25, 26
obtained problem-solving ability, 9, 26-27, 193
operant conditioning, 315
oral reading, 309
order center, 272

paranoia, 21, 24-25
parent group-dynamics, 333
parental influence, 182-184
parental permission, 252, 340-341
Peabody Individual Achievement Test (PIAT), 35
Peabody Picture Vocabulary Test, 32
percentage baseline measurement procedure, 307
perseveration, 50-51
Physical Arrangement of the Classroom, 272-279

P.L. 94-142, 213, 227, 339-347
postintervention target-behavior frequency, 302, 305-306
potential problem solving ability, 9, 26-7, 193
precise presenting problem, 261-262, 350-351
Precision Referral Form, 261-262
preintervention baseline, 302, 305-306
pretest as posttest, 360-361
privacy, invasion of, 10, 16
problem solving ability, obtained, 9, 26-27, 193
problem solving ability, potential, 9, 26-27, 193
prophesy, self fulfilling, 10-11, 193
pseudomental retardation, 44, 92
psychodeterminism, 199-200, 313
psychodrama, 331-332
psychodynamics, 198-199
psychoeducational test, informal, 9
psychoeducational tests, formal, 9
Psychoeducational Testing and Assessment, 9-196
psychosis, 26, 46 & 48, 93, 180
punishment, 324-325

random time sampling, 302
random within fixed time, sampling, 303
rate of target behavior counting procedure, 306
re-evaluation, 263
Regional Resource Center, 251
reinforcement, 313-322
reinforcement, double, 322
reinforcement, negative, 320-321, 336
reinforcement, positive, 313-322
reinforcement, social, 317-318
reinforcement, tally system, 320
reinforcement, token system, 320
reinforcement consistency, 316
Reinforcement Inventory, 191-192
reinforcers, primary, 318
reinforcers, secondary, 318
reinforcers, tertiary, 318-319
reinforcers and aversive stimuli, 324
Request for Service Form, 253
resource teacher, 264
Retrogression, 50
role playing, 331
Rorschach Test, 89
rubella, 151, 176

sample IEPs 364-382
Sample Task Analyses, 220-224
satiation, 325
school readiness, 46, 92
score, scaled, 22, 23, 27
self-contained teacher, 264
sequential steps of Diagnostic-Prescriptive Teaching, 227
sex education, 243
skill continua, 232
Skinnerian model, 315
sound blending, 137
sound location, 136
special education identity, 251
special education, non-categorical, 3, 264, 349-354
Stanford-Binet Intelligence Scale, 30-31
Stellern-Shaw Informal Learning Inventory (SILI), 124-172
Stellern-Shaw Informal Learning Inventory record form, 161-166
structured classroom, 335
Student Referral Form, 254-257
subject anxiety, 11, 20, 46, 93, 176, 202, 352
subject developmental history, 176-179
subject emotional factors, 179-182
subject hyperactivity, 179
subject perplexity, 12
subject school history, 182
success criteria, 207, 209-212
symbolism, 51-52, 67

tally sampling, 303
tally system, 320, 329
target behavior counting procedure, 305-308
task analysis, 4, 217-224
teacher aides, 333-334
terminal behavior, 207
testing, confidentiality, 16, 17
testing, ethics, 16-17
testing, parental permission, 340-341
testing, phenomonology, 14, 89
testing, reality, 26, 183
tests, criterion referenced, 10
tests, norm-referenced, 9
tests, standardized, 9-10
Theoretical Orientation to Understanding of Personality, 197-204
Thorndikian model, 315
time-out, 329-330
time out area, 272
token economy, 320, 328
token system, 320

toxoplasmosis, 177

VAKT center, 274, 361
verbal output, 138
visual acuity, 135
visual closure, 149
visual discrimination, 139
visual figure ground, 150
visual learning center, 274
visual tracking, 138

WAIS, 28
Wechsler Adult Intelligence Scale-Revised, 29
WISC, 18-28
WISC-R, 28
withdrawal, 46, 93
withdrawal of rewards, 325
WPPSI, 28-29
WRAT, 34

X-work, 244-250